Ascent of Mount Carmel
by St. John of the Cross
Edited by Anthony Uyl

Woodstock, Ontario, 2016

Ascent of Mount Carmel
Ascent of Mount Carmel
by St. John of the Cross
Doctor of the Church
Edited by Anthony Uyl

Translated and edited, with an Introduction, by E. Allison Peers
from the critical edition of P. Silverio De Santa Teresa, C.D.

Nihil Obstat: Ceorgivs Smith, S.T.D., PH.D.
Censor Depvtatvs
Imprimatvr: E. Morrogh Bernard
Vicarivs Generalis
Westmonstarii: Die XXIV Septembris MCMLII

To the Discalced Carmelites of Castile,
With abiding memories of their hospitality and kindness in Madrid, Ávila and Burgos, but above all of their devotion to Saint John of the Cross, I dedicate this translation
    - E. Allison Peers

The text of Ascent of Mount Carmel is all in the Public Domain. This edition is published by Devoted Publishing a division of 2165467 Ontario Inc.

What kind of philosophies do you have?
Let us know!

Contact us at: devotedpub@hotmail.com
Visit us on Facebook: Devoted Publishing
Get more products via our website: www.devotedpublishing.com

Published in Woodstock, Ontario, Canada 2016.

For bulk educational rates, please contact us at the above email address.

ISBN: 978-1-988297-58-3

Table of Contents

"the greatest of all mystical theologians" 9
TRANSLATOR'S PREFACE TO THE FIRST EDITION 10
   II 11
   III 12
      Footnotes: 12
TRANSLATOR'S PREFACE TO THE SECOND EDITION 13
PRINCIPAL ABBREVIATIONS 14
AN OUTLINE OF THE LIFE OF ST. JOHN OF THE CROSS [2] 15
      Footnotes: 16
GENERAL INTRODUCTION TO THE WORKS OF ST. JOHN OF THE CROSS 17
   I - DATES AND METHODS OF COMPOSITION 17
   II - OUTSTANDING QUALITIES AND DEFECTS OF THE SAINT'S STYLE 23
   III - DIFFUSION OF THE WRITINGS OF ST. JOHN OF THE CROSS -- LOSS OF THE AUTOGRAPHS -- GENERAL CHARACTERISTICS OF THE MANUSCRIPTS 24
   IV - INTEGRITY OF THE SAINT'S WORK -- INCOMPLETE CONDITION OF THE 'ASCENT' AND THE 'NIGHT' -- DISPUTED QUESTIONS 26
   V - HISTORY OF THE PUBLICATION OF ST. JOHN OF THE CROSS'S WRITINGS -- THE FIRST EDITION 29
   VI - DENUNCIATION OF THE WORKS' TO THE INQUISITION -- DEFENCE OF THEM MADE BY FR. BASILO PONCE DE LEÓN -- EDITIONS OF THE SEVENTEENTH AND EIGHTEENTH CENTURIES 30
   VII - NEW DENUNCIATIONS AND DEFENCES -- FRAY NICOLÁS DE JESÚS MARÍA -- THE CARMELITE SCHOOL AND THE INQUISITION 32
   VIII - FURTHER HISTORY OF THE EDITIONS -- P. ANDRÉS DE LA ENCARNACIÓN -- EDITIONS OF THE NINETEENTH AND TWENTIETH CENTURIES 34
      Footnotes: 36
INTRODUCTION 38
      Footnotes: 40
THE MANUSCRIPTS [63] 41
      Footnotes: 42
ASCENT OF MOUNT CARMEL 43
   ARGUMENT 43
   STANZAS[66] 43
      Footnotes: 43
PROLOGUE 44
      Footnotes: 45
BOOK THE FIRST 46
   CHAPTER I 46
      Footnotes: 47
   CHAPTER II 48
      Footnotes: 48
   CHAPTER III 49

Ascent of Mount Carmel

- Footnotes: 50
- CHAPTER IV 51
  - Footnotes: 53
- CHAPTER V 54
  - Footnotes: 55
- CHAPTER VI 57
  - Footnotes: 58
- CHAPTER VII 59
  - Footnotes: 60
- CHAPTER VIII 61
  - Footnotes: 62
- CHAPTER IX 63
  - Footnotes: 64
- CHAPTER X 65
  - Footnotes: 65
- CHAPTER XI 66
  - Footnotes: 68
- CHAPTER XII 69
  - Footnotes: 70
- CHAPTER XIII 71
  - Footnotes: 72
- CHAPTER XIV 73
  - Footnotes: 73
- CHAPTER XV 74
  - Footnotes: 74

BOOK THE SECOND 75
- STANZA THE SECOND 76
- CHAPTER I 76
  - Footnotes: 77
- CHAPTER II 78
  - Footnotes: 78
- CHAPTER III 79
  - Footnotes: 80
- CHAPTER IV 81
  - Footnotes: 82
- CHAPTER V 83
  - Footnotes: 85
- CHAPTER VI 86
  - Footnotes: 87
- CHAPTER VII 88
  - Footnotes: 90

CHAPTER VIII	91
Footnotes:	92
CHAPTER IX	93
Footnotes:	94
CHAPTER X	95
CHAPTER XI	96
Footnotes:	98
CHAPTER XII	100
Footnotes:	102
CHAPTER XIII	103
Footnotes:	104
CHAPTER XIV	105
Footnotes:	108
CHAPTER XV	110
Footnotes:	111
CHAPTER XVI	112
CHAPTER XVII	116
CHAPTER XVIII	119
Footnotes:	120
CHAPTER XIX	121
Footnotes:	124
CHAPTER XX	125
Footnotes:	126
CHAPTER XXI	127
Footnotes:	130
CHAPTER XXII	131
Footnotes:	135
CHAPTER XXIII	136
Footnotes:	137
CHAPTER XXIV	138
Footnotes:	140
CHAPTER XXV	141
CHAPTER XXVI	142
Footnotes:	145
CHAPTER XXVII	146
Footnotes:	147
CHAPTER XXVIII	148
Footnotes:	148
CHAPTER XXIX	149
Footnotes:	151
CHAPTER XXX	152

Ascent of Mount Carmel

- Footnotes: 153
- CHAPTER XXXI 154
- Footnotes: 155
- CHAPTER XXXII 156
- Footnotes: 157
- BOOK THE THIRD 158
  - CHAPTER I 158
  - Footnotes: 158
  - CHAPTER II 159
  - Footnotes: 161
  - CHAPTER III 163
  - Footnotes: 164
  - CHAPTER IV 165
  - Footnotes: 165
  - CHAPTER V 166
  - CHAPTER VI 167
  - Footnotes: 167
  - CHAPTER VII 168
  - Footnotes: 168
  - CHAPTER VIII 169
  - Footnotes: 169
  - CHAPTER IX 170
  - Footnotes: 170
  - CHAPTER X 171
  - Footnotes: 171
  - CHAPTER XI 172
  - Footnotes: 172
  - CHAPTER XII 173
  - Footnotes: 173
  - CHAPTER XIII 174
  - Footnotes: 176
  - CHAPTER XIV 177
  - Footnotes: 177
  - CHAPTER XV 178
  - Footnotes: 178
  - CHAPTER XVI 179
  - Footnotes: 180
  - CHAPTER XVII 181
  - Footnotes: 181
  - CHAPTER XVIII 182
  - Footnotes: 183

CHAPTER XIX	184
Footnotes:	186
CHAPTER XX	187
CHAPTER XXI	189
Footnotes:	189
CHAPTER XXII	190
Footnotes:	191
CHAPTER XXIII	192
Footnotes:	192
CHAPTER XXIV	193
Footnotes:	194
CHAPTER XXV	195
Footnotes:	195
CHAPTER XXVI	196
Footnotes:	197
CHAPTER XXVII	198
Footnotes:	199
CHAPTER XXVIII	200
Footnotes:	201
CHAPTER XXIX	202
Footnotes:	202
CHAPTER XXX	203
Footnotes:	204
CHAPTER XXXI	205
Footnotes:	206
CHAPTER XXXII	208
Footnotes:	208
CHAPTER XXXIII	209
Footnotes:	209
CHAPTER XXXIV	210
CHAPTER XXXV	211
Footnotes:	212
CHAPTER XXXVI	213
Footnotes:	214
CHAPTER XXXVII	215
CHAPTER XXXVIII	216
Footnotes:	217
CHAPTER XXXIX	217
Footnotes:	218
CHAPTER XL	219
Footnotes:	219

Ascent of Mount Carmel

CHAPTER XLI 220

CHAPTER XLII 221

Footnotes: 222

CHAPTER XLIII 223

Footnotes: 223

CHAPTER XLIV 224

Footnotes: 225

CHAPTER XLV 226

"the greatest of all mystical theologians"

Thus has Thomas Merton described St. John of the Cross, echoing the considered judgment of most authorities on the spiritual life; and here in this volume is the great mystic's most widely appealing work. Ascent of Mount Carmel is an incomparable guide to the spiritual life -- because its author has lived his own counsel. Addressed to informed Christians who aspire to grow in union with God, it examines every category of spiritual experience, the spurious as well as the authentic. With rare insight into human psychology it not only tells how to become more closely united with God, but spells out in vivid detail the pitfalls to avoid.

In his Apostolic Letter proclaiming St. John of the Cross a Doctor of the Church, Pope Pius XI wrote that he "points out to souls the way of perfection as though illumined by light from on high, in his limpidly clear analysis of mystical experience. And although [his works] deal with difficult and hidden matters, they are nevertheless replete with such lofty spiritual doctrine and are so well adapted to the understanding of those who study them that they can rightly be called a guide and handbook for the man of faith who proposes to embrace a life of perfection."

This translation by E. Allison Peers was hailed by the London Times as "the most faithful that has appeared in any European language."

St. John of the Cross was perhaps the greatest mystical writer the world has ever known. Bossuet's famous tribute -- that his writings "possess the same authority in mystical theology as the writings of St. Thomas possess in dogmatic theology" -- remains the most fitting testimonial to his august place among spiritual writers.

John was born in Castile in 1542 -- eve of Spain's century of greatness, to which he himself was to add such lustre. He studied under the Jesuits and worked for six years in a hospital. Entering the Carmelites in 1563, he was professed a year later and sent to the great University of Salamanca. He was ordained in 1567 but, shrinking from the apostolate of a priest in the world, considered entering the Carthusians, a hermitical order.

Then came the turning point in his life. He met St. Teresa of Ávila, who was pursuing her epic work of restoring the pristine, stricter observance of the Carmelite rule. John and two other members of the order took the vows of the Discalced (or reformed) Carmelites the following year, binding themselves to a more rigorous way of life which included daily (and nightly) recitation of the Divine Office in choir, perpetual abstinence from meat, and additional fasting.

Yet his religious vows were but a part of the rigors John was to undergo. The main branch of the order, the Calced Carmelites, so opposed the Reform that they twice had John kidnapped and jailed -- providentially, so it proved, for much of his writing was done in prison.

The greater part of his twenty-three years as a Discalced Carmelite, however, was spent in filling a number of important posts in the order, among them Rector of two colleges, Prior, Definator, and Vicar-Provincial. But it was in one of his lesser offices that he was to spend the most decisive years of his life: he was confessor to the Carmelite nuns at Ávila, where St. Teresa was Superior.

The secret of St. John's unique contribution to mystical theology was not simply his mysticism, for there have been other mystics; not even his profound grasp of Scripture, dogma, Thomism, and spiritual literature, for there have also been learned mystics. What sets him apart is his extraordinary poetic vision. To write of mystical experience is to try to express the inexpressible. Because he was a great poet St. John of the Cross was able, in the realm of mysticism, to push the frontiers of human expression beyond where any writer has succeeded in venturing before or since. This poetic intensity is found even in his prose, the major works of which are Ascent of Mount Carmel, Dark Night of the Soul, Spiritual Canticle, and Living Flame of Love.

St. John of the Cross died in 1591, was beatified less than a century later in 1675, was canonized in 1726, and was named a Doctor of the Church by Pope Pius XI in 1926.

TRANSLATOR'S PREFACE TO THE FIRST EDITION

FOR at least twenty years, a new translation of the works of St. John of the Cross has been an urgent necessity. The translations of the individual prose works now in general use go back in their original form to the eighteen-sixties, and, though the later editions of some of them have been submitted to a certain degree of revision, nothing but a complete retranslation of the works from their original Spanish could be satisfactory. For this there are two reasons.

First, the existing translations were never very exact renderings of the original Spanish text even in the form which held the field when they were first published. Their great merit was extreme readableness: many a disciple of the Spanish mystics, who is unacquainted with the language in which they wrote, owes to these translations the comparative ease with which he has mastered the main lines of St. John of the Cross's teaching. Thus for the general reader they were of great utility; for the student, on the other hand, they have never been entirely adequate. They paraphrase difficult expressions, omit or add to parts of individual sentences in order (as it seems) to facilitate comprehension of the general drift of the passages in which these occur, and frequently retranslate from the Vulgate the Saint's Spanish quotations from Holy Scripture instead of turning into English the quotations themselves, using the text actually before them.

A second and more important reason for a new translation, however, is the discovery of fresh manuscripts and the consequent improvements which have been made in the Spanish text of the works of St. John of the Cross, during the present century. Seventy years ago, the text chiefly used was that of the collection known as the Biblioteca de Autores Españoles (1853), which itself was based, as we shall later see, upon an edition going back as far as 1703, published before modern methods of editing were so much as imagined. Both the text of the B.A.E. edition and the unimportant commentary which accompanied it were highly unsatisfactory, yet until the beginning of the present century nothing appreciably better was attempted.

In the last twenty years, however, we have had two new editions, each based upon a close study of the extant manuscripts and each representing a great advance upon the editions preceding it. The three-volume Toledo edition of P. Gerardo de San Juan de la Cruz, C.D. (1912-14), was the first attempt made to produce an accurate text by modern critical methods. Its execution was perhaps less laudable than its conception, and faults were pointed out in it from the time of its appearance, but it served as a new starting-point for Spanish scholars and stimulated them to a new interest in St. John of the Cross's writings. Then, seventeen years later, came the magnificent five-volume edition of P. Silverio de Santa Teresa, C.D. (Burgos, 1929-31), which forms the basis of this present translation. So superior is it, even on the most casual examination, to all its predecessors that to eulogize it in detail is superfluous. It is founded upon a larger number of texts than has previously been known and it collates them with greater skill than that of any earlier editor. It can hardly fail to be the standard edition of the works of St. John of the Cross for generations.

Thanks to the labours of these Carmelite scholars and of others whose findings they have incorporated in their editions, Spanish students can now approach the work of the great Doctor with the reasonable belief that they are reading, as nearly as may be, what he actually wrote. English-reading students, however, who are unable to master sixteenth-century Spanish, have hitherto had no grounds for such a belief. They cannot tell whether, in any particular passage, they are face to face with the Saint's own words, with a translator's free paraphrase of them or with a gloss made by some later copyist or early editor in the supposed interests of orthodoxy. Indeed, they cannot be sure that some whole paragraph is not one of the numerous interpolations which has its rise in an early printed edition -- i.e., the timorous qualifications of statements which have seemed to the interpolator over-bold. Even some of the most distinguished writers in English on St. John of the Cross have been misled in this way and it has been impossible for any but those who read Spanish with ease to make a systematic and reliable study of such an important question as the alleged dependence of Spanish quietists upon the Saint, while his teaching on the mystical life has quite unwittingly been distorted by persons who would least wish to misrepresent it in any particular.

It was when writing the chapter on St. John of the Cross in the first volume of my Studies of the Spanish Mystics (in which, as it was published in 1927, I had not the advantage of using P. Silverio's edition) that I first realized the extent of the harm caused by the lack of an accurate and modern translation. Making my own versions of all the passages quoted, I had sometimes occasion to compare them with those of other translators, which at their worst were almost unrecognizable as versions of the same originals. Then and there I resolved that, when time allowed, I would make a fresh translation of the works of a saint to whom I have long had great devotion -- to whom, indeed, I owe more than to any other writer outside the Scriptures. Just at that time I happened to visit the Discalced Carmelites at Burgos, where I first met P. Silverio, and found, to my gratification, that his edition of St. John of the Cross was much nearer publication than I had imagined. Arrangements for sole permission to translate the new edition were quickly made and work on the early volumes was begun even before the last volume was published.

II

These preliminary notes will explain why my chief preoccupation throughout the performance of this task has been to present as accurate and reliable a version of St. John of the Cross's works as it is possible to obtain. To keep the translation, line by line, au pied de la lettre, is, of course, impracticable: and such constantly occurring Spanish habits as the use of abstract nouns in the plural and the verbal construction ir + present participle' introduce shades of meaning which cannot always be reproduced. Yet wherever, for stylistic or other reasons, I have departed from the Spanish in any way that could conceivably cause a misunderstanding, I have scrupulously indicated this in a footnote. Further, I have translated, not only the text, but the variant readings as given by P. Silverio, [1] except where they are due merely to slips of the copyist's pen or where they differ so slightly from the readings of the text that it is impossible to render the differences in English. I beg students not to think that some of the smaller changes noted are of no importance; closer examination will often show that, however slight they may seem, they are, in relation to their context, or to some particular aspect of the Saint's teaching, of real interest; in other places they help to give the reader an idea, which may be useful to him in some crucial passage, of the general characteristics of the manuscript or edition in question. The editor's notes on the manuscripts and early editions which he has collated will also be found, for the same reason, to be summarized in the introduction to each work; in consulting the variants, the English-reading student has the maximum aid to a judgment of the reliability of his authorities.

Concentration upon the aim of obtaining the most precise possible rendering of the text has led me to sacrifice stylistic elegance to exactness where the two have been in conflict; it has sometimes been difficult to bring oneself to reproduce the Saint's often ungainly, though often forceful, repetitions of words or his long, cumbrous parentheses, but the temptation to take refuge in graceful paraphrases has been steadily resisted. In the same interest, and also in that of space, I have made certain omissions from, and abbreviations of, other parts of the edition than the text. Two of P. Silverio's five volumes are entirely filled with commentaries and documents. I have selected from the documents those of outstanding interest to readers with no detailed knowledge of Spanish religious history and have been content to summarize the editor's introductions to the individual works, as well as his longer footnotes to the text, and to omit such parts as would interest only specialists, who are able, or at least should be obliged, to study them in the original Spanish.

The decision to summarize in these places has been made the less reluctantly because of the frequent unsuitability of P. Silverio's style to English readers. Like that of many Spaniards, it is so discursive, and at times so baroque in its wealth of epithet and its profusion of imagery, that a literal translation, for many pages together, would seldom have been acceptable. The same criticism would have been applicable to any literal translation of P. Silverio's biography of St. John of the Cross which stands at the head of his edition (Vol. I, pp. 7-130). There was a further reason for omitting these biographical chapters. The long and fully documented biography by the French Carmelite, P. Bruno de Jésus-Marie, C.D., written from the same standpoint as P. Silverio's, has recently been translated into English, and any attempt to rival this in so short a space would be foredoomed to failure. I have thought, however, that a brief outline of the principal events in St. John of the Cross's life would be a useful preliminary to this edition; this has therefore been substituted for the biographical sketch referred to.

In language, I have tried to reproduce the atmosphere of a sixteenth-century text as far as is consistent with clarity. Though following the paragraph divisions of my original, I have not scrupled, where this has seemed to facilitate understanding, to divide into shorter sentences the long and sometimes straggling periods in which the Saint so frequently indulged. Some attempt has been made to show the contrast between the highly adorned, poetical language of much of the commentary on the Spiritual Canticle' and the more closely shorn and eminently practical, though always somewhat discursive style of the Ascent and Dark Night. That the Living Flame occupies an intermediate position in this respect should also be clear from the style of the translation.

Quotations, whether from the Scriptures or from other sources, have been left strictly as St. John of the Cross made them. Where he quotes in Latin, the Latin has been reproduced; only his quotations in

Ascent of Mount Carmel

Spanish have been turned into English. The footnote references are to the Vulgate, of which the Douai Version is a direct translation; if the Authorized Version differs, as in the Psalms, the variation has been shown in square brackets for the convenience of those who use it.

A word may not be out of place regarding the translations of the poems as they appear in the prose commentaries. Obviously, it would have been impossible to use the comparatively free verse renderings which appear in Volume II of this translation, since the commentaries discuss each line and often each word of the poems. A literal version of the poems in their original verse-lines, however, struck me as being inartistic, if not repellent, and as inviting continual comparison with the more polished verse renderings which, in spirit, come far nearer to the poet's aim. My first intention was to translate the poems, for the purpose of the commentaries, into prose. But later I hit upon the long and metrically unfettered verse-line, suggestive of Biblical poetry in its English dress, which I have employed throughout. I believe that, although the renderings often suffer artistically from their necessary literalness, they are from the artistic standpoint at least tolerable.

III

The debts I have to acknowledge, though few, are very large ones. My gratitude to P. Silverio de Santa Teresa for telling me so much about his edition before its publication, granting my publishers the sole translation rights and discussing with me a number of crucial passages cannot be disjoined from the many kindnesses I have received during my work on the Spanish mystics, which is still proceeding, from himself and from his fellow-Carmelites in the province of Castile. In dedicating this translation to them, I think particularly of P. Silverio in Burgos, of P. Florencio del Ni-o Jesús in Madrid, and of P. Crisógono de Jesús Sacramentado, together with the Fathers of the Convento de la Santa' in vila.

The long and weary process of revising the manuscript and proofs of this translation has been greatly lightened by the co-operation and companionship of P. Edmund Gurdon, Prior of the Cartuja de Miraflores, near Burgos, with whom I have freely discussed all kinds of difficulties, both of substance and style, and who has been good enough to read part of my proofs. From the quiet library of his monastery, as well as from his gracious companionship, I have drawn not only knowledge, but strength, patience and perseverance. And when at length, after each of my visits, we have had to part, we have continued our labours by correspondence, shaking hands, as it were, over a vast' and embracing from the ends of opposd winds.'

Finally, I owe a real debt to my publishers for allowing me to do this work without imposing any such limitations of time as often accompany literary undertakings. This and other considerations which I have received from them have made that part of the work which has been done outside the study unusually pleasant and I am correspondingly grateful.

E. ALLISON PEERS.
University of Liverpool.
Feast of St. John of the Cross,
November 24, 1933.

Note. -- Wherever a commentary by St. John of the Cross is referred to, its title is given in italics (e.g. Spiritual Canticle); where the corresponding poem is meant, it is placed between quotation marks (e.g. Spiritual Canticle'). The abbreviation e.p.' stands for editio princeps throughout.

Footnotes:

1. The footnotes are P. Silverio's except where they are enclosed in square brackets.

TRANSLATOR'S PREFACE TO THE SECOND EDITION

DURING the sixteen years which have elapsed since the publication of the first edition, several reprints have been issued, and the demand is now such as to justify a complete resetting. I have taken advantage of this opportunity to revise the text throughout, and hope that in some of the more difficult passages I may have come nearer than before to the Saint's mind. Recent researches have necessitated a considerable amplification of introductions and footnotes and greatly increased the length of the bibliography.

The only modification which has been made consistently throughout the three volumes relates to St. John of the Cross's quotations from Scripture. In translating these I still follow him exactly, even where he himself is inexact, but I have used the Douia Version (instead of the Authorized, as in the first edition) as a basis for all Scriptural quotations, as well as in the footnote references and the Scriptural index in Vol. III.

Far more is now known of the life and times of St. John of the Cross than when this translation of the Complete Works was first published, thanks principally to the Historia del Carmen Descalzo of P. Silverio de Santa Teresa, C.D, now General of his Order, and to the admirably documented Life of the Saint written by P. Crisógono de Jesus Sacramentado, C.D., and published (in Vida y Obras de San Juan de la Cruz) in the year after his untimely death. This increased knowledge is reflected in many additional notes, and also in the Outline of the Life of St. John of the Cross' (Vol. I, pp. xxv-xxviii), which, for this edition, has been entirely recast. References are given to my Handbook to the Life and Times of St. Teresa and St. John of the Cross, which provides much background too full to be reproduced in footnotes and too complicated to be compressed. The Handbook also contains numerous references to contemporary events, omitted from the Outline' as being too remote from the main theme to justify inclusion in a summary necessarily so condensed.

My thanks for help in revision are due to kindly correspondents, too numerous to name, from many parts of the world, who have made suggestions for the improvement of the first edition; to the Rev. Professor David Knowles, of Cambridge University, for whose continuous practical interest in this translation I cannot be too grateful; to Miss I.L. McClelland, of Glasgow University, who has read a large part of this edition in proof; to Dom Philippe Chevallier, for material which I have been able to incorporate in it; to P. José Antonio de Sobrino, S.J., for allowing me to quote freely from his recently published Estudios; and, most of all, to M.R.P. Silverio de Santa Teresa, C.D., and the Fathers of the International Carmelite College at Rome, whose learning and experience, are, I hope, faintly reflected in this new edition.

E.A.P.
June 30, 1941.

PRINCIPAL ABBREVIATIONS

A.V.--Authorized Version of the Bible (1611).

D.V.--Douai Version of the Bible (1609).

C.W.S.T.J.--The Complete Works of Saint Teresa of Jesus, translated and edited by E. Allison Peers from the critical edition of P. Silverio de Santa Teresa, C.D. London, Sheed and Ward, 1946. 3 vols.

H.-E. Allison Peers: Handbook to the Life and Times of St. Teresa and St. John of the Cross. London, Burns Oates and Washbourne, 1953.

LL.--The Letters of Saint Teresa of Jesus, translated and edited by E. Allison Peers from the critical edition of P. Silverio de Santa Teresa, C.D. London, Burns Oates and Washburne, 1951. 2 vols.

N.L.M.--National Library of Spain (Biblioteca Nacional), Madrid.

Obras (P. Silv.)--Obras de San Juan de la Cruz, Doctor de la Iglesia, editadas y anotadas pot el P. Silverio de Santa Teresa, C.D. Burgos, 1929-31. 5 vols.

S.S.M.--E. Allison Peers: Studies of the Spanish Mystics. Vol. I, London, Sheldon Press, 1927; 2nd ed., London, S.P.C.K., 1951. Vol. II, London, Sheldon Press, 1930.

Sobrino.-José Antonio de Sobrino, S.J.: Estudios sobre San Juan de la Cruz y nuevos textos de su obra. Madrid, 1950.

AN OUTLINE OF THE LIFE OF ST. JOHN OF THE CROSS [2]

1542. Birth of Juan de Yepes at Fontiveros (Hontiveros), near vila.
The day generally ascribed to this event is June 24 (St. John Baptist's Day). No documentary evidence for it, however, exists, the parish registers having been destroyed by a fire in 1544. The chief evidence is an inscription, dated 1689, on the font of the parish church at Fontiveros.

? c. 1543. Death of Juan's father. After some years' the mother removes, with her family, to Arévalo, and later to Medina del Campo.

? c. 1552-6. Juan goes to school at the Colegio de los Ni-os de la Doctrina, Medina.

c. 1556-7. Don Antonio lvarez de Toledo takes him into a Hospital to which he has retired, with the idea of his (Juan's) training for Holy Orders under his patronage.

? c. 1559-63. Juan attends the College of the Society of Jesus at Medina.

c. 1562. Leaves the Hospital and the patronage of lvarez de Toledo.

1563. Takes the Carmelite habit at St. Anne's, Medina del Campo, as Juan de San Matías (Santo Matía).

The day is frequently assumed (without any foundation) to have been the feast of St. Matthias (February 24), but P. Silverio postulates a day in August or September and P. Crisógono thinks February definitely improbable.

1564. Makes his profession in the same priory -- probably in August or September and certainly not earlier than May 21 and not later than October.

1564 (November). Enters the University of Salamanca as an artista. Takes a three-year course in Arts (1564-7).

1565 (January 6). Matriculates at the University of Salamanca.

1567. Receives priest's orders (probably in the summer).

1567 (? September). Meets St. Teresa at Medina del Campo. Juan is thinking of transferring to the Carthusian Order. St. Teresa asks him to join her Discalced Reform and the projected first foundation for friars. He agrees to do so, provided the foundation is soon made.

1567 (November). Returns to the University of Salamanca, where he takes a year's course in theology.

1568. Spends part of the Long Vacation at Medina del Campo. On August 10, accompanies St. Teresa to Valladolid. In September, returns to Medina and later goes to Avila and Duruelo.

1568 (November 28). Takes the vows of the Reform Duruelo as St. John of the Cross, together with Antonio de Heredia (Antonio de Jesus), Prior of the Calced Carmelites at Medina, and José de Cristo, another Carmelite from Medina.

1570 (June 11). Moves, with the Duruelo community, to Mancera de Abajo.

1570 (October, or possibly February 1571). Stays for about a month at Pastrana, returning thence to Mancera.

1571 (? January 25). Visits Alba de Tormes for the inauguration of a new convent there.

1571 (? April). Goes to Alcalá de Henares as Rector of the College of the Reform and directs the Carmelite nuns.

1572 (shortly after April 23). Recalled to Pastrana to correct the rigours of the new novice-master, Angel de San Gabriel.

1572 (between May and September). Goes to vila as confessor to the Convent of the Incarnation. Remains there till 1577.

1574 (March). Accompanies St. Teresa from vila to Segovia, arriving on March 18. Returns to vila about the end of the month.

1575-6 (Winter of: before February 1576). Kidnapped by the Calced and imprisoned at Medina del Campo. Freed by the intervention of the Papal Nuncio, Ormaneto.

1577 (December 2 or 3). Kidnapped by the Calced and carried off to the Calced Carmelite priory at Toledo as a prisoner.

1577-8. Composes in prison 17 (or perhaps 30) stanzas of the Spiritual Canticle' (i.e., as far as the stanza: Daughters of Jewry'); the poem with the refrain Although tis night'; and the stanzas beginning In

Ascent of Mount Carmel

principio erat verbum.' He may also have composed the paraphrase of the psalm Super flumina and the poem Dark Night.' (Note: All these poems, in verse form, will be found in Vol. II of this edition.)

1578 (August 16 or shortly afterwards). Escapes to the convent of the Carmelite nuns in Toledo, and is thence taken to his house by D. Pedro González de Mendoza, Canon of Toledo.

1578 (October 9). Attends a meeting of the Discalced superiors at Almodóvar. Is sent to El Calvario as Vicar, in the absence in Rome of the Prior.

1578 (end of October). Stays for a few days' at Beas de Segura, near El Calvario. Confesses the nuns at the Carmelite Convent of Beas.

1578 (November). Arrives at El Calvario.

1578-9 (November-June). Remains at El Calvario as Vicar. For a part of this time (probably from the beginning of 1579), goes weekly to the convent of Beas to hear confessions. During this period, begins his commentaries entitled The Ascent of Mount Carmel (cf. pp. 9-314, below) and Spiritual Canticle (translated in Vol. I).

1579 (June 14). Founds a college of the Reform at Baeza. 1579-82. Resides at Baeza as Rector of the Carmelite college. Visits the Beas convent occasionally. Writes more of the prose works begun at El Calvario and the rest of the stanzas of the Spiritual Canticle' except the last five, possibly with the commentaries to the stanzas.

1580. Death of his mother.

1581 (March 3). Attends the Alcalá Chapter of the Reform. Appointed Third Definitor and Prior of the Granada house of Los Mártires. Takes up the latter office only on or about the time of his election by the community in March 1582.

1581 (November 28). Last meeting with St. Teresa, at vila. On the next day, sets out with two nuns for Beas (December 8-January 15) and Granada.

1582 (January 20). Arrives at Los Mártires.

1582-8. Mainly at Granada. Re-elected (or confirmed) as Prior of Los Mártires by the Chapter of Almodóvar, 1583. Resides at Los Mártires more or less continuously till 1584 and intermittently afterwards. Visits the Beas convent occasionally. Writes the last five stanzas of the Spiritual Canticle' during one of these visits. At Los Mártires, finishes the Ascent of Mount Carmel and composes his remaining prose treatises. Writes Living Flame of Love about 1585, in fifteen days, at the request of Doña Ana de Peñalosa.

1585 (May). Lisbon Chapter appoints him Second Definitor and (till 1587) Vicar-Provincial of Andalusia. Makes the following foundations: Málaga, February 17, 1585; Córdoba, May 18, 1586; La Manchuela (de Jaén), October 12, 1586; Caravaca, December 18, 1586; Bujalance, June 24, 1587.

1587 (April). Chapter of Valladolid re-appoints him Prior of Los Mártires. He ceases to be Definitor and Vicar-Provincial.

1588 (June 19). Attends the first Chapter-General of the Reform in Madrid. Is elected First Definitor and a consiliario.

1588 (August 10). Becomes Prior of Segovia, the central house of the Reform and the headquarters of the Consulta. Acts as deputy for the Vicar-General, P. Doria, during the latter's absences.

1590 (June 10). Re-elected First Definitor and a consiliario at the Chapter-General Extraordinary, Madrid.

1591 (June 1). The Madrid Chapter-General deprives him of his offices and resolves to send him to Mexico. (This latter decision was later revoked.)

1591 (August 10). Arrives at La Pe-uela.

1591 (September 12). Attacked by fever. (September Leaves La Pe-uela for beda. (December 14) Dies at beda.

January 25, 1675. Beatified by Clement X.

December 26, 1726. Canonized by Benedict XIII.

August 24, 1926. Declared Doctor of the Church Universal by Pius XI.

Footnotes:

2. Cf. Translator's Preface to the First Edition, II.

GENERAL INTRODUCTION TO THE WORKS OF ST. JOHN OF THE CROSS

I - DATES AND METHODS OF COMPOSITION

GENERAL CHARACTERISTICS

WITH regard to the times and places at which the works of St. John of the Cross were written, and also with regard to the number of these works, there have existed, from a very early date, considerable differences of opinion. Of internal evidence from the Saint's own writings there is practically none, and such external testimony as can be found in contemporary documents needs very careful examination.

There was no period in the life of St. John of the Cross in which he devoted himself entirely to writing. He does not, in fact, appear to have felt any inclination to do so: his books were written in response to the insistent and repeated demands of his spiritual children. He was very much addicted, on the other hand, to the composition of apothegms or maxims for the use of his penitents and this custom he probably began as early as the days in which he was confessor to the Convent of the Incarnation at vila, though his biographers have no record of any maxims but those written at Beas. One of his best beloved daughters however, Ana María de Jesús, of the Convent of the Incarnation, declared in her deposition, during the process of the Saint's canonization, that he was accustomed to comfort those with whom he had to do, both by his words and by his letters, of which this witness received a number, and also by certain papers concerning holy things which this witness would greatly value if she still had them.' Considering, the number of nuns to whom the Saint was director at vila, it is to be presumed that M. Ana María was not the only person whom he favoured. We may safely conclude, indeed, that there were many others who shared the same privileges, and that, had we all these papers,' they would comprise a large volume, instead of the few pages reproduced elsewhere in this translation.

There is a well-known story, preserved in the documents of the canonization process, of how, on a December night of 1577, St. John, of the Cross was kidnapped by the Calced Carmelites of vila and carried off from the Incarnation to their priory. [3] Realizing that he had left behind him some important papers, he contrived, on the next morning, to escape, and returned to the Incarnation to destroy them while there was time to do so. He was missed almost immediately and he had hardly gained his cell when his pursuers were on his heels. In the few moments that remained to him he had time to tear up these papers and swallow some of the most compromising. As the original assault had not been unexpected, though the time of it was uncertain, they would not have been very numerous. It is generally supposed that they concerned the business of the infant Reform, of which the survival was at that time in grave doubt. But it seems at least equally likely that some of them might have been these spiritual maxims, or some more extensive instructions which might be misinterpreted by any who found them. It is remarkable, at any rate, that we have none of the Saint's writings belonging to this period whatever.

All his biographers tell us that he wrote some of the stanzas of the Spiritual Canticle,' together with a few other poems, while he was imprisoned at Toledo. When he left the prison,' says M. Magdalena del Espíritu Santo, he took with him a little book in which he had written, while there, some verses based upon the Gospel In principio erat Verbum, together with some couplets which begin: "How well I know the fount that freely flows, Although tis night," and the stanzas or liras that begin "Whither has vanishd?" as far as the stanzas beginning "Daughters of Jewry." The remainder of them the Saint composed later when he was Rector of the College at Baeza. Some of the expositions were written at Beas, as answers to questions put to him by the nuns; others at Granada. This little book, in which the Saint wrote while in prison, he left in the Convent of Beas and on various occasions I was commanded to copy it. Then someone took it from my cell -- who, I never knew. The freshness of the words in this book, together with their beauty and subtlety, caused me great wonder, and one day I asked the Saint if God gave him those words which were so comprehensive and so lovely. And he answered: "Daughter, sometimes God gave them to me and at other times I sought them."' [4]

M. Isabel de Jesús María, who was a novice at Toledo when the Saint escaped from his

Ascent of Mount Carmel

imprisonment there, wrote thus from Cuerva on November 2, 1614. I remember, too, that, at the time we had him hidden in the church, he recited to us some lines which he had composed and kept in his mind, and that one of the nuns wrote them down as he repeated them. There were three poems -- all of them upon the Most Holy Trinity, and so sublime and devout that they seem to enkindle the reader. In this house at Cuerva we have some which begin:

"Far away in the beginning,
Dwelt the Word in God Most High.'" [5]

The frequent references to keeping his verses in his head and the popular exaggeration of the hardships (great though these were) which the Saint had to endure in Toledo have led some writers to affirm that he did not in fact write these poems in prison but committed them to memory and transferred them to paper at some later date. The evidence of M. Magdalena, however, would appear to be decisive. We know, too, that the second of St. John of the Cross's gaolers, Fray Juan de Santa María, was a kindly man who did all he could to lighten his captive's sufferings; and his superiors would probably not have forbidden him writing materials provided he wrote no letters. [6]

It seems, then, that the Saint wrote in Toledo the first seventeen (or perhaps thirty) stanzas of the Spiritual Canticle,' the nine parts of the poem Far away in the beginning . . .,' the paraphrase of the psalm Super flumina Babylonis and the poem How well I know the fount . . .' This was really a considerable output of work, for, except perhaps when his gaoler allowed him to go into another room, he had no light but that of a small oil-lamp or occasionally the infiltration of daylight that penetrated a small interior window.

Apart from the statement of M. Magdalena already quoted, little more is known of what the Saint wrote in El Calvario than of what he wrote in Toledo. From an amplification made by herself of the sentences to which we have referred it appears that almost the whole of what she had copied was taken from her; as the short extracts transcribed by her are very similar to passages from the Saint's writings we may perhaps conclude that much of the other material was also incorporated in them. In that case he may well have completed a fair proportion of the Ascent of Mount Carmel before leaving Beas.

It was in El Calvario, too, and for the nuns of Beas, that the Saint drew the plan called the Mount of Perfection' (referred to by M. Magdalena [7] and in the Ascent of Mount Carmel and reproduced as the frontispiece to this volume) of which copies were afterwards multiplied and distributed among Discalced houses. Its author wished it to figure at the head of all his treatises, for it is a graphical representation of the entire mystic way, from the starting-point of the beginner to the very summit of perfection. His first sketch, which still survives, is a rudimentary and imperfect one; before long, however, as M. Magdalena tells us, he evolved another that was fuller and more comprehensive.

Mount Carmel

Just as we owe to PP. Gracián and Salazar many precious relics of St. Teresa, so we owe others of St. John of the Cross to M. Magdalena. Among the most valuable of these is her own copy of the Mount,' which, after her death, went to the Desert' [8] of Our Lady of the Snows established by the Discalced province of Upper Andalusia in the diocese of Granada. It was found there by P. Andrés de la Encarnación, of whom we shall presently speak, and who immediately made a copy of it, legally certified as an exact one and now in the National Library of Spain (MS. 6,296).

The superiority of the second plan over the first is very evident. The first consists simply of three parallel lines corresponding to three different paths -- one on either side of the Mount, marked Road of the spirit of imperfection' and one in the centre marked Path of Mount Carmel. Spirit of perfection.' In the spaces between the paths are written the celebrated maxims which appear in Book I, Chapter xiii, of the Ascent of Mount Carmel, in a somewhat different form, together with certain others. At the top of the drawing are the words Mount Carmel,' which are not found in the second plan, and below them is the legend: There is no road here, for there is no law for the righteous man,' together with other texts from Scripture.

The second plan represents a number of graded heights, the loftiest of which is planted with trees. Three paths, as in the first sketch, lead from the base of the mount, but they are traced more artistically and have a more detailed ascetic and mystical application. Those on either side, which denote the roads of imperfection, are broad and somewhat tortuous and come to an end before the higher stages of the mount are reached. The centre road, that of perfection, is at first very narrow but gradually broadens and leads right up to the summit of the mountain, which only the perfect attain and where they enjoy the iuge convivium -- the heavenly feast. The different zones of religious perfection, from which spring various virtues, are portrayed with much greater detail than in the first plan. As we have reproduced the second plan in this volume, it need not be described more fully.

We know that St. John of the Cross used the Mount' very, frequently for all kinds of religious instruction. By means of this drawing,' testified one of his disciples, he used to teach us that, in order to attain to perfection, we must not desire the good things of earth, nor those of Heaven; but that we must desire naught save to seek and strive after the glory and honour of God our Lord in all things . . . and this "Mount of Perfection" the said holy father himself expounded to this Witness when he was his superior in the said priory of Granada.' [9]

It seems not improbable that the Saint continued writing chapters of the Ascent and the Spiritual Canticle while he was Rector at Baeza, [10] whether in the College itself, or in El Castellar, where he was accustomed often to go into retreat. It was certainly here that he wrote the remaining stanzas of the Canticle (as M. Magdalena explicitly tells us in words already quoted), except the last five, which he composed rather later, at Granada. One likes to think that these loveliest of his verses were penned by the banks of the Guadalimar, in the woods of the Granja de Santa Ann, where he was in the habit of passing long hours in communion with God. At all events the stanzas seem more in harmony with such an atmosphere than with that of the College.

With regard to the last five stanzas, we have definite evidence from a Beas nun, M. Francisca de la Madre de Dios, who testifies in the Beatification process (April 2, 1618) as follows:

> And so, when the said holy friar John of the Cross was in this convent one Lent (for his great love for it brought him here from the said city of Granada, where he was prior, to confess the nuns and preach to them) he was preaching to them one day in the parlour, and this witness observed that on two separate occasions he was rapt and lifted up from the ground; and when he came to himself he dissembled and said: You saw how sleep overcame me!' And one day he asked this witness in what her prayer consisted, and she replied: In considering the beauty of God and in rejoicing that He has such beauty.' And the Saint was so pleased with this that for some days he said the most sublime things concerning the beauty of God, at which all marvelled. And thus, under the influence of this love, he composed five stanzas, beginning Beloved, let us sing, And in thy beauty see ourselves portray'd.' And in all this he showed that there was in his breast a great love of God.

From a letter which this nun wrote from Beas in 1629 to P. Jerónimo de San José, we gather that the stanzas were actually written at Granada and brought to Beas, where

> . . . with every word that we spoke to him we seemed to be opening a door to the fruition of the great treasures and riches which God had stored up in his soul.

If there is a discrepancy here, however, it is of small importance; there is no doubt as to the approximate date of the composition of these stanzas and of their close connection with Beas.

The most fruitful literary years for St. John of the Cross were those which he spent at Granada. Here he completed the Ascent and wrote all his remaining treatises. Both M. Magdalena and the Saint's closest disciple, P. Juan Evangelista, bear witness to this. The latter writes from Granada to P. Jerónimo de San José, the historian of the Reform:

> With regard to having seen our venerable father write the books, I saw him write them all; for, as I have said, I was ever at his side. The Ascent of Mount Carmel and the Dark Night he wrote here at Granada, little by little, continuing them only with many breaks. The Living Flame of Love he also wrote in this house, when he was Vicar-Provincial, at the request of Doña Ana de Peñalosa, and he wrote it in fifteen days when he was very busy here with an abundance of occupations. The first thing that he wrote was Whither hast vanishd? and that too he wrote here; the stanzas he had written in the prison at Toledo. [11]

In another letter (February 18, 1630), he wrote to the same correspondent:

> With regard to our holy father's having written his books in this home, I will say what is undoubtedly true -- namely, that he wrote here the commentary on the stanzas Whither hast vanishd? and the Living Flame of Love, for he began and ended them in my time. The Ascent of Mount Carmel I found had been begun when I came here to take the habit, which was a year and a half after the foundation of this house; he may have brought it from yonder already begun. But the Dark Night he certainly wrote here, for I saw him writing a part of it, and this is certain, because I saw it. [12]

These and other testimonies might with advantage be fuller and more concrete, but at least they place beyond doubt the facts that we have already set down. Summarizing our total findings, we may assert that part of the Spiritual Canticle,' with perhaps the Dark Night,' and the other poems enumerated, were written in the Toledo prison; that at the request of some nuns he wrote at El Calvario (1578-79) a few chapters of the Ascent and commentaries on some of the stanzas of the Canticle'; that he composed further stanzas at Baeza (1579-81), perhaps with their respective commentaries; and that, finally, he completed the Canticle and the Ascent at Granada and wrote the whole of the Dark Night and of the Living Flame -- the latter in a fortnight. All these last works he wrote before the end of 1585, the first year in which he was Vicar-Provincial.

Other writings, most of them brief, are attributed to St. John of the Cross; they will be discussed in the third volume of this edition, in which we shall publish the minor works which we accept as genuine. The authorship of his four major prose works -- the Ascent, Dark Night, Spiritual Canticle and Living Flame -- no one has ever attempted to question, even though the lack of extant autographs and the large number of copies have made it difficult to establish correct texts. To this question we shall return later.

The characteristics of the writings of St. John of the Cross are so striking that it would be difficult to confuse them with those of any other writer. His literary personality stands out clearly from that of his Spanish contemporaries who wrote on similar subjects. Both his style and his methods of exposition bear the marks of a strong individuality.

If some of these derive from his native genius and temperament, others are undoubtedly reflections of his education and experience. The Aristotelian-Thomistic philosophy, then at the height of its splendour, which he learned so thoroughly in the classrooms of Salamanca University, characterizes the whole of his writings, giving them a granite-like solidity even when their theme is such as to defy human speculation. Though the precise extent of his debt to this Salamancan training in philosophy has not yet been definitely assessed, the fact of its influence is evident to every reader. It gives massiveness, harmony and unity to both the ascetic and the mystical work of St. John of the Cross -- that is to say, to all his scientific writing.

Deeply, however, as St. John of the Cross drew from the Schoolmen, he was also profoundly indebted to many other writers. He was distinctly eclectic in his reading and quotes freely (though less than some of his Spanish contemporaries) from the Fathers and from the mediaeval mystics, especially from St. Thomas, St. Bonaventura, Hugh of St. Victor and the pseudo-Areopagite. All that he quotes, however, he makes his own, with the result that his chapters are never a mass of citations loosely strung together, as are those of many other Spanish mystics of his time.

When we study his treatises -- principally that great composite work known as the Ascent of Mount Carmel and the Dark Night -- we have the impression of a master-mind that has scaled the heights of mystical science and from their summit looks down upon and dominates the plain below and the paths leading upward. We may well wonder what a vast contribution to the subject he would have made had he been able to expound all the eight stanzas of his poem since he covered so much ground in expounding no more than two. Observe with what assurance and what mastery of subject and method he defines his themes and divides his arguments, even when treating the most abstruse and controversial questions. The most obscure phenomena he appears to illumine, as it were, with one lightning flash of understanding, as though the explanation of them were perfectly natural and easy. His solutions of difficult problems are not timid, questioning and loaded with exceptions, but clear, definite and virile like the man who proposes them. No scientific field, perhaps, has so many zones which are apt to become vague and obscure as has that of mystical theology; and there are those among the Saint's predecessors who seem to have made their permanent abode in them. They give the impression of attempting to cloak vagueness in verbosity, in order to avoid being forced into giving solutions of problems which they find insoluble. Not so St. John of the Cross. A scientific dictator, if such a person were conceivable, could hardly express himself with greater clarity. His phrases have a decisive, almost a chiselled quality; where he errs on the side of redundance, it is not with the intention of cloaking uncertainty, but in order that he may drive home with double force the truths which he desires to impress.

No less admirable are, on the one hand, his synthetic skill and the logic of his arguments, and, on the other, his subtle and discriminating analyses, which weigh the finest shades of thought and dissect each subject with all the accuracy of science. To his analytical genius we owe those finely balanced statements, orthodox yet bold and fearless, which have caused clumsier intellects to misunderstand him. It is not remarkable that this should have occurred. The ease with which the unskilled can misinterpret genius is shown in the history of many a heresy.

How much of all this St. John of the Cross owed to his studies of scholastic philosophy in the University of Salamanca, it is difficult to say. If we examine the history of that University and read of its severe discipline we shall be in no danger of under-estimating the effect which it must have produced upon so agile and alert an intellect. Further, we note the constant parallelisms and the comparatively infrequent (though occasionally important) divergences between the doctrines of St. John of the Cross and St. Thomas, to say nothing of the close agreement between the views of St. John of the Cross and those of the Schoolmen on such subjects as the passions and appetites, the nature of the soul, the relations between soul and body. Yet we must not forget the student tag: Quod natura non dat, Salamtica non praestat. Nothing but natural genius could impart the vigour and the clarity which enhance all St. John of the Cross's arguments and nothing but his own deep and varied experience could have made him what he may well be termed -- the greatest psychologist in the history of mysticism.

Eminent, too, was St. John of the Cross in sacred theology. The close natural connection that exists between dogmatic and mystical theology and their continual interdependence in practice make it impossible for a Christian teacher to excel in the latter alone. Indeed, more than one of the heresies that have had their beginnings in mysticism would never have developed had those who fell into them been well grounded in dogmatic theology. The one is, as it were, the lantern that lights the path of the other, as St. Teresa realized when she began to feel the continual necessity of consulting theological teachers. If St. John of the Cross is able to climb the greatest heights of mysticism and remain upon them without stumbling or dizziness it is because his feet are invariably well shod with the truths of dogmatic theology. The great mysteries -- those of the Trinity, the Creation, the Incarnation and the Redemption -- and such dogmas as those concerning grace, the gifts of the Spirit, the theological virtues, etc., were to him guide-posts for those who attempted to scale, and to lead others to scale, the symbolic mount of sanctity.

It will be remembered that the Saint spent but one year upon his theological course at the University of Salamanca, for which reason many have been surprised at the evident solidity of his attainments. But, apart from the fact that a mind so keen and retentive as that of Fray Juan de San Matías could absorb in a year what others would have failed to imbibe in the more usual two or three, we must of necessity assume a far longer time spent in private study. For in one year he could not have studied all the treatises of which he clearly demonstrates his knowledge -- to say nothing of many others which he must have known. His own works, apart from any external evidence, prove him to have been a theologian of distinction.

In both fields, the dogmatic and the mystical he was greatly aided by his knowledge of Holy Scripture, which he studied continually, in the last years of his life, to the exclusion, as it would seem, of all else. Much of it he knew by heart; the simple devotional talks that he was accustomed to give were invariably studded with texts, and he made use of passages from the Bible both to justify and to illustrate his teaching. In the mystical interpretation of Holy Scripture, as every student of mysticism knows, he has had few equals even among his fellow Doctors of the Church Universal.

Testimonies to his mastery of the Scriptures can be found in abundance. P. Alonso de la Madre de Dios, el Asturicense, for example, who was personally acquainted with him, stated in 1603 that he had a great gift and facility for the exposition of the Sacred Scripture, principally of the Song of Songs, Ecclesiasticus, Ecclesiastes, the Proverbs and the Psalms of David.'[13] His spiritual daughter, that same Magdalena del Espíritu Santo to whom we have several times referred, affirms that St. John of the Cross would frequently read the Gospels to the nuns of Beas and expound the letter and the spirit to them.[14] Fray Juan Evangelista says in a well-known passage:

He was very fond of reading in the Scriptures, and I never once saw him read any other books than the Bible,[15] *almost all of which he knew by heart, St. Augustine Contra Haereses and the Flos Sanctorum. When occasionally he preached (which was seldom) or gave informal addresses [pláticas], as he more commonly did, he never read from any book save the Bible. His conversation, whether at recreation or at other times, was continually of God, and he spoke so delightfully that, when he discoursed upon sacred things at recreation, he would make us all laugh and we used greatly to enjoy going out. On occasions when we held chapters, he would usually give devotional addresses (pláticas divinas) after supper, and he never failed to give an address every night.*[16]

Fray Pablo de Santa María, who had also heard the Saint's addresses, wrote thus:

He was a man of the most enkindled spirituality and of great insight into all that concerns mystical theology and matters of prayer; I consider it impossible that he could have spoken so well about all the virtues if he had not been most proficient in the spiritual life, and I really think he knew the whole Bible by heart, so far as one could judge from the various Biblical passages which he would quote at chapters and in the refectory, without any great effort, but as one who goes where the Spirit leads him.[17]

Nor was this admiration for the expository ability of St. John of the Cross confined to his fellow-friars, who might easily enough have been led into hero-worship. We know that he was thought highly of in this respect by the University of Alcalá de Henares, where he was consulted as an authority. A Dr. Villegas, Canon of Segovia Cathedral, has left on record his respect for him. And Fray Jerónimo de San José relates the esteem in which he was held at the University of Baeza, which in his day enjoyed a considerable reputation for Biblical studies:

Ascent of Mount Carmel

> There were at that time at the University of Baeza many learned and spiritually minded persons, disciples of that great father and apostle Juan de vila.[18] ... All these doctors ... would repair to our venerable father as to an oracle from heaven and would discuss with him both their own spiritual progress and that of souls committed to their charge, with the result that they were both edified and astonished at his skill. They would also bring him difficulties and delicate points connected with Divine letters, and on these, too, he spoke with extraordinary energy and illumination. One of these doctors, who had consulted him and listened to him on various occasions, said that, although he had read deeply in St. Augustine and St. John Chrysostom and other saints, and had found in them greater heights and depths, he had found in none of them that particular kind of spirituality in exposition which this great father applied to Scriptural passages.[19]

The Scriptural knowledge of St. John of the Cross was, as this passage makes clear, in no way merely academic. Both in his literal and his mystical interpretations of the Bible, he has what we may call a Biblical sense,' which saves him from such exaggerations as we find in other expositors, both earlier and contemporary. One would not claim, of course, that among the many hundreds of applications of Holy Scripture made by the Carmelite Doctor there are none that can be objected to in this respect; but the same can be said of St. Augustine, St. Ambrose, St. Gregory or St. Bernard, and no one would assert that, either with them or with him, such instances are other than most exceptional.

To the three sources already mentioned in which St. John of the Cross found inspiration we must add a fourth -- the works of ascetic and mystical writers. It is not yet possible to assert with any exactness how far the Saint made use of these; for, though partial studies of this question have been attempted, a complete and unbiased treatment of it has still to be undertaken. Here we can do no more than give a few indications of what remains to be done and summarize the present content of our knowledge.[20]

We may suppose that, during his novitiate in Medina, the Saint read a number of devotional books, one of which would almost certainly have been the Imitation of Christ, and others would have included works which were translated into Spanish by order of Cardinal Cisneros. The demands of a University course would not keep him from pursuing such studies at Salamanca; the friar who chose a cell from the window of which he could see the Blessed Sacrament, so that he might spend hours in its company, would hardly be likely to neglect his devotional reading. But we have not a syllable of direct external evidence as to the titles of any of the books known to him.

Nor, for that matter, have we much more evidence of this kind for any other part of his life. Both his early Carmelite biographers and the numerous witnesses who gave evidence during the canonization process describe at great length his extraordinary penances, his love for places of retreat beautified by Nature, the long hours that he spent in prayer and the tongue of angels with which he spoke on things spiritual. But of his reading they say nothing except to describe his attachment to the Bible, nor have we any record of the books contained in the libraries of the religious houses that he visited. Yet if, as we gather from the process, he spent little more than three hours nightly in sleep, he must have read deeply of spiritual things by night as well as by day.

Some clues to the nature of his reading may be gained from his own writings. It is true that the clues are slender. He cites few works apart from the Bible and these are generally liturgical books, such as the Breviary. Some of his quotations from St. Augustine, St. Gregory and other of the Fathers are traceable to these sources. Nevertheless, we have not read St. John of the Cross for long before we find ourselves in the full current of mystical tradition. It is not by means of more or less literal quotations that the Saint produces this impression; he has studied his precursors so thoroughly that he absorbs the substance of their doctrine and incorporates it so intimately in his own that it becomes flesh of his flesh. Everything in his writings is fully matured: he has no juvenilia. The mediaeval mystics whom he uses are too often vague and undisciplined; they need someone to select from them and unify them, to give them clarity and order, so that their treatment of mystical theology may have the solidity and substance of scholastic theology. To have done this is one of the achievements of St. John of the Cross.

We are convinced, then, by an internal evidence which is chiefly of a kind in which no chapter and verse can be given, that St. John of the Cross read widely in mediaeval mystical theology and assimilated a great part of what he read. The influence of foreign writers upon Spanish mysticism, though it was once denied, is to-day generally recognized. It was inevitable that it should have been considerable in a country which in the sixteenth century had such a high degree of culture as Spain. Plotinus, in a diluted form, made his way into Spanish mysticism as naturally as did Seneca into Spanish asceticism. Plato and Aristotle entered it through the two greatest minds that Christianity has known -- St. Augustine and St. Thomas. The influence of the Platonic theories of love and beauty and of such basic Aristotelian theories as the origin of knowledge is to be found in most of the Spanish mystics, St. John of the Cross among them.

The pseudo-Dionysius was another writer who was considered a great authority by the Spanish mystics. The importance attributed to his works arose partly from the fact that he was supposed to have been one of the first disciples of the Apostles; many chapters from mystical works of those days all over Europe are no more than glosses of the pseudo-Areopagite. He is followed less, however, by St. John of the Cross than by many of the latter's contemporaries.

Other influences upon the Carmelite Saint were St. Gregory, St. Bernard and Hugh and Richard of St. Victor, many of whose maxims were in the mouths of the mystics in the sixteenth century. More important, probably, than any of these was the Fleming, Ruysbroeck, between whom and St. John of the Cross there were certainly many points of contact. The Saint would have read him, not in the original, but in Surius' Latin translation of 1552, copies of which are known to have been current in Spain. [21] Together with Ruysbroeck may be classed Suso, Denis the Carthusian, Herp, Kempis and various other writers.

Many of the ideas and phrases which we find in St. John of the Cross, as in other writers, are, of course, traceable to the common mystical tradition rather than to any definite individual influence. The striking metaphor of the ray of light penetrating the room, for example, which occurs in the first chapter of the pseudo-Areopagite's De Mystica Theologia, has been used continually by mystical writers ever since his time. The figures of the wood consumed by fire, of the ladder, the mirror, the flame of love and the nights of sense and spirit had long since become naturalized in mystical literature. There are many more such examples.

The originality of St. John of the Cross is in no way impaired by his employment of this current mystical language: such an idea might once have been commonly held, but has long ceased to be put forward seriously. His originality, indeed, lies precisely in the use which he made of language that he found near to hand. It is not going too far to liken the place taken by St. John of the Cross in mystical theology to that of St. Thomas in dogmatic; St. Thomas laid hold upon the immense store of material which had accumulated in the domain of dogmatic theology and subjected it to the iron discipline of reason. That St. John of the Cross did the same for mystical theology is his great claim upon our admiration. Through St. Thomas speaks the ecclesiastical tradition of many ages on questions of religious belief; through St. John speaks an equally venerable tradition on questions of Divine love. Both writers combined sainthood with genius. Both opened broad channels to be followed of necessity by Catholic writers through the ages to come till theology shall lose itself in that vast ocean of truth and love which is God. Both created instruments adequate to the greatness of their task: St. Thomas' clear, decisive reasoning processes give us the formula appropriate to each and every need of the understanding; St. John clothes his teaching in mellower and more appealing language, as befits the exponent of the science of love. We may describe the treatises of St. John of the Cross as the true Summa Angelica of mystical theology.

II - OUTSTANDING QUALITIES AND DEFECTS OF THE SAINT'S STYLE

The profound and original thought which St. John of the Cross bestowed upon so abstruse a subject, and upon one on which there was so little classical literature in Spanish when he wrote, led him to clothe his ideas in a language at once energetic, precise and of a high degree of individuality. His style reflects his thought, but it reflects the style of no school and of no other writer whatsoever.

This is natural enough, for thought and feeling were always uppermost in the Saint: style and language take a place entirely subordinate to them. Never did he sacrifice any idea to artistic combinations of words; never blur over any delicate shade of thought to enhance some rhythmic cadence of musical prose. Literary form (to use a figure which he himself might have coined) is only present at all in his works in the sense in which the industrious and deferential servant is present in the ducal apartment, for the purpose of rendering faithful service to his lord and master. This subordination of style to content in the Saint's work is one of its most eminent qualities. He is a great writer, but not a great stylist. The strength and robustness of his intellect everywhere predominate.

This to a large extent explains the negligences which we find in his style, the frequency with which it is marred by repetitions and its occasional degeneration into diffuseness. The long, unwieldy sentences, one of which will sometimes run to the length of a reasonably sized paragraph, are certainly a trial to many a reader. So intent is the Saint upon explaining, underlining and developing his points so that they shall be apprehended as perfectly as may be, that he continually recurs to what he has already said, and repeats words, phrases and even passages of considerable length without scruple. It is only fair to remind the reader that such things were far commoner in the Golden Age than they are to-day; most didactic Spanish prose of that period would be notably improved, from a modern standpoint, if its volume were cut down by about one-third.

Be that as it may, these defects in the prose of St. John of the Cross are amply compensated by the fullness of his phraseology, the wealth and profusion of his imagery, the force and the energy of his argument. He has only to be compared with the didactic writers who were his contemporaries for this to become apparent. Together with Luis de Granada, Luis de León, Juan de los Ángeles and Luis de la Puente,[22] he created a genuinely native language, purged of Latinisms, precise and eloquent, which Spanish writers have used ever since in writing of mystical theology.

The most sublime of all the Spanish mystics, he soars aloft on the wings of Divine love to heights known to hardly any of them. Though no words can express the loftiest of the experiences which he describes, we are never left with the impression that word, phrase or image has failed him. If it does not exist, he appears to invent it, rather than pause in his description in order to search for an expression of the idea that is in his mind or be satisfied with a prolix paraphrase. True to the character of his thought, his style is always forceful and energetic, even to a fault.

We have said nothing of his poems, for indeed they call for no purely literary commentary. How full of life the greatest of them are, how rich in meaning, how unforgettable and how inimitable, the individual reader may see at a glance or may learn from his own experience. Many of their exquisite figures their author owes, directly or indirectly, to his reading and assimilation of the Bible. Some of them, however, have acquired a new life in the form which he has given them. A line here, a phrase there, has taken root in the mind of some later poet or essayist and has given rise to a new work of art, to many lovers of which the Saint who lies behind it is unknown.

It is perhaps not an exaggeration to say that the verse and prose works combined of St. John of the Cross form at once the most grandiose and the most melodious spiritual canticle to which any one man has ever given utterance. It is impossible, in the space at our disposal, to quote at any length from the Spanish critics who have paid tribute to its comprehensiveness and profundity. We must content ourselves with a short quotation characterizing the Saint's poems, taken from the greatest of these critics, Marcelino Menéndez Pelayo, who, besides referring frequently to St. John of the Cross in such of his mature works as the Heterodoxos, Ideas Estéticas and Ciencia Española, devoted to him a great part of the address which he delivered as a young man at his official reception into the Spanish Academy under the title of Mystical Poetry.'

So sublime,' wrote Menéndez Pelayo, is this poetry [of St. John of the Cross] that it scarcely seems to belong to this world at all; it is hardly capable of being assessed by literary criteria. More ardent in its passion than any profane poetry, its form is as elegant and exquisite, as plastic and as highly figured as any of the finest works of the Renaissance. The spirit of God has passed through these poems every one, beautifying and sanctifying them on its way.'

III - DIFFUSION OF THE WRITINGS OF ST. JOHN OF THE CROSS -- LOSS OF THE AUTOGRAPHS -- GENERAL CHARACTERISTICS OF THE MANUSCRIPTS

The outstanding qualities of St. John of the Cross's writings were soon recognized by the earliest of their few and privileged readers. All such persons, of course, belonged to a small circle composed of the Saint's intimate friends and disciples. As time went on, the circle widened repeatedly; now it embraces the entire Church, and countless individual souls who are filled with the spirit of Christianity.

First of all, the works were read and discussed in those loci of evangelical zeal which the Saint had himself enkindled, by his word and example, at Beas, El Calvario, Baeza and Granada. They could not have come more opportunely. St. Teresa's Reform had engendered a spiritual alertness and energy reminiscent of the earliest days of Christianity. Before this could in any way diminish, her first friar presented the followers of them both with spiritual food to nourish and re-create their souls and so to sustain the high degree of zeal for Our Lord which He had bestowed upon them.

In one sense, St. John of the Cross took up his pen in order to supplement the writings of St. Teresa; on several subjects, for example, he abstained from writing at length because she had already treated of them.[23] Much of the work of the two Saints, however, of necessity covers the same ground, and thus the great mystical school of the Spanish Carmelites is reinforced at its very beginnings in a way which must be unique in the history of mysticism. The writings of St. Teresa and St. John of the Cross, though of equal value and identical aim, are in many respects very different in their nature; together they cover almost the entire ground of orthodox mysticism, both speculative and experimental. The Carmelite mystics who came after them were able to build upon a broad and sure foundation.

The writings of St. John of the Cross soon became known outside the narrow circle of his sons and daughters in religion. In a few years they had gone all over Spain and reached Portugal, France and Italy. They were read by persons of every social class, from the Empress Maria of Austria, sister of

Philip II, to the most unlettered nuns of St. Teresa's most remote foundations. One of the witnesses at the process for the beatification declared that he knew of no works of which there existed so many copies, with the exception of the Bible.

We may fairly suppose (and the supposition is confirmed by the nature of the extant manuscripts) that the majority of the early copies were made by friars and nuns of the Discalced Reform. Most Discalced houses must have had copies and others were probably in the possession of members of other Orders. We gather, too, from various sources, that even lay persons managed to make or obtain copies of the manuscripts.

How many of these copies, it will be asked, were made directly from the autographs? So vague is the available evidence on this question that it is difficult to attempt any calculation of even approximate reliability. All we can say is that the copies made by, or for, the Discalced friars and nuns themselves are the earliest and most trustworthy, while those intended for the laity were frequently made at third or fourth hand. The Saint himself seems to have written out only one manuscript of each treatise and none of these has come down to us. Some think that he destroyed the manuscripts copied with his own hand, fearing that they might come to be venerated for other reasons than that of the value of their teaching. He was, of course, perfectly capable of such an act of abnegation; once, as we know, in accordance with his own principles, he burned some letters of St. Teresa, which he had carried with him for years, for no other reason than that he realized that he was becoming attached to them. [24]

The only manuscript of his that we possess consists of a few pages of maxims, some letters and one or two documents which he wrote when he was Vicar-Provincial of Andalusia. [25] So numerous and so thorough have been the searches made for further autographs during the last three centuries that further discoveries of any importance seem most unlikely. We have, therefore, to console ourselves with manuscripts, such as the Sanlúcar de Barrameda Codex of the Spiritual Canticle, which bear the Saint's autograph corrections as warrants of their integrity.

The vagueness of much of the evidence concerning the manuscripts to which we have referred extends to the farthest possible limit -- that of using the word original' to indicate autograph' and copy' indifferently. Even in the earliest documents we can never be sure which sense is intended. Furthermore, there was a passion in the seventeenth and eighteenth centuries for describing all kinds of old manuscripts as autographs, and thus we find copies so described in which the hand bears not the slightest resemblance to that of the Saint, as the most superficial collation with a genuine specimen of his hand would have made evident. We shall give instances of this in describing the extant copies of individual treatises. One example of a general kind, however, may be quoted here to show the extent to which the practice spread. In a statement made, with reference to one of the processes, at the convent of Discalced Carmelite nuns of Valladolid, a certain M. María de la Trinidad deposed that a servant of God, a Franciscan tertiary named Ana María, possesses the originals of the books of our holy father, and has heard that he sent them to the Order.' Great importance was attached to this deposition and every possible measure was taken to find the autographs -- needless to say, without result. [26]

With the multiplication of the number of copies of St. John of the Cross's writings, the number of variants naturally multiplied also. The early copies having all been made for devotional purposes, by persons with little or no palaeographical knowledge, many of whom did not even exercise common care, it is not surprising that there is not a single one which can compare in punctiliousness with certain extant eighteenth-century copies of documents connected with St. John of the Cross and St. Teresa. These were made by a painstaking friar called Manuel de Santa María, whose scrupulousness went so far that he reproduced imperfectly formed letters exactly as they were written, adding the parts that were lacking (e.g., the tilde over the letter ñ) with ink of another colour.

We may lament that this good father had no predecessor like himself to copy the Saint's treatises, but it is only right to say that the copies we possess are sufficiently faithful and numerous to give us reasonably accurate versions of their originals. The important point about them is that they bear no signs of bad faith, nor even of the desire (understandable enough in those unscientific days) to clarify the sense of their original, or even to improve upon its teaching. Their errors are often gross ones, but the large majority of them are quite easy to detect and put right. The impression to this effect which one obtains from a casual perusal of almost any of these copies is quite definitely confirmed by a comparison of them with copies corrected by the Saint or written by the closest and most trusted of his disciples. It may be added that some of the variants may, for aught we know to the contrary, be the Saint's own work, since it is not improbable that he may have corrected more than one copy of some of his writings, and not been entirely consistent.

There are, broadly speaking, two classes into which the copies (more particularly those of the Ascent and the Dark Night) may be divided. One class aims at a more or less exact transcription; the other definitely sets out to abbreviate. Even if the latter class be credited with a number of copies which hardly merit the name, the former is by far the larger, and, of course, the more important, though it must not be supposed that the latter is unworthy of notice. The abbreviators generally omit whole chapters, or passages, at a time, and, where they are not for the moment doing this, or writing the connecting phrases necessary to repair their mischief, they are often quite faithful to their originals. Since they do not, in general, attribute anything to their author that is not his, no objection can be taken, on moral grounds, to their proceeding, though, in actual fact, the results are not always happy. Their ends were purely practical and devotional and they made no attempt to pass their compendia as full-length transcriptions.

With regard to the Spiritual Canticle and the Living Flame of Love, of each of which there are two redactions bearing indisputable marks of the author's own hand, the classification of the copies will naturally depend upon which redaction each copy the more nearly follows. This question will be discussed in the necessary detail in the introduction to each of these works, and to the individual introductions to the four major treatises we must refer the reader for other details of the manuscripts. In the present pages we have attempted only a general account of these matters. It remains to add that our divisions of each chapter into paragraphs follow the manuscripts throughout except where indicated. The printed editions, as we shall see, suppressed these divisions, but, apart from their value to the modern reader, they are sufficiently nearly identical in the various copies to form one further testimony to their general high standard of reliability.

IV - INTEGRITY OF THE SAINT'S WORK -- INCOMPLETE CONDITION OF THE ASCENT' AND THE NIGHT' -- DISPUTED QUESTIONS

The principal lacuna in St. John of the Cross's writings, and, from the literary standpoint, the most interesting, is the lack of any commentary to the last five stanzas [27] of the poem Dark Night.' Such a commentary is essential to the completion of the plan which the Saint had already traced for himself in what was to be, and, in spite of its unfinished condition, is in fact, his most rigorously scientific treatise. All the doctrine,' he wrote in the Argument of the Ascent, whereof I intend to treat in this Ascent of Mount Carmel is included in the following stanzas, and in them is also described the manner of ascending to the summit of the Mount, which is the high estate of perfection which we here call union of the soul with God.' This leaves no doubt but that the Saint intended to treat the mystical life as one whole, and to deal in turn with each stage of the road to perfection, from the beginnings of the Purgative Way to the crown and summit of the life of Union. After showing the need for such a treatise as he proposes to write, he divides the chapters on Purgation into four parts corresponding to the Active and Passive nights of Sense and of Spirit. These, however, correspond only to the first two stanzas of his poem; they are not, as we shall shortly see, complete, but their incompleteness is slight compared with that of the work as a whole.

Did St. John of the Cross, we may ask, ever write a commentary on those last five stanzas, which begin with a description of the state of Illumination:

Twas that light guided me, More surely than the noonday's brightest glare --

and end with that of the life of Union:

All things for me that day Ceas'd, as I slumber'd there, Amid the lilies drowning all my care?

If we suppose that he did, we are faced with the question of its fate and with the strange fact that none of his contemporaries makes any mention of such a commentary, though they are all prolific in details of far less importance.

Conjectures have been ventured on this question ever since critical methods first began to be applied to St. John of the Cross's writings. A great deal was written about it by P. Andrés de la Encarnación, to whom his superiors entrusted the task of collecting and editing the Saint's writings, and whose findings, though they suffer from the defects of an age which from a modern standpoint must be called unscientific, and need therefore to be read with the greatest caution, are often surprisingly just and accurate. P. Andrés begins by referring to various places where St. John of the Cross states that he has treated certain subjects and proposes to treat others, about which nothing can be found in his writings. This, he says, may often be due to an oversight on the writer's part or to changes which new experiences might have brought to his mode of thinking. On the other hand, there are sometimes signs that these promises have been fulfilled: the sharp truncation of the argument, for example, at the end of Book III of the Ascent suggests that at least a few pages are missing, in which case the original manuscript must have been mutilated, [28] for almost all the extant copies break off at the same word. It is unthinkable, as P. Andrés says, that the Saint 'should have gone on to write the Night without completing the Ascent, for all these five books [29] are integral parts of one whole, since they all treat of different stages of one spiritual path.'[30]

It may be argued in the same way that St. John of the Cross would not have gone on to write the commentaries on the Spiritual Canticle' and the Living Flame of Love' without first completing the Dark Night. P. Andrés goes so far as to say that the very unwillingness which the Saint displayed towards writing commentaries on the two latter poems indicates that he had already completed the others; otherwise, he could easily have excused himself from the later task on the plea that he had still to finish the earlier.

Again, St. John of the Cross declares very definitely, in the prologue to the Dark Night, that, after describing in the commentary on the first two stanzas the effects of the two passive purgations of the sensual and the spiritual part of man, he will devote the six remaining stanzas to expounding various and wondrous effects of the spiritual illumination and union of love with God.' Nothing could be clearer than this. Now, in the commentary on the Living Flame,' argues P. Andrés, he treats at considerable length of simple contemplation and adds that he has written fully of it in several chapters of the Ascent and the Night, which he names; but not only do we not find the references in two of the chapters enumerated by him, but he makes no mention of several other chapters in which the references are of considerable fullness. The proper deductions from these facts would seem to be, first, that we do not possess the Ascent and the Night in the form in which the Saint wrote them, and, second, that in the missing chapters he referred to the subject under discussion at much greater length than in the chapters we have.

Further, the practice of St. John of the Cross was not to omit any part of his commentaries when for any reason he was unable or unwilling to write them at length, but rather to abbreviate them. Thus, he runs rapidly through the third stanza of the Night and through the fourth stanza of the Living Flame: we should expect him in the same way to treat the last three stanzas of the Night with similar brevity and rapidity, but not to omit them altogether.

Such are the principal arguments used by P. Andrés which have inclined many critics to the belief that St. John of the Cross completed these treatises. Other of his arguments, which to himself were even more convincing, have now lost much weight. The chief of these are the contention that, because a certain Fray Agustín Antolínez (b. 1554), in expounding these same poems, makes no mention of the Saint's having failed to expound five stanzas of the Night, he did therefore write an exposition of them;[31] and the supposition that the Living Flame was written before the Spiritual Canticle, and that therefore, when the prologue to the Living Flame says that the author has already described the highest state of perfection attainable in this life, it cannot be referring to the Canticle and must necessarily allude to passages, now lost, from the Dark Night.[32]

Our own judgment upon this much debated question is not easily delivered. On the one hand, the reasons why St. John of the Cross should have completed his work are perfectly sound ones and his own words in the Ascent and the Dark Night are a clear statement of his intentions. Furthermore, he had ample time to complete it, for he wrote other treatises at a later date and he certainly considered the latter part of the Dark Night to be more important than the former. On the other hand, it is disconcerting to find not even the briefest clear reference to this latter part in any of his subsequent writings, when both the Living Flame and the Spiritual Canticle offered so many occasions for such a reference to an author accustomed to refer his readers to his other treatises. Again, his contemporaries, who were keenly interested in his work, and mention such insignificant things as the Cautions, the Maxims and the Mount of Perfection,' say nothing whatever of the missing chapters. None of his biographers speaks of them, nor does P. Alonso de la Madre de Dios, who examined the Saint's writings in detail immediately after his death and was in touch with his closest friends and companions. We are inclined, therefore, to think that the chapters in question were never written.[33] Is not the following sequence of probable facts the most tenable? We know from P. Juan Evangelista that the Ascent and the Dark Night were written at different times, with many intervals of short or long duration. The Saint may well have entered upon the Spiritual Canticle, which was a concession to the affectionate importunity of M. Ann de Jesús, with every intention of returning later to finish his earlier treatise. But, having completed the Canticle, he may equally well have been struck with the similarity between a part of it and the unwritten commentary on the earlier stanzas, and this may have decided him that the Dark Night needed no completion, especially as the Living Flame also described the life of Union. This hypothesis will explain all the facts, and seems completely in harmony with all we know of St. John of the Cross, who was in no sense, as we have already said, a writer by profession. If we accept it, we need not necessarily share the views which we here assume to have been his. Not only would the completion of the Dark Night have given us new ways of approach to so sublime and intricate a theme, but this would have been treated in a way more closely connected with the earlier stages of the mystical life than was possible in either the Living Flame or the Canticle.

We ought perhaps to notice one further supposition of P. Andrés, which has been taken up by a number of later critics: that St. John of the Cross completed the commentary which we know as the Dark Night, but that on account of the distinctive nature of the contents of the part now lost he gave it a separate title.[34] The only advantage of this theory seems to be that it makes the hypothesis of the loss of the commentary less improbable. In other respects it is as unsatisfactory as the theory of P. Andrés,[35] of which we find a variant in M. Baruzi,[36] that the Saint thought the commentary too bold, and too sublime, to be perpetuated, and therefore destroyed it, or, at least, forbade its being copied. It is surely unlikely that the sublimity of these missing chapters would exceed that of the Canticle or the Living Flame.

This seems the most suitable place to discuss a feature of the works of St. John of the Cross to which allusion is often made -- the little interest which he took in their division into books and chapters and his lack of consistency in observing such divisions when he had once made them. A number of examples may be cited. In the first chapter of the Ascent of Mount Carmel, using the words part' and book' as synonyms, he makes it clear that the Ascent and the Dark Night are to him one single treatise. The first night or purgation,' he writes, is of the sensual part of the soul, which is treated in the present stanza, and will be treated in the first part of this book. And the second is of the spiritual part; of this speaks the second stanza, which follows; and of this we shall treat likewise, in the second and the third part, with respect to the activity of the soul; and in the fourth part, with respect to its passivity.'[37] The author's intention here is evident. Purgation may be sensual or spiritual, and each of these kinds may be either active or passive. The most logical proceeding would be to divide the whole of the material into four parts or books: two to be devoted to active purgation and two to passive.[38] St. John of the Cross, however, devotes two parts to active spiritual purgation -- one to that of the understanding and the other to that of the memory and the will. In the Night, on the other hand, where it would seem essential to devote one book to the passive purgation of sense and another to that of spirit, he includes both in one part, the fourth. In the Ascent, he divides the content of each of his books into various chapters; in the Night, where the argument is developed like that of the Ascent, he makes a division into paragraphs only, and a very irregular division at that, if we may judge by the copies that have reached us. In the Spiritual Canticle and the Living Flame he dispenses with both chapters and paragraphs. The commentary on each stanza here corresponds to a chapter.

Another example is to be found in the arrangement of his expositions. As a rule, he first writes down the stanzas as a whole, then repeats each in turn before expounding it, and repeats each line also in its proper place in the same way. At the beginning of each treatise he makes some general observations -- in the form either of an argument and prologue, as in the Ascent; of a prologue and general exposition, as in the Night; of a prologue alone, as in the first redaction of the Canticle and in the Living Flame; or of a prologue and argument, as in the second redaction of the Canticle. In the Ascent and the Night, the first chapter of each book contains the exposition of the stanzas,' though some copies describe this, in Book III of the Ascent, as an argument.' In the Night, the book dealing with the Night of Sense begins with the usual exposition'; that of the Night of the Spirit, however, has nothing to correspond with it.

In the first redaction of the Spiritual Canticle, St. John of the Cross first sets down the poem, then a few lines of exposition' giving the argument of the stanza, and finally the commentary upon each line. Sometimes he comments upon two or three lines at once. In the second redaction, he prefaces almost every stanza with an annotation,' of which there is none in the first redaction except before the commentary on the thirteenth and fourteenth stanzas. The chief purpose of the annotation' is to link the argument of each stanza with that of the stanza preceding it; occasionally the annotation and the exposition are combined.

It is clear from all this that, in spite of his orderly mind, St. John of the Cross was no believer in strict uniformity in matters of arrangement which would seem to demand such uniformity once they had been decided upon. They are, of course, of secondary importance, but the fact that the inconsistencies are the work of St. John of the Cross himself, and not merely of careless copyists, who have enough else to account for, is of real moment in the discussion of critical questions which turn on the Saint's accuracy.

Another characteristic of these commentaries is the inequality of length as between the exposition of certain lines and stanzas. While some of these are dealt with fully, the exposition of others is brought to a close with surprising rapidity, even though it sometimes seems that much more needs to be said: we get the impression that the author was anxious to push his work forward or was pressed for time. He devotes fourteen long chapters of the Ascent to glossing the first two lines of the first stanza and dismisses the three remaining lines in a few sentences. In both the Ascent and the Night, indeed, the stanzas appear to serve only as a pretext for introducing the great wealth of ascetic and mystical teaching which the Saint has gathered together. In the Canticle and the Living Flame, on the other hand, he keeps much closer to his stanzas, though here, too, there is a considerable inequality. One result of the difference in nature between these two pairs of treatises is that the Ascent and the Night are more solidly built and more rigidly doctrinal, whereas in the Canticle and the Flame there is more movement and more poetry.

V - HISTORY OF THE PUBLICATION OF ST. JOHN OF THE CROSS'S WRITINGS -- THE FIRST EDITION

It seems strange that mystical works of such surpassing value should not have been published till twenty-seven years after their author's death, for not only were the manuscript copies insufficient to propagate them as widely as those who made them would have desired, but the multiplication of these copies led to an ever greater number of variants in the text. Had it but been possible for the first edition of them to have been published while their author still lived, we might to-day have a perfect text. But the probability is that, if such an idea had occurred to St. John of the Cross, he would have set it aside as presumptuous. In allowing copies to be made he doubtless never envisaged their going beyond the limited circle of his Order.

We have found no documentary trace of any project for an edition of these works during their author's lifetime. The most natural time for a discussion of the matter would have been in September 1586, when the Definitors of the Order, among whom was St. John of the Cross, met in Madrid and decided to publish the works of St. Teresa. [39] Two years earlier, when he was writing the Spiritual Canticle, St. John of the Cross had expressed a desire for the publication of St. Teresa's writings and assumed that this would not be long delayed. [40] As we have seen, he considered his own works as complementary to those of St. Teresa, [41] and one would have thought that the simultaneous publication of the writings of the two Reformers would have seemed to the Definitors an excellent idea.

After his death, it is probable that there was no one at first who was both able and willing to undertake the work of editor; for, as is well known, towards the end of his life the Saint had powerful enemies within his Order who might well have opposed the project, though, to do the Discalced Reform justice, it was brought up as early as ten years after his death. A resolution was passed at the Chapter-General of the Reform held in September 1601, to the effect that the works of Fr. Juan de la Cruz be printed and that the Definitors, Fr. Juan de Jesús María and Fr. Tomás [de Jesús], be instructed to examine and approve them.' [42] Two years later (July 4, 1603), the same Chapter, also meeting in Madrid, gave leave to the Definitor, Fr. Tomás [de Jesús], for the printing of the works of Fr. Juan de la Cruz, first friar of the Discalced Reform.' [43]

It is not known (since the Chapter Book is no longer extant) why the matter lapsed for two years, but Fr. Tomás de Jesús, the Definitor to whom alone it was entrusted on the second occasion, was a most able man, well qualified to edit the works of his predecessor. [44] Why, then, we may wonder, did he not do so? The story of his life in the years following the commission may partly answer this question. His definitorship came to an end in 1604, when he was elected Prior of the desert' of San José de las Batuecas. After completing the customary three years in this office, during which time he could have done no work at all upon the edition, he was elected Prior of the Discalced house at Zaragoza. But at this point Paul V sent for him to Rome and from that time onward his life followed other channels.

The next attempt to accomplish the project was successful. The story begins with a meeting between the Definitors of the Order and Fr. José de Jesús María, the General, at Vélez-Málaga, where a new decision to publish the works of St. John of the Cross was taken and put into effect (as a later resolution has it) without any delay or condition whatsoever.' [45] The enterprise suffered a setback, only a week after it had been planned, in the death of the learned Jesuit P. Suárez, who was on terms of close friendship with the Discalced and had been appointed one of the censors. But P. Diego de Jesús (Salablanca), Prior of the Discalced house at Toledo, to whom its execution was entrusted, lost no time in accomplishing his task; indeed, one would suppose that he had begun it long before, since early in the next year it was completed and published in Alcalá. The volume, entitled Spiritual Works which lead a soul to perfect union with God, has 720 pages and bears the date 1618. The works are preceded by a preface addressed to the reader and a brief summary of the author's life and virtues.' An engraving of the Mount of Perfection' is included. [46]

There are several peculiarities about this editio princeps. In the first place, although the pagination is continuous, it was the work of two different printers; the reason for this is quite unknown, though various reasons might be suggested. The greatest care was evidently taken so that the work should be well and truly approved: it is recommended, in terms of the highest praise, by the authorities of the University of Alcalá, who, at the request of the General of the Discalced Carmelites, had submitted it for examination to four of the professors of that University. No doubt for reasons of safety, the Spiritual Canticle was not included in that edition: it was too much like a commentary on the Song of Songs for such a proceeding to be just then advisable.

We have now to enquire into the merits of the edition of P. Salablanca, which met with such warm approval on its publication, yet very soon afterwards began to be recognized as defective and is little

Ascent of Mount Carmel
esteemed for its intrinsic qualities to-day.

It must, of course, be realized that critical standards in the early seventeenth century were low and that the first editor of St. John of the Cross had neither the method nor the available material of the twentieth century. Nor were the times favourable for the publication of the works of a great mystic who attempted fearlessly and fully to describe the highest stages of perfection on the road to God. These two facts are responsible for most of the defects of the edition.

For nearly a century, the great peril associated with the mystical life had been that of Illuminism, a gross form of pseudo-mysticism which had claimed many victims among the holiest and most learned, and of which there was such fear that excessive, almost unbelievable, precautions had been taken against it. These precautions, together with the frequency and audacity with which Illuminists invoked the authority and protection of well-known contemporary ascetic and mystical writers, give reality to P. Salablanca's fear lest the leaders of the sect might shelter themselves behind the doctrines of St. John of the Cross and so call forth the censure of the Inquisition upon passages which seemed to him to bear close relation to their erroneous teaching. It was for this definite reason, and not because of an arbitrary meticulousness, that P. Salablanca omitted or adapted such passages as those noted in Book I, Chapter viii of the Ascent of Mount Carmel and in a number of chapters in Book II. A study of these, all of which are indicated in the footnotes to our text, is of great interest.

Less important are a large number of minor corrections made with the intention of giving greater precision to some theological concept; the omission of lines and even paragraphs which the editor considered redundant, as in fact they frequently are; and corrections made with the aim of lending greater clearness to the argument or improving the style. A few changes were made out of prudery: such are the use of sensitivo for sensual, the suppression of phrases dealing with carnal vice and the omission of several paragraphs from that chapter of the Dark Night -- which speaks of the third deadly sin of beginners. There was little enough reason for these changes: St. John of the Cross is particularly inoffensive in his diction and may, from that point of view, be read by a child.

The sum total of P. Salablanca's mutilations is very considerable. There are more in the Ascent and the Living Flame than in the Dark Night; but hardly a page of the editio princeps is free from them and on most pages they abound. It need not be said that they are regrettable. They belong to an age when the garments of dead saints were cut up into small fragments and distributed among the devout and when their cells were decked out with indifferent taste and converted into oratories. It would not have been considered sufficient had the editor printed the text of St. John of the Cross as he found it and glossed it to his liking in footnotes; another editor would have put opposite interpretations upon it, thus cancelling out the work of his predecessor. Even the radical mutilations of P. Salablanca did not suffice, as will now be seen, to protect the works of the Saint from the Inquisition.

VI - DENUNCIATION OF THE WORKS' TO THE INQUISITION -- DEFENCE OF THEM MADE BY FR. BASILO PONCE DE LEÓN -- EDITIONS OF THE SEVENTEENTH AND EIGHTEENTH CENTURIES

Neither the commendations of University professors nor the scissors of a meticulous editor could save the treatises of St. John of the Cross from that particular form of attack which, more than all others, was feared in the seventeenth century. We shall say nothing here of the history, nature and procedure of the Spanish Inquisition, which has had its outspoken antagonists and its unreasoning defenders but has not yet been studied with impartiality. It must suffice to set down the facts as they here affect our subject.

Forty propositions, then, were extracted from the edition of 1618 and presented to the Holy Office for condemnation with the object of causing the withdrawal of the edition from circulation. The attempt would probably have succeeded but for the warm, vigorous and learned defence put up by the Augustinian Fray Basilio Ponce de León, a theological professor in the University of Salamanca and a nephew of the Luis de León who wrote the Names of Christ and took so great an interest in the works of St. Teresa. [47]

It was in the very convent of San Felipe in Madrid where thirty-five years earlier Fray Luis had written his immortal eulogy of St. Teresa [48] that Fray Basilio, on July 11, 1622, signed a most interesting Reply' to the objections which had been raised to the Alcalá edition of St. John of the Cross. Although we propose, in our third volume, to reproduce Fray Basilio's defence, it is necessary to our narrative to say something of it here, for it is the most important of all extant documents which reveal the vicissitudes in the history of the Saint's teaching.

Before entering upon an examination of the censured propositions, the learned Augustinian makes some general observations, which must have carried great weight as coming from so high a theological authority. He recalls the commendations of the edition by the professors of the University of Alcalá where the faculty of theology is so famous,' and by many others, including several ministers of the Holy Office and two Dominicans who without dispute are among the most learned of their Order.' Secondly, he refers to the eminently saintly character of the first friar of the Discalced Reform: it is not to be presumed that God would set a man whose teaching is so evil . . . as is alleged, to be the corner-stone of so great a building.' Thirdly, he notes how close a follower was St. John of the Cross of St. Teresa, a person who was singularly free from any taint of unorthodoxy. And finally he recalls a number of similar attacks on works of this kind, notably that on Laredo's Ascent of Mount Sion, [49] which have proved to be devoid of foundation, and points out that isolated propositions' need to be set in their context before they can be fairly judged.

Fray Basilio next refutes the charges brought against the works of St. John of the Cross, nearly all of which relate to his teaching on the passivity of the faculties in certain degrees of contemplation. Each proposition he copies and afterwards defends, both by argument and by quotations from the Fathers, from the medieval mystics and from his own contemporaries. It is noteworthy that among these authorities he invariably includes St. Teresa, who had been beatified in 1614, and enjoyed an undisputed reputation. This inclusion, as well as being an enhancement of his defence, affords a striking demonstration of the unity of thought existing between the two great Carmelites.

Having expounded the orthodox Catholic teaching in regard to these matters, and shown that the teaching of St. John of the Cross is in agreement with it, Fray Basilio goes on to make clear the true attitude of the Illuminists and thus to reinforce his contentions by showing how far removed from this is the Saint's doctrine.

Fray Basilio's magnificent defence of St. John of the Cross appears to have had the unusual effect of quashing the attack entirely: the excellence of his arguments, backed by his great authority, was evidently unanswerable. So far as we know, the Inquisition took no proceedings against the Alcalá edition whatsoever. Had this at any time been prohibited, we may be sure that Llorente would have revealed the fact, and, though he refers to the persecution of St. John of the Cross during his lifetime,[50] he is quite silent about any posthumous condemnation of his writings.

The editio princeps was reprinted in 1619, with a different pagination and a few corrections, in Barcelona.[51] Before these two editions were out of print, the General of the Discalced Carmelites had entrusted an able historian of the Reform, Fray Jerónimo de San José, with the preparation of a new one. This was published at Madrid, in 1630. It has a short introduction describing its scope and general nature, a number of new and influential commendations and an admirable fifty-page 'sketch' of St. John of the Cross by the editor which has been reproduced in most subsequent editions and has probably done more than any other single work to make known the facts of the Saint's biography. The great feature of this edition, however, is the inclusion of the Spiritual Canticle, placed (by an error, as a printer's note explains) at the end of the volume, instead of before the Living Flame, which is, of course, its proper position.

The inclusion of the Canticle is one of the two merits that the editor claims for his new edition. The other is that he prints both the Canticle and the other works according to their original manuscripts, written in the hand of the same venerable author.' This claim is, of course, greatly exaggerated, as what has been said above with regard to the manuscripts will indicate. Not only does Fray Jerónimo appear to have had no genuine original manuscript at all, but of the omissions of the editio princeps it is doubtful if he makes good many more than one in a hundred. In fact, with very occasional exceptions, he merely reproduces the princeps -- omissions, interpolations, well-meant improvements and all.[52]

In Fray Jerónimo's defence it must be said that the reasons which moved his predecessor to mutilate his edition were still potent, and the times had not changed. It is more surprising that for nearly three centuries the edition of 1630 should have been followed by later editors. The numerous versions of the works which saw the light in the later seventeenth and the eighteenth century added a few poems, letters and maxims to the corpus of work which he presented and which assumed great importance as the Saint became better known and more deeply venerated. But they did no more. It suffices, therefore, to enumerate the chief of them.

The Barcelona publisher of the 1619 edition produced a new edition in 1635, which is a mere reproduction of that of 1630. A Madrid edition of 1649, which adds nine letters, a hundred maxims and a small collection of poems, was reproduced in 1672 (Madrid), 1679 (Madrid), 1693 (Barcelona) and 1694 (Madrid), the last reproduction being in two volumes. An edition was also published in Barcelona in 1700.

If we disregard a compendium' of the Saint's writings published in Seville in 1701, the first eighteenth-century edition was published in Seville in 1703 -- the most interesting of those that had seen the light since 1630. It is well printed on good paper in a folio volume and its editor, Fr. Andrés de Jesús María, claims it, on several grounds, as an advance on preceding editions. First, he says, innumerable errors of great importance' have been corrected in it; then, the Spiritual Canticle has been amended according to its original manuscript in the hand of the same holy doctor, our father, kept and venerated in our convent of Discalced Carmelite nuns at Jaén'; next, he adds two new poems and increases the number of maxims from 100 to 365; and lastly, the letters are increased from nine to seventeen, all of which are found in P. Jerónimo de San José's history. The first of these claims is as great an exaggeration as was P. Jerónimo's; to the second we shall refer in our introduction to the Spiritual Canticle. The third and fourth, however, are justified, and for these, as for a few minor improvements, the editor deserves every commendation.

The remaining years of the eighteenth century produced few editions; apart from a reprint (1724) of the compendium of 1701, the only one known to us is that published at Pamplona in 1774, after which nearly eighty years were to pass before any earlier edition was so much as reprinted. Before we resume this bibliographical narrative, however, we must go back over some earlier history.

VII - NEW DENUNCIATIONS AND DEFENCES -- FRAY NICOLÁS DE JESÚS MARÍA -- THE CARMELITE SCHOOL AND THE INQUISITION

We remarked, apropos of the edition of 1630, that the reasons which led Fray Diego de Jesús to mutilate his texts were still in existence when Fray Jerónimo de San José prepared his edition some twelve years later. If any independent proof of this statement is needed, it may be found in the numerous apologias that were published during the seventeenth century, not only in Spain, but in Italy, France, Germany and other countries of Europe. If doctrines are not attacked, there is no occasion to write vigorous defences of them.

Following the example of Fray Basilio Ponce de León, a professor of theology in the College of the Reform at Salamanca, Fray Nicholás de Jesús María, wrote a learned Latin defence of St. John of the Cross in 1631, often referred to briefly as the Elucidatio. [53] It is divided into two parts, the first defending the Saint against charges of a general kind that were brought against his writings, and the second upholding censured propositions taken from them. On the general ground, P. Nicholás reminds his readers that many writers who now enjoy the highest possible reputation were in their time denounced and unjustly persecuted. St. Jerome was attacked for his translation of the Bible from Hebrew into Latin; St. Augustine, for his teaching about grace and free-will. The works of St. Gregory the Great were burned at Rome; those of St. Thomas Aquinas at Paris. Most mediaeval and modern mystics have been the victims of persecution -- Ruysbroeck, Tauler and even St. Teresa. Such happenings, he maintains, have done nothing to lessen the eventual prestige of these authors, but rather have added to it.

Nor, he continues, can the works of any author fairly be censured, because misguided teachers make use of them to propagate their false teaching. No book has been more misused by heretics than Holy Scripture and few books of value would escape if we were to condemn all that had been so treated. Equally worthless is the objection that mystical literature is full of difficulties which may cause the ignorant and pusillanimous to stumble. Apart from the fact that St. John of the Cross is clearer and more lucid than most of his contemporaries, and that therefore the works of many of them would have to follow his own into oblivion, the same argument might again be applied to the Scriptures. Who can estimate the good imparted by the sacred books to those who read them in a spirit of uprightness and simplicity? Yet what books are more pregnant with mystery and with truths that are difficult and, humanly speaking, even inaccessible?

But (continues P. Nicolás), even if we allow that parts of the work of St. John of the Cross, for all the clarity of his exposition, are obscure to the general reader, it must be remembered that much more is of the greatest attraction and profit to all. On the one hand, the writings of the Saint represent the purest sublimation of Divine love in the pilgrim soul, and are therefore food for the most advanced upon the mystic way. On the other, every reader, however slight his spiritual progress, can understand the Saint's ascetic teaching: his chapters on the purgation of the senses, mortification, detachment from all that belongs to the earth, purity of conscience, the practice of the virtues, and so on. The Saint's greatest enemy is not the obscurity of his teaching but the inflexible logic with which he deduces, from the fundamental principles of evangelical perfection, the consequences which must be observed by those who would scale the Mount. So straight and so hard is the road which he maps out for the climber that the majority of those who see it are at once dismayed.

These are the main lines of P. Nicolás' argument, which he develops at great length. We must refer briefly to the chapter in which he makes a careful synthesis of the teaching of the Illuminists, to show how far it is removed from that of St. John of the Cross. He divides these false contemplatives into four classes. In the first class he places those who suppress all their acts, both interior and exterior, in prayer. In the second, those who give themselves up to a state of pure quiet, with no loving attention to God. In the third, those who allow their bodies to indulge every craving and maintain that, in the state of spiritual intoxication which they have reached, they are unable to commit sin. In the fourth, those who consider themselves to be instruments of God and adopt an attitude of complete passivity, maintaining also that they are unable to sin, because God alone is working in them. The division is more subtle than practical, for the devotees of this sect, with few exceptions, professed the same erroneous beliefs and tended to the same degree of licence in their conduct. But, by isolating these tenets, P. Nicolás is the better able to show the antithesis between them and those of St. John of the Cross.

In the second part of the Elucidatio, he analyses the propositions already treated by Fray Basilio Ponce de León, reducing them to twenty and dealing faithfully with them in the same number of chapters. His defence is clear, methodical and convincing and follows similar lines to those adopted by Fray Basilio, to whom its author acknowledges his indebtedness.

Another of St. John of the Cross's apologists is Fray José de Jesús María (Quiroga), who, in a number of his works, [54] both defends and eulogizes him, without going into any detailed examination of the propositions. Fray José is an outstanding example of a very large class of writers, for, as Illuminism gave place to Quietism, the teaching of St. John of the Cross became more and more violently impugned and almost all mystical writers of the time referred to him. Perhaps we should single out, from among his defenders outside the Carmelite Order, that Augustinian father, P. Antolínez, to whose commentary on three of the Saint's works we have already made reference.

As the school of mystical writers within the Discalced Carmelite Reform gradually grew -- a school which took St. John of the Cross as its leader and is one of the most illustrious in the history of mystical theology -- it began to share in the same persecution as had befallen its founder. It is impossible, in a few words, to describe this epoch of purgation, and indeed it can only be properly studied in its proper context -- the religious history of the period as a whole. For our purpose, it suffices to say that the works of St. John of the Cross were once more denounced to the Inquisition, though, once more, no notice appears to have been taken of the denunciations, for there exists no record ordering the expurgation or prohibition of the books referred to. The Elucidatio was also denounced, together with several of the works of P. José de Jesús María, at various times in the seventeenth century, and these attacks were of course equivalent to direct attacks on St. John of the Cross. One of the most vehement onslaughts made was levelled against P. José's Subida del Alma a Dios (Ascent of the Soul to God'), which is in effect an elaborate commentary on St. John of the Cross's teaching. The Spanish Inquisition refusing to censure the book, an appeal against it was made to the Inquisition at Rome. When no satisfaction was obtained in this quarter, P. José's opponents went to the Pope, who referred the matter to the Sacred Congregation of the Index; but this body issued a warm eulogy of the book and the matter thereupon dropped.

In spite of such defeats, the opponents of the Carmelite school continued their work into the eighteenth century. In 1740, a new appeal was made to the Spanish Inquisition to censure P. José's Subida. A document of seventy-three folios denounced no less than one hundred and sixty-five propositions which it claimed to have taken direct from the work referred to, and this time, after a conflict extending over ten years, the book (described as falsely attributed' to P. José [55]) was condemned (July 4, 1750), as containing doctrine most perilous in practice, and propositions similar and equivalent to those condemned in Miguel de Molinos.'

We set down the salient facts of this controversy, without commenting upon them, as an instance of the attitude of the eighteenth century towards the mystics in general, and, in particular, towards the school of the Discalced Carmelites. In view of the state and tendencies of thought in these times, the fact of the persecution, and the degree of success that it attained, is not surprising. The important point to bear in mind is that it must be taken into account continually by students of the editions of the Saint's writings and of the history of his teaching throughout the eighteenth and nineteenth centuries.

VIII - FURTHER HISTORY OF THE EDITIONS -- P. ANDRÉS DE LA ENCARNACIÓN -- EDITIONS OF THE NINETEENTH AND TWENTIETH CENTURIES

What has just been said will fully explain the paucity of the editions of St. John of the Cross which we find in the eighteenth century. This century, however, was, scientifically speaking, one of great progress. Critical methods of study developed and became widespread; and there was a great desire to obtain purer and more nearly perfect texts and to discover the original sources of the ideas of great thinkers. These tendencies made themselves felt within the Discalced Carmelite Order, and there also arose a great ambition to republish in their original forms the works both of St. Teresa and of St. John of the Cross. The need was greater in the latter case than in the former; so urgent was it felt to be as to admit of no delay. 'There have been discovered in the works [of St. John of the Cross],' says a document of about 1753, 'many errors, mutilations and other defects the existence of which cannot be denied.'[56] The religious who wrote thus to the Chapter-General of the Reform set out definite and practical schemes for a thorough revision of these works, which were at once accepted. There thus comes into our history that noteworthy friar, P. Andrés de la Encarnación, to whom we owe so much of what we know about the Saint to-day. P. Andrés was no great stylist, nor had he the usual Spanish fluency of diction. But he was patient, modest and industrious, and above all he was endowed with a double portion of the critical spirit of the eighteenth century. He was selected for the work of investigation as being by far the fittest person who could be found for it. A decree dated October 6, 1754 ordered him to set to work. As a necessary preliminary to the task of preparing a corrected text of the Saint's writings, he was to spare no effort in searching for every extant manuscript; accordingly he began long journeys through La Mancha and Andalusia, going over all the ground covered by St. John of the Cross in his travels and paying special attention to the places where he had lived for any considerable period. In those days, before the religious persecutions of the nineteenth century had destroyed and scattered books and manuscripts, the archives of the various religious houses were intact. P. Andrés and his amanuensis were therefore able to copy and collate valuable manuscripts now lost to us and they at once began to restore the phrases and passages omitted from the editions. Unhappily, their work has disappeared and we can judge of it only at second hand; but it appears to have been in every way meritorious. So far as we can gather from the documents which have come down to us, it failed to pass the rigorous censorship of the Order. In other words, the censors, who were professional theologians, insisted upon making so many corrections that the Superiors, who shared the enlightened critical opinions of P. Andrés, thought it better to postpone the publication of the edition indefinitely.

The failure of the project, however, to which P. Andrés devoted so much patient labour, did not wholly destroy the fruits of his skill and perseverance. He was ordered to retire to his priory, where he spent the rest of his long life under the burden of a trial the magnitude of which any scholar or studiously minded reader can estimate. He did what he could in his seclusion to collect, arrange and recopy such notes of his work as he could recover from those to whom they had been submitted. His defence of this action to the Chapter-General is at once admirable in the tranquillity of its temper and pathetic in the eagerness and affection which it displays for the task that he has been forbidden to continue:

Inasmuch as I was ordered, some years ago . . . to prepare an exact edition of the works of our holy father, and afterwards was commanded to suspend my labours for just reasons which presented themselves to these our fathers and prevented its accomplishment at the time, I obeyed forthwith with the greatest submissiveness, but, as I found that I had a rich store of information which at some future time might contribute to the publication of a truly illustrious and perfect edition, it seemed to me that I should not be running counter to the spirit of the Order if I gave it some serviceable form, so that I should not be embarrassed by seeing it in a disorderly condition if at some future date it should be proposed to carry into effect the original decisions of the Order. With humility and submissiveness, therefore, I send to your Reverences these results of my private labours, not because it is in my mind that the work should be recommended, or that, if this is to be done, it should be at any particular time, for that I leave to the disposition of your Reverences and of God, but to the end that I may return to the Order that which belongs to it; for, since I was excused from religious observances for nearly nine years so that I might labour in this its own field, the Order cannot but have a right to the fruits of my labours, nor can I escape the obligation of delivering what I have discovered into its hand. . . .[57]

We cannot examine the full text of the interesting memorandum to the Censors which follows this humble exordium. One of their allegations had been that the credit of the Order would suffer if it became known that passages of the Saint's works had been suppressed by Carmelite editors. P. Andrés makes the sage reply: There is certainly the risk that this will become known if the edition is made; but there is also a risk that it will become known in any case. We must weigh the risks against each other and decide which proceeding will bring the Order into the greater discredit if one of them materializes.' He fortifies this argument with the declaration that the defects of the existing editions were common knowledge outside the Order as well as within it, and that, as manuscript copies of the Saint's works were also in the possession of many others than Carmelites, there was nothing to prevent a correct edition being made at any time. This must suffice as a proof that P. Andrés could be as acute as he was submissive.

    Besides collecting this material, and leaving on record his opposition to the short-sighted decision of the Censors, P. Andrés prepared 'some Disquisitions on the writings of the Saint, which, if a more skilful hand should correct and improve their style, cannot but be well received.' Closely connected with the Disquisitions are the Preludes in which he glosses the Saint's writings. These studies, like the notes already described, have all been lost -- no doubt, together with many other documents from the archives of the Reform in Madrid, they disappeared during the pillaging of the religious houses in the early nineteenth century.

    The little of P. Andrés' work that remains to us gives a clear picture of the efforts made by the Reform to bring out a worthy edition of St. John of the Cross's writings in the eighteenth century; it is manifestly insufficient, however, to take a modern editor far along the way. Nor, as we have seen, are his judgments by any means to be followed otherwise than with the greatest caution; he greatly exaggerates, too, the effect of the mutilations of earlier editors, no doubt in order to convince his superiors of the necessity for a new edition. The materials for a modern editor are to be found, not in the documents left by P. Andrés, but in such Carmelite archives as still exist, and in the National Library of Spain, to which many Carmelite treasures found their way at the beginning of the last century.

    The work sent by P. Andrés to his superiors was kept in the archives of the Discalced Carmelites, but no new edition was prepared till a hundred and fifty years later. In the nineteenth century such a task was made considerably more difficult by religious persecution; which resulted in the loss of many valuable manuscripts, some of which P. Andrés must certainly have examined. For a time, too, the Orders were expelled from Spain, and, on their return, had neither the necessary freedom, nor the time or material means, for such undertakings. In the twenty-seventh volume of the well-known series of classics entitled Biblioteca de Autores Españoles (1853) the works of St. John of the Cross were reprinted according to the 1703 edition, without its engravings, indices and commendations, and with a critical estimate' of the Saint by Pi y Margall, which has some literary value but in other respects fails entirely to do justice to its subject.

    Neither the Madrid edition of 1872 nor the Barcelona edition of 1883 adds anything to our knowledge and it was not till the Toledo edition of 1912-14 that a new advance was made. This edition was the work of a young Carmelite friar, P. Gerardo de San Juan de la Cruz, who died soon after its completion. It aims, according to its title, which is certainly justified, at being the most correct and complete edition of all that have been published down to the present date.' If it was not as successful as might have been wished, this could perhaps hardly have been expected of a comparatively inexperienced editor confronted with so gigantic a task -- a man, too, who worked almost alone and was by temperament and predilection an investigator rather than a critic. Nevertheless, its introductions, footnotes, appended documents, and collection of apocryphal works of the Saint, as well as its text, were all considered worthy of extended study and the edition was rightly received with enthusiasm. Its principal merit will always lie in its having restored to their proper places, for the first time in a printed edition, many passages which had theretofore remained in manuscript.

    We have been anxious that this new edition [Burgos, 1929-31] should represent a fresh advance in the task of establishing a definitive text of St. John of the Cross's writings. For this reason we have examined, together with two devoted assistants, every discoverable manuscript, with the result, as it seems to us, that both the form and the content of our author's works are as nearly as possible as he left them.

    In no case have we followed any one manuscript exclusively, preferring to assess the value of each by a careful preliminary study and to consider each on its merits, which are described in the introduction to each of the individual works. Since our primary aim has been to present an accurate text, our footnotes will be found to be almost exclusively textual. The only edition which we cite, with the occasional exception of that of 1630, is the princeps, from which alone there is much to be learned. The Latin quotations from the Vulgate are not, of course, given except where they appear in the manuscripts, and, save for the occasional correction of a copyist's error, they are reproduced in exactly the form in which we have found them. Orthography and punctuation have had perforce to be modernized, since the manuscripts differ widely and we have so few autographs that nothing conclusive can be learned of the Saint's own practice.[58]

Footnotes:

3. [H., III, ii.]

4. M. Magdalena is a very reliable witness, for she was not only a most discreet and able woman, but was also one of those who were very near to the saint and gained most from his spiritual direction. The quotation is from MS. 12,944.

5. MS. 12,738, fol. 835. Ft. Jerónimo de S. José, too, says that the nuns of Toledo also copied certain poems from the Saint's dictation. M. Ana de S. Alberto heard him say of his imprisonment: God sought to try me, but His mercy forsook me not. I made some stanzas there which begin: "Whither hast vanishd, Beloved"; and also those other verses, beginning "Far above the many rivers That in Babylon abound." All these verses 1 sent to Fray José de Jesús María, who told me that he was interested in them and was keeping them in his memory in order to write them out.'

6. [H., III, ii.]

7. MS. 12,944. He also occasionally wrote spiritual things that were of great benefit. There, too, he composed the Mount and drew a copy with his own hand for each of our breviaries; later, he added to these copies and made some changes.'

8. [See, on this term, S.S.M., II, 282, and Catholic Encyclopedia, sub. Carmelites.']

9. Fray Martin de San José in MS. 12,738, fol. 125.

10. [H., IV, i.]

11. MS. 12,738, fol. 1,431. The letter is undated as to the year.

12. MS. 12,738, fol. 1,435.

13. MS. 12,738, fol. 3. Cf. a letter of April 28, 1614, by the same friar (ibid., fol. 865), which describes the Saint's knowledge of the Holy Scriptures, and skill in expounding them, as inspired' and Divine.'

14. Ibid., fol. 18.

15. Jerónimo de la Cruz (ibid., fol. 639) describes the Saint on his journeys as frequently reading the Bible' as he went along on his beast.'

16. MS. 12,738, fol. 559. P. Alonso writes similarly in a letter to Fray Jerónimo de San José: And in this matter of speaking of God and expounding passages from Scripture he made everyone marvel, for they never asked him about a passage which he could not explain in great detail, and sometimes at recreation the whole hour and much more went by in the explanation of passages about which they asked him' (fol. 1,431).

17. Ibid., fol. 847.

18. [Cf. S.S.M., II, 123-48.]

19. Vida, Bk. IV, Chap. xiv, 1.

20. [On this subject cf. P. Crisógono de Jesús Sacramentado: San Juan de la Cruz, Madrid, 1929, Vol. II, pp. 17-34 et passim.]

21. On Flemish influences on Spanish mysticism, see P. Groult: Les Mystiques des Pays-Bas et la littérature espagnole du seizième siècle, Louvain, 1927 [, and Joaquín Sanchis Alventosa, O.F.M.: La Escuela mística alemana y sus relaciones con nuestros místicos del Siglo de Oro, Madrid, 1946].

22. Cf. S.S.M., I (1927), 33-76, 291-405; (1951), 25-61, 235-328; II (1930), 309-43.]

23. One well-known example will be found in the commentary on the Spiritual Canticle,' Chap. xii (cf. V below).

24. MS. 12,738, fol. 639.

25. To these we shall refer in the third volume of this edition.

26. If any single person could have spoken from knowledge of this matter it would be P. Alonso de la Madre de Dios, as all papers connected with St. John of the Cross passed through his hands and he took hundreds of depositions in connection with the Beatification process. His statements, however (MS. 19,404, fol. 176 [P. Silverio, I, 179]), are as vague as any others. Rather more reliable are the Saint's two early biographers, P. José de Jesús María (Quiroga) and P. Jerónimo de San José. The former states in one place that he is using an autograph on the Ascent of Mount Carmel, but again it seems likely that he was mistaken, since the archives of the Reform were still intact in the next century and no genuine autograph of any length was found in them.

27. [The commentary on the third stanza is begun in ii, xxv of Dark Night. If this be not counted, the number of stanzas left uncommented is six.]

28. This is not so unlikely as it may seem, for the early manuscripts were all either unbound, or very roughly stitched together, and several of the extant copies have leaves missing. It was not till the time of the Beatification Process that greater care began to be taken of the Saint's writings, and they were bound strongly and even luxuriously.

29. I.e., the three books of the Ascent and the two of the Night.

30. MS. 3,180, Adición B.

31. It would be natural enough, of course, for Fray Agustín Antolínez to have noted this fact, but,

as he makes no mention of St. John of the Cross at all, nothing can be safely inferred from his silence. It may be added that Fray Agustín's commentary is to be published by the Spanish Augustinians [and that P. Silverio (I, 190-3) gives a specimen of it which shows how well it deserves publication].

32. As we shall later see, the Living Flame was written after the first redaction of the Spiritual Canticle, but before the second redaction, which mentions the Living Flame in the exposition of Stanza XXXI, thus misleading P. Andrés as to its date. There is no doubt, in our mind, that the reference in the preface to the Living Flame is to the Canticle: the description fits it exactly.

33. [P. Silverio's words are: For my own part, I think it very probable that he never composed them.' I myself give a little less weight to the negative evidence brought forward, and, though I too am inclined to the negative solution, I should hold the scales between the two rather more evenly.]

34. If this were so, we might even hazard a guess that the title was that given in the Living Flame (I, 21) and not exactly applicable to any of the existing treatises, viz. The Dark Night of the Ascent of Mount Carmel.

35. Memorias Historiales, C. 1 3.

36. Saint Jean de la Croix, pp. 1 3-15.

37. Cf. Ascent, I, i, below.

38. Some manuscripts do in fact divide the treatise in this way; but apart from the fact that we have the authority of St. John of the Cross himself, in the passage just quoted (confirmed in Ascent, I, xiii), for a different division, the Alcaudete MS., which we believe to be the most reliable, follows the division laid down by the Saint. We may add that St. John of the Cross is not always a safe guide in these matters, no doubt because he trusted too much to his memory; in Ascent, II, xi, for example, he calls the fourth book the third.

39. [H., V, iii.]

40. Spiritual Canticle, Stanza XII, 6 [Second Redaction, XIII, 7].

41. In the same passage as that referred to in the last note he declares his intention of not repeating what she has said (cf. General Introduction, III, above).

42. Our authority for this statement is P. Andres de la Encarnación (Memorias Historiales, B. 32), who found the Chapter Book in the General Archives of the Reform at Madrid.

43. Op. cit. (B. 33).

44. [For a study of Tomás de Jesús, see S.S.M., II, 281-306.]

45. Memorias Historiales, B. 35.

46. Cf. General Introduction, I, above.

47. [Cf. S.S.M., I (1927), 291-344; (1951), 235-79. An abridged English edition of the Names of Christ, translated by a Benedictine of Stanbrook, was published by Messrs. Burns Oates and Washbourne in 1926.]

48. [Cf. S.S.M., I (1927), 295-6; (1951), 240.]

49. [Cf. S.S.M., II, 41-76.]

50. Historia crítica de la Inquisición de España, Vol. V, Chap. xxx, and elsewhere. [The original of this work is in French: Histoire critique de l'Inquisition d'Espagñe, 1817-18.]

51. Here we have a curious parallelism with the works of St. Teresa, first published at Salamanca in 1588 and also reprinted in Barcelona in the year following.

52. He also supplies the Latin text of Scriptural quotations which St. John of the Cross gives in the vernacular, corrects the punctuation and spelling of the princeps and substitutes his Sketch' of the Saint's life for the biographical notes of that edition. The treatise in which he corrects most of the defects of the princeps is the Ascent of Mount Carmel.

53. Phrasium mysticae Theologiae V.P. Fr. Joannis a Cruce, Carmelitarum excalceatorum Parentis primi elucidatio. Compluti, 1631.

54. Subida del Alma a Dios; Apología mística en defensa de la contemplación divina; Don que tuvo San Juan de la Cruz para guiar las almas, etc.

55. This phrase, no doubt, was inserted in order to save the reputation of P. José's earlier supporters, and out of respect to his uncle, who had been a Cardinal and Inquisitor-General.

56. Quoted by P. Andrés de la Encarnación (MS. 3,653, Previo 1).

57. MS. 3,653, Previo 1.

58. [The last two paragraphs form P. Silverio's description of his own edition. The lines followed in the present translation have been described in the Translator's Preface.]

INTRODUCTION

AS will be seen from the biographical outline which we have given of the life of St. John of the Cross, this was the first of the Saint's treatises to be written; it was begun at El Calvario, and, after various intervals, due to the author's preoccupation with the business of government and the direction and care of souls, was completed at Granada.

The treatise presents a remarkable outline of Christian perfection from the point at which the soul first seeks to rise from the earth and soar upward towards union with God. It is a work which shows every sign of careful planning and great attention to detail, as an ascetic treatise it is noteworthy for its detailed psychological analysis; as a contribution to mystical theology, for the skill with which it treats the most complicated and delicate questions concerning the Mystic Way.

Both the great Carmelite reformers pay close attention to the early stages of the mystical life, beyond which many never pass, and both give the primacy to prayer as a means of attaining perfection. To St. Teresa prayer is the greatest of all blessings of this life, the channel through which all the favours of God pass to the soul, the beginning of every virtue and the plainly marked highroad which leads to the summit of Mount Carmel. She can hardly conceive of a person in full spiritual health whose life is not one of prayer. Her coadjutor in the Carmelite Reform writes in the same spirit. Prayer, for St. John of the Cross as for St. Teresa, is no mere exercise made up of petition and meditation, but a complete spiritual life which brings in its train all the virtues, increases all the soul's potentialities and may ultimately lead to deification' or transformation in God through love. It may be said that the exposition of the life of prayer, from its lowest stages to its highest, is the common aim of these two Saints, which each pursues and accomplishes in a peculiarly individual manner.

St. John of the Cross assumes his reader to be familiar with the rudiments of the spiritual life and therefore omits detailed description of the most elementary of the exercises incumbent upon all Christians. The plan of the Ascent of Mount Carmel (which, properly speaking, embraces its sequel, the Dark Night) follows the lines of the poem with the latter title (p. 10). Into two stanzas of five lines each, St. John of the Cross has condensed all the instruction which he develops in this treatise. In order to reach the Union of Light, the soul must pass through the Dark Night -- that is to say, through a series of purifications, during which it is walking, as it were, through a tunnel of impenetrable obscurity and from which it emerges to bask in the sunshine of grace and to enjoy the Divine intimacy.

Through this obscurity the thread which guides the soul is that of emptiness' or negation.' Only by voiding ourselves of all that is not God can we attain to the possession of God, for two contraries cannot co-exist in one individual, and creature-love is darkness, while God is light, so that from any human heart one of the two cannot fail to drive out the other. [59]

Now the soul, according to the Saint's psychology, is made up of interior and exterior senses and of the faculties. All these must be free from creature impurities in order to be prepared for Divine union. The necessary self-emptying may be accomplished in two ways: by our own efforts, with the habitual aid of grace, and by the action of God exclusively, in which the individual has no part whatsoever. Following this order, the Ascent is divided into two parts, which deal respectively with the Active' night and the Passive.' Each of these parts consists of several books. Since the soul must be purified in its entirety, the Active Night is logically divided into the Night of Sense and the Night of the Spirit; a similar division is observed in treating of the Passive Night. One book is devoted to the Active Night of Sense; two are needed for the Active Night of the Spirit. Unhappily, however, the treatise was never finished; not only was its author unable to take us out of the night into the day, as he certainly intended to do, but he has not even space to describe the Passive Night in all the fullness of its symbolism.

A brief glance at the outstanding parts of the Ascent of Mount Carmel will give some idea of its nature. The first obstacle which the pilgrim soul encounters is the senses, upon which St. John of the Cross expends his analytical skill in Book I. Like any academic professor (and it will be recalled that he had undergone a complete university course at Salamanca), he outlines and defines his subject, goes over the necessary preliminary ground before expounding it, and treats it, in turn, under each of its natural divisions. He tells us, that is to say, what he understands by the dark night'; describes its causes and its stages; explains how necessary it is to union with God; enumerates the perils which beset the soul that enters it; and shows how all desires must be expelled, however small they be,' if the soul is to travel through it safely. Finally he gives a complete synthesis of the procedure that must be adopted by the pilgrim in relation to this part of his journey: the force of this is intensified by those striking maxims and distichs which make Chapter xiii of Book I so memorable.

The first thirteen chapters of the Ascent are perhaps the easiest to understand (though they are anything but easy to put into practice) in the entire works of St. John of the Cross. They are all a commentary on the very first line of the poem. The last two chapters of the first book glance at the remaining lines, rather than expound them, and the Saint takes us on at once to Book II, which expounds the second stanza and enters upon the Night of the Spirit.

Here the Saint treats of the proximate means to union with God -- namely, faith. He uses the same careful method of exposition, showing clearly how faith is to the soul as a dark night, and how, nevertheless, it is the safest of guides. A parenthetical chapter (v) attempts to give some idea of the nature of union, so that the reader may recognize from afar the goal to which he is proceeding. The author then goes on to describe how the three theological virtues -- faith, hope and charity -- must void and dispose for union' the three faculties of the soul -- understanding, memory and will.

He shows how narrow is the way that leads to life and how nothing that belongs to the understanding can guide the soul to union. His illustrations and arguments are far more complicated and subtle than are those of the first book, and give the reader some idea of his knowledge, not only of philosophy and theology, but also of individual souls. Without this last qualification he could never have written those penetrating chapters on the impediments to union -- above all, the passages on visions, locutions and revelations -- nor must we overlook his description (Chapter xiii) of the three signs that the soul is ready to pass from meditation to contemplation. It may be doubted if in its own field this second book has ever been surpassed. There is no mystic who gives a more powerful impression than St. John of the Cross of an absolute mastery of his subject. No mistiness, vagueness or indecision clouds his writing: he is as clear-cut and definite as can be.

In his third book St. John of the Cross goes on to describe the obstacles to union which come from the memory and the will. Unlike St. Thomas, he considered the memory as a distinct and separate faculty of the soul. Having written, however, at such length of the understanding, he found it possible to treat more briefly of that other faculty, which is so closely related to it. [60] Fourteen chapters (ii-xv) describe the dark night to be traversed by the memory; thirty (xvi-xlv) the passage of the will, impelled by love. [61] The latter part is the more strikingly developed. Four passions -- joy, hope, sorrow and fear -- invade the will, and may either encompass the soul's perdition, or, if rightly directed, lead it to virtue and union. Once more St. John of the Cross employs his profound familiarity with the human soul to turn it away from peril and guide it into the path of safety. Much that he says, in dealing with passions so familiar to us all, is not only purely ascetic, but is even commonplace to the instructed Christian. Yet these are but parts of a greater whole.

Of particular interest, both intrinsically and as giving a picture of the Saint's own times, are the chapters on ceremonies and aids to devotion -- the use of rosaries, medals, pilgrimages, etc. It must be remembered, of course, that he spent most of his active life in the South of Spain, where exaggerations of all kinds, even to-day, are more frequent than in the more sober north. In any case there is less need, in this lukewarm age, to warn Christians against the abuse of these means of grace, and more need, perhaps, to urge them to employ aids that will stimulate and quicken their devotion.

In the seventeenth chapter of this third book, St. John of the Cross enumerates the 'six kinds of good' which can give rise to rejoicing and sets down his intention of treating each of them in turn. He carries out his purpose, but, on entering his last division, subdivides it at considerable length and subsequently breaks off with some brusqueness while dealing with one of these sub-heads, just as he is introducing another subject of particular interest historically -- namely, pulpit methods considered from the standpoint of the preacher. In all probability we shall never know what he had to say about the hearers of sermons, or what were his considered judgments on confessors and penitents -- though of these judgments he has left us examples elsewhere in this treatise, as well as in others.

We cannot estimate of how much the sudden curtailment of the Ascent of Mount Carmel has robbed us. [62] Orderly as was the mind of St. John of the Cross, he was easily carried away in his expositions, which are apt to be unequal. No one would have suspected, for example, that, after going into such length in treating the first line of his first stanza, he would make such short work of the remaining four. Nor can we disregard the significance of his warning that much of what he had written on the understanding was applicable also to the memory and the will. He may, therefore, have been nearer the end of his theme than is generally supposed. Yet it is equally possible that much more of his subtle analysis was in store for his readers. Any truncation, when the author is a St. John of the Cross, must be considered irreparable.

Footnotes:

59. Ascent, Bk. III, Chap. ii.
60. Ascent, Bk. III, Chap. iii, 1.
61. Cf. Ascent, Bk. III, Chap. xvi, 1-2.
62. [On the question of the curtailment of the Ascent, see Sobrino, pp. 159-66.]

THE MANUSCRIPTS [63]

Unfortunately there is no autograph of this treatise extant, though there are a number of early copies, some of which have been made with great care. Others, for various reasons, abbreviate the original considerably. The MSS. belonging to both classes will be enumerated.

Alba de Tormes. The Discalced Carmelite priory of Alba de Tormes has a codex which contains the four principal treatises of St. John of the Cross (Ascent, Dark Night, Spiritual Canticle and Living Flame). This codex belonged from a very early date (perhaps from a date not much later than that of the Saint's death) to the family of the Duke of Alba, which was greatly devoted to the Discalced Carmelite Reform and to St. Teresa, its foundress. It remained in the family until the beginning of the eighteenth century, when it came into the hands of a learned Carmelite, Fray Alonso de la Madre de Dios, who presented it to the Alba monastery on April 15, 1705. The details of this history are given by Fray Alonso himself in a note bearing this date.

For over half a century the MS. was believed to be an autograph, partly, no doubt, on account of its luxurious binding and the respect paid to the noble house whence it came. In February 1761, however, it was examined carefully by P. Manuel de Santa María, who, by his Superiors' orders, was assisting P. Andrés de la Encarnación in his search for, and study of, manuscripts of the Saint's writings. P. Manuel soon discovered that the opinion commonly held was erroneous -- greatly, it would seem, to the disillusionment of his contemporaries. Among the various reasons which he gives in a statement supporting his conclusions is that in two places the author is described as 'santo' -- a proof not only that the MS. is not an autograph but also that the copyist had no intention of representing it as such.

Although this copy is carefully made and richly bound -- which suggests that it was a gift from the Reform to the house of Alba -- it contains many errors, of a kind which indicate that the copyist, well educated though he was, knew little of ascetic or mystical theology. A number of omissions, especially towards the end of the book, give the impression that the copy was finished with haste and not compared with the original on its completion. There is no reason, however, to suppose that the errors and omissions are ever intentional; indeed, they are of such a kind as to suggest that the copyist had not the skill necessary for successful adulteration.

MS. 6,624. This copy, like the next four, is in N.L.M. [National Library of Spain, Madrid], and contains the same works as that of Alba de Tormes. It was made in 1755, under the direction of P. Andrés de la Encarnación, from a manuscript, now lost, which was venerated by the Benedictines of Burgos: this information is found at the end of the volume. P. Andrés had evidently a good opinion of the Burgos MS., as he placed this copy in the archives of the Discalced Reform, whence it passed to the National Library early in the nineteenth century.

As far as the Ascent is concerned, this MS. is very similar to that of Alba. With a few notable exceptions, such as the omission of the second half of Book I, Chapter iv, the errors and omissions are so similar as to suggest a definite relationship, if not a common source.

MS. 13,498. This MS., which gives us the Ascent and the Dark Night, also came from the Archives of the Reform and is now in the National Library. The handwriting might be as early as the end of the sixteenth century. The author did not attempt to make a literal transcription of the Ascent, but summarized where he thought advisable, reducing the number of chapters and abbreviating many of them -- this last not so much by the method of paraphrase as by the free omission of phrases and sentences.

MS. 2,201. This, as far as the Ascent is concerned, is an almost literal transcription of the last MS., in a seventeenth-century hand; it was bound in the eighteenth century, when a number of other treatises were added to it, together with some poems by St. John of the Cross and others. The variants as between this MS. and 13,498 are numerous, but of small importance, and seem mainly to have been due to carelessness.

MS. 18,160. This dates from the end of the sixteenth century and contains the four treatises named above, copied in different hands and evidently intended to form one volume. Only the first four chapters of the Ascent are given, together with the title and the first three lines of the fifth chapter. The transcription is poorly done.

MS. 13,507. An unimportant copy, containing only a few odd chapters of the Ascent and others from the remaining works of St. John of the Cross and other writers.

Ascent of Mount Carmel

Pamplona. A codex in an excellent state of preservation is venerated by the Discalced Carmelite nuns of Pamplona. It was copied, at the end of the sixteenth century, by a Barcelona Carmelite, M. Magdalena de la Asunción, and contains a short summary of the four treatises enumerated above, various poems by St. John of the Cross and some miscellaneous writings. The Ascent is abbreviated to the same extent as in 13,498 and 2,201 and by the same methods; many chapters, too, are omitted in their entirety.

Alcaudete. This MS., which contains the Ascent only, was copied by St. John of the Cross's close friend and companion, P. Juan Evangelista, as a comparison with manuscripts (N.L.M., 12,738) written in his well-known and very distinctive hand, puts beyond all doubt. P. Juan, who took the habit of the Reform at Christmas 1582, knew the Saint before this date; was professed by him at Granada in 1583; accompanied him on many of his journeys; saw him write most of his books; and, as his close friend and confessor, was consulted repeatedly by his biographers. [64] It is natural that he should also have acted as the Saint's copyist, and, in the absence of autographs, we should expect no manuscripts to be more trustworthy than copies made by him. Examination of this MS. shows that it is in fact highly reliable. It corrects none of those unwieldy periods in which the Saint's work abounds, and which the editio princeps often thought well to amend, nor, like the early editions and even some manuscripts, does it omit whole paragraphs and substitute others for them. Further, as this copy was being made solely for the use of the Order, no passages are omitted or altered in it because they might be erroneously interpreted as illuministic. It is true that P. Juan Evangelista is not, from the technical standpoint, a perfect copyist, but, frequently as are his slips, they are always easy to recognize.

The Alcaudete MS. was found in the Carmelite priory in that town by P. Andrés de la Encarnación, who first made use of it for his edition. When the priory was abandoned during the religious persecutions of the early nineteenth century, the MS. was lost. Nearly a hundred years passed before it was re-discovered by P. Silverio de Santa Teresa in a second-hand bookshop [and forms a most important contribution to that scholar's edition, which normally follows it]. It bears many signs of frequent use; eleven folios are missing from the body of the MS. (corresponding approximately to Book III, Chapters xxii to xxvi) and several more from its conclusion.

In the footnotes to the Ascent, the following abbreviations are used:
A = MS. of the Discalced Carmelite Friars of Alba.
Alc. = Alcaudete MS.
B = MS. of the Benedictines of Burgos.
C = N.L.M., MS. 13,498.
D = N.L.M., MS. 2,201.
P = MS. of the Discalced Carmelite Nuns of Pamplona.
E.p. = Editio princeps (Alcalá, 1618).

Other editions or manuscripts cited are referred to without abbreviation.

Footnotes:

63. [On MSS. not described by P. Silverio, see Ephemerides Carmeliticae, Florence, 1950, IV, 95-148, and in particular p. 103, n. 9. As the variants and annotations in these MSS. will be of interest only to specialists, and few of them can be reproduced in a translation, those who wish to study them are referred to that article.]

64. [H, sub Juan Evangelista (2)]

ASCENT OF MOUNT CARMEL

Treats of how the soul may prepare itself in order to attain in a short time to Divine union. Gives very profitable counsels and instruction, both to beginners and to proficients, that they may know how to disencumber themselves of all that is temporal and not to encumber themselves with the spiritual, and to remain in complete detachment and liberty of spirit, as is necessary for Divine union.

ARGUMENT

ALL the doctrine whereof I intend to treat in this Ascent of Mount Carmel is included in the following stanzas, and in them is also described the manner of ascending to the summit of the Mount, which is the high estate of perfection which we here call union of the soul with God. And because I must continually base upon them that which I shall say, I have desired to set them down here together, to the end that all the substance of that which is to be written may be seen and comprehended together; although it will be fitting to set down each stanza separately before expounding it, and likewise the lines of each stanza, according as the matter and the exposition require. The poem, then, runs as follows: [65]

STANZAS[66]

Wherein the soul sings of the happy chance which it had in passing through the dark night of faith, in detachment and purgation of itself, to union with the Beloved.

1. On a dark night, Kindled [67] in love with yearnings -- oh, happy chance! --
   I went forth without being observed, My house being now at rest. [68]
2. In darkness and secure, By the secret ladder, disguised -- oh, happy chance! --
   In darkness and in concealment, My house being now at rest.
3. In the happy night, In secret, when none saw me,
   Nor I beheld aught, Without light or guide, save that which burned in my heart.
4. This light guided me More surely than the light of noonday,
   To the place where he (well I knew who!) was awaiting me -- A place where none appeared.
5. Oh, night that guided me, Oh, night more lovely than the dawn,
   Oh, night that joined Beloved with lover, Lover transformed in the Beloved!
6. Upon my flowery breast, Kept wholly for himself alone,
   There he stayed sleeping, and I caressed him, And the fanning of the cedars made a breeze.
7. The breeze blew from the turret As I parted his locks;
   With his gentle hand he wounded my neck And caused all my senses to be suspended.
8. I remained, lost in oblivion; [69] My face I reclined on the Beloved.
   All ceased and I abandoned myself, Leaving my cares forgotten among the lilies.

Footnotes:

65. [Lit.: It says, then, thus.']
66. For a verse translation in the metre of the original, see Vol. II.
67. [The adjectives are feminine throughout.]
68. [The word translated at rest' is a past participle: more literally, stilled.']
69. [Lit.: I remained and forgot.']

PROLOGUE

IN order to expound and describe this dark night, through which the soul passes in order to attain to the Divine light of the perfect union of the love of God, as far as is possible in this life, it would be necessary to have illumination of knowledge and experience other and far greater than mine; for this darkness and these trials, both spiritual and temporal, through which happy souls are wont to pass in order to be able to attain to this high estate of perfection, are so numerous and so profound that neither does human knowledge suffice for the understanding of them, nor experience for the description of them; for only he that passes this way can understand it, and even he cannot describe it.

2. Therefore, in order to say a little about this dark night, I shall trust neither to experience nor to knowledge, since both may fail and deceive; but, while not omitting to make such use as I can of these two things, I shall avail myself, in all that, with the Divine favour, I have to say, or at the least, in that which is most important and dark to the understanding, of Divine Scripture; for, if we guide ourselves by this, we shall be unable to stray, since He Who speaks therein is the Holy Spirit. And if aught I stray, whether through my imperfect understanding of that which is said in it or of matters uncollected with it, it is not my intention to depart from the sound sense and doctrine of our Holy Mother the Catholic Church; for in such a case I submit and resign myself wholly, not only to her command, but to whatever better judgment she may pronounce concerning it.

3. To this end I have been moved, not by any possibility that I see in myself of accomplishing so arduous a task, but by the confidence which I have in the Lord that He will help me to say something to relieve the great necessity which is experienced by many souls, who, when they set out upon the road of virtue, and Our Lord desires to bring them into this dark night that they may pass through it to Divine union, make no progress. At times this is because they have no desire to enter it or to allow themselves to be led into it; at other times, because they understand not themselves and lack competent and alert directors [70] who will guide them to the summit. And so it is sad to see many souls to whom God gives both aptitude and favour with which to make progress (and who, if they would take courage, could attain to this high estate), remaining in an elementary stage [71] of communion with God, for want of will, or knowledge, or because there is none who will lead them in the right path or teach them how to get away from these beginnings. And at length, although Our Lord grants them such favour as to make them to go onward without this hindrance or that, they arrive at their goal very much later, and with greater labour, yet with less merit, because they have not conformed themselves to God, and allowed themselves to be brought freely into the pure and sure road of union. For, although it is true that God is leading them, and that He can lead them without their own help, they will not allow themselves to be led; and thus they make less progress, because they resist Him Who is leading them, and they have less merit, because they apply not their will, and on this account they suffer more. For these are souls who, instead of committing themselves to God and making use of His help, rather hinder God by the indiscretion of their actions or by their resistance; like children who, when their mothers desire to carry them in their arms, start stamping and crying, and insist upon being allowed to walk, with the result that they can make no progress; and, if they advance at all, it is only at the pace of a child.

4. Wherefore, to the end that all, whether beginners or proficients, may know how to commit themselves to God's guidance, when His Majesty desires to lead them onward, we shall give instruction and counsel, by His help, so that they may be able to understand His will, or, at the least, allow Him to lead them. For some confessors and spiritual fathers, having no light and experience concerning these roads, are wont to hinder and harm such souls rather than to help them on the road; they are like the builders of Babel, who, when told to furnish suitable material, gave and applied other very different material, because they understood not the language, and thus nothing was done. Wherefore, it is a difficult and troublesome thing at such seasons for a soul not to understand itself or to find none who understands it. For it will come to pass that God will lead the soul by a most lofty path of dark contemplation and aridity, wherein it seems to be lost, and, being thus full of darkness and trials, constraints and temptations, will meet one who will speak to it like Job's comforters, and say that it is suffering from melancholy, or low spirits, or a morbid disposition, or that it may have some hidden sin, and that it is for this reason that God has forsaken it. Such comforters are wont to declare immediately that that soul must have been very evil, since such things as these are befalling it.

5. And there will likewise be those who tell the soul to retrace its steps, since it is finding no

pleasure or consolation in the things of God as it did aforetime. And in this way they double the poor soul's trials; for it may well be that the greatest affliction which it is feeling is that of the knowledge of its own miseries, thinking that it sees itself, more clearly than daylight, to be full of evils and sins, for God gives it that light of knowledge in that night of contemplation, as we shall presently show. And, when the soul finds someone whose opinion agrees with its own, and who says that these things must be due to its own fault, its affliction and trouble increase infinitely and are wont to become more grievous than death. And, not content with this, such confessors, thinking that these things proceed from sin, make these souls go over their lives and cause them to make many general confessions, and crucify them afresh; not understanding that this may quite well not be the time for any of such things, and that their penitents should be left in the state of purgation which God gives them, and be comforted and encouraged to desire it until God be pleased to dispose otherwise; for until that time, no matter what the souls themselves may do and their confessors may say, there is no remedy for them.

6. This, with the Divine favour, we shall consider hereafter, and also how the soul should conduct itself at such a time, and how the confessor must treat it, and what signs there will be whereby it may be known if this is the purgation of the soul; and, in such case, whether it be of sense or of spirit (which is the dark night whereof we speak), and how it may be known if it be melancholy or some other imperfection with respect to sense or to spirit. For there may be some souls who will think, or whose confessors will think, that God is leading them along this road of the dark night of spiritual purgation, whereas they may possibly be suffering only from some of the imperfections aforementioned. And, again, there are many souls who think that they have no aptitude for prayer, when they have very much; and there are others who think that they have much when they have hardly any.

7. There are other souls who labour and weary themselves to a piteous extent, and yet go backward, seeking profit in that which is not profitable, but is rather a hindrance; and there are still others who, by remaining at rest and in quietness, continue to make great progress. There are others who are hindered and disturbed and make no progress, because of the very consolations and favours that God is granting them in order that they may make progress. And there are many other things on this road that befall those who follow it, both joys and afflictions and hopes and griefs: some proceeding from the spirit of perfection and others from imperfection. Of all these, with the Divine favour, we shall endeavour to say something, so that each soul who reads this may be able to see something of the road that he ought to follow, if he aspire to attain to the summit of this Mount.

8. And, since this introduction relates to the dark night through which the soul must go to God, let not the reader marvel if it seem to him somewhat dark also. This, I believe, will be so at the beginning when he begins to read; but, as he passes on, he will find himself understanding the first part better, since one part will explain another. And then, if he read it a second time, I believe it will seem clearer to him and the instruction will appear sounder. And if any persons find themselves disagreeing with this instruction, it will be due to my ignorance and poor style; for in itself the matter is good and of the first importance. But I think that, even were it written in a more excellent and perfect manner than it is, only the minority would profit by it, for we shall not here set down things that are very moral and delectable[72] for all spiritual persons who desire to travel toward God by pleasant and delectable ways, but solid and substantial instruction, as well suited to one kind of person as to another, if they desire to pass to the detachment of spirit which is here treated.

9. Nor is my principal intent to address all, but rather certain persons of our sacred Order of Mount Carmel of the primitive observance, both friars and nuns -- since they have desired me to do so -- to whom God is granting the favour of setting them on the road to this Mount; who, as they are already detached from the temporal things of this world, will better understand the instruction concerning detachment of spirit.

Footnotes:

70. [Lit. and wideawake guides.']
71. [Lit., a low manner.']
72. Needless to say, the Saint does not here mean that he will not write in conformity with moral standards -- no writer is more particular in this respect -- nor that he will deal with no delectable matters at all, but rather that he will go to the very roots of spiritual teaching and expound the 'solid and substantial instruction,' which not only forms its basis but also leads the soul toward the most intimate union with God in love.

BOOK THE FIRST

Wherein is described the nature of dark night and how necessary it is to pass through it to Divine union; and in particular this book describes the dark night of sense, and desire, and the evils which these work in the soul. [73]

CHAPTER I

Sets down the first stanza. Describes two different nights through which spiritual persons pass, according to the two parts of man, the lower and the higher. Expounds the stanza which follows.

Stanza The First

On a dark night, Kindled in love with yearnings -- oh, happy chance! --
I went forth without being observed, My house being now at rest.

In this first stanzas the soul sings of the happy fortune and chance which it experienced in going forth from all things that are without, and from the desires [74] and imperfections that are in the sensual [75] part of man because of the disordered state of his reason. For the understanding of this it must be known that, for a soul to attain to the state of perfection, it has ordinarily first to pass through two principal kinds of night, which spiritual persons call purgations or purifications of the soul; and here we call them nights, for in both of them the soul journeys, as it were, by night, in darkness.

2. The first night or purgation is of the sensual part of the soul, which is treated in the present stanza, and will be treated in the first part of this book. And the second is of the spiritual part; of this speaks the second stanza, which follows; and of this we shall treat likewise, in the second and the third part, [76] with respect to the activity of the soul; and in the fourth part, with respect to its passitivity.

3. And this first night pertains to beginners, occurring at the time when God begins to bring them into the state of contemplation; in this night the spirit likewise has a part, as we shall say in due course. And the second night, or purification, pertains to those who are already proficient, occurring at the time when God desires to bring them to the state of union with God. And this latter night is a more obscure and dark and terrible purgation, as we shall say afterwards.

4. Briefly, then, the soul means by this stanza that it went forth (being led by God) for love of Him alone, enkindled in love of Him, upon a dark night, which is the privation and purgation of all its sensual desires, with respect to all outward things of the world and to those which were delectable to its flesh, and likewise with respect to the desires of its will. This all comes to pass in this purgation of sense; for which cause the soul says that it went forth while its house was still at rest; [77] which house is its sensual part, the desires being at rest and asleep in it, as it is to them. [78] For there is no going forth from the pains and afflictions of the secret places of the desires until these be mortified and put to sleep. And this, the soul says, was a happy chance for it -- namely, its going forth without being observed: that is, without any desire of its flesh or any other thing being able to hinder it. And likewise, because it went out by night -- which signifies the privation of all these things wrought in it by God, which privation was night for it.

5. And it was a happy chance that God should lead it into this night, from which there came to it so much good; for of itself the soul would not have succeeded in entering therein, because no man of himself can succeed in voiding himself of all his desires in order to come to God.

6. This is, in brief, the exposition of the stanza; and we shall now have to go through it, line by line, setting down one line after another, and expounding that which pertains to our purpose. And the same method is followed in the other stanzas, as I said in the Prologue [79] -- namely, that each stanza will be set down and expounded, and afterwards each line.

Footnotes:

73. The Codices give neither title nor sub-title: both were inserted in e.p. ['Desire' is to be taken as the direct object of 'describes'; 'these' refers to 'sense' and 'desire,' not to the dark night.]

74. [Lit., 'appetites,' but this word is uniformly translated 'desires,' as the Spanish context frequently will not admit the use of the stronger word in English.]

75. [The word translated 'sensual' is sometimes sensual, and sometimes, as here, sensitivo. The meaning in either case is simply 'of sense.']

76. So Alc. The other authorities read: 'and of this we shall treat likewise, in the second part with respect to the activity [of the soul] [these last three words are not contained in the Spanish of any authority], and in the third and the fourth part with respect to its passivity.' E.p. follows this division. Alc., however, seems to correspond more closely with the Saint's intentions; for he did not divide each of his 'books' into 'parts' and appears therefore to indicate by 'part' what we know as 'book.' Now Book I is in fact devoted to the active purgation of sense, as are Books II and III to the active purgation of the spirit. For the 'fourth book,' see General Introduction, IV above.

77. [The word translated 'at rest' is a past participle: more literally, 'stilled.']

78. [Lit., 'and it in them.' This 'it' means the soul; the preceding 'it,' the house.]

79. I.e., in the Argument.'

CHAPTER II

Explains the nature of this dark night through which the soul says that it has passed on the road to union.

On A Dark Night

We may say that there are three reasons for which this journey [80] made by the soul to union with God is called night. The first has to do with the point from which the soul goes forth, for it has gradually to deprive itself of desire for all the worldly things which it possessed, by denying them to itself; [81] the which denial and deprivation are, as it were, night to all the senses of man. The second reason has to do with the mean, [82] or the road along which the soul must travel to this union -- that is, faith, which is likewise as dark as night to the understanding. The third has to do with the point to which it travels -- namely, God, Who, equally, is dark night to the soul in this life. These three nights must pass through the soul -- or, rather, the soul must pass through them -- in order that it may come to Divine union with God.

2. In the book of the holy Tobias these three kinds of night were shadowed forth by the three nights which, as the angel commanded, were to pass ere the youth Tobias should be united with his bride. In the first he commanded him to burn the heart of the fish in the fire, which signifies the heart that is affectioned to, and set upon, the things of the world; which, in order that one may begin to journey toward God, must be burned and purified from all that is creature, in the fire of the love of God. And in this purgation the devil flees away, for he has power over the soul only when it is attached to things corporeal and temporal.

3. On the second night the angel told him that he would be admitted into the company of the holy patriarchs, who are the fathers of the faith. For, passing through the first night, which is self-privation of all objects of sense, the soul at once enters into the second night, and abides alone in faith to the exclusion, not of charity, but of other knowledge acquired by the understanding, as we shall say hereafter, which is a thing that pertains not to sense.

4. On the third night the angel told him that he would obtain a blessing, which is God; Who, by means of the second night, which is faith, continually communicates Himself to the soul in such a secret and intimate manner that He becomes another night to the soul, inasmuch as this said communication is far darker than those others, as we shall say presently. And, when this third night is past, which is the complete accomplishment of the communication of God in the spirit, which is ordinarily wrought in great darkness of the soul, there then follows its union with the Bride, which is the Wisdom of God. Even so the angel said likewise to Tobias that, when the third night was past, he should be united with his bride in the fear of the Lord; for, when this fear of God is perfect, love is perfect, and this comes to pass when the transformation of the soul is wrought through its love.

5. These three parts of the night are all one night; but, after the manner of night, it has three parts. For the first part, which is that of sense, is comparable to the beginning of night, the point at which things begin to fade from sight. And the second part, which is faith, is comparable to midnight, which is total darkness. And the third part is like the close of night, which is God, the which part is now near to the light of day. And, that we may understand this the better, we shall treat of each of these reasons separately as we proceed.

Footnotes:

80. [More exactly, this passage' or transition' (tránsito).]
81. [Lit., in negation of them.']
82. [By the mean' is meant the middle, or main part, of the journey.]

CHAPTER III

Speaks of the first cause of this night, which is that of the privation of the desire in all things, and gives the reason for which it is called night.

We here describe as night the privation of every kind of pleasure which belongs to the desire; for, even as night is naught but the privation of light, and, consequently, of all objects that can be seen by means of light, whereby the visual faculty remains unoccupied [83] and in darkness, even so likewise the mortification of desire may be called night to the soul. For, when the soul is deprived of the pleasure of its desire in all things, it remains, as it were, unoccupied and in darkness. For even as the visual faculty, by means of light, is nourished and fed by objects which can be seen, and which, when the light is quenched, are not seen, even so, by means of the desire, the soul is nourished and fed by all things wherein it can take pleasure according to its faculties; and, when this also is quenched, or rather, mortified, the soul ceases to feed upon the pleasure of all things, and thus, with respect to its desire, it remains unoccupied and in darkness.

2. Let us take an example from each of the faculties. When the soul deprives its desire of the pleasure of all that can delight the sense of hearing, the soul remains unoccupied and in darkness with respect to this faculty. And, when it deprives itself of the pleasure of all that can please the sense of sight, it remains unoccupied and in darkness with respect to this faculty also. And, when it deprives itself of the pleasure of all the sweetness of perfumes which can give it pleasure through the sense of smell, it remains equally unoccupied and in darkness according to this faculty. And, if it also denies itself the pleasure of all food that can satisfy the palate, the soul likewise remains unoccupied and in darkness. And finally, when the soul mortifies itself with respect to all the delights and pleasures that it can receive from the sense of touch, it remains, in the same way, unoccupied and in darkness with respect to this faculty. So that the soul that has denied and thrust away from itself the pleasures which come from all these things, and has mortified its desire with respect to them, may be said to be, as it were, in the darkness of night, which is naught else than an emptiness within itself of all things.

3. The reason for this is that, as the philosophers say, the soul, as soon as God infuses it into the body, is like a smooth, blank board [84] upon which nothing is painted; and, save for that which it experiences through the senses, nothing is communicated to it, in the course of nature, from any other source. And thus, for as long as it is in the body, it is like one who is in a dark prison and who knows nothing, save what he is able to see through the windows of the said prison; and, if he saw nothing through them, he would see nothing in any other way. And thus the soul, save for that which is communicated to it through the senses, which are the windows of its prison, could acquire nothing, in the course of nature, in any other way.

4. Wherefore, if the soul rejects and denies that which it can receive through the senses, we can quite well say that it remains, as it were, in darkness and empty; since, as appears from what has been said, no light can enter it, in the course of nature, by any other means of illumination than those aforementioned. For, although it is true that the soul cannot help hearing and seeing and smelling and tasting and touching, this is of no greater import, nor, if the soul denies and rejects the object, is it hindered more than if it saw it not, heard it not, etc. Just so a man who desires to shut his eyes will remain in darkness, like the blind man who has not the faculty of sight. And to this purpose David says these words: Pauper sum ego, et in laboribus a indenture mea. [85] Which signifies: I am poor and in labours from my youth. He calls himself poor, although it is clear that he was rich, because his will was not set upon riches, and thus it was as though he were really poor. But if he had not been really poor and had not been so in his will, he would not have been truly poor, for his soul, as far as its desire was concerned, would have been rich and replete. For that reason we call this detachment night to the soul, for we are not treating here of the lack of things, since this implies no detachment on the part of the soul if it has a desire for them; but we are treating of the detachment from them of the taste and desire, for it is this that leaves the soul free and void of them, although it may have them; for it is not the things of this world that either occupy the soul or cause it harm, since they enter it not, but rather the will and desire for them, for it is these that dwell within it.

5. This first kind of night, as we shall say hereafter, belongs to the soul according to its sensual part, which is one of the two parts, whereof we spoke above, through which the soul must pass in order to attain to union.

6. Let us now say how meet it is for the soul to go forth from its house into this dark night of

Ascent of Mount Carmel
sense, in order to travel to union with God.

Footnotes:

83. [Lit., without anything (sc. to do).']
84. ['Blank board': Sp., tabla rasa; Lat., tabula rasa.]
85. Psalm lxxxvii, 16 [A.V., lxxxviii, 15].

CHAPTER IV

Wherein is declared how necessary it is for the soul truly to pass through this dark night of sense, which is mortification of desire, in order that it may journey to union with God.

The reason for which it is necessary for the soul, in order to attain to Divine union with God, to pass through this dark night of mortification of the desires and denial of pleasures in all things, is because all the affections which it has for creatures are pure darkness in the eyes of God, and, when the soul is clothed in these affections, it has no capacity for being enlightened and possessed by the pure and simple light of God, if it first cast them not from it; for light cannot agree with darkness; since, as Saint John says: Tenebroe eam non comprehenderunt. [86] That is: The darkness could not receive the light.

2. The reason is that two contraries (even as philosophy teaches us) cannot coexist in one person; and that darkness, which is affection set upon the creatures, and light, which is God, are contrary to each other, and have no likeness or accord between one another, even as Saint Paul taught the Corinthians, saying: Quoe conventio luci ad tenebras? [87] That is to say: What communion can there be between light and darkness? Hence it is that the light of Divine union cannot dwell in the soul if these affections first flee not away from it.

3. In order that we may the better prove what has been said, it must be known that the affection and attachment which the soul has for creatures renders the soul like to these creatures; and, the greater is its affection, the closer is the equality and likeness between them; for love creates a likeness between that which loves and that which is loved. For which reason David, speaking of those who set their affections upon idols, said thus: Similes illis fiant qui faciunt ea: et omnes qui confidunt in eis. [88] Which signifies: Let them that set their heart upon them be like to them. And thus, he that loves a creature becomes as low as that creature, and, in some ways, lower; for love not only makes the lover equal to the object of his love, but even subjects him to it. Hence in the same way it comes to pass that the soul that loves anything else becomes incapable of pure union with God and transformation in Him. For the low estate of the creature is much less capable of union with the high estate of the Creator than is darkness with light. For all things of earth and heaven, compared with God, are nothing, as Jeremias says in these words: Aspexi terram, et ecce vacua erat, et nihil; et coelos, et non erat lux in eis. [89] I beheld the earth,' he says, 'and it was void, and it was nothing; and the heavens, and saw that they had no light.' In saying that he beheld the earth void, he means that all its creatures were nothing, and that the earth was nothing likewise. And, in saying that he beheld the heavens and saw no light in them, he says that all the luminaries of heaven, compared with God, are pure darkness. So that in this way all the creatures are nothing; and their affections, we may say, are less than nothing, since they are an impediment to transformation in God and the privation thereof, even as darkness is not only nothing, but less than nothing, since it is privation of light. And even as he that is in darkness comprehends not the light, so the soul that sets its affection upon creatures will be unable to comprehend God; and, until it be purged, it will neither be able to possess Him here below, through pure transformation of love, nor yonder in clear vision. And, for greater clarity, we will now speak in greater detail.

4. All the being of creation, then, compared with the infinite Being of God, is nothing. And therefore the soul that sets its affection upon the being of creation is likewise nothing in the eyes of God, and less than nothing; for, as we have said, love makes equality and similitude, and even sets the lover below the object of his love. And therefore such a soul will in no wise be able to attain to union with the infinite Being of God; for that which is not can have no communion with that which is. And, coming down in detail to some examples, all the beauty of the creatures, compared with the infinite beauty of God, is the height of deformity [90] even as Solomon says in the Proverbs: Fallax gratia, et vana est pulchritudo. [91] Favour is deceitful and beauty is vain.' And thus the soul that is affectioned to the beauty of any creature is the height of deformity in the eyes of God. And therefore this soul that is deformed will be unable to become transformed in beauty, which is God, since deformity cannot attain to beauty; and all the grace and beauty of the creatures, compared with the grace of God, is the height of misery [92] and of uncomeliness. Wherefore the soul that is ravished by the graces and beauties of the creatures has only supreme [93] misery and unattractiveness in the eyes of God; and thus it cannot be capable of the infinite grace and loveliness of God; for that which has no grace is far removed from that which is infinitely gracious; and all the goodness of the creatures of the world, in comparison with the infinite goodness of God, may be described as wickedness. For there is naught good, save only God.' [94]

Ascent of Mount Carmel

And therefore the soul that sets its heart upon the good things of the world is supremely evil in the eyes of God. And, even as wickedness comprehends not goodness, even so such a soul cannot be united with God, Who is supreme goodness.

5. All the wisdom of the world and all human ability, compared with the infinite wisdom of God, are pure and supreme ignorance, even as Saint Paul writes ad Corinthios, saying: Sapientia hujus mundi stultitia est apud Deum. [95] The wisdom of this world is foolishness with God.' Wherefore any soul that makes account of all its knowledge and ability in order to come to union with the wisdom of God is supremely ignorant in the eyes of God and will remain far removed from that wisdom; for ignorance knows not what wisdom is, even as Saint Paul says that this wisdom seems foolishness to God; since, in the eyes of God, those who consider themselves to be persons with a certain amount of knowledge are very ignorant, so that the Apostle, writing to the Romans, says of them: Dicentes enim se esse sapientes, stulti facti sunt. That is: Professing themselves to be wise, they became foolish. [96] And those alone acquire wisdom of God who are like ignorant children, and, laying aside their knowledge, walk in His service with love. This manner of wisdom Saint Paul taught likewise ad Corinthios: Si quis videtur inter vos sapiens esse in hoc soeculo, stultus fiat ut sit sapiens. Sapientia enim hujus mundi stultitia est apud Deum. [97] That is: If any man among you seem to be wise, let him become ignorant that he may be wise; for the wisdom of this world is foolishness with God. So that, in order to come to union with the wisdom of God, the soul has to proceed rather by unknowing than by knowing; and all the dominion and liberty of the world, compared with the liberty and dominion of the Spirit of God, is the most abject [98] slavery, affliction and captivity.

6. Wherefore the soul that is enamoured of prelacy, [99] or of any other such office, and longs for liberty of desire, is considered and treated, in the sight of God, not as a son, but as a base slave and captive, since it has not been willing to accept His holy doctrine, wherein He teaches us that whoso would be greater must be less, and whoso would be less must be greater. And therefore such a soul will be unable to attain to that true liberty of spirit which is attained in His Divine union. For slavery can have no part with liberty; and liberty cannot dwell in a heart that is subject to desires, for this is the heart of a slave; but it dwells in the free man, because he has the heart of a son. It was for this cause that Sara bade her husband Abraham cast out the bondwoman and her son, saying that the son of the bondwoman should not be heir with the son of the free woman. [100]

7. And all the delights and pleasures of the will in all the things of the world, in comparison with all those delights which are God, are supreme affliction, torment and bitterness. And thus he that sets his heart upon them is considered, in the sight of God, as worthy of supreme affliction, torment and bitterness; and thus he will be unable to attain to the delights of the embrace of union with God, since he is worthy of affliction and bitterness. All the wealth and glory of all creation, in comparison with the wealth which is God, is supreme poverty and wretchedness. Thus the soul that loves and possesses creature wealth is supremely poor and wretched in the sight of God, and for that reason will be unable to attain to that wealth and glory which is the state of transformation in God; for that which is miserable and poor is supremely far removed from that which is supremely rich and glorious.

8. And therefore Divine Wisdom, grieving for such as these, who make themselves vile, low, miserable and poor, because they love the things in this world which seem to them so rich and beautiful, addresses an exclamation to them in the Proverbs, saying: O viri, ad vos clamito, et vox mea ad filios hominum. Intelligite, parvuli, astutiam, et insipientes, animadvertite. Audite quia de rebus magnis locutura sum. And farther on he continues: Mecum sunt divitiae, et gloria, opes superbae et justicia. Melior est fructus meus auro, et lapide pretioso, et genimina mea argento electo. In viis justitiae ambulo, in medio semitarum judicii, ut ditem diligentes me, et thesauros eorum repleam. [101] Which signifies: O ye men, to you I call, and my voice is to the sons of men. Attend, little ones, to subtlety and sagacity; ye that are foolish, take notice. Hear, for I have to speak of great things. With me are riches and glory, high riches and justice. Better is the fruit that ye will find in me than gold and precious stones; and my generation -- namely, that which ye will engender of me in your souls -- is better than choice silver. I walk in the ways of justice, in the midst of the paths of judgment, that I may enrich those that love me and fill their treasures perfectly. -- Herein Divine Wisdom speaks to all those that set their hearts and affections upon anything of the world, according as we have already said. And she calls them little ones,' because they make themselves like to that which they love, which is little. And therefore she tells them to be subtle and to take note that she is treating of great things and not of things that are little like themselves. That the great riches and the glory that they love are with her and in her, and not where they think. And that high riches and justice dwell in her; for, although they think the things of this world to be all this, she tells them to take note that her things are better, saying that the fruit that they will find in them will be better for them than gold and precious stones; and that which she engenders in souls is better than the choice silver which they love; by which is understood any kind of affection that can be possessed in this life.

Footnotes:

86. St. John i, 5.
87. 2 Corinthians vi, 14.
88. Psalm cxiv, 9 [A.V., cxv, 8].
89. Jeremias iv, 23.
90. [The words often translated deformity,' deformed,' or vileness,' vile,' are the ordinary contraries of beauty,' beautiful,' and might be rendered, more literally but less elegantly, ugliness,' ugly.']
91. Proverbs xxxi, 30.
92. [For grace . . . misery' the Spanish has gracia . . . desgracia. The latter word, however, does not, as might be supposed, correspond to English disgrace.']
93. E.p. omits 'supreme'; the Spanish word [having a more literally superlative force than the English] can hardly be applied, save in a restricted sense, to what is finite.
94. St. Luke xviii, 19.
95. 1 Corinthians iii, 19.
96. Romans i, 22.
97. 1 Corinthians iii, 18-19.
98. [Lit., is supreme.']
99. [The word is applicable to any kind of preferential position.]
100. Genesis xxi, 10.
101. Proverbs viii, 4-6, 18-21.

CHAPTER V

Wherein the aforementioned subject is treated and continued, and it is shown by passages and figures from Holy Scripture how necessary it is for the soul to journey to God through this dark night of the mortification of desire in all things.

From what has been said it may be seen in some measure how great a distance there is between all that the creatures are in themselves and that which God is in Himself, and how souls that set their affections upon any of these creatures are at as great a distance as they from God; for, as we have said, love produces equality and likeness. This distance was clearly realized by Saint Augustine, who said in the Sololoquies, speaking with God: Miserable man that I am, when will my littleness and imperfection be able to have fellowship with Thy uprightness? Thou indeed art good, and I am evil; Thou art merciful, and I am impious; Thou art holy, I am miserable; Thou art just, I am unjust; Thou art light, I am blind; Thou, life, I, death; Thou, medicine, I, sick; Thou, supreme truth, I, utter vanity.' All this is said by this Saint. [102]

2. Wherefore, it is supreme ignorance for the soul to think that it will be able to pass to this high estate of union with God if first it void not the desire of all things, natural and supernatural, which may hinder it, according as we shall explain hereafter; [103] for there is the greatest possible distance between these things and that which comes to pass in this estate, which is naught else than transformation in God. For this reason Our Lord, when showing us this path, said through Saint Luke: Qui non renuntiat omnibus quae possidet, non potest meus esse discipulus. [104] This signifies: He that renounces not all things that he possesses with his will cannot be My disciple. And this is evident; for the doctrine that the Son of God came to teach was contempt for all things, whereby a man might receive as a reward the Spirit of God in himself. For, as long as the soul rejects not all things, it has no capacity to receive the Spirit of God in pure transformation.

3. Of this we have a figure in Exodus, wherein we read that God gave not the children of Israel the food from Heaven, which was manna, until the flour which they had brought from Egypt failed them. By this is signified that first of all it is meet to renounce all things, for this angels' food is not fitting for the palate that would find delight in the food of men. And not only does the soul become incapable of receiving the Divine Spirit when it stays and pastures on other strange pleasures, but those souls greatly offend the Divine Majesty who desire spiritual food and are not content with God alone, but desire rather to intermingle desire and affection for other things. This can likewise be seen in the same book of Holy Scripture, [105] wherein it is said that, not content with that simplest of food, they desired and craved fleshly food. [106] And that Our Lord was greatly wroth that they should desire to intermingle a food that was so base and so coarse with one that was so noble [107] and so simple; which, though it was so, had within itself the sweetness and substance of all foods. [108] Wherefore, while they yet had the morsels in their mouths, as David says likewise: Ira Dei descendit super eos. [109] The wrath of God came down upon them, sending fire from Heaven and consuming many thousands of them; for God held it an unworthy thing that they should have a desire for other food when He had given them food from Heaven.

4. Oh, did spiritual persons but know how much good and what great abundance of spirit they lose through not seeking to raise up their desires above childish things, and how in this simple spiritual food they would find the sweetness of all things, if they desired not to taste those things! But such food gives them no pleasure, for the reason why the children of Israel received not the sweetness of all foods that was contained in the manna was that they would not reserve their desire for it alone. So that they failed to find in the manna all the sweetness and strength that they could wish, not because it was not contained in the manna, but because they desired some other thing. Thus he that will love some other thing together with God of a certainty makes little account of God, for he weighs in the balance against God that which, as we have said, is at the greatest possible distance from God.

5. It is well known by experience that, when the will of a man is affectioned to one thing, he prizes it more than any other; although some other thing may be much better, he takes less pleasure in it. And if he wishes to enjoy both, he is bound to wrong the more important, because he makes an equality between them. Wherefore, since there is naught that equals God, the soul that loves some other thing together with Him, or clings to it, does Him a grievous wrong. And if this is so, what would it be doing if it loved anything more than God?

6. It is this, too, that was denoted by the command of God to Moses that he should ascend the

Mount to speak with Him: He commanded him not only to ascend it alone, leaving the children of Israel below, but not even to allow the beasts to feed over against the Mount. [110] By this He signified that the soul that is to ascend this mount of perfection, to commune with God, must not only renounce all things and leave them below, but must not even allow the desires, which are the beasts, to pasture over against this mount -- that is, upon other things which are not purely God, in Whom -- that is, in the state of perfection -- every desire ceases. So he that journeys on the road and makes the ascent to God must needs be habitually careful to quell and mortify the desires; and the greater the speed wherewith a soul does this, the sooner will it reach the end of its journey. Until these be quelled, it cannot reach the end, however much it practise the virtues, since it is unable to attain to perfection in them; for this perfection consists in voiding and stripping and purifying the soul of every desire. Of this we have another very striking figure in Genesis, where we read that, when the patriarch Jacob desired to ascend Mount Bethel, in order to build an altar there to God whereon he should offer Him sacrifice, he first commanded all his people to do three things: one was that they should cast away from them all strange gods; the second, that they should purify themselves; the third, that they should change their garments. [111]

7. By these three things it is signified that any soul that will ascend this mount in order to make of itself an altar whereon it may offer to God the sacrifice of pure love and praise and pure reverence, must, before ascending to the summit of the mount, have done these three things aforementioned perfectly. First, it must cast away all strange gods -- namely, all strange affections and attachments; secondly, it must purify itself of the remnants which the desires aforementioned have left in the soul, by means of the dark night of sense whereof we are speaking, habitually denying them and repenting itself of them; and thirdly, in order to reach the summit of this high mount, it must have changed its garments, which, through its observance of the first two things, God will change for it, from old to new, by giving it a new understanding of God in God, the old human understanding being cast aside; and a new love of God in God, the will being now stripped of all its old desires and human pleasures, and the soul being brought into a new state of knowledge and profound delight, all other old images and forms of knowledge having been cast away, and all that belongs to the old man, which is the aptitude of the natural self, quelled, and the soul clothed with a new supernatural aptitude with respect to all its faculties. So that its operation, which before was human, has become Divine, which is that that is attained in the state of union, wherein the soul becomes naught else than an altar whereon God is adored in praise and love, and God alone is upon it. For this cause God commanded that the altar whereon the Ark of the Covenant was to be laid should be hollow within; [112] so that the soul may understand how completely empty of all things God desires it to be, that it may be an altar worthy of the presence of His Majesty. On this altar it was likewise forbidden that there should be any strange fire, or that its own fire should ever fail; and so essential was this that, because Nadab and Abiu, who were the sons of the High Priest Aaron, offered strange fire upon His Altar, Our Lord was wroth and slew them there before the altar. [113] By this we are to understand that the love of God must never fail in the soul, so that the soul may be a worthy altar, and so that no other love must be mingled with it.

8. God permits not that any other thing should dwell together with Him. Wherefore we read in the First Book the Kings that, when the Philistines put the Ark of the Covenant into the temple where their idol was, the idol was cast down upon the ground at the dawn of each day, and broken to pieces. [114] And He permits and wills that there should be only one desire where He is, which is to keep the law of God perfectly, and to bear upon oneself the Cross of Christ. And thus naught else is said in the Divine Scripture to have been commanded by God to be put in the Ark, where the manna was, save the book of the Law, [115] and the rod Moses, [116] which signifies the Cross. For the soul that aspires naught else than the keeping of the law of the Lord perfectly and the bearing of the Cross of Christ will be a true Ark, containing within itself the true manna, which is God, when that soul attains to a perfect possession within itself of this law and this rod, without any other thing soever.

Footnotes:

102. Soliloq., chap. ii (Migne: Patr. lat., Vol. XL, p. 866).

103. So Alc. The other authorities have merely: which may pertain to it,' and e.p. adds to this: through self-love.' Even when softened by Diego de Pesús this phrase of the Saint did not escape denunciation, and it was the first of the propositions' condemned in his writings (cf. General Introduction, VI, above). It was defended by P. Basilio Ponce de León in his Reply (p. lx), and more extensively by P. Nicolás de Jesús María (Elucidatio, Pt. II, Chap i, pp. 125-40). In reality, little defence is needed other than that contained in the last chapters of the Ascent of Mount Carmel, which clearly show the harm caused by supernatural favours, when these are abused, to the memory, the understanding and the will. Who, after all, can doubt that we may abuse things supernatural' and by such abuse hinder the soul from attaining union with God?

104. St. Luke xiv, 33.

105. E.p. alters this to: in the same Scripture.' [It does not, in fact, occur in the same book.]

Ascent of Mount Carmel
    106. Numbers xi, 4.
    107. [Lit., 'so high.']
    108. [Wisdom xvi, 20.]
    109. Psalm lxxvii, 31 [A.V., lxxviii, 31].
    110. [Exodus xxxiv, 2-3.] E.p.: within sight of the Mount.' A, B: near the Mount.'
    111. Gen. xxxv, 2.
    112. Exodus xxvii, 8.
    113. Leviticus x, 1-2.
    114. 1 Kings [A.V., 1 Samuel] v, 3-5.
    115. Deut. xxxi, 26.
    116. Numbers xvii, 10. [More properly, the rod of Aaron.']

CHAPTER VI

Wherein are treated two serious evils caused in the soul by the desires, the one evil being privative and the other positive.

In order that what we have said may be the more clearly and fully understood, it will be well to set down here and state how these desires are the cause of two serious evils in the soul: the one is that they deprive it of the Spirit of God, and the other is that the soul wherein they dwell is wearied, tormented, darkened, defiled and weakened, according to that which is said in Jeremias, Chapter II: Duo mala fecit Populus meus: dereliquerunt fontem aquae vivae, ut foderunt sibi cisternas, dissipatas, quae continere non valent aquas. Which signifies: They have forsaken Me, Who am the fountain of living water, and they have hewed them out broken cisterns, that can hold no water. [117] Those two evils -- namely, the privative and the positive -- may be caused by any disordered act of the desire. And, speaking first of all, of the privative, it is clear from the very fact that the soul becomes affectioned to a thing which comes under the head of creature, that the more the desire for that thing fills the soul, [118] the less capacity has the soul for God; inasmuch as two contraries, according to the philosophers, cannot coexist in one person; and further, since, as we said in the fourth chapter, affection for God and affection for creatures are contraries, there cannot be contained within one will affection for creatures and affection for God. For what has the creature to do with the Creator? What has sensual to do with spiritual? Visible with invisible? Temporal with eternal? Food that is heavenly, spiritual and pure with food that is of sense alone and is purely sensual? Christlike poverty of spirit with attachment to aught soever?

2. Wherefore, as in natural generation no form can be introduced unless the preceding, contrary form is first expelled from the subject, which form, while present, is an impediment to the other by reason of the contrariety which the two have between each other; even so, for as long as the soul is subjected to the sensual spirit, the spirit which is pure and spiritual cannot enter it. Wherefore our Saviour said through Saint Matthew: Non est bonum sumere panem filiorum, et mittere canibus. [119] That is: It is not meet to take the children's bread and to cast it to the dogs. And elsewhere, too, he says through the same Evangelist: Nolite sanctum dare canibus. [120] Which signifies: Give not that which is holy to the dogs. In these passages Our Lord compares those who renounce their creature-desires, and prepare themselves to receive the Spirit of God in purity, to the children of God; and those who would have their desire feed upon the creatures, to dogs. For it is given to children to eat with their father at table and from his dish, which is to feed upon His Spirit, and to dogs are given the crumbs which fall from the table.

3. From this we are to learn that all created things are crumbs that have fallen from the table of God. Wherefore he that feeds ever upon [121] the creatures is rightly called a dog, and therefore the bread is taken from the children, because they desire not to rise above feeding upon the crumbs, which are created things, to the Uncreated Spirit of their Father. Therefore, like dogs, they are ever hungering, and justly so, because the crumbs serve to whet their appetite rather than to satisfy their hunger. And thus David says of them: Famem patientur ut canes, et circuibunt civitatem. Si vero non fuerint saturati, et murmurabunt. [122] Which signifies: They shall suffer hunger like dogs and shall go round about the city, and, if they find not enough to fill them, they shall murmur. For this is the nature of one that has desires, that he is ever discontented and dissatisfied, like one that suffers hunger; for what has the hunger which all the creatures suffer to do with the fullness which is caused by the Spirit of God? Wherefore this fullness that is uncreated cannot enter the soul, if there be not first cast out that other created hunger which belongs to the desire of the soul; for, as we have said two contraries cannot dwell in one person, the which contraries in this case are hunger and fullness.

4. From what has been said it will be seen how much greater is the work of God [123] in the cleansing and the purging of a soul from these contrarieties than in the creating of that soul from nothing. For thee contrarieties, these contrary desires and affections, are more completely opposed to God and offer Him greater resistance than does nothingness; for nothingness resists not at all. And let this suffice with respect to the first of the important evils which are inflicted upon the soul by the desires -- namely, resistance to the Spirit of God -- since much has been said of this above.

5. Let us now speak of the second effect which they cause in the soul. This is of many kinds, because the desires weary the soul and torment and darken it, and defile it and weaken it. Of these five things we shall speak separately, in their turn.

6. With regard to the first, it is clear that the desires weary and fatigue the soul; for they are like

Ascent of Mount Carmel

restless and discontented children, who are ever demanding this or that from their mother, and are never contented. And even as one that digs because he covets a treasure is wearied and fatigued, even so is the soul weary and fatigued in order to attain that which its desires demand of it; and although in the end it may attain it, it is still weary, because it is never satisfied; for, after all, the cisterns which it is digging are broken, and cannot hold water to satisfy thirst. And thus, as Isaias says: Lassus adhuc sitit, et anima ejus vacua est. [124] Which signifies: His desire is empty. And the soul that has desires is wearied and fatigued; for it is like a man that is sick of a fever, who finds himself no better until the fever leaves him, and whose thirst increases with every moment. For, as is said in the Book of Job: Cum satiatus fuerit, artabitur, aestuabit, et omnis dolor inruet super eum. [125] Which signifies: When he has satisfied his desire, he will be the more oppressed and straitened; the heat of desire hath increased in his soul and thus every sorrow will fall upon him. The soul is wearied and fatigued by its desires, because it is wounded and moved and disturbed by them as is water by the winds; in just the same way they disturb it, allowing it not to rest in any place or in any thing soever. And of such a soul says Isaias: Cor impii quasi mare fervens. [126] The heart of the wicked man is like the sea when it rages.' And he is a wicked man that conquers not his desires. The soul that would fain satisfy its desires grows wearied and fatigued; for it is like one that, being an hungered, opens his mouth that he may sate himself with wind, whereupon, instead of being satisfied, his craving becomes greater, for the wind is no food for him. To this purpose said Jeremias: In desiderio animae sum attraxit ventum amoris sui. [127] As though he were to say: In the desire of his will he snuffed up the wind of his affection. And he then tries to describe the aridity wherein such a soul remains, and warns it, saying: Prohibe pedem tuum a nuditate, et guttur tuum a siti. [128] Which signifies: Keep thy foot (that is, thy thought) from being bare and thy throat from thirst (that is to say, thy will from the indulgence of the desire which causes greater dryness); and, even as the lover is wearied and fatigued upon the day of his hopes, when his attempt has proved to be vain, so the soul is wearied and fatigued by all its desires and by indulgence in them, since they all cause it greater emptiness and hunger; for, as is often said, desire is like the fire, which increases as wood is thrown upon it, and which, when it has consumed the wood, must needs die.

7. And in this regard it is still worse with desire; for the fire goes down when the wood is consumed, but desire, though it increases when fuel is added to it, decreases not correspondingly when the fuel is consumed; on the contrary, instead of going down, as does the fire when its fuel is consumed, it grows weak through weariness, for its hunger is increased and its food diminished. And of this Isaias speaks, saying: Declinabit ad dexteram, et esuriet: et comedet ad sinistram, et non saturabitur. [129] This signifies: He shall turn to the right hand, and shall be hungry; and he shall eat on the left hand, and shall not be filled. For they that mortify not their desires, when they turn,' justly see the fullness of the sweetness of spirit of those who are at the right hand of God, which fullness is not granted to themselves; and justly, too, when they eat on the left hand, [130] by which is meant the satisfaction of their desire with some creature comfort, they are not filled, for, leaving aside that which alone can satisfy, they feed on that which causes them greater hunger. It is clear, then, that the desires weary and fatigue the soul.

Footnotes:

117. Jeremias ii, 13.
118. [Lit., the greater the bulk that that desire has in the soul.']
119. St. Matthew xv, 26.
120. St. Matthew vii, 6.
121. [Lit., he that goes feeding upon.']
122. Psalm lviii, 15-16 [A.V., lix, 14-15].
123. [Lit., how much more God does.']
124. Isaias xxix, 8. The editions supply the translation of the first part of the Latin text, which the Saint and the Codices omitted: After being wearied and fatigued, he yet thirsteth,' etc.
125. Job xx, 22.
126. Isaias lvii, 20.
127. Jeremias ii, 24.
128. Jeremias ii, 25.
129. Isaias ix, 20.
130. Thus Alc. [with run' for eat']. A, B, e.p. read: . . . when they turn from the way of God (which is the right hand) are justly hungered, for they merit not the fullness of the sweetness of spirit. And justly, too, when they eat on the left hand,' etc. [While agreeing with P. Silverio that Alc. gives the better reading, I prefer eat' to run': it is nearer the Scriptural passage and the two Spanish words, comen and corren, could easily be confused in MS.]

CHAPTER VII

Wherein is shown how the desires torment the soul. This is proved likewise by comparison and quotations.

The second kind of positive evil which the desires cause the soul is in their tormenting and afflicting of it, after the manner of one who is in torment through being bound with cords from which he has no relief until he be freed. And of these David says: Funes peccatorum circumplexi sunt me. [131] The cords of my sins, which are my desires, have constrained me round about. And, even as one that lies naked upon thorns and briars is tormented and afflicted, even so is the soul tormented and afflicted when it rests upon its desires. For they take hold upon it and distress it and cause it pain, even as do thorns. Of these David says likewise: Circumdederunt me sicut apes: et exarserunt sicut ignis in spinis. [132] Which signifies: They compassed me about like bees, wounding me with their stings, and they were enkindled against me, like fire among thorns; for in the desires, which are the thorns, increases the fire of anguish and torment. And even as the husbandman, coveting the harvest for which he hopes, afflicts and torments the ox in the plough, even so does concupiscence afflict a soul that is subject to its desire to attain that for which it longs. This can be clearly seen in that desire which Dalila had to know whence Samson derived his strength that was so great, for the Scripture says that it fatigued and tormented her so much that it caused her to swoon, almost to the point of death, and she said: Defecit anima ejus, et ad mortem usque lassata est. [133]

2. The more intense is the desire, the greater is the torment which it causes the soul. So that the torment increases with the desire; and the greater are the desires which possess the soul, the greater are its torments; for in such a soul is fulfilled, even in this life, that which is said in the Apocalypse concerning Babylon, in these words: Quantum glorificavit se, et in deliciis fuit, tantum date illi tormentum, et luctum. [134] That is: As much as she has wished to exalt and fulfil her desires, so much give ye to her torment and anguish. And even as one that falls into the hands of his enemies is tormented and afflicted, even so is the soul tormented and afflicted that is led away by its desires. Of this there is a figure in the Book of the Judges, wherein it may be read that that strong man, Samson, who at one time was strong and free and a judge of Israel, fell into the power of his enemies, and they took his strength from him, and put out his eyes, and bound him in a mill, to grind corn, [135] wherein they tormented and afflicted him greatly; [136] and thus it happens to the soul in which these its enemies, the desires, live and rule; for the first thing that they do is to weaken the soul and blind it, as we shall say below; and then they afflict and torment it, binding it to the mill of concupiscence; and the bonds with which it is bound are its own desires.

3. Wherefore God, having compassion on these that with such great labour, and at such cost to themselves, go about endeavouring to satisfy the hunger and thirst of their desire in the creatures, says to them through Isaias: Omnes sitientes, venite ad aquas; et qui non habetis argentum, properate, emite, el comedite: venite, emite absque argento vinum et lac. Quare appenditis argentum non in panibus, et laborem vestrum non in saturitate? [137] As though He were to say: All ye that have thirst of desire, come to the waters, and all ye that have no silver of your own will and desires, make haste; buy from Me and eat; come and buy from Me wine and milk (that is, spiritual sweetness and peace) without the silver of your own will, and without giving Me any labour in exchange for it, as ye give for your desires. Wherefore do ye give the silver of your will for that which is not bread -- namely, that of the Divine Spirit -- and set the labour of your desires upon that which cannot satisfy you? Come, hearkening to Me, and ye shall eat the good that ye desire and your soul shall delight itself in fatness.

4. This attaining to fatness is a going forth from all pleasures of the creatures; for the creatures torment, but the Spirit of God refreshes. And thus He calls us through Saint Matthew, saying: Venite ad me omnes, qui laboratis et onerati estis, et ego reficiam vos, et invenietis requiem animabus vestris. [138] As though He were to say: All ye that go about tormented, afflicted and burdened with the burden of your cares and desires, go forth from them, come to Me, and I will refresh you and ye shall find for your souls the rest which your desires take from you, wherefore they are a heavy burden, for David says of them: Sicut onus grave gravatae sunt super me. [139] Psalm xxxvii, 5 [A.V., xxxviii, 4].

Ascent of Mount Carmel
Footnotes:
131. Psalm cxviii, 61 [A.V., cxix, 61].
132. Psalm cxvii, 12 [A.V., cxviii, 12].
133. Judges xvi, 16. [Actually it was Samson, not Dalila, who was wearied even until death.']
134. Apocalypse xviii, 7.
135. [Lit., bound him to grind in a mill.']
136. Judges xvi, 21.
137. Isaias lv, 1-2.
138. St. Matthew xi, 28-9.
139.

CHAPTER VIII

Wherein is shown how the desires darken and blind the soul.

The third evil that the desires cause in the soul is that they blind and darken it. Even as vapours darken the air and allow not the bright sun to shine; or as a mirror that is clouded over cannot receive within itself a clear image; or as water defiled by mud reflects not the visage of one that looks therein; even so the soul that is clouded by the desires is darkened in the understanding and allows neither [140] the sun of natural reason nor that of the supernatural Wisdom of God to shine upon it and illumine it clearly. And thus David, speaking to this purpose, says: Comprehenderunt me iniquitates meae, et non potui, ut viderem. [141] Which signifies: Mine iniquities have taken hold upon me, and I could have no power to see.

2. And, at this same time, when the soul is darkened in the understanding, it is benumbed also in the will, and the memory becomes dull and disordered in its due operation. For, as these faculties in their operations depend upon the understanding, it is clear that, when the understanding is impeded, they will become disordered and troubled. And thus David says: Anima mea turbata est valde. [142] That is: My soul is sorely troubled. Which is as much as to say, disordered in its faculties.' For, as we say, the understanding has no more capacity for receiving enlightenment from the wisdom of God than has the air, when it is dark, for receiving enlightenment from the sun; neither has the will any power to embrace God within itself in pure love, even as the mirror that is clouded with vapour has no power to reflect clearly within itself any visage, [143] and even less power has the memory which is clouded by the darkness of desire to take clearly upon itself the form of the image of God, just as the muddled water cannot show forth clearly the visage of one that looks at himself therein.

3. Desire blinds and darkens the soul; for desire, as such, is blind, since of itself it has no understanding in itself, the reason being to it always, as it were, a child leading a blind man. And hence it comes to pass that, whensoever the soul is guided by its desire, it becomes blind; for this is as if one that sees were guided by one that sees not, which is, as it were, for both to be blind. And that which follows from this is that which Our Lord says through Saint Matthew: Si caecus caeco ducatum praestet, ambo in foveam cadunt. [144] If the blind lead the blind, both fall into the pit.' Of little use are its eyes to a moth, since desire for the beauty of the light dazzles it and leads it into the flame. [145] And even so we may say that one who feeds upon desire is like a fish that is dazzled, upon which the light acts rather as darkness, preventing it from seeing the snares which the fishermen are preparing for it. This is very well expressed by David himself, where he says of such persons: Supercecidit ignis, et non viderunt solem. [146] Which signifies: There came upon them the fire, which burns with its heat and dazzles with its light. And it is this that desire does to the soul, enkindling its concupiscence and dazzling its understanding so that it cannot see its light. For the cause of its being thus dazzled is that when another light of a different kind is set before the eye, the visual faculty is attracted by that which is interposed so that it sees not the other; and, as the desire is set so near to the soul as to be within the soul itself, the soul meets this first light and is attracted by it; and thus it is unable to see the light of clear understanding, neither will see it until the dazzling power of desire is taken away from it.

4. For this reason one must greatly lament the ignorance of certain men, who burden themselves with extraordinary penances and with many other voluntary practices, and think that this practice or that will suffice to bring them to the union of Divine Wisdom; but such will not be the case if they endeavour not diligently to mortify their desires. If they were careful to bestow half of that labour on this, they would profit more in a month than they profit by all the other practices in many years. For, just as it is necessary to till the earth if it is to bear fruit, and unless it be tilled it bears naught but weeds, just so is mortification of the desires necessary if the soul is to profit. Without this mortification, I make bold to say, the soul no more achieves progress on the road to perfection and to the knowledge of God of itself, however many efforts it may make, than the seed grows when it is cast upon untilled ground. Wherefore the darkness and rudeness of the soul will not be taken from it until the desires be quenched. For these desires are like cataracts, or like motes in the eye, which obstruct the sight until they be taken away.

5. And thus David, realizing how blind are these souls, and how completely impeded from beholding the light of truth, and how wroth is God with them, speaks to them, saying: Priusquam intelligerent spinae vestrae rhamnum: sicut viventes, sic in ira absorber eos. [147] And this is as though He had said: Before your thorns (that is, your desires) harden and grow, changing from tender thorns into a

Ascent of Mount Carmel

thick hedge and shutting out the sight of God even as oft-times the living find their thread of life broken in the midst of its course, even so will God swallow them up in His wrath. For the desires that are living in the soul, so that it cannot understand Him, [148] will be swallowed up by God by means of chastisement and correction, either in this life or in the next, and this will come to pass through purgation. And He says that He will swallow them up in wrath, because that which is suffered in the mortification of the desires is punishment for the ruin which they have wrought in the soul.

6. Oh, if men but knew how great is the blessing of Divine light whereof they are deprived by this blindness which proceeds from their affections and desires, and into what great hurts and evils these make them to fall day after day, for so long as they mortify them not! For a man must not rely upon a clear understanding, or upon gifts that he has received from God, and think that he may indulge his affection or desire, and will not be blinded and darkened, and fall gradually into a worse estate. For who would have said that a man so perfect in wisdom and the gifts of God as was Solomon would have been reduced to such blindness and torpor of the will as to make altars to so many idols and to worship them himself, when he was old? [149] Yet no more was needed to bring him to this than the affection which he had for women and his neglect to deny the desires and delights of his heart. For he himself says concerning himself, in Ecclesiastes, that he denied not his heart that which it demanded of him. [150] And this man was capable of being so completely led away by his desires that, although it is true that at the beginning he was cautious, nevertheless, because he denied them not, they gradually blinded and darkened his understanding, so that in the end they succeeded in quenching that great light of wisdom which God had given him, and therefore in his old age he foresook God.

7. And if unmortified desires could do so much in this man who knew so well the distance that lies between good and evil, what will they not be capable of accomplishing by working upon our ignorance? For we, as God said to the prophet Jonas concerning the Ninivites, cannot discern between [151] our right hand and our left. [152] At every step we hold evil to be good, and good, evil, and this arises from our own nature. What, then, will come to pass if to our natural darkness is added the hindrance of desire? [153] Naught but that which Isaias describes thus: Palpavimus, sicut caeci parietem, et quasi absque oculis adtrectavimus: impegimus meridie, quasi in tenebris. [154] The prophet is speaking with those who love to follow these their desires. It is as if he had said: We have groped for the wall as though we were blind, and we have been groping as though we had no eyes, and our blindness has attained to such a point that we have stumbled at midday as though it were in the darkness. For he that is blinded by desire has this property, that, when he is set in the midst of truth and of that which is good for him, he can no more see them than if he were in darkness.

Footnotes:

140. [Lit., gives no occasion either for,' etc.]
141. Psalm xxxix, 13 [A.V., xl, 12.]
142. Psalm vi, 4 [A.V., vi, 3].
143. [Lit., the present visage.']
144. St. Matthew xv, 14.
145. [hoguera. More exactly: fire,' bonfire,' blaze.']
146. Psalm lvii, 9 [cf. A.V., lviii, 8].
147. Psalm lvii, 10 [A.V., lviii, 9].
148. [Lit., before it can understand God.']
149. 3 Kings [A.V., 1 Kings] xi, 4.
150. Ecclesiastes ii, 10.
151. [Lit., we . . . know not what there is between.']
152. Jonas iv, 11.
153. [Lit., is added desire.']
154. Isaias lix, 10.

CHAPTER IX

Wherein is described how the desires defile the soul. This is proved by comparisons and quotations from Holy Scripture.

The fourth evil which the desires cause in the soul is that they stain and defile it, as is taught in Ecclesiasticus, in these words: Qui tetigerit picem, inquinabitur ab ea. [155] This signifies: He that toucheth pitch shall be defiled with it. And a man touches pitch when he allows the desire of his will to be satisfied by any creature. Here it is to be noted that the Wise Man compares the creatures to pitch; for there is more difference between excellence of soul and the best of the creatures [156] than there is between pure diamond, [157] or fine gold, and pitch. And just as gold or diamond, if it were heated and placed upon pitch, would become foul and be stained by it, inasmuch as the heat would have cajoled and allured the pitch, even so the soul that is hot with desire for any creature draws forth foulness from it through the heat of its desire and is stained by it. And there is more difference between the soul and other corporeal creatures than between a liquid that is highly clarified and mud that is most foul. Wherefore, even as such a liquid would be defiled if it were mingled with mud, so is the soul defiled that clings to creatures, since by doing this it becomes like to the said creatures. And in the same way that traces of soot would defile a face that is very lovely and perfect, even in this way do disordered desires befoul and defile the soul that has them, the which soul is in itself a most lovely and perfect image of God.

2. Wherefore Jeremias, lamenting the ravages of foulness which these disordered affections cause in the soul, speaks first of its beauty, and then of its foulness, saying: Candidiores sunt Nazaraei ejus nive, nitidiores lacte, rubicundiores ebore antiquo, sapphiro pulchriores. Denigrata est super carbones facies eorum, et non sunt cogniti in plateis. [158] Which signifies: Its hair -- that is to say, that of the soul -- is more excellent in whiteness than the snow, clearer [159] than milk, and ruddier than old ivory, and lovelier than the sapphire stone. Their face has now become blacker than coal and they are not known in the streets. [160] By the hair we here understand the affections and thoughts of the soul, which, ordered as God orders them -- that is, in God Himself -- are whiter than snow, and clearer [161] than milk, and ruddier than ivory, and lovelier than the sapphire. By these four things is understood every kind of beauty and excellence of corporeal creatures, higher than which, says the writer, are the soul and its operations, which are the Nazarites or the hair aforementioned; the which Nazarites, being unruly, [162] with their lives ordered in a way that God ordered not -- that is, being set upon the creatures -- have their face (says Jeremias) made and turned blacker than coal.

3. All this harm, and more, is done to the beauty of the soul by its unruly desires for the things of this world; so much so that, if we set out to speak of the foul and vile appearance that the desires can give the soul, we should find nothing, however full of cobwebs and worms it might be, not even the corruption of a dead body, nor aught else that is impure and vile, nor aught that can exist and be imagined in this life, to which we could compare it. For, although it is true that the unruly soul, in its natural being, is as perfect as when God created it, yet, in its reasonable being, it is vile, abominable, foul, black and full of all the evils that are here being described, and many more. For, as we shall afterwards say, a single unruly desire, although there be in it no matter of mortal sin, suffices to bring a soul into such bondage, foulness and vileness that it can in no wise come to accord with God in union [163] until the desire be purified. What, then, will be the vileness of the soul that is completely unrestrained with respect to its own passions and given up to its desires, and how far removed will it be from God and from His purity?

4. It is impossible to explain in words, or to cause to be understood by the understanding, what variety of impurity is caused in the soul by a variety of desires. For, if it could be expressed and understood, it would be a wondrous thing, and one also which would fill us with pity, to see how each desire, in accordance with its quality and degree, be it greater or smaller, leaves in the soul its mark and deposit of impurity and vileness, and how one single disorder of the reason can be the source of innumerable different impurities, some greater, some less, each one after its kind. For, even as the soul of the righteous man has in one single perfection, which is uprightness of soul, innumerable gifts of the greatest richness, and many virtues of the greatest loveliness, each one different and full of grace after its kind according to the multitude and the diversity of the affections of love which it has had in God, even so the unruly soul, according to the variety of the desires which it has for the creatures, has in itself a miserable variety of impurities and meannesses, wherewith it is endowed [164] by the said desires.

Ascent of Mount Carmel

5. The variety of these desires is well illustrated in the Book of Ezechiel, where it is written that God showed this Prophet, in the interior of the Temple, painted around its walls, all likenesses of creeping things which crawl on the ground, and all the abomination of unclean beasts.[165] And then God said to Ezechiel: Son of man, hast thou not indeed seen the abominations that these do, each one in the secrecy of his chamber?'[166] And God commanded the Prophet to go in farther and he would see greater abominations; and he says that he there saw women seated, weeping for Adonis, the god of love.[167] And God commanded him to go in farther still, and he would see yet greater abominations, and he says that he saw there five-and-twenty old men whose backs were turned toward the Temple.[168]

6. The diversity of creeping things and unclean beasts that were painted in the first chamber of the Temple are the thoughts and conceptions which the understanding fashions from the lowly things of earth, and from all the creatures, which are painted, just as they are, in the temple of the soul, when the soul embarrasses its understanding with them, which is the soul's first habitation. The women that were farther within, in the second habitation, weeping for the god Adonis, are the desires that are in the second faculty of the soul, which is the will; the which are, as it were, weeping, inasmuch as they covet that to which the will is affectioned, which are the creeping things painted in the understandings. And the men that were in the third habitation are the images and representations of the creatures, which the third part of the soul -- namely memory -- keeps and reflects upon[169] within itself. Of these it is said that their backs are turned toward the Temple because when the soul, according to these three faculties, completely and perfectly embraces anything that is of the earth, it can be said to have its back turned toward the Temple of God, which is the right reason of the soul, which admits within itself nothing that is of creatures.

7. And let this now suffice for the understanding of this foul disorder of the soul with respect to its desires. For if we had to treat in detail of the lesser foulness which these imperfections and their variety make and cause in the soul, and that which is caused by venial sins, which is still greater than that of the imperfections, and their great variety, and likewise that which is caused by the desires for mortal sin, which is complete foulness of the soul, and its great variety, according to the variety and multitude of all these three things, we should never end, nor would the understanding of angels suffice to understand it. That which I say, and that which is to the point for my purpose, is that any desire, although it be for but the smallest imperfection, stains and defiles the soul.

Footnotes:

155. Ecclesiasticus xiii, 1.

156. [More literally: and all the best that is of the creatures.' Best' is neuter and refers to qualities, appurtenances, etc.]

157. [Lit., bright diamond.']

158. Lamentations iv, 7-8.

159. [Lit., más resplandecientes, more brilliant,' more luminous.']

160. [Lit., plazas (derived from the Latin plateas), which now, however, has the meaning of 'squares,' (market) places.']

161. [Clearer' here is más claros; the adjective is rendered bright' elsewhere.]

162. [The words translated unruly,' disordered,' here and elsewhere, and occasionally unrestrained,' are the same in the original: desordenado.]

163. [The Spanish of the text reads literally: in a union.']

164. [The verb is pintar, paint': perhaps corrupt' is intended. The same verb occurs in the following sentence.]

165. Ezechiel viii, 10.

166. [Ezechiel viii, 12.]

167. Ezechiel viii, 14.

168. Ezechiel viii, 16.

169. [Lit., revolves'--turns over in its mind' in our common idiom.]

CHAPTER X

Wherein is described how the desires weaken the soul in virtue and make it lukewarm.

The fifth way in which the desires harm the soul is by making it lukewarm and weak, so that it has no strength to follow after virtue and to persevere therein. For as the strength of the desire, when it is set upon various aims, is less than if it were set wholly on one thing alone, and as, the more are the aims whereon it is set, the less of it there is for each of them, for this cause philosophers say that virtue in union is stronger than if it be dispersed. Wherefore it is clear that, if the desire of the will be dispersed among other things than virtue, it must be weaker as regards virtue. And thus the soul whose will is set upon various trifles is like water, which, having a place below wherein to empty itself, never rises; and such a soul has no profit. For this cause the patriarch Jacob compared his son Ruben to water poured out, because in a certain sin he had given rein to his desires. And he said: Thou art poured out like water; grow thou not.' [170] As though he had said: Since thou art poured out like water as to the desires, thou shalt not grow in virtue. And thus, as hot water, when uncovered, readily loses heat, and as aromatic spices, when they are unwrapped, gradually lose the fragrance and strength of their perfume, even so the soul that is not recollected in one single desire for God loses heat and vigour in its virtue. This was well understood by David, when he said, speaking with God: I will keep my strength for Thee. [171] That is, concentrating the strength of my desires upon Thee alone.

2. And the desires weaken the virtue of the soul, because they are to it like the shoots that grow about a tree, and take away its virtue so that it cannot bring forth so much fruit. And of such souls as these says the Lord: Vae praegnantibus, et nutrientibus in illis diebus. [172] That is: Woe to them that in those days are with child and to them that give suck. This being with child and giving suck is understood with respect to the desires; which, if they be not pruned, will ever be taking more virtue from the soul, and will grow to the harm of the soul, like the shoots upon the tree. Wherefore Our Lord counsels us, saying: Have your loins girt about [173] -- the loins signifying here the desires. And indeed, they are also like leeches, which are ever sucking the blood from the veins, for thus the Preacher terms them when he says: The leeches are the daughters -- that is, the desires -- saying ever: Daca, daca. [174]

3. From this it is clear that the desires bring no good to the soul but rather take from it that which it has; and, if it mortify them not, they will not cease till they have wrought in it that which the children of the viper are said to work in their mother; who, as they are growing within her womb, consume her and kill her, and they themselves remain alive at her cost. Just so the desires that are not mortified grow to such a point that they kill the soul with respect to God because it has not first killed them. And they alone live in it. Wherefore the Preacher says: Aufer a me Domine ventris concupiscentias. [175]

4. And, even though they reach not this point, it is very piteous to consider how the desires that live in this poor soul treat it, how unhappy it is with regard to itself, how dry with respect to its neighbours, and how weary and slothful with respect to the things of God. For there is no evil humour that makes it as wearisome and difficult for a sick man to walk, or gives him a distaste for eating comparable to the weariness and distaste for following virtue which is given to a soul by desire for creatures. And thus the reason why many souls have no diligence and eagerness to gain virtue is, as a rule, that they have desires and affections which are not pure and are not fixed upon God. [176]

Footnotes:

170. Genesis xlix, 4.
171. Psalm lviii, 10 [A.V., lix, 9].
172. St. Matthew xxix, 19.
173. St. Luke xii, 35.
174. Proverbs xxx, 15.
175. Ecclesiasticus xxiii, 6. [In the original the last two sentences are transposed.]
176. [Lit., not pure on (or in') God.']

CHAPTER XI

Wherein it is proved necessary that the soul that would attain to Divine union should be free from desires, however slight they be.

I expect that for a long time the reader has been wishing to ask whether it be necessary, in order to attain to this high estate of perfection, to undergo first of all total mortification in all the desires, great and small, or if it will suffice to mortify some of them and to leave others, those at least which seem of little moment. For it appears to be a severe and most difficult thing for the soul to be able to attain to such purity and detachment that it has no will and affection for anything.

2. To this I reply: first, that it is true that all the desires are not equally hurtful, nor do they all equally embarrass the soul. I am speaking of those that are voluntary, for the natural desires hinder the soul little, if at all, from attaining to union, when they are not consented to nor pass beyond the first movements (I mean, [177] all those wherein the rational will has had no part, whether at first or afterward); and to take away these -- that is, to mortify them wholly in this life -- is impossible. And these hinder not the soul in such a way as to prevent its attainment to Divine union, even though they be not, as I say, wholly mortified; for the natural man may well have them, and yet the soul may be quite free from them according to the rational spirit. For it will sometimes come to pass that the soul will be in the full [178] union of the prayer of quiet in the will at the very time when these desires are dwelling in the sensual part of the soul, and yet the higher part, which is in prayer, will have nothing to do with them. But all the other voluntary desires, whether they be of mortal sin, which are the gravest, or of venial sin, which are less grave, or whether they be only of imperfections, which are the least grave of all, must be driven away every one, and the soul must be free from them all, howsoever slight they be, if it is to come to this complete union; and the reason is that the state of this Divine union consists in the soul's total transformation, according to the will, in the will of God, so that, there may be naught in the soul that is contrary to the will of God, but that, in all and through all, its movement may be that of the will of God alone.

3. It is for this reason that we say of this state that it is the making of two wills into one -- namely, into the will of God, which will of God is likewise the will of the soul. For if this soul desired any imperfection that God wills not, there would not be made one will of God, since the soul would have a will for that which God has not. It is clear, then, that for the soul to come to unite itself perfectly with God through love and will, it must first be free from all desire of the will, howsoever slight. That is, that it must not intentionally and knowingly consent with the will to imperfections, and it must have power and liberty to be able not so to consent intentionally. I say knowingly, because, unintentionally and unknowingly, or without having the power to do otherwise, it may well fall into imperfections and venial sins, and into the natural desires whereof we have spoken; for of such sins as these which are not voluntary and surreptitious it is written that the just man shall fall seven times in the day and shall rise up again. [179] But of the voluntary desires, which, though they be for very small things, are, as I have said, intentional venial sins, any one that is not conquered suffices to impede union. [180] I mean, if this habit be not mortified; for sometimes certain acts of different desires have not as much power when the habits are mortified. Still, the soul will attain to the stage of not having even these, for they likewise proceed from a habit of imperfection. But some habits of voluntary imperfections, which are never completely conquered, prevent not only the attainment of Divine union, but also progress in perfection.

4. These habitual imperfections are, for example, a common custom of much speaking, or some slight attachment which we never quite wish to conquer -- such as that to a person, a garment, a book, a cell, a particular kind of food, tittle-tattle, fancies for tasting, knowing or hearing certain things, and suchlike. Any one of these imperfections, if the soul has become attached and habituated to it, is of as great harm to its growth and progress in virtue as though it were to fall daily into many other imperfections and usual venial sins which proceed not from a habitual indulgence in any habitual and harmful attachment, and will not hinder it so much as when it has attachment to anything. For as long as it has this there is no possibility that it will make progress in perfection, even though the imperfection be extremely slight. For it comes to the same thing whether a bird be held by a slender cord or by a stout one; since, even if it be slender, the bird will be well held as though it were stout, for so long as it breaks it not and flies not away. It is true that the slender one is the easier to break; still, easy though it be, the bird will not fly away if it be not broken. And thus the soul that has attachment to anything, however much virtue it possess, will not attain to the liberty of Divine union. For the desire and the attachment of

the soul have that power which the sucking-fish [181] is said to have when it clings to a ship; for, though but a very small fish, if it succeed in clinging to the ship, it makes it incapable of reaching the port, or of sailing on at all. It is sad to see certain souls in this plight; like rich vessels, they are laden with wealth and good works and spiritual exercises, and with the virtues and the favours that God grants them; and yet, because they have not the resolution to break with some whim or attachment or affection (which all come to the same thing), they never make progress or reach the port of perfection, though they would need to do no more than make one good flight and thus to snap that cord of desire right off, or to rid themselves of that sucking-fish of desire which clings to them.

5. It is greatly to be lamented that, when God has granted them strength to break other and stouter cords [182] -- namely, affections for sins and vanities -- they should fail to attain to such blessing because they have not shaken off some childish thing which God had bidden them conquer for love of Him, and which is nothing more than a thread or a hair. [183] And, what is worse, not only do they make no progress, but because of this attachment they fall back, lose that which they have gained, and retrace that part of the road along which they have travelled at the cost of so much time and labour; for it is well known that, on this road, not to go forward is to turn back, and not to be gaining is to be losing. This Our Lord desired to teach us when He said: He that is not with Me is against Me; and he that gathereth not with Me scattereth.' [184] He that takes not the trouble to repair the vessel, however slight be the crack in it, is likely to spill all the liquid that is within it. The Preacher taught us this clearly when he said: He that contemneth small things shall fall by little and little. [185] For, as he himself says, a great fire cometh from a single spark. [186] And thus one imperfection is sufficient to lead to another; and these lead to yet more; wherefore you will hardly ever see a soul that is negligent in conquering one desire, and that has not many more arising from the same weakness and imperfection that this desire causes. In this way they are continually filling; we have seen many persons to whom God has been granting the favour of leading them a long way, into a state of great detachment and liberty, yet who, merely through beginning to indulge some slight attachment, under the pretext of doing good, or in the guise of conversation and friendship, often lose their spirituality and desire for God and holy solitude, fall from the joy and wholehearted devotion which they had in their spiritual exercises, and cease not until they have lost everything; and this because they broke not with that beginning of sensual desire and pleasure and kept not themselves in solitude for God.

6. Upon this road we must ever journey in order to attain our goal; which means that we must ever be mortifying our desires and not indulging them; and if they are not all completely mortified we shall not completely attain. For even as a log of wood may fail to be transformed in the fire because a single degree of heat is wanting to it, even so the soul will not be transformed in God if it have but one imperfection, although it be something less than voluntary desire; for, as we shall say hereafter concerning the night of faith, the soul has only one will, and that will, if it be embarrassed by aught and set upon by aught, is not free, solitary, and pure, as is necessary for Divine transformation.

7. Of this that has been said we have a figure in the Book of the Judges, where it is related that the angel came to the children of Israel and said to them that, because they had not destroyed that forward people, but had made a league with some of them, they would therefore be left among them as enemies, that they might be to them an occasion of stumbling and perdition. [187] And just so does God deal with certain souls: though He has taken them out of the world, and slain the giants, their sins, and destroyed the multitude of their enemies, which are the occasions of sin that they encountered in the world, solely that they may enter this Promised Land of Divine union with greater liberty, yet they harbour friendship and make alliance with the insignificant peoples [188] -- that is, with imperfections -- and mortify them not completely; therefore Our Lord is angry, and allows them to fall into their desires and go from bad to worse.

8. In the Book of Josue, again, we have a figure of what has just been said -- where we read that God commanded Josue, at the time that he had to enter into possession of the Promised Land, to destroy all things that were in the city of Jericho, in such wise as to leave therein nothing alive, man or woman, young or old, and to slay all the beasts, and to take naught, neither to covet aught, of all the spoils. [189] This He said that we may understand how, if a man is to enter this Divine union, all that lives in his soul must die, both little and much, small and great, and that the soul must be without desire for all this, and detached from it, even as though it existed not for the soul, neither the soul for it. This Saint Paul teaches us clearly in his epistle ad Corinthios, saying: This I say to you, brethren, that the time is short; it remains, and it behoves you, that they that have wives should be as if they had none; and they that weep for the things of this world, as though they wept not; and they that rejoice, as if they rejoiced not; and they that buy, as though they possessed not; and they that use this world, as if they used it not.' [190] This the Apostle says to us in order to teach us how complete must be the detachment of our soul from all things if it is to journey to God.

Footnotes:

177. [The original has no such explanatory phrase.]
178. [That is, will be enjoying all the union that the prayer of quiet gives.]
179. Proverbs xxiv, 16.
180. [The original omits union.']
181. [Or remora.']
182. [cordeles: a stronger word than that used above (hilo), which, if the context would permit, might better be translated 'string' -- its equivalent in modern speech. Below, hilo is translated thread.']
183. [Hilo, rendered thread,' as explained in n. 4 above, can also be taken in the stronger sense of cord.']
184. St. Matthew xii, 30.
185. Ecclesiasticus xix, 1.
186. [Lit., the fire is increased by a single spark.'] Ecclesiasticus xi, 34 [A.V., xi, 32].
187. Judges ii, 3.
188. [The original phrase (gente menuda) means little folk.' It is used of children and sometimes also of insects and other small creatures. There is a marked antithesis between the giants,' or sins, and the little folk,' or imperfections.]
189. Josue vi, 21.
190. 1 Corinthians vii, 29-31.

CHAPTER XII

Which treats of the answer to another question, explaining what the desires are that suffice to cause the evils aforementioned in the soul.

We might write at greater length upon this matter of the night of sense, saying all that there is to say concerning the harm which is caused by the desires, not only in the ways aforementioned, but in many others. But for our purpose that which has been said suffices; for we believe we have made it clear in what way the mortification of these desires is called night, and how it behoves us to enter this night in order to journey to God. The only thing that remains, before we treat of the manner of entrance therein, in order to bring this part to a close, is a question concerning what has been said which might occur to the reader.

2. It may first be asked if any desire can be sufficient to work and produce in the soul the two evils aforementioned -- namely, the privative, which consists in depriving the soul of the grace of God, and the positive, which consists in producing within it the five serious evils whereof we have spoken. Secondly, it may be asked if any desire, however slight it be and of whatever kind, suffices to produce all these together, or if some desires produce some and others produce others. If, for example, some produce torment; others, weariness; others, darkness, etc.

3. Answering this question, I say, first of all, that with respect to the privative evil -- which consists in the soul's being deprived of God -- this is wrought wholly, and can only be wrought, by the voluntary desires, which are of the matter of mortal sin; for they deprive the soul of grace in this life, and of glory, which is the possession of God, in the next. In the second place, I say that both those desires which are of the matter of mortal sin, and the voluntary desires, which are of the matter of venial sin, and those that are of the matter of imperfection, are each sufficient to produce in the soul all these positive evils together; the which evils, although in a certain way they are privative, we here call positive, since they correspond to a turning towards the creature, even as the privative evils correspond to a turning away from God. But there is this difference, that the desires which are of mortal sin produce total blindness, torment, impurity, weakness, etc. Those others, however, which are of the matter of venial sin or imperfection, produce not these evils in a complete and supreme degree, since they deprive not the soul of grace, upon the loss of which depends the possession of them, since the death of the soul is their life; but they produce them in the soul remissly, proportionately to the remission of grace which these desires produce in the soul. [191] So that desire which most weakens grace will produce the most abundant torment, blindness and defilement.

4. It should be noted, however, that, although each desire produces all these evils, which we here term positive, there are some which, principally and directly, produce some of them, and others which produce others, and the remainder are produced consequently upon these. For, although it is true that one sensual desire produces all these evils, yet its principal and proper effect is the defilement of soul and body. And, although one avaricious desire produces them all, its principal and direct result is to produce misery. And, although similarly one vainglorious desire produces them all, its principal and direct result is to produce darkness and blindness. And, although one gluttonous desire produces them all, its principal result is to produce lukewarmness in virtue. And even so is it with the rest.

5. And the reason why any act of voluntary desire produces in the soul all these effects together lies in the direct contrariety which exists between them and all the acts of virtue which produce the contrary effects in the soul. For, even as an act of virtue produces and begets in the soul sweetness, peace, consolation, light, cleanness and fortitude altogether, even so an unruly desire causes torment, fatigue, weariness, blindness and weakness. All the virtues grow through the practice of any one of them, and all the vices grow through the practice of any one of them likewise, and the remnants [192] of each grow in the soul. And although all these evils are not evident at the moment when the desire is indulged, since the resulting pleasure gives no occasion for them, yet the evil remnants which they leave are clearly perceived, whether before or afterwards. This is very well illustrated by that book which the angel commanded Saint John to eat, in the Apocalypse, the which book was sweetness to his mouth, and in his belly bitterness. [193] For the desire, when it is carried into effect, is sweet and appears to be good, but its bitter taste is felt afterwards; the truth of this can be clearly proved by anyone who allows himself to be led away by it. Yet I am not ignorant that there are some men so blind and insensible as not to feel this, for, as they do not walk in God, they are unable to perceive that which hinders them from approaching Him.

6. I am not writing here of the other natural desires which are not voluntary, and of thoughts that go not beyond the first movements, and other temptations to which the soul is not consenting; for these produce in the soul none of the evils aforementioned. For, although a person who suffers from them may think that the passion and disturbance which they then produce in him are defiling and blinding him, this is not the case; rather they are bringing him the opposite advantages. For, in so far as he resists them, he gains fortitude, purity, light and consolation, and many blessings, even as Our Lord said to Saint Paul: That virtue was made perfect in weakness. [194] But the voluntary desires work all the evils aforementioned, and more. Wherefore the principal care of spiritual masters is to mortify their disciples immediately with respect to any desire soever, by causing them to remain without the objects of their desires, in order to free them from such great misery.

Footnotes:

191. [The word here translated remissness' is rendered remission' in the text, where it seems to have a slightly different meaning.]

192. [The word translated remnants' also means after-taste.']

193. Apocalypse x, 9.

194. 2 Corinthians xii, 9. [Virtue' had often, in the author's day, much of the meaning of the modern word 'strength.']

CHAPTER XIII

Wherein is described the manner and way which the soul must follow in order to enter this night of sense.

It now remains for me to give certain counsels whereby the soul may know how to enter this night of sense and may be able so to do. To this end it must be known that the soul habitually enters this night of sense in two ways: the one is active; the other passive. The active way consists in that which the soul can do, and does, of itself, in order to enter therein, whereof we shall now treat in the counsels which follow. The passive way is that wherein the soul does nothing, and God works in it, and it remains, as it were, patient. Of this we shall treat in the fourth book, where we shall be treating of beginners. And because there, with the Divine favour, we shall give many counsels to beginners, according to the many imperfections which they are apt to have while on this road, I shall not spend time in giving many here. And this, too, because it belongs not to this place to give them, as at present we are treating only of the reasons for which this journey is called a night, and of what kind it is, and how many parts it has. But, as it seems that it would be incomplete, and less profitable than it should be, if we gave no help or counsel here for walking in this night of desires, I have thought well to set down briefly here the way which is to be followed: and I shall do the same at the end of each of the next two parts, or causes, of this night, whereof, with the help of the Lord, I have to treat.

2. These counsels for the conquering of the desires, which now follow, albeit brief and few, I believe to be as profitable and efficacious as they are concise; so that one who sincerely desires to practice them will need no others, but will find them all included in these.

3. First, let him have an habitual desire [195] to imitate Christ in everything that he does, conforming himself to His life; upon which life he must meditate so that he may know how to imitate it, and to behave in all things as Christ would behave.

4. Secondly, in order that he may be able to do this well, every pleasure that presents itself to the senses, if it be not purely for the honour and glory of God, must be renounced and completely rejected for the love of Jesus Christ, Who in this life had no other pleasure, neither desired any, than to do the will of His Father, which He called His meat and food. [196] I take this example. If there present itself to a man the pleasure of listening to things that tend not to the service and honour of God, let him not desire that pleasure, nor desire to listen to them; and if there present itself the pleasure of looking at things that help him not Godward, let him not desire the pleasure or look at these things; and if in conversation or in aught else soever such pleasure present itself, let him act likewise. And similarly with respect to all the senses, in so far as he can fairly avoid the pleasure in question; if he cannot, it suffices that, although these things may be present to his senses, he desires not to have this pleasure. And in this wise he will be able to mortify and void his senses of such pleasure, as though they were in darkness. If he takes care to do this, he will soon reap great profit.

5. For the mortifying and calming of the four natural passions, which are joy, hope, fear and grief, from the concord and pacification whereof come these and other blessings, the counsels here following are of the greatest help, and of great merit, and the source of great virtues.

6. Strive always to prefer, not that which is easiest, but that which is most difficult;
Not that which is most delectable, but that which is most unpleasing;
Not that which gives most pleasure, but rather that which gives least;
Not that which is restful, but that which is wearisome;
Not that which is consolation, but rather that which is disconsolateness;
Not that which is greatest, but that which is least;
Not that which is loftiest and most precious, but that which is lowest and most despised;
Not that which is [197] a desire for anything, but that which is a desire for nothing;
Strive to go about seeking not the best of temporal things, but the worst.
Strive thus to desire to enter into complete detachment and emptiness and poverty, with respect to everything that is in the world, for Christ's sake.

7. And it is meet that the soul embrace these acts with all its heart and strive to subdue its will thereto. For, if it perform them with its heart, it will very quickly come to find in them great delight and consolation, and to act with order and discretion.

8. These things that have been said, if they be faithfully put into practice, are quite sufficient for entrance into the night of sense; but, for greater completeness, we shall describe another kind of

Ascent of Mount Carmel

exercise which teaches us to mortify the concupiscence of the flesh and the concupiscence of the eyes, and the pride of life, which, says Saint John, [198] are the things that reign in the world, from which all the other desires proceed.

9. First, let the soul strive to work in its own despite, and desire all to do so. Secondly, let it strive to speak in its own despite and desire all to do so. Third, let it strive to think humbly of itself, in its own despite, and desire all to do so.

10. To conclude these counsels and rules, it will be fitting to set down here those lines which are written in the Ascent of the Mount, which is the figure that is at the beginning of this book; the which lines are instructions for ascending to it, and thus reaching the summit of union. For, although it is true that that which is there spoken of is spiritual and interior, there is reference likewise to the spirit of imperfection according to sensual and exterior things, as may be seen by the two roads which are on either side of the path of perfection. It is in this way and according to this sense that we shall understand them here; that is to say, according to that which is sensual. Afterwards, in the second part of this night, they will be understood according to that which is spiritual. [199]

11. The lines are these:
In order to arrive at having pleasure in everything,
Desire to have pleasure in nothing.
In order to arrive at possessing everything,
Desire to possess nothing.
In order to arrive at being everything,
Desire to be nothing.
In order to arrive at knowing everything,
Desire to know nothing. [200]
In order to arrive at that wherein thou hast no pleasure,
Thou must go by a way wherein thou hast no pleasure.
In order to arrive at that which thou knowest not,
Thou must go by a way that thou knowest not.
In order to arrive at that which thou possessest not,
Thou must go by a way that thou possessest not.
In order to arrive at that which thou art not,
Thou must go through that which thou art not.

12. When thy mind dwells upon anything,
Thou art ceasing to cast thyself upon the All. For, in order to pass
from the all to the All, Thou hast to deny thyself wholly [201] in
all. And, when thou comest to possess it wholly, Thou must possess
it without desiring anything. For, if thou wilt have anything in
having all, [202] Thou hast not thy treasure purely in God.

13. In this detachment the spiritual soul finds its quiet and repose; for, since it covets nothing, nothing wearies it when it is lifted up, and nothing oppresses it when it is cast down, because it is in the centre of its humility; but when it covets anything, at that very moment it becomes wearied.

Footnotes:

195. [The word used for desire is apetito, which has been used in the past chapters for desires of sense (cf. chap. I, above).]
196. [St. John iv, 34.]
197. Lit., Not that which is to desire anything, etc.']
198. [1 St. John ii, 16.]
199. The Saint does not, however, allude to these lines again. The order followed below is that of Alc., which differs somewhat from that followed in the diagram.
200. [This line, like ll. 6, 8 of the paragraph, reads more literally: Desire not to possess (be, know) anything in anything.' It is more emphatic than l. 2.]
201. [There is a repetition here which could only be indicated by translating all-ly.' So, too, in the next couplet.]
202. [Lit. anything in all.']

CHAPTER XIV

Wherein is expounded the second line of the stanza.
Kindled in love with yearnings.

Now that we have expounded the first line of this stanza, which treats of the night of sense, explaining what this night of sense is, and why it is called night; and now that we have likewise described the order and manner which are to be followed for a soul to enter therein actively, the next thing to be treated in due sequence is its properties and effects, which are wonderful, and are described in the next lines of the stanza aforementioned, upon which I will briefly touch for the sake of expounding the said lines, as I promised in the Prologue; [203] and I will then pass on at once to the second book, treating of the other part of this night, which is the spiritual.

2. The soul, then, says that, kindled in love with yearnings,' it passed through this dark night of sense and came out thence to the union of the Beloved. For, in order to conquer all the desires and to deny itself the pleasures which it has in everything, and for which its love and affection are wont to enkindle the will that it may enjoy them, it would need to experience another and a greater enkindling by an other and a better love, which is that of its Spouse; to the end that, having its pleasure set upon Him and deriving from Him its strength, it should have courage and constancy to deny itself all other things with ease. And, in order to conquer the strength of the desires of sense, it would need, not only to have love for its Spouse, but also to be enkindled by love and to have yearnings. For it comes to pass, and so it is, that with such yearnings of desire the sensual nature is moved and attracted toward sensual things, so that, if the spiritual part be not enkindled with other and greater yearnings for that which is spiritual, it will be unable to throw off the yoke of nature [204] or to enter this night of sense, neither will it have courage to remain in darkness as to all things, depriving itself of desire for them all.

3. And the nature and all the varieties of these yearnings of love which souls experience in the early stages of this road to union; and the diligent means and contrivances which they employ in order to leave their house, which is self-will, during the night of the mortification of their senses; and how easy, and even sweet and delectable, these yearnings for the Spouse make all the trials and perils of this night to appear to them, this is not the place to describe, neither is such description possible; for it is better to know and meditate upon these things than to write of them. And so we shall pass on to expound the remaining lines in the next chapter.

Footnotes:

203. This confirms our point (Bk. I, chap. ii, 6, above) that the Saint considers the Argument as part of the Prologue.
204. Lit., to conquer the natural yoke.']

CHAPTER XV

Wherein are expounded the remaining lines of the aforementioned stanza.

... oh, happy chance! --
I went forth without being observed, My house being now at rest.

These lines take as a metaphor the miserable estate of captivity, a man's deliverance from which, when none of the gaolers' hinder his release, he considers a happy chance.' For the soul, on account of [205] original sin, is truly as it were a captive in this mortal body, subject to the passions and desires of nature, from bondage and subjection to which it considers its having gone forth without being observed as a happy chance' -- having gone forth, that is, without being impeded or engulfed [206] by any of them.

2. For to this end the soul profited by going forth upon a dark night' -- that is, in the privation of all pleasures and mortification of all desires, after the manner whereof we have spoken. And by its house being now at rest' is meant the sensual part, which is the house of all the desires, and is now at rest because they have all been overcome and lulled to sleep. For until the desires are lulled to sleep through the mortification of the sensual nature, and until at last the sensual nature itself is at rest from them, so that they make not war upon the spirit, the soul goes not forth to true liberty and to the fruition of union with its Beloved.

END OF THE FIRST BOOK

Footnotes:

205. [Lit., after.']
206. [Lit., comprehended.']

BOOK THE SECOND
OF THE ASCENT OF MT. CARMEL'

    Wherein is treated the proximate means of ascending to union with God, which is faith; and wherein therefore is described the second part of this night, which, as we said, belongs to the spirit, and is contained in the second stanza, which is as follows.

STANZA THE SECOND

CHAPTER I

In darkness and secure, By the secret ladder, disguised -- oh, happy chance! -- In darkness and in concealment, My house being now at rest.

In this second stanza the soul sings of the happy chance which it experienced in stripping the spirit of all spiritual imperfections and desires for the possession of spiritual things. This was a much greater happiness to, by reason of the greater difficulty that there is in putting to rest this house of the spiritual part, and of being able to enter this interior darkness, which is spiritual detachment from all things, whether sensual or spiritual, and leaning on pure faith alone and an ascent thereby to God. The soul here calls this a ladder,' and 'secret,' because all the rungs and parts of it [207] are secret and hidden from all sense and understanding. And thus the soul has remained in darkness as to all light of sense and understanding, going forth beyond all limits of nature and reason in order to ascend by this Divine ladder of faith, which attains [208] and penetrates even to the heights [209] of God. The soul says that it was travelling disguised,' because the garments and vesture which it wears and its natural condition are changed into the Divine, as it ascends by faith. And it was because of this disguise that it was not recognized or impeded, either by time or by reason or by the devil; for none of these things can harm one that journeys in faith. And not only so, but the soul travels in such wise concealed and hidden and is so far from all the deceits of the devil that in truth it journeys (as it also says here) in darkness and in concealment' -- that is to say, hidden from the devil, to whom the light of faith is more than darkness.

2. And thus the soul that journeys through this night, we may say, journeys in concealment and in hiding from the devil, as will be more clearly seen hereafter. Wherefore the soul says that it went forth in darkness and secure'; for one that has such happiness as to be able to journey through the darkness of faith, taking faith for his guide, like to one that is blind, [210] and leaving behind all natural imaginings and spiritual reasonings, journeys very securely, as we have said. And so the soul says furthermore that it went forth through this spiritual night, its house being now at rest' -- that is to say, its spiritual and rational parts. When, therefore, the soul attains to union which is of God, its natural faculties are at rest, as are likewise its impulses and yearnings of the senses, in its spiritual part. For this cause the soul says not here that it went forth with yearnings, as in the first night of sense. For, in order to journey in the night of sense, and to strip itself of that which is of sense, it needed yearnings of sense-love so that it might go forth perfectly; but, in order to put to rest the house of its spirit, it needs no more than denial [211] of all faculties and pleasures and desires of the spirit in pure faith. This attained, the soul is united with the Beloved in a union of simplicity and purity and love and similitude.

3. And it must be remembered that the first stanza, speaking of the sensual part, says that the soul went forth upon a dark night,' and here, speaking of the spiritual part, it says that it went forth in darkness.' For the darkness of the spiritual part is by far the greater, even as darkness is a greater obscurity than that of night. For, however dark a night may be, something can always be seen, but in true darkness nothing can be seen; and thus in the night of sense there still remains some light, for the understanding and reason remain, and are not blinded. But this spiritual night, which is faith, deprives the soul of everything, both as to understanding and as to sense. And for this cause the soul in this night says that it was journeying in darkness and secure,' which it said not in the other. For, the less the soul works with its own ability, the more securely it journeys, because it journeys more in faith. And this will be expounded at length in the course of this second book, wherein it will be necessary for the devout reader to proceed attentively, because there will be said herein things of great importance to the person that is truly spiritual. [212] And, although they are somewhat obscure, some of them will pave the way to others, so that I believe they will all be quite clearly understood.

Footnotes:

207. [Lit., all the steps and articles that it has.']
208. [Lit., climbs': the verb (escala) is identical with the noun ladder' (escala).]
209. [Lit., to the depths.']
210. [The literal translation is shorter, viz. taking faith for a blind man's guide.']
211. [Lit., negation.'] This is the reading of Alc. Affirmation' is found in A, B, C, D, e.p. Though the two words are antithetical, they express the same underlying concept. [The affirmation, or establishment, of all the powers and desires of the spirit upon pure faith, so that they may be ruled by pure faith alone, is equivalent to the denial, or negation, of those powers and desires in so far as they are not ruled by pure faith.]
212. [Lit., to true spirit.']

CHAPTER II

Which begins to treat of the second part or cause of this night, which is faith. Proves by two arguments how it is darker than the first and than the third.

We now go on to treat of the second part of this night, which is faith; this is the wondrous means which, as we said, leads to the goal, which is God, Who, as we said, [213] is also to the soul, naturally, the third cause or part of this night. For faith, which is the means, [214] is compared with midnight. And thus we may say that it is darker for the soul either than the first part or, in a way, than the third; for the first part, which is that of sense, is compared to the beginning of night, or the time when sensible objects can no longer be seen, and thus it is not so far removed from light as is midnight. The third part, which is the period preceding the dawn, is quite close to the light of day, and it, too, therefore, is not so dark as midnight; for it is now close to the enlightenment and illumination of the light of day, which is compared with God. For, although it is true, if we speak after a natural manner, that God is as dark a night to the soul as is faith, still, when these three parts of the night are over, which are naturally night to the soul, God begins to illumine the soul by supernatural means with the ray of His Divine light; which is the beginning of the perfect union that follows, when the third night is past, and it can thus be said to be less dark.

2. It is likewise darker than the first night, for this belongs to the lower part of man, which is the sensual part, and, consequently, the more exterior; and this second part, which is of faith, belongs to the higher part of man, which is the rational part, and, in consequence, more interior and more obscure, since it deprives it of the light of reason, or, to speak more clearly, blinds it; [215] and thus it is aptly compared to midnight, which is the depth of night and the darkest part thereof.

3. We have now to prove how this second part, which is faith, is night to the spirit, even as the first part is night to sense. And we shall then also describe the things that are contrary to it, and how the soul must prepare itself actively to enter it. For, concerning the passive part, which is that which God works in it, when He brings it into that night, we shall speak in its place, which I intend shall be the third book.

Footnotes:

213. [I, ii, above.]
214. [Cf. I, ii, above.]
215. This was another of the propositions which were cited by those who denounced the writings of St. John of the Cross to the Holy Office. It is interpretable, nevertheless, in a sense that is perfectly true and completely in conformity with Catholic doctrine. The Saint does not, in these words, affirm that faith destroys nature or quenches the light of human reason (St. Thomas, Summa, Pt. 1, q. 1, a. 8, et alibi); what he endeavors to show is that the coming of knowledge through faith excludes a simultaneous coming of natural knowledge through reason. It is only in this way that, in the act of faith, the soul is deprived of the light of reason, and left, as it were, in blindness, so that it may be raised to another nobler and sublimer kind of knowledge, which, far from destroying reason, gives it dignity and perfection. Philosophy teaches that the proper and connatural object of the understanding, in this life, is things visible, material and corporeal. By his nature, man inclines to knowledge of this kind, but cannot lay claim to such knowledge as regards the things which belong to faith. For, to quote a famous verse of Scripture: Fides est sperandarum substantia rerum, argumentum non apparientium (Hebrews xi, 1). This line of thought is not confined to St. John of the Cross, but is followed by all the mystics and is completely in agreement with theological doctrine. Cf. Respuesta [Reply] of P. Basilio Ponce de León and Dilucidatio, Pt. II, Chap. ii, and also the following chapter in this present book.

CHAPTER III

How faith is dark night to the soul. This is proved with arguments and quotations and figures from Scripture.

Faith, say the theologians, is a habit of the soul, certain and obscure. And the reason for its being an obscure habit is that it makes us believe truths revealed by God Himself, which transcend all natural light, and exceed all human understanding, beyond all proportion. Hence it follows that, for the soul, this excessive light of faith which is given to it is thick darkness, for it overwhelms greater things and does away with small things, even as the light of the sun overwhelms all other lights whatsoever, so that when it shines and disables our visual faculty they appear not to be lights at all. So that it blinds it and deprives it of the sight that has been given to it, inasmuch as its light is great beyond all proportion and transcends the faculty of vision. Even so the light of faith, by its excessive greatness, oppresses and disables that of the understanding; for the latter, of its own power, extends only to natural knowledge, although it has a faculty [216] for the supernatural, whenever Our Lord is pleased to give it supernatural activity.

2. Wherefore a man can know nothing by himself, save after a natural manner, [217] which is only that which he attains by means of the senses. For this cause he must have the phantasms and the forms of objects present in themselves and in their likenesses; otherwise it cannot be, for, as philosophers say: Ab objecto et potentia paritur notitia. That is: From the object that is present and from the faculty, knowledge is born in the soul. Wherefore, if one should speak to a man of things which he has never been able to understand, and whose likeness he has never seen, he would have no more illumination from them whatever than if naught had been said of them to him. I take an example. If one should say to a man that on a certain island there is an animal which he has never seen, and give him no idea of the likeness of that animal, that he may compare it with others that he has seen, he will have no more knowledge of it, or idea of its form, than he had before, however much is being said to him about it. And this will be better understood by another and a more apt example. If one should describe to a man that was born blind, and has never seen any colour, what is meant by a white colour or by a yellow, he would understand it but indifferently, however fully one might describe it to him; for, as he has never seen such colours or anything like them by which he may judge them, only their names would remain with him; for these he would be able to comprehend through the ear, but not their forms or figures, since he has never seen them.

3. Even so is faith with respect to the soul; it tells us of things which we have never seen or understood, nor have we seen or understood aught that resembles them, since there is naught that resembles them at all. And thus we have no light of natural knowledge concerning them, since that which we are told of them bears no relation to any sense of ours; we know it by the ear alone, believing that which we are taught, bringing our natural light into subjection and treating it as if it were not. [218] For, as Saint Paul says, Fides ex auditu. [219] As though he were to say: Faith is not knowledge which enters by any of the senses, but is only the consent given by the soul to that which enters through the ear.

4. And faith far transcends even that which is indicated by the examples given above. For not only does it give no information and knowledge, but, as we have said, it deprives us of all other information and knowledge, and blinds us to them, so that they cannot judge it well. For other knowledge can be acquired by the light of the understanding; but the knowledge that is of faith is acquired without the illumination of the understanding, which is rejected for faith; and in its own light, if that light be not darkened, it is lost. Wherefore Isaias said: Si non credideritis, non intelligetis. [220] That is: If ye believe not, ye shall not understand. It is clear, then, that faith is dark night for the soul, and it is in this way that it gives it light; and the more the soul is darkened, the greater is the light that comes to it. For it is by blinding that it gives light, according to this saying of Isaias. For if ye believe not, ye shall not (he says) have light. [221] And thus faith was foreshadowed by that cloud which divided the children of Israel and the Egyptians when the former were about to enter the Red Sea, whereof Scripture says: Erat nubes tenebrosa, et illuminans noctem. [222] This is to say that that cloud was full of darkness and gave light to the night.

5. A wondrous thing it is that, though it was dark, it should give light to the night. This was said to show that faith, which is a black and dark cloud to the soul (and likewise is night, since in the presence of faith the soul is deprived of its natural light and is blinded), can with its darkness give light and

illumination to the darkness of the soul, for it was fitting that the disciples should thus be like the master. For man, who is in darkness, could not fittingly be enlightened save by other darkness, even as David teaches us, saying: Dies diei eructat verbum et nox nocti indicat scientiam. [223] Which signifies: Day unto day uttereth and aboundeth in speech, and night unto night showeth knowledge. Which, to speak more clearly, signifies: The day, which is God in bliss, where it is day to the blessed angels and souls who are now day, communicates and reveals to them the Word, which is His Son, that they may know Him and enjoy Him. And the night, which is faith in the Church Militant, where it is still night, shows knowledge is night to the Church, and consequently to every soul, which knowledge is night to it, since it is without clear beatific wisdom; and, in the presence of faith, it is blind as to its natural light.

6. So that which is to be inferred from this that faith, because it is dark night, gives light to the soul, which is in darkness, that there may come to be fulfilled that which David likewise says to this purpose, in these works: Et nox illuminatio mea in deliciis meis. [224] Which signifies: the night will be illumination in my delights. Which is as much as to say: In the delights of my pure contemplation and union with God, the night of faith shall be my guide. Wherein he gives it clearly to be understood that the soul must be in darkness in order to have light for this road.

Footnotes:

216. E .p.: an obediential faculty' [potencia obediencial]: this phrase is borrowed from the Schoolmen. Among the various divisions of the faculty are two, natural and obediential. The first is that which is directed towards an act within the sphere of nature, such as the cooling action of water and the heating action of fire; the second is directed towards an act which exceeds these powers, brought about by God, Who is outside the laws of nature and can therefore work outside the natural domain. This obediential faculty (called also receptive' or passive') frequently figures in mystical theology, since it is this that disposes the faculties of the soul for the supernatural reception of the gifts of grace, all of which exceed natural capacity.

217. E.p.: a natural manner which has its beginning in the senses.' Here the Saint expounds a principle of scholastic philosophy summarized in the axiom: Nihil est in intellectu quin prius non fuerit in sensu. This principle, like many other great philosophical questions, has continually been debated. St. John of the Cross will be found as a rule to follow the philosophy most favored by the Church and is always rigidly orthodox.

218. [Lit., 'subjecting and blinding our natural light.']
219. Romans x, 17.
220. Isaias vii, 9. So Alc. The passage seems to be taken from the Septuagint. [The Vulgate has non permanebitis.]
221. [Lit., If ye believe not, that is, ye shall not have light.']
222. Exodus xiv, 20.
223. Psalm xviii, 3 [A.V., xix, 2].
224. Psalm cxxxviii, 11 [A.V., cxxxix, 11].

CHAPTER IV

Treats in general of how the soul likewise must be in darkness, in so far as this rests with itself, to the end that it may be effectively guided by faith to the highest contemplation.

It is now, I think, becoming clear how faith is dark night to the soul, and how the soul likewise must be dark, or in darkness as to its own light so that it may allow itself to be guided by faith to this high goal of union. But, in order that the soul may be able to do this, it will now be well to continue describing, in somewhat greater detail, this darkness which it must have, in order that it may enter into this abyss of faith. And thus in this chapter I shall speak of it in a general way; and hereafter, with the Divine favour, I shall continue to describe more minutely the way in which the soul is to conduct itself that it may neither stray therein nor impede this guide.

2. I say, then, that the soul, in order to be effectively guided to this state by faith, must not only be in darkness with respect to that part that concerns the creatures and temporal things, which is the sensual and the lower part (whereof we have already treated), but that likewise it must be blinded and darkened according to the part which has respect to God and to spiritual things, which is the rational and higher part, whereof we are now treating. For, in order that one may attain supernatural transformation, it is clear that he must be plunged into darkness and carried far away from all contained in his nature that is sensual and rational. For the word supernatural means that which soars above the natural self; the natural self, therefore, remains beneath it. For, although this transformation and union is something that cannot be comprehended by human ability and sense, the soul must completely and voluntarily void itself of all that can enter into it, whether from above or from below -- I mean according to the affection and will -- so far as this rests with itself. For who shall prevent God from doing that which He will in the soul that is resigned, annihilated and detached? But the soul must be voided of all such things as can enter its capacity, so that, however many supernatural experiences it may have, it will ever remain as it were detached from them and in darkness. It must be like to a blind man, leaning upon dark faith, taking it for guide and light, and leaning upon none of the things that he understands, experiences, feels and imagines. For all these are darkness, which will cause him to stray; and faith is above all that he understands and experiences and feels and imagines. And, if he be not blinded as to this, and remain not in total darkness, he attains not to that which is greater -- namely, that which is taught by faith.

3. A blind man, if he be not quite blind, refuses to be led by a guide; and, since he sees a little, he thinks it better to go in whatever happens to be the direction which he can distinguish, because he sees none better; and thus he can lead astray a guide who sees more than he, for after all it is for him to say where he shall go rather than for the guide. In the same way a soul may lean upon any knowledge of its own, or any feeling or experience of God, yet, however great this may be, it is very little and far different from what God is; and, in going along this road, a soul is easily led astray, or brought to a standstill, because it will not remain in faith like one that is blind, and faith is its true guide.

4. It is this that was meant by Saint Paul when he said: Accedentem ad Deum oportet credere quod est. [225] Which signifies: He that would journey towards union with God must needs believe in His Being. As though he had said: He that would attain to being joined in a union with God must not walk by understanding, neither lean upon experience or feeling or imagination, but he must believe in His being, which is not perceptible to the understanding, neither to the desire nor to the imagination nor to any other sense, neither can it be known in this life at all. Yea, in this life, the highest thing that can be felt and experienced concerning God is infinitely remote from God and from the pure possession of Him. Isaias and Saint Paul say: Nec oculus vidit, nec auris audivit, nec in cor hominis ascendit, qua praeparavit Deus iis, qui diligunt illum. [226] Which signifies: That which God hath prepared for them that love Him neither eye hath seen, nor ear heard, neither hath it entered into the heart or thought of man. So, however much the soul aspires to be perfectly united through grace in this life with that to which it will be united through glory in the next (which, as Saint Paul here says, eye hath not seen, nor ear heard, neither hath it entered into the heart of man in the flesh), it is clear that, in order perfectly to attain to union in this life through grace and through love, a soul must be in darkness with respect to all that can enter through the eye, and to all that can be received through the ear, and can be imagined with the fancy, and understood with the heart, which here signifies the soul. And thus a soul is greatly impeded from reaching this high estate of union with God when it clings to any understanding or feeling or imagination or appearance or will or manner of its own, or to any other act or to anything of its own, and cannot detach and strip itself of all these. For, as we say, the goal which it seeks lies beyond all this,

yea, beyond even the highest thing that can be known or experienced; and thus a soul must pass beyond everything to unknowing.

5. Wherefore, upon this road, to enter upon the road is to leave the road; or, to express it better, it is to pass on to the goal and to leave one's own way, [227] and to enter upon that which has no way, which is God. For the soul that attains to this state has no longer any ways or methods, still less is it attached to ways and methods, or is capable of being attached to them. I mean ways of understanding, or of perception, or of feeling. Nevertheless it has within itself all ways, after the way of one that possesses nothing, yet possesses all things. [228] For, if it have courage to pass beyond its natural limitations, both interiorly and exteriorly, it enters within the limits of the supernatural, which has no way, yet in substance has all ways. Hence for the soul to arrive at these limits is for it to leave these limits, in each case going forth out of itself a great way, from this lowly state to that which is high above all others.

6. Wherefore, passing beyond all that can be known and understood, both spiritually and naturally, the soul will desire with all desire to come to that which in this life cannot be known, neither can enter into its heart. And, leaving behind all that it experiences and feels, both temporally and spiritually, and all that it is able to experience and feel in this life, it will desire with all desire to come to that which surpasses all feeling and experience. And, in order to be free and void to that end, it must in no wise lay hold upon that which it receives, either spiritually or sensually, within itself [229] (as we shall explain presently, when we treat this in detail), considering it all to be of much less account. For the more emphasis the soul lays upon what it understands, experiences and imagines, and the more it esteems this, whether it be spiritual or no, the more it loses of the supreme good, and the more it is hindered from attaining thereto. And the less it thinks of what it may have, however much this be, in comparison with the highest good, the more it dwells upon that good and esteems it, and, consequently, the more nearly it approaches it. And in this wise the soul approaches a great way towards union, in darkness, by means of faith, which is likewise dark, and in this wise faith wondrously illumines it. It is certain that, if the soul should desire to see, it would be in darkness much more quickly, with respect to God, than would one who opens his eyes to look upon the great brightness of the sun.

7. Wherefore, by blinding itself in its faculties upon this road, the soul will see the light, even as the Saviour says in the Gospel, in this wise: In judicium veni in hunc mundum: ut qui non vident, videant, et qui vident, caeci fiant. [230] That is: I am come into this world for judgment; that they which see not may see, and that they which see may become blind. This, as it will be supposed, is to be understood of this spiritual road, where the soul that is in darkness, and is blinded as regards all its natural and proper lights, will see supernaturally; and the soul that would depend upon any light of its own will become the blinder and will halt upon the road to union.

8. And, that we may proceed with less confusion, I think it will be necessary to describe, in the following chapter, the nature of this that we call union of the soul with God; for, when this is understood, that which we shall say hereafter will become much clearer. And so I think the treatment of this union comes well at this point, as in its proper place. For, although the thread of that which we are expounding is interrupted thereby, this is not done without a reason, since it serves to illustrate in this place the very thing that is being described. The chapter which follows, then, will be a parenthetical one, placed, as it were, between the two terms of an enthymeme, since we shall afterwards have to treat in detail of the three faculties of the soul, with respect to the three logical virtues, in relation to this second night.

Footnotes:

225. Hebrews xi, 6.
226. Isaias lxiv, 4; 1 Corinthians ii, 9.
227. [The word translated 'way' is modo, which, in the language of scholastic philosophy, would rather be translated 'mode.']
228. [2 Corinthians vi, 10.]
229. [Lit., either spiritually or sensually, in its soul.']
230. St. John ix, 39.

CHAPTER V

Wherein is described what is meant by union of the soul with God. A comparison is given. [231]

From what has been said above it becomes clear to some extent what we mean by union of the soul with God; what we now say about it, therefore, will be the better understood. It is not my intention here to treat of the divisions of this union, nor of its parts, for I should never end if I were to begin now to explain what is the nature of union of the understanding, and what is that of union according to the will, and likewise according to the memory; and likewise what is transitory and what permanent in the union of the said faculties; and then what is meant by total union, transitory and permanent, with regard to the said faculties all together. All this we shall treat gradually in our discourse -- speaking first of one and then of another. But here this is not to the point in order to describe what we have to say concerning them; it will be explained much more fittingly in its place, when we shall again be treating the same matter, and shall have a striking illustration to add to the present explanation, so that everything will then be considered and explained and we shall judge of it better.

2. Here I treat only of this permanent and total union according to the substance of the soul and its faculties with respect to the obscure habit of union: for with respect to the act, we shall explain later, with the Divine favour, how there can be no permanent union in the faculties, in this life, but a transitory union only.

3. In order, then, to understand what is meant by this union whereof we are treating, it must be known that God dwells and is present substantially in every soul, even in that of the greatest sinner in the world. And this kind of union is ever wrought between God and all the creatures, for in it He is preserving their being: if union of this kind were to fail them, they would at once become annihilated and would cease to be. And so, when we speak of union of the soul with God, we speak not of this substantial union which is continually being wrought, but of the union and transformation of the soul with God, which is not being wrought continually, but only when there is produced that likeness that comes from love; we shall therefore term this the union of likeness, even as that other union is called substantial or essential. The former is natural, the latter supernatural. And the latter comes to pass when the two wills -- namely that of the soul and that of God -- are conformed together in one, and there is naught in the one that repugnant to the other. And thus, when the soul rids itself totally of that which is repugnant to the Divine will and conforms not with it, it is transformed in God through love.

4. This is to be understood of that which is repugnant, not only in action, but likewise in habit, so that not only must the voluntary acts of imperfection cease, but the habits of any such imperfections must be annihilated. And since no creature whatsoever, and none of its actions or abilities, can conform or can attain to that which is God, therefore must the soul be stripped of all things created, and of its own actions and abilities -- namely, of its understanding, perception and feeling -- so that, when all that is unlike God and unconformed to Him is cast out, the soul may receive the likeness of God; and nothing will then remain in it that is not the will of God and it will thus be transformed in God. Wherefore, although it is true that, as we have said, God is ever in the soul, giving it, and through His presence conserving within it, its natural being, yet He does not always communicate supernatural being to it. For this is communicated only by love and grace, which not all souls possess; and all those that possess it have it not in the same degree; for some have attained more degrees of love and others fewer. Wherefore God communicates Himself most to that soul that has progressed farthest in love; namely, that has its will in closest conformity with the will of God. And the soul that has attained complete conformity and likeness of will is totally united and transformed in God supernaturally. Wherefore, as has already been explained, the more completely a soul is wrapped up in [232] the creatures and in its own abilities, by habit and affection, the less preparation it has for such union; for it gives not God a complete opportunity to transform it supernaturally. The soul, then, needs only to strip itself of these natural dissimilarities and contrarieties, so that God, Who is communicating Himself naturally to it, according to the course of nature, may communicate Himself to it supernaturally, by means of grace.

5. And it is this that Saint John desired to explain when he said: Qui non ex sanguinibus, neque ex voluntate carnis, neque ex voluntate viri, sed ex Deo nati sunt. [233] As though he had said: He gave power to be sons of God -- that is, to be transformed in God -- only to those who are born, not of blood -- that is, not of natural constitution and temperament -- neither of the will of the flesh -- that is, of the free will of natural capacity and ability -- still less of the will of man -- wherein is included every way and manner of judging and comprehending with the understanding. He gave power to none of these to

become sons of God, but only to those that are born of God -- that is, to those who, being born again through grace, and dying first of all to everything that is of the old man, are raised above themselves to the supernatural, and receive from God this rebirth and adoption, which transcends all that can be imagined. For, as Saint John himself says elsewhere: Nisi quis renatus fuerit ex aqua, et Spiritu Sancto, non potest videre regnum Dei.[234] This signifies: He that is not born again in the Holy Spirit will not be able to see this kingdom of God, which is the state of perfection; and to be born again in the Holy Spirit in this life is to have a soul most like to God in purity, having in itself no admixture of imperfection, so that pure transformation can be wrought in it through participation of union, albeit not essentially.

6. In order that both these things may be the better understood, let us make a comparison. A ray of sunlight is striking a window. If the window is in any way stained or misty, the sun's ray will be unable to illumine it and transform it into its own light, totally, as it would if it were clean of all these things, and pure; but it will illumine it to a lesser degree, in proportion as it is less free from those mists and stains; and will do so to a greater degree, in proportion as it is cleaner from them, and this will not be because of the sun's ray, but because of itself; so much so that, if it be wholly pure and clean, the ray of sunlight will transform it and illumine it in such wise that it will itself seem to be a ray and will give the same light as the ray. Although in reality the window has a nature distinct from that of the ray itself, however much it may resemble it, yet we may say that that window is a ray of the sun or is light by participation. And the soul is like this window, whereupon is ever beating (or, to express it better, wherein is ever dwelling) this Divine light of the Being of God according to nature, which we have described.

7. In thus allowing God to work in it, the soul (having rid itself of every mist and stain of the creatures, which consists in having its will perfectly united with that of God, for to love is to labour to detach and strip itself for God's sake of all that is not God) is at once illumined and transformed in God, and God communicates to it His supernatural Being, in such wise that it appears to be God Himself, and has all that God Himself has. And this union comes to pass when God grants the soul this supernatural favour, that all the things of God and the soul are one in participant transformation; and the soul seems to be God rather than a soul, and is indeed God by participation; although it is true that its natural being, though thus transformed, is as distinct from the Being of God as it was before, even as the window has likewise a nature distinct from that of the ray, though the ray gives it brightness.

8. This makes it clearer that the preparation of the soul for this union, as we said, is not that it should understand or perceive or feel or imagine anything, concerning either God or aught else, but that it should have purity and love -- that is, perfect resignation and detachment from everything for God's sake alone; and, as there can be no perfect transformation if there be not perfect purity, and as the enlightenment, illumination and union of the soul with God will be according to the proportion of its purity, in greater or in less degree; yet the soul will not be perfect, as I say, if it be not wholly and perfectly[235] bright and clean.

9. This will likewise be understood by the following comparison. A picture is truly perfect, with many and most sublime beauties and delicate and subtle illuminations, and some of its beauties are so fine and subtle that they cannot be completely realized, because of their delicacy and excellence. Fewer beauties and less delicacy will be seen in this picture by one whose vision is less clear and refined; and he whose vision is somewhat more refined will be able to see in it more beauties and perfections; and, if another person has a vision still more refined, he will see still more perfection; and, finally, he who has the clearest and purest faculties will see the most beauties and perfections of all; for there is so much to see in the picture that, however far one may attain, there will ever remain higher degrees of attainment.

10. After the same manner we may describe the condition of the soul with relation to God in this enlightenment or transformation. For, although it is true that a soul, according to its greater or lesser capacity, may have attained to union, yet not all do so in an equal degree, for this depends upon what the Lord is pleased to grant to each one. It is in this way that souls see God in Heaven; some more, some less; but all see Him, and all are content, for their capacity is satisfied.

11. Wherefore, although in this life here below we find certain souls enjoying equal peace and tranquillity in the state of perfection, and each one of them satisfied, yet some of them may be many degrees higher than others. All, however, will be equally satisfied, because the capacity of each one is satisfied. But the soul that attains not to such a measure of purity as is in conformity with its capacity never attains true peace and satisfaction, since it has not attained to the possession of that detachment and emptiness in its faculties which is required for simple union.

Footnotes:

231. As the Saint has explained above, this is a parenthetical chapter necessary to an understanding of the following chapters on the active purification of the three faculties of the soul; for, in order to make an intelligent use of the means to an end, it is important to know what that end is. St. John of the Cross begins by setting aside the numerous divisions under which the mystics speak of union with God and deals only with that which most usually concerns the soul, namely union which is active, and acquired by our own efforts, together with the habitual aid of grace. This is the kind of union which is most suitably described in this treatise, which deals with the intense activity of the soul as regards the purgation of the senses and faculties as a necessary means for the loving transformation of the soul in God -- the end and goal of all the Saint's writings. In order to forestall any grossly erroneous pantheistic interpretations, we point out, with the author of the Médula Mística (Trat. V, Chap. i, No. 2), that by union the Saint understands a linking and conjoining of two things which, though united, are still different, each, as St. Thomas teaches (Pt. III, q. 2, a. 1), keeping its own nature, for otherwise there would not be union but identity. Union of the soul with God, therefore, will be a linking and conjoining of the soul with God and of God with the soul, for the one cannot be united with the other if the other be not united with the one, so that the soul is still the soul and God is still God. But just as, when two things are united, the one which has the most power, virtue and activity communicates its properties to the other, just so, since God has greater strength, virtue and activity than the soul, He communicates His properties to it and makes it, as it were, deific, and leaves it, as it were, divinized, to a greater or a lesser degree, corresponding to the greater or the lesser degree of union between the two.' This conception, which is a basic one in Christian mysticism, is that of St. John of the Cross. Had all his commentators understood that fact, some of them would have been saved from making ridiculous comparisons of him with Gnostics, Illuminists or even the Eastern seekers after Nirvana. Actually, this Saint and Doctor of the Church applies the tenets of Catholic theology to the union of the soul with God, presenting them in a condensed and vigorous form and keeping also to strict psychological truth, as in general do the other Spanish mystics. This is one of his greatest merits. In this chapter he is speaking, not of essential union, which has nothing to do with his subject, but (presupposing the union worked through sanctifying grace received in the substance of the soul, which is the source of the infused virtues, such as faith, hope and charity, and the gifts of the Holy Spirit) of active actual union, after which we can and should strive, so that we may will what God wills and abhor what He abhors. Though not the only kind of union, it is this which chiefly concerns the soul; and, when once this is attained, God readily grants all other mystical gifts. Cf. St. Teresa's Interior Castle, V, iii [C.W.S.T.J., II, 259-60].

232. [Lit., is clothed with.']
233. St. John i, 13.
234. St. John iii, 5.
235. [Lit., wholly perfect and . . .']

CHAPTER VI

Wherein is described how it is the three theological virtues that perfect the three faculties of the soul, and how the said virtues produce emptiness and darkness within them.

Having now to endeavour to show how [236] the three faculties of the soul -- understanding, memory and will -- are brought into this spiritual night, which is the means to Divine union, it is necessary first of all to explain in this chapter how the three theological virtues -- faith, hope and charity -- which have respect to the three faculties aforesaid as their proper supernatural objects, and by means whereof the soul is united with God according to its faculties, produce the same emptiness and darkness, each one in its own faculty. Faith, in the understanding; hope, in the memory; and charity, in the will. And afterwards we shall go on to describe how the understanding is perfected in the darkness of faith; and the memory in the emptiness of hope; and likewise how the will must be buried by withdrawing and detaching every affection so that the soul may journey to God. This done, it will be clearly seen how necessary it is for the soul, if it is to walk securely on this spiritual road, to travel through this dark night, leaning upon these three virtues, which empty it of all things and make it dark with respect to them. For, as we have said, the soul is not united with God in this life through understanding, nor through enjoyment, nor through the imagination, nor through any sense whatsoever; but only through faith, according to the understanding; and through hope, according to the memory; and through love, according to the will.

2. These three virtues, as we have said, all cause emptiness in the faculties: faith, in the understanding, causes an emptiness and darkness with respect to understanding; hope, in the memory, causes emptiness of all possessions; and charity causes emptiness in the will and detachment from all affection and from rejoicing in all that is not God. For, as we see, faith tells us what cannot be understood with the understanding. Wherefore Saint Paul spoke of it ad Hebraeos after this manner: Fides est sperandarum substantia rerum, argumentum non apparentium. [237] This we interpret as meaning that faith is the substance of things hoped for; and, although the understanding may be firmly and certainly consenting to them, they are not things that are revealed to the understanding, since, if they were revealed to it, there would be no faith. So faith, although it brings certainty to the understanding, brings it not clearness, but obscurity.

3. Then, as to hope, there is no doubt but that it renders the memory empty and dark with respect both to things below and to things above. For hope always relates to that which is not possessed; for, if it were possessed, there would be no more hope. Wherefore Saint Paul says ad Romanos: Spes, quae videtur, non est spes: nam quod videt quis, quid sperat? [238] That is to say: Hope that is seen is not hope; for what a man seeth -- that is, what a man possesseth -- how doth he hope for it? This virtue, then, also produces emptiness, for it has to do with that which is not possessed and not with that which is possessed.

4. Similarity, charity causes emptiness in the will with respect to all things, since it obliges us to love God above them all; which cannot be unless we withdraw our affection from them in order to set it wholly upon God. Wherefore Christ says, through Saint Luke: Qui non renuntiat omnibus quae possidet, non potest meus esse discipulus. [239] Which signifies: He that renounces not all that he possesses with the will cannot be My disciple. And thus all these three virtues set the soul in obscurity and emptiness with respect to all things.

5. And here we must consider that parable which our Redeemer related in the eleventh chapter of Saint Luke, wherein He said that a friend had to go out at midnight in order to ask his friend for three loaves; [240] the which loaves signify these three virtues. And he said that he asked for them at midnight in order to signify that the soul that is in darkness as to all things must acquire these three virtues according to its faculties and must perfect itself in them in this night. In the sixth chapter of Isaias we read that the two seraphim whom this Prophet saw on either side of God had each six wings; with two they covered their feet, which signified the blinding and quenching of the affections of the will with respect to all things for the sake of God; and with two they covered their face, which signified the darkness of the understanding in the presence of God; and with the other two they flew. [241] This is to signify the flight of hope to the things that are not possessed, when it is raised above all that it can possess, whether below or above, apart from God.

6. To these three virtues, then, we have to lead the three faculties of the soul, informing each faculty by each one of them, and stripping it and setting it in darkness concerning all things save only

these three virtues. And this is the spiritual night which just now we called active; for the soul does that which in it lies in order to enter therein. And even as, in the night of sense, we described a method of voiding the faculties of sense of their sensible objects, with regard to the desire, so that the soul might go forth from the beginning of its course to the mean, [242] which is faith; even so, in this spiritual night, with the favour of God, we shall describe a method whereby the spiritual faculties are voided and purified of all that is not God, and are set in darkness concerning these three virtues, which, as we have said, are the means and preparation for the union of the soul with God.

7. In this method is found all security against the crafts of the devil and against the efficacy of self-love and its ramifications, which is wont most subtly to deceive and hinder spiritual persons on their road, when they know not how to become detached and to govern themselves according to these three virtues; and thus they are never able to reach the substance and purity of spiritual good, nor do they journey by so straight and short a road as they might.

8. And it must be noted that I am now speaking particularly to those who have begun to enter the state of contemplation, because as far as this concerns beginners it must be described somewhat more amply, as we shall note in the second book, God willing, when we treat of the properties of these beginners.

Footnotes:

236. [Lit., to lead . . . into,' as at the beginning of 6, below.]
237. Hebrews xi, 1.
238. Romans viii, 24.
239. St. Luke xiv, 33.
240. Luke xi, 5.
241. Isaias vi, 2.
242. [Or middle.' Cf. Bk. I, chap. ii, above.]

CHAPTER VII

Wherein is described how strait is the way that leads to eternal life and how completely detached and disencumbered must be those that will walk in it. We begin to speak of the detachment of the understanding.

We have now to describe the detachment and purity of the three faculties of the soul and for this are necessary a far greater knowledge and spirituality than mine, in order to make clear to spiritual persons how strait is this road which, said Our Saviour, leads to life; so that, persuaded of this, they may not marvel at the emptiness and detachment to which, in this night, we have to abandon the faculties of the soul.

2. To this end must be carefully noted the words which Our Saviour used, in the seventh chapter of Saint Matthew, concerning this road, as follows: Quam angusta porta, et arcta via est, quae ducit ad vitam, et pauci sunt, qui inveniunt eam. [243] This signifies: How strait is the gate and how narrow the way that leadeth unto life, and few there are that find it! In this passage we must carefully note the emphasis and insistence which are contained in that word Quam. For it is as if He had said: In truth the way is very strait, more so than you think. And likewise it is to be noted that He says first that the gate is strait, to make it clear that, in order for the soul to enter by this gate, which is Christ, and which comes at the beginning of the road, the will must first be straitened and detached in all things sensual and temporal, and God must be loved above them all; which belongs to the night of sense, as we have said.

3. He then says that the way is narrow -- that is to say, the way of perfection -- in order to make it clear that, to travel upon the way of perfection, the soul has not only to enter by the strait gate, emptying itself of things of sense, but has also to straiten [244] itself, freeing and disencumbering itself completely in that which pertains to the spirit. And thus we can apply what He says of the strait gate to the sensual part of man; and what He says of the narrow road we can understand of the spiritual or the rational part; and, when He says Few there are that find it,' the reason of this must be noted, which is that there are few who can enter, and desire to enter, into this complete detachment and emptiness of spirit. For this path ascending the high mountain of perfection leads upward, and is narrow, and therefore requires travellers that have no burden weighing upon them with respect to lower things, neither aught that embarrasses them with respect to higher things: and, as this is a matter wherein we must seek after and attain to God alone, God alone must be the object of our search and attainment.

4. Hence it is clearly seen that the soul must not only be disencumbered from that which belongs to the creatures, but likewise, as it travels, must be annihilated and detached from all that belongs to its spirit. Wherefore Our Lord, instructing us and leading us into this road, gave, in the eighth chapter of St. Mark, that wonderful teaching of which I think it may almost be said that, the more necessary it is for spiritual persons, the less it is practised by them. As this teaching is so important and so much to our purpose, I shall reproduce it here in full, and expound it according to its genuine, spiritual sense. He says, then, thus: Si quis vult me sequi, deneget semetipsum: et tollat crucem suam, et sequatur me. Qui enim voluerit animam suam salvam facere, perdet eam: qui autem perdiderit animam suam propter me. . . salvam lacier eam. [245] This signifies: If any man will follow My road, let him deny himself and take up his cross and follow Me. For he that will save his soul shall lose it; but he that loses it for My sake, shall gain it.

5. Oh, that one could show us how to understand, practise and experience what this counsel is which our Saviour here gives us concerning self-denial, [246] so that spiritual persons might see in how different a way they should conduct themselves upon this road from that which many of them think proper! For they believe that any kind of retirement and reformation of life suffices; and others are content with practising the virtues and continuing in prayer and pursuing mortification; but they attain not to detachment and poverty or selflessness [247] or spiritual purity (which are all one), which the Lord here commends to us; for they prefer feeding and clothing their natural selves with spiritual feelings and consolations, to stripping themselves of all things, and denying themselves all things, for God's sake. For they think that it suffices to deny themselves worldly things without annihilating and purifying themselves of spiritual attachment. Wherefore it comes to pass that, when there presents itself to them any of this solid and perfect spirituality, consisting in the annihilation of all sweetness in God, in aridity, distaste and trial, which is the true spiritual cross, and the detachment of the spiritual poverty of Christ, they flee from it as from death, and seek only sweetness and delectable communion with God. This is not self-denial and detachment of spirit, but spiritual gluttony. Herein, spiritually, they become enemies

of the Cross of Christ; for true spirituality seeks for God's sake that which is distasteful rather than that which is delectable; and inclines itself rather to suffering than to consolation; and desires to go without all blessings for God's sake rather than to possess them; and to endure aridities and afflictions rather than to enjoy sweet communications, knowing that this is to follow Christ and to deny oneself, and that the other is perchance to seek oneself in God, which is clean contrary to love. For to seek oneself in God is to seek the favours and refreshments of God; but to seek God in oneself is not only to desire to be without both of these for God's sake, but to be disposed to choose, for Christ's sake, all that is most distasteful, whether in relation to God or to the world; and this is love of God.

6. Oh, that one could tell us how far Our Lord desires this self-denial to be carried! It must certainly be like to death and annihilation, temporal, natural and spiritual, in all things that the will esteems, wherein consists all self-denial. And it is this that Our Lord meant when He said: He that will save his life, the same shall lose it.' That is to say: He that will possess anything or seek anything for himself, the same shall lose it; and he that loses his soul for My sake, the same shall gain it. That is to say: He who for Christ's sake renounces all that his will can desire and enjoy, and chooses that which is most like to the Cross (which the Lord Himself, through Saint John, describes as hating his soul [248]), the same shall gain it. And this His Majesty taught to those two disciples who went and begged Him for a place on His right hand and on His left; when, giving no countenance to their request for such glory, He offered them the chalice which He had to drink, as a thing more precious and more secure upon this earth than is fruition. [249]

7. This chalice is death to the natural self, a death attained through the detachment and annihilation of that self, in order that the soul may travel by this narrow path, with respect to all its connections with sense, as we have said, and according to the spirit, as we shall now say; that is, in its understanding and in its enjoyment and in its feeling. And, as a result, not only has the soul made its renunciation as regards both sense and spirit, but it is not hindered, even by that which is spiritual, in taking the narrow way, on which there is room only for self-denial (as the Saviour explains), and the Cross, which is the staff wherewith one may reach one's goal, and whereby the road is greatly lightened and made easy. Wherefore Our Lord said through Saint Matthew: My yoke is easy and My burden is light'; which burden is the cross. For if a man resolve to submit himself to carrying this cross -- that is to say, if he resolve to desire in truth to meet trials and to bear them in all things for God's sake, he will find in them all great relief and sweetness wherewith he may travel upon this road, detached from all things and desiring nothing. Yet, if he desire to possess anything -- whether it come from God or from any other source -- with any feeling of attachment, he has not stripped and denied himself in all things; and thus he will be unable to walk along this narrow path or to climb upward by it.

8. I would, then, that I could convince spiritual persons that this road to God consists not in a multiplicity of meditations nor in ways or methods of such, nor in consolations, although these things may in their own way be necessary to beginners; but that it consists only in the one thing that is needful, which is the ability to deny oneself truly, according to that which is without and to that which is within, giving oneself up to suffering for Christ's sake, and to total annihilation. For the soul that practises this suffering and annihilation will achieve all that those other exercises can achieve, and that can be found in them, and even more. And if a soul be found wanting in this exercise, which is the sum and root of the virtues, all its other methods are so much beating about the bush, and profiting not at all, although its meditations and communications may be as lofty as those of the angels. For progress comes not save through the imitation of Christ, Who is the Way, the Truth and the Life, and no man comes to the Father but by Him, even as He Himself says through Saint John. [250] And elsewhere He says: I am the door; by Me if any man enter he shall be saved.' [251] Wherefore, as it seems to me, any spirituality that would fain walk in sweetness and with ease, and flees from the imitation of Christ, is worthless.

9. And, as I have said that Christ is the Way, and that this Way is death to our natural selves, in things both of sense and of spirit, I will now explain how we are to die, following the example of Christ, for He is our example and light.

10. In the first place, it is certain that He died as to sense, spiritually, in His life, besides dying naturally, at His death. For, as He said, He had not in His life where to lay His head, and at His death this was even truer.

11. In the second place, it is certain that, at the moment of His death, He was likewise annihilated in His soul, and was deprived of any relief and consolation, since His Father left Him in the most intense aridity, according to the lower part of His nature. Wherefore He had perforce to cry out, saying: My God! My God! Why hast Thou forsaken Me?' [252] This was the greatest desolation, with respect to sense, that He had suffered in His life. And thus He wrought herein the greatest work that He had ever wrought, whether in miracles or in mighty works, during the whole of His life, either upon earth or in Heaven, which was the reconciliation and union of mankind, through grace, with God. And this, as I say, was at the moment and the time when this Lord was most completely annihilated in everything. Annihilated, that is to say, with respect to human reputation; since, when men saw Him die, they mocked Him rather than esteemed Him; and also with respect to nature, since His nature was

Ascent of Mount Carmel

annihilated when He died; and further with respect to the spiritual consolation and protection of the Father, since at that time He forsook Him, that He might pay the whole of man's debt and unite him with God, being thus annihilated and reduced as it were to nothing. Wherefore David says concerning Him: Ad nihilum redactus sum, et nescivi. [253] This he said that the truly spiritual man may understand the mystery of the gate and of the way of Christ, and so become united with God, and may know that, the more completely he is annihilated for God's sake, according to these two parts, the sensual and the spiritual, the more completely is he united to God and the greater is the work which he accomplishes. And when at last he is reduced to nothing, which will be the greatest extreme of humility, spiritual union will be wrought between the soul and God, which in this life is the greatest and the highest state attainable. This consists not, then, in refreshment and in consolations and spiritual feelings, but in a living death of the Cross, both as to sense and as to spirit -- that is, both inwardly and outwardly.

12. I will not pursue this subject farther, although I have no desire to finish speaking of it, for I see that Christ is known very little by those who consider themselves His friends: we see them seeking in Him their own pleasures and consolations because of their great love for themselves, but not loving His bitter trials and His death because of their great love for Him. I am speaking now of those who consider themselves His friends; for such as live far away, withdrawn from Him, men of great learning and influence, and all others who live yonder, with the world, and are eager about their ambitions and their prelacies, may be said not to know Christ; and their end, however good, will be very bitter. Of such I make no mention in these lines; but mention will be made of them on the Day of Judgment, for to them it was fitting to speak first this word of God, [254] as to those whom God set up as a target for it, [255] by reason of their learning and their high position.

13. But let us now address the understanding of the spiritual man, and particularly that of the man to whom God has granted the favour of leading him into the state of contemplation (for, as I have said, I am now speaking to these in particular), and let us say how such a man must direct himself toward God in faith, and purify himself from contrary things, constraining himself that he may enter upon this narrow path of obscure contemplation.

Footnotes:

243. St. Matthew vii, 14.

244. [The Spanish verb, used also at the end of the preceding paragraph, is derived from the adjective.]

245. St. Mark viii, 34-5.

246. [Lit., the denial of ourselves to our very selves.']

247. [enagenación, a word which to-day means alienation,' rapture,' derangement (of mind),' but in Covarrubias' dictionary (1611) is also defined as giving to another what is one's own.']

248. St. John xii, 25.

249. St. Matthew xx, 22.

250. John xiv, 6.

251. St. John x, 9.

252. St. Matthew xxvii, 46.

253. Psalm lxxii, 22 [A.V., lxxiii, 22].

254. [The reference seems to be to Acts xiii, 46, the point of it being in the second part of that verse. The Spanish will also bear the interpretation: for them it behoved first (i.e., before others) to speak this word of God, as (being) those whom God set up as guides, etc.']

255. [By this vivid phrase the author seems to mean: whom God held to be suitable recipients of it.']

CHAPTER VIII

Which describes in a general way how no creature and no knowledge that can be comprehended by the understanding can serve as a proximate means of Divine union with God.

Before we treat of the proper and fitting means of union with God, which is faith, it behoves us to prove how no thing, created or imagined, can serve the understanding as a proper means of union with God; and how all that the understanding can attain serves it rather as an impediment than as such a means, if it should desire to cling to it. And now, in this chapter, we shall prove this in a general way, and afterwards we shall begin to speak in detail, treating in turn of all kinds of knowledge that the understanding may receive from any sense, whether inward or outward, and of the inconveniences and evils that may result from all these kinds of inward and outward knowledge, when it clings not, as it progresses, to the proper means, which is faith.

2. It must be understood, then, that, according to a rule of philosophy, all means must be proportioned to the end; that is to say, they must have some connection and resemblance with the end, such as is enough and sufficient for the desired end to be attained through them. I take an example. A man desires to reach a city; he has of necessity to travel by the road, which is the means that brings him to this same city and connects [256] him with it. Another example. Fire is to be combined and united with wood; it is necessary that heat, which is the means, shall first prepare the wood, by conveying to it so many degrees of warmth that it will have great resemblance and proportion to fire. Now if one would prepare the wood by any other than the proper means -- namely, with heat -- as, for example, with air or water or earth, it would be impossible for the wood to be united with the fire, just as it would be to reach the city without going by the road that leads to it. Wherefore, in order that the understanding may be united with God in this life, so far as is possible, it must of necessity employ that means that unites it with Him and that bears the greatest resemblance to Him.

3. Here it must be pointed out that, among all the creatures, the highest or the lowest, there is none that comes near to God or bears any resemblance to His Being. For, although it is true that all creatures have, as theologians say, a certain relation to God, and bear a Divine impress (some more and others less, according to the greater or lesser excellence of their nature), yet there is no essential resemblance or connection between them and God -- on the contrary, the distance between their being and His Divine Being is infinite. Wherefore it is impossible for the understanding to attain to God by means of the creatures, whether these be celestial or earthly, inasmuch as there is no proportion or resemblance between them. Wherefore, when David speaks of the heavenly creatures, he says: There is none among the gods like unto Thee, O Lord'; [257] meaning by the gods the angels and holy souls. And elsewhere: O God, Thy way is in the holy place. What God is there so great as our God?' [258] As though he were to say: The way of approach to Thee, O God, is a holy way -- that is, the purity of faith. For what God can there be so great? That is to say: What angel will there be so exalted in his being, and what saint so exalted in glory, as to be a proportionate and sufficient road by which a man may come to Thee? And the same David, speaking likewise of earthly and heavenly things both together, says: The Lord is high and looketh on lowly things, and the high things He knoweth afar off' [259] As though he had said: Lofty in His own Being, He sees that the being of things here below is very low in comparison with His lofty Being; and the lofty things, which are the celestial creatures, He sees and knows to be very far from His Being. All the creatures, then, cannot serve as a proportionate means to the understanding whereby it may reach God.

4. Just so all that the imagination can imagine and the understanding can receive and understand in this life is not, nor can it be, a proximate means of union with God. For, if we speak of natural things, since understanding can understand naught save that which is contained within, and comes under the category of, forms and imaginings of things that are received through the bodily senses, the which things, we have said, cannot serve as means, it can make no use of natural intelligence. And, if we speak of the supernatural (in so far as is possible in this life of our ordinary faculties), the understanding in its bodily prison has no preparation or capacity for receiving the clear knowledge of God; for such knowledge belongs not to this state, and we must either die or remain without receiving it. Wherefore Moses, when he entreated God for this clear knowledge, was told by God that he would be unable to see Him, in these words: No man shall see Me and remain alive.' [260] Wherefore Saint John says: No man hath seen God at any time, [261] neither aught that is like to Him.' And Saint Paul says, with Isaias: Eye hath not seen Him, nor hath ear heard Him, neither hath it entered into the heart of man.' [262] And it is for

this reason that, as is said in the Acts of the Apostles, [263] Moses, in the bush, durst not consider for as long as God was present; for he knew that his understanding could make no consideration that was fitting concerning God, corresponding to the sense which he had of God's presence. And of Elias, our father, it is said that he covered his face on the Mount in the presence of God [264] -- an action signifying the blinding of his understanding, which he wrought there, daring not to lay so base a hand upon that which was so high, and seeing clearly that whatsoever he might consider or understand with any precision would be very far from God and completely unlike Him.

5. Wherefore no supernatural apprehension or knowledge in this mortal state can serve as a proximate means to the high union of love with God. For all that can be understood by the understanding, that can be tasted by the will, and that can be invented by the imagination is most unlike to God and bears no proportion to Him, as we have said. All this Isaias admirably explained in that most noteworthy passage, where he says: To what thing have ye been able to liken God? Or what image will ye make that is like to Him? Will the workman in iron perchance be able to make a graven image? Or will he that works gold be able to imitate Him [265] with gold, or the silversmith with plates of silver?' [266] By the workman in iron is signified the understanding, the office of which is to form intelligences and strip them of the iron of species and images. By the workman in gold is understood the will, which is able to receive the figure and the form of pleasure, caused by the gold of love. By the silversmith, who is spoken of as being unable to form [267] Him with plates of silver, is understood the memory, with the imagination, whereof it may be said with great propriety that its knowledge and the imaginings that it can invent [268] and make are like plates of silver. And thus it is as though he had said: Neither the understanding with its intelligence will be able to understand aught that is like Him, nor can the will taste pleasure and sweetness that bears any resemblance to that which is God, neither can the memory set in the imagination ideas and images that represent Him. It is clear, then, that none of these kinds of knowledge can lead the understanding direct to God; and that, in order to reach Him, a soul must rather proceed by not understanding than by desiring to understand; and by blinding itself and setting itself in darkness, rather than by opening its eyes, in order the more nearly to approach the ray Divine.

6. And thus it is that contemplation, whereby the understanding has the loftiest knowledge of God, is called mystical theology, which signifies secret wisdom of God; for it is secret even to the understanding that receives it. For that reason Saint Dionysius calls it a ray of darkness. Of this the prophet Baruch says: There is none that knoweth its way, nor any that can think of its paths.' [269] It is clear, then, that the understanding must be blind to all paths that are open to it in order that it may be united with God. Aristotle says that, even as are the eyes of the bat with regard to the sun, which is total darkness to it, even so is our understanding to that which is greater light in God, which is total darkness to us. And he says further that, the loftier and clearer are the things of God in themselves, the more completely unknown and obscure are they to us. This likewise the Apostle affirms, saying: The lofty things of God are the least known unto men.' [270]

7. But we should never end if we continued at this rate to quote authorities and arguments to prove and make clear that among all created things, and things that can be apprehended by the understanding, there is no ladder whereby the understanding can attain to this high Lord. Rather it is necessary to know that, if the understanding should seek to make use of all these things, or of any of them, as a proximate means to such union, they would be not only a hindrance, but even an occasion of numerous errors and delusions in the ascent of this mount.

Footnotes:

256. [Lit., unite.']
257. Psalm lxxxv, 8 [A.V., lxxxvi, 8].
258. Psalm lxxvi, 14 [A.V., lxxvii, 13] [lit., in that which is holy'].
259. Psalm cxxxvii, 6 [A.V., cxxxviii, 6].
260. Exodus xxxiii, 20.
261. St. John i, 18.
262. 1 Corinthians ii, 9; Isaias lxiv, 4.
263. Acts vii, 32.
264. 3 Kings [A.V., 1 Kings] xix, 13.
265. [Lit., feign Him.']
266. Isaias xl, 18-19.
267. [All authorities read form' (or figure') here. Cf. n. 7, above.]
268. [This is the word (fingir, feign'), translated above as imitate.' Cf. n. 7, above.]
269. Baruch iii, 23.
270. [Possibly a further reference to 1 Corinthians ii, 9-10, quoted above.]

CHAPTER IX

How faith is the proximate and proportionate means to the understanding whereby the soul may attain to the Divine union of love. This is proved by passages and figures from Divine Scripture.

From what has been said it is to be inferred that, in order for the understanding to be prepared for this Divine union, it must be pure and void of all that pertains to sense, and detached and freed from all that can clearly be apprehended by the understanding, profoundly hushed and put to silence, and leaning upon faith, which alone is the proximate and proportionate means whereby the soul is united with God; for such is the likeness between itself and God that there is no other difference, save that which exists between seeing God and believing in Him. For, even as God is infinite, so faith sets Him before us as infinite; and, as He is Three and One, it sets Him before us as Three and One; and, as God is darkness to our understanding, even so does faith likewise blind and dazzle our understanding. And thus, by this means alone, God manifests Himself to the soul in Divine light, which passes all understanding. And therefore, the greater is the faith of the soul, the more closely is it united with God. It is this that Saint Paul meant in the passage which we quoted above, where he says: He that will be united with God must believe.' [271] That is, he must walk by faith as he journeys to Him, the understanding being blind and in darkness, walking in faith alone; for beneath this darkness the understanding is united with God, and beneath it God is hidden, even as David said in these words: He set darkness under His feet. And He rose upon the cherubim, and flew upon the wings of the wind. And He made darkness, and the dark water, His hiding-place.' [272]

2. By his saying that He set darkness beneath His feet, and that He took the darkness for a hiding-place, and that His tabernacle round about Him was in the dark water, is denoted the obscurity of the faith wherein He is concealed. And by his saying that He rose upon the cherubim and flew upon the wings of the winds, is understood His soaring above all understanding. For the cherubim denote those who understand or contemplate. And the wings of the winds signify the subtle and lofty ideas and conceptions of spirits, above all of which is His Being, and to which none, by his own power, can attain.

3. This we learn from an illustration in the Scriptures. When Solomon had completed the building of the Temple, God came down in darkness and filled the Temple so that the children of Israel could not see; whereupon Solomon spake and said: The Lord hath promised that He will dwell in darkness'. [273] Likewise He appeared in darkness to Moses on the Mount, where God was concealed. And whensoever God communicated Himself intimately, He appeared in darkness, as may be seen in Job, where the Scripture says that God spoke with him from the darkness of the air. [274] All these mentions of darkness signify the obscurity of the faith wherein the Divinity is concealed, when It communicates Itself to the soul; which will be ended when, as Saint Paul says, that which is in part shall be ended, [275] which is this darkness of faith, and that which is perfect shall come, which is the Divine light. Of this we have a good illustration in the army of Gedeon, whereof it is said all the soldiers had lamps in their hands, which they saw not, because they had them concealed in the darkness of the pitchers; but, when these pitchers were broken, the light was seen. [276] Just so does faith, which is foreshadowed by those pitchers, contain within itself Divine light; which, when it is ended and broken, at the ending and breaking of this mortal life, will allow the glory and light of the Divinity, which was contained in it, to appear.

4. It is clear, then, that, if the soul in this life is to attain to union with God, and commune directly with Him, it must unite itself with the darkness whereof Solomon spake, wherein God had promised to dwell, and must draw near to the darkness of the air wherein God was pleased to reveal His secrets to Job, and must take in its hands, in darkness, the jars of Gedeon, that it may have in its hands (that is, in the works of its will) the light, which is the union of love, though it be in the darkness of faith, so that, when the pitchers of this life are broken, which alone have kept from it the light of faith, it may see God face to face in glory.

5. It now remains to describe in detail all the types of knowledge and the apprehensions which the understanding can receive; the hindrance and the harm which it can receive upon this road of faith; and the way wherein the soul must conduct itself so that, whether they proceed from the senses or from the spirit, they may cause it, not harm, but profit.

Footnotes:

271. Hebrews xi, 6.
272. Psalm xvii, 10-12 [A.V., xviii, 9-11].
273. 3 Kings [A.V., 1 Kings] viii, 12.
274. Job xxxviii, 1; xl, 1.
275. 1 Corinthians xiii, 10.
276. Judges viii, 16.

CHAPTER X

Wherein distinction is made between all apprehensions and types of knowledge which can be comprehended by the understanding.

In order to treat in detail of the profit and the harm which may come to the soul, with respect to this means to Divine union which we have described -- namely, faith -- through the ideas and apprehensions of the understanding, it is necessary here to make a distinction between all the apprehensions, whether natural or supernatural, that the soul may receive, so that then, with regard to each of them in order, we may direct the understanding with greater clearness into the night and obscurity of faith. This will be done with all possible brevity.

2. It must be known, then, that the understanding can receive knowledge and intelligence by two channels: the one natural and the other supernatural. By the natural channel is meant all that the understanding can understand, whether by means of the bodily senses or by its own power. [277] The supernatural channel is all that is given to the understanding over and above its natural ability and capacity.

3. Of these kinds of supernatural knowledge, some are corporeal and some are spiritual. The corporeal are two in number: some are received by means of the outward bodily senses; others, by means of the inward bodily senses, wherein is comprehended all that the imagination can comprehend, form and conceive.

4. The spiritual supernatural knowledge is likewise of two kinds: that which is distinct and special in its nature, and that which is confused, general and dark. Of the distinct and special kind there are four manners of apprehension which are communicated to the spirit without the aid of any bodily sense: these are visions, revelations, locutions and spiritual feelings. The obscure and general type of knowledge is of one kind alone, which is contemplation that is given in faith. To this we have to lead the soul by bringing it thereto through all these other means, beginning with the first and detaching it from them.

Footnotes:
  277. [Lit., 'by itself.']

CHAPTER XI

Of the hindrance and harm that may be caused by apprehensions of the understanding which proceed from that which is supernaturally represented to the outward bodily senses; and how the soul is to conduct itself therein.

The first kinds of knowledge whereof we have spoken in the preceding chapter are those that belong to the understanding and come through natural channels. Of these, since we have treated them already in the first book, where we led the soul into the night of sense, we shall here say not a word, for in that place we gave suitable instruction to the soul concerning them. What we have to treat, therefore, in the present chapter, will be solely those kinds of knowledge and those apprehensions which belong to the understanding and come supernaturally, by way of the outward bodily senses -- namely, by seeing, hearing, smelling, tasting and touching. With respect to all these there may come, and there are wont to come, to spiritual persons representations and objects of a supernatural kind. With respect to sight, they are apt to picture figures and forms of persons belonging to the life to come -- the forms of certain saints, and representations of angels, good and evil, and certain lights and brightnesses of an extraordinary kind. And with the ears they hear certain extraordinary words, sometimes spoken by those figures that they see, sometimes without seeing the person who speaks them. As to the sense of smell, they sometimes perceive the sweetest perfumes with the senses, without knowing whence they proceed. Likewise, as to taste, it comes to pass that they are conscious of the sweetest savours, and, as to touch, they experience great delight -- sometimes to such a degree that it is as though all the bones and the marrow rejoice and sing [278] and are bathed in delight; this is like that which we call spiritual unction, which in pure souls proceeds from the spirit and flows into the very members. And this sensible sweetness is a very ordinary thing with spiritual persons, for it comes to them from their sensible affection and devotion, [279] to a greater or a lesser degree, to each one after his own manner.

2. And it must be known that, although all these things may happen to the bodily senses in the way of God, we must never rely upon them or accept them, but must always fly from them, without trying to ascertain whether they be good or evil; for, the more completely exterior and corporeal they are, the less certainly are they of God. For it is more proper and habitual to God to communicate Himself to the spirit, wherein there is more security and profit for the soul, than to sense, wherein there is ordinarily much danger and deception; for bodily sense judges and makes its estimate of spiritual things by thinking that they are as it feels them to be, whereas they are as different as is the body from the soul and sensuality [280] from reason. For the bodily sense is as ignorant of spiritual things as is a beast of rational things, and even more so.

3. So he that esteems such things errs greatly and exposes himself to great peril of being deceived; in any case he will have within himself a complete impediment to the attainment of spirituality. For, as we have said, between spiritual things and all these bodily things there exists no kind of proportion whatever. And thus it may always be supposed that such things as these are more likely to be of the devil than of God; for the devil has more influence in that which is exterior and corporeal, and can deceive a soul more easily thereby than by that which is more interior and spiritual.

4. And the more exterior are these corporeal forms and objects in themselves, the less do they profit the interior and spiritual nature, because of the great distance and the lack of proportion existing between the corporeal and the spiritual. For, although there is communicated by their means a certain degree of spirituality, as is always the case with things that come from God, much less is communicated than would be the case if the same things were more interior and spiritual. And thus they very easily become the means whereby error and presumption and vanity grow in the soul; since, as they are so palpable and material, they stir the senses greatly, and it appears to the judgment of the soul that they are of greater importance because they are more readily felt. Thus the soul goes after them, abandoning faith and thinking that the light which it receives from them is the guide and means to its desired goal, which is union with God. But the more attention it pays to such things, the farther it strays from the true way and means, which are faith.

5. And, besides all this, when the soul sees that such extraordinary things happen to it, it is often visited, insidiously and secretly by a certain complacency, so that it thinks itself to be of some importance in the eyes of God; which is contrary to humility. The devil, too, knows how to insinuate into the soul a secret satisfaction with itself, which at times becomes very evident; wherefore he frequently represents these objects to the senses, setting before the eyes figures of saints and most

beauteous lights; and before the ears words very much dissembled; and representing also sweetest perfumes, delicious tastes [281] and things delectable to the touch; to the end that, by producing desires for such things, he may lead the soul into much evil. These representations and feelings, therefore, must always be rejected; for, even though some of them be of God, He is not offended by their rejection, nor is the effect and fruit which He desires to produce in the soul by means of them any the less surely received because the soul rejects them and desires them not.

6. The reason for this is that corporeal vision, or feeling in respect to any of the other senses, or any other communication of the most interior kind, if it be of God, produces its effect upon the spirit at the very moment when it appears or is felt, without giving the soul time or opportunity to deliberate whether it will accept or reject it. For, even as God gives these things supernaturally, without effort on the part of the soul, and independently of its capacity, even so likewise, without respect to its effort or capacity, God produces in it the effect that He desires by means of such things; for this is a thing that is wrought and brought to pass in the spirit passively; and thus its acceptance or non-acceptance consists not in the acceptance or the rejection of it by the will. It is as though fire were applied to a person's naked body: it would matter little whether or no he wished to be burned; the fire would of necessity accomplish its work. Just so is it with visions and representations that are good: even though the soul desire it not, they work their effect upon it, chiefly and especially in the soul, rather than in the body. And likewise those that come from the devil (without the consent of the soul) cause it disturbance or aridity or vanity or presumption in the spirit. Yet these are not so effective to work evil as are those of God to work good; for those of the devil can only set in action the first movements of the will, [282] and move it no farther, unless the soul be consenting thereto; and such trouble continues not long unless the soul's lack of courage and prudence be the occasion of its continuance. But the visions that are of God penetrate the soul and move the will to love, and produce their effect, which the soul cannot resist even though it would, any more than the window can resist the sun's rays when they strike

7. The soul, then, must never presume to desire to receive them, even though, as I say, they be of God; for, if it desire to receive them, there follow six inconveniences.

The first is that faith grows gradually less; for things that are experienced by the senses derogate from faith; since faith, as we have said, transcends every sense. And thus the soul withdraws itself from the means of union with God when it closes not its eyes to all these things of sense.

Secondly, if they be not rejected, they are a hindrance to the spirit, for the soul rests in them and its spirit soars not to the invisible. This was one of the reasons why the Lord said to His disciples that it was needful for Him to go away that the Holy Spirit might come; so, too, He forbade Mary Magdalene to touch His feet, after His resurrection, that she might be grounded in faith.

Thirdly, the soul becomes attached to these things and advances not to true resignation and detachment of spirit.

Fourthly, it begins to lose the effect of them and the inward spirituality which they cause it, because it sets its eyes upon their sensual aspect, which is the least important. And thus it receives not so fully the spirituality which they cause, which is impressed and preserved more securely when all things of sense are rejected, since these are very different from pure spirit.

Fifthly, the soul begins to lose the favours of God, because it accepts them as though they belonged to it and profits not by them as it should. And to accept them in this way and not to profit by them is to seek after them; but God gives them not that the soul may seek after them; nor should the soul take upon itself to believe that they are of God. [283]

Sixthly, a readiness to accept them opens the door to the devil that he may deceive the soul by other things like to them, which he very well knows how to dissimulate and disguise, so that they may appear to be good; for, as the Apostle says, he can transform himself into an angel of light. [284] Of this we shall treat hereafter, by the Divine favour, in our third book, in the chapter upon spiritual gluttony.

8. It is always well, then, that the soul should reject these things, and close its eyes to them, whencesoever they come. For, unless it does so, it will prepare the way for those things that come from the devil, and will give him such influence that, not only will his visions come in place of God's, but his visions will begin to increase, and those of God to cease, in such manner that the devil will have all the power and God will have none. So it has happened to many incautious and ignorant souls, who rely on these things to such an extent that many of them have found it hard to return to God in purity of faith; and many have been unable to return, so securely has the devil rooted himself in them; for which reason it is well to resist and reject them all. For, by the rejection of evil visions, the errors of the devil are avoided, and by the rejection of good visions no hindrance is offered to faith and the spirit harvests the fruit of them. And just as, when the soul allows them entrance, God begins to withhold them because the soul is becoming attached to them and is not profiting by them as it should, while the devil insinuates and increases his own visions, where he finds occasion and cause for them; just so, when the soul is resigned, or even averse to them, the devil begins to desist, since he sees that he is working it no harm; and contrariwise God begins to increase and magnify His favours in a soul that is so humble and detached, making it ruler over [285] many things, even as He made the servant who was faithful in small

Ascent of Mount Carmel
things. [286]

9. In these favours, if the soul be faithful and humble, [287] the Lord will not cease until He has raised it from one step to another, even to Divine union and transformation. For Our Lord continues to prove the soul and to raise it ever higher, so that He first gives it things that are very unpretentious and exterior and in the order of sense, in conformity with the smallness of its capacity; to the end that, when it behaves as it should, and receives these first morsels with moderation for its strength and sustenance, He may grant it further and better food. If, then, the soul conquer the devil upon the first step, it will pass to the second; and if upon the second likewise, it will pass to the third; and so onward, through all seven mansions, [288] which are the seven steps of love, until the Spouse shall bring it to the cellar of wine of His perfect charity.

10. Happy the soul that can fight against that beast of the Apocalypse, [289] which has seven heads, set over against these seven steps of love, and which makes war therewith against each one, and strives therewith against the soul in each of these mansions, wherein the soul is being exercised and is mounting step by step in the love of God. And undoubtedly if it strive faithfully against each of these heads, and gain the victory, it will deserve to pass from one step to another, and from one mansion to another, even unto the last, leaving the beast vanquished after destroying its seven heads, wherewith it made so furious a war upon it. So furious is this war that Saint John says in that place [290] that it was given unto the beast to make war against the saints and to be able to overcome them upon each one of these steps of love, arraying against each one many weapons and munitions of war. And it is therefore greatly to be lamented that many who engage in this spiritual battle against the beast do not even destroy its first head by denying themselves the sensual things of the world. And, though some destroy and cut off this head, they destroy not the second head, which is that of the visions of sense whereof we are speaking. But what is most to be lamented is that some, having destroyed not only the first and the second but even the third, which is that of the interior senses, pass out of the state of meditation, and travel still farther onward, and are overcome by this spiritual beast at the moment of their entering into purity of spirit, for he rises up against them once more, and even his first head comes to life again, and the last state of those souls is worse than the first, since, when they fall back, the beast brings with him seven other spirits worse then himself. [291]

11. The spiritual person, then, has to deny himself all the apprehensions, and the temporal delights, that belong to the outward senses, if he will destroy the first and the second head of this beast, and enter into the first chamber of love, and the second, which is of living faith, desiring neither to lay hold upon, nor to be embarrassed by, that which is given to the senses, since it is this that derogates most from faith.

12. It is clear, then, that these sensual apprehensions and visions cannot be a means to union, since they bear no proportion to God; and this was one of the reasons why Christ desired that the Magdalene and Saint Thomas should not touch Him. And so the devil rejoices greatly when a soul desires to receive revelations, and when he sees it inclined to them, for he has then a great occasion and opportunity to insinuate errors and, in so far as he is able, to derogate from faith; for, as I have said, he renders the soul that desires them very gross, and at times even leads it into many temptations and unseemly ways.

13. I have written at some length of these outward apprehensions in order to throw and shed rather more light on the others, whereof we have to treat shortly. There is so much to say on this part of my subject that I could go on and never end. I believe, however, that I am summarizing it sufficiently by merely saying that the soul must take care never to receive these apprehensions, save occasionally on another person's advice, which should very rarely be given, and even then it must have no desire for them. I think that on this part of my subject what I have said is sufficient.

Footnotes:

278. [Lit., and blossom.']
279. [Lit., from the affection and devotion of the sensible spirit.']
280. [P. Silverio remarks here that] we must understand [as frequently elsewhere] 'sensibility' and not sensuality in the grosser sense.
281. [Lit., and sweetnesses in the mouth.']
282. E.p.: for those of the devil stop at the first movements and cannot move the will.' This, no doubt, was the Saint's meaning, for the Church teaches that the devil cannot influence the will directly, though he may do so indirectly, principally through the senses and the imagination.
283. St. John of the Cross means that the soul should not rely upon its own judgment in such matters but upon some discreet and learned director.
284. 2 Corinthians xi, 14.
285. [Lit., making it over.'] E.p. has: 'setting it and placing it over.'
286. [St. Matthew xxv, 21.]

287. [Lit., and retired.']
288. [The phrase is suggestive of St. Teresa, though the Spanish word is not moradas, but mansiones.]
289. [Apocalypse xiii, 1.]
290 [Apocalypse xiii, 7.]
291. [St. Luke xi, 26.]

CHAPTER XII

Which treats of natural imaginary apprehensions. Describes their nature and proves that they cannot be a proportionate means of attainment to union with God. Shows the harm which results from inability to detach oneself from them.

Before we treat of the imaginary visions which are wont to occur supernaturally to the interior sense, which is the imagination and the fancy, it is fitting here, so that we may proceed in order, to treat of the natural apprehensions of this same interior bodily sense, in order that we may proceed from the lesser to the greater, and from the more exterior to the more interior, until we reach the most interior [292] recollection wherein the soul is united with God; this same order we have followed up to this point. For we treated first of all the detachment of the exterior senses from the natural apprehensions of objects, and, in consequence, from the natural power of the desires -- this was contained in the first book, wherein we spoke of the night of sense. We then began to detach these same senses from supernatural exterior apprehensions (which, as we have just shown in the last chapter, affect the exterior senses), in order to lead the soul into the night of the spirit.

2. In this second book, the first thing that has now to be treated is the interior bodily sense -- namely, the imagination and the fancy; this we must likewise void of all the imaginary apprehensions and forms that may belong to it by nature, and we must prove how impossible it is that the soul should attain to union with God until its operation cease in them, since they cannot be the proper and proximate means of this union.

3. It is to be known, then, that the senses whereof we are here particularly speaking are two interior bodily senses which are called imagination and fancy, which subserve each other in due order. For the one sense reasons, as it were, by imagining, and the other forms the imagination, or that which is imagined, by making use of the fancy. [293] For our purpose the discussion of the one is equivalent to that of the other, and, for this reason, when we name them not both, it must be understood that we are speaking of either, as we have here explained. All the things, then, that these senses can receive and fashion are known as imaginations and fancies, which are forms that are represented to these senses by bodily figures and images. This can happen in two ways. The one way is supernatural, wherein representation can be made, and is made, to these senses passively, without any effort of their own; these we call imaginary visions, produced after a supernatural manner, and of these we shall speak hereafter. The other way is natural, wherein, through the ability of the soul, these things can be actively fashioned in it through its operation, beneath forms, figures and images. And thus to these two faculties belongs meditation, which is a discursive action wrought by means of images, forms and figures that are fashioned and imagined by the said senses, as when we imagine Christ crucified, or bound to the column, or at another of the stations; or when we imagine God seated upon a throne with great majesty; or when we consider and imagine glory to be like a most beauteous light, etc.; or when we imagine all kinds of other things, whether Divine or human, that can belong to the imagination. All these imaginings must be cast out from the Soul, which will remain in darkness as far as this sense is concerned, that it may attain to Divine union; for they can bear no proportion to proximate means of union with God, any more than can the bodily imaginings, which serve as objects to the five exterior senses.

4. The reason of this is that the imagination cannot fashion or imagine anything whatsoever beyond that which it has experienced through its exterior senses -- namely, that which it has seen with the eyes, or heard with the ears, etc. At most it can only compose likenesses of those things that it has seen or heard or felt, which are of no more consequence than those which have been received by the senses aforementioned, nor are they even of as much consequence. For, although a man imagines palaces of pearls and mountains of gold, because he has seen gold and pearls, all this is in truth less than the essence of a little gold or of a single pearl, although in the imagination it be greater in quantity and in beauty. And since, as has already been said, no created things can bear any proportion to the Being of God, it follows that nothing that is imagined in their likeness can serve as proximate means to union with Him, but, as we say, quite the contrary.

5. Wherefore those that imagine God beneath any of these figures, or as a great fire or brightness, or in any other such form, and think that anything like this will be like to Him, are very far from approaching Him. For, although these considerations and forms and manners of meditation are necessary to beginners, in order that they may gradually feed and enkindle their souls with love by

means of sense, as we shall say hereafter, and although they thus serve them as remote means to union with God, through which a soul has commonly to pass in order to reach the goal and abode of spiritual repose, yet they must merely pass through them, and not remain ever in them, for in such a manner they would never reach their goal, which does not resemble these remote means, neither has aught to do with them. The stairs of a staircase have naught to do with the top of it and the abode to which it leads, yet are means to the reaching of both; and if the climber left not behind the stairs below him until there were no more to climb, but desired to remain upon any one of them, he would never reach the top of them nor would he mount to the pleasant [294] and peaceful room which is the goal. And just so the soul that is to attain in this life to the union of that supreme repose and blessing, by means of all these stairs of meditations, forms and ideas, must pass though them and have done with them, since they have no resemblance and bear no proportion to the goal to which they lead, which is God. Wherefore Saint Paul says in the Acts of the Apostles: Non debemus aestimare, auro, vel argento, aut lapidi sculpturae artis, et cogitationis hominis, Divinum esse similem. [295] Which signifies: We ought not to think of the Godhead by likening Him to gold or to silver, neither to stone that is formed by art, nor to aught that a man can fashion with his imagination.

6. Great, therefore, is the error of many spiritual persons who have practised approaching God by means of images and forms and meditations, as befits beginners. God would now lead them on to [296] further spiritual blessings, which are interior and invisible, by taking from them the pleasure and sweetness of discursive meditation; but they cannot, or dare not, or know not how to detach themselves from those palpable methods to which they have grown accustomed. They continually labour to retain them, desiring to proceed, as before, by the way of consideration and meditation upon forms, for they think that it must be so with them always. They labour greatly to this end and find little sweetness or none; rather the aridity and weariness and disquiet of their souls are increased and grow, in proportion as they labour for that earlier sweetness. They cannot find this in that earlier manner, for the soul no longer enjoys that food of sense, as we have said; it needs not this but another food, which is more delicate, more interior and partaking less of the nature of sense; it consists not in labouring with the imagination, but in setting the soul at rest, and allowing it to remain in its quiet and repose, which is more spiritual. For, the farther the soul progresses in spirituality, the more it ceases from the operation of the faculties in particular acts, since it becomes more and more occupied in one act that is general and pure; and thus the faculties that were journeying to a place whither the soul has arrived cease to work, even as the feet stop and cease to move when their journey is over. For if all were motion, one would never arrive, and if all were means, where or when would come the fruition of the end and goal?

7. It is piteous, then, to see many a one who [297] though his soul would fain tarry in this peace and rest of interior quiet, where it is filled with the peace and refreshment of God, takes from it its tranquillity, and leads it away to the most exterior things, and would make it return and retrace the ground it has already traversed, to no purpose, and abandon the end and goal wherein it is already reposing for the means which led it to that repose, which are meditations. This comes not to pass without great reluctance and repugnance of the soul, which would fain be in that peace that it understands not, as in its proper place; even as one who has arrived, with great labour, and is now resting, suffers pain if he is made to return to his labour. And, as such souls know not the mystery of this new experience, the idea comes to them that they are being idle and doing nothing; and thus they allow not themselves to be quiet, but endeavor to meditate and reason. Hence they are filled with aridity and affliction, because they seek to find sweetness where it is no longer to be found; we may even say of them that the more they strive the less they profit, for, the more they persist after this manner, the worse is the state wherein they find themselves, because their soul is drawn farther away from spiritual peace; and this is to leave the greater for the less, and to retrace the ground already traversed, and to seek to do that which has been done.

8. To such as these the advice must be given to learn to abide attentively and wait lovingly upon God in that state of quiet, and to pay no heed either to imagination or to its working; for here, as we say, the faculties are at rest, and are working, not actively, but passively, by receiving that which God works in them; and, if they work at times, it is not with violence or with carefully elaborated meditation, but with sweetness of love, moved less by the ability of the soul itself than by God, as will be explained hereafter. But let this now suffice to show how fitting and necessary it is for those who aim at making further progress to be able to detach themselves from all these methods and manners and works of the imagination at the time and season when the profit of the state which they have reached demands and requires it.

9. And, that it may be understood how this is to be, and at what season, we shall give in the chapter following certain signs which the spiritual person will see in himself and whereby he may know at what time and season he may freely avail himself of the goal mentioned above, and may cease from journeying by means of meditation and the work of the imagination.

Footnotes:

292. [Lit., the intimate'; but the superlative idea is clearly present.]
293. [Lit., by fancying.']
294. [Lit., the level' -- i.e., by contrast with the steep stairs.]
295. Acts xvii, 29.
296. [The verb, recoger, of which the derived noun is translated recollection,' has more accurately the meaning of gather,' take inwards.']
297. [Lit., to see that there are many who.']

CHAPTER XIII

Wherein are set down the signs which the spiritual person will find in himself whereby he may know at what season it behoves him to leave meditation and reasoning and pass to the state of contemplation.

In order that there may be no confusion in this instruction it will be meet in this chapter to explain at what time and season it behoves the spiritual person to lay aside the task of discursive meditation as carried on through the imaginations and forms and figures above mentioned, in order that he may lay them aside neither sooner nor later than when the Spirit bids him; for, although it is meet for him to lay them aside at the proper time in order that he may journey to God and not be hindered by them, it is no less needful for him not to lay aside the said imaginative meditation before the proper time lest he should turn backward. For, although the apprehensions of these faculties serve not as proximate means of union to the proficient, they serve nevertheless as remote means to beginners in order to dispose and habituate the spirit to spirituality by means of sense, and in order to void the sense, in the meantime, of all the other low forms and images, temporal, worldly and natural. We shall therefore speak here of certain signs and examples which the spiritual person will find in himself, whereby he may know whether or not it will be meet for him to lay them aside at this season.

2. The first sign is his realization that he can no longer meditate or reason with his imagination, neither can take pleasure therein as he was wont to do aforetime; he rather finds aridity in that which aforetime was wont to captivate his senses and to bring him sweetness. But, for as long as he finds sweetness in meditation, and is able to reason, he should not abandon this, save when his soul is led into the peace and quietness [298] which is described under the third head.

3. The second sign is a realization that he has no desire to fix his mediation or his sense upon other particular objects, exterior or interior. I do not mean that the imagination neither comes nor goes (for even at times of deep [299] recollection it is apt to move freely), but that the soul has no pleasure in fixing it of set purpose upon other objects.

4. The third and surest sign is that the soul takes pleasure in being alone, and waits with loving attentiveness upon God, without making any particular meditation, in inward peace and quietness and rest, and without acts and exercises of the faculties -- memory, understanding and will -- at least, without discursive acts, that is, without passing from one thing to another; the soul is alone, with an attentiveness and a knowledge, general and loving, as we said, but without any particular understanding, and adverting not to that which it is contemplating.

5. These three signs, at least, the spiritual person must observe in himself, all together, before he can venture safely to abandon the state of meditation and sense, [300] and to enter that of contemplation and spirit.

6. And it suffices not for a man to have the first alone without the second, for it might be that the reason for his being unable to imagine and meditate upon the things of God, as he did aforetime, was distraction on his part and lack of diligence; for the which cause he must observe in himself the second likewise, which is the absence of inclination or desire to think upon other things; for, when the inability to fix the imagination and sense upon the things of God proceeds from distraction or lukewarmness, the soul then has the desire and inclination to fix it upon other and different things, which lead it thence altogether. Neither does it suffice that he should observe in himself the first and second signs, if he observe not likewise, together with these, the third; for, although he observe his inability to reason and think upon the things of God, and likewise his distaste for thinking upon other and different things, this might proceed from melancholy or from some other kind of humour in the brain or the heart, which habitually produces a certain absorption and suspension of the senses, causing the soul to think not at all, nor to desire or be inclined to think, but rather to remain in that pleasant state of reverie. [301] Against this must be set the third sign, which is loving attentiveness and knowledge, in peace, etc., as we have said.

7. It is true, however, that, when this condition first begins, the soul is hardly aware of this loving knowledge, and that for two reasons. First, this loving knowledge is apt at the beginning to be very subtle and delicate, and almost imperceptible to the senses. Secondly, when the soul has been accustomed to that other exercise of meditation, which is wholly perceptible, it is unaware, and hardly conscious, of this other new and imperceptible condition, which is purely spiritual; especially when, not understanding it, the soul allows not itself to rest in it, but strives after the former, which is more readily

perceptible; so that abundant though the loving interior peace may be, the soul has no opportunity of experiencing and enjoying it. But the more accustomed the soul grows to this, by allowing itself to rest, the more it will grow therein and the more conscious it will become of that loving general knowledge of God, in which it has greater enjoyment than in aught else, since this knowledge causes it peace, rest, pleasure and delight without labour.

8. And, to the end that what has been said may be the clearer, we shall give, in this chapter following, the causes and reasons why the three signs aforementioned appear to be necessary for the soul that is journeying to pure spirit. [302]

Footnotes:

298. E.p. omits: and quietness.' The Saint's description of this first sign at which a soul should pass from meditation to contemplation was denounced as disagreeing with Catholic doctrine, particularly the phrase: that he can no longer meditate or reason with his imagination, neither can take pleasure therein as he was wont to do aforetime.' This language, however, is common to mystics and theologians, not excluding St. Thomas (2a 2ae, q. 180, a. 6) and Suárez (De Oratione, Bk. II, Chap. x), as is proved, with eloquence and erudition, by P. Basilio Ponce de León and the Elucidatio, in their refutations of the Saint's critics. All agree that, in the act of contemplation of which St. John of the Cross here speaks, the understanding must be stripped of forms and species of the imagination and that the reasonings and reflections of meditation must be set aside. This is to be understood, both of the contemplation that transcends all human methods, and also of that which is practised according to these human methods with the ordinary aid of grace. But there is this important difference, that those who enjoy the first kind of contemplation set aside all intellectual reasoning as well as processes of the fancy and the imagination, whereas, for the second kind, reasoning prior to the act of contemplation is normally necessary, though it ceases at the act of contemplation, and there is then substituted for it simple and loving intuition of eternal truth. It should be clearly understood that this is not of habitual occurrence in the contemplative soul, but occurs only during the act of contemplation, which is commonly of short duration. St. Teresa makes this clear in Chap. xxvii of her Life, and treats this same doctrinal question in many other parts of her works--e.g., Life, Chaps. x, xii; Way of Perfection, Chap. xxvi; Interior Castle, IV, Chap. iii, etc.

299. [Lit., much.']

300. E.p. omits: and sense.' Since sense plays so great a part in meditation, St. John of the Cross places it in contradistinction to contemplation, which, the more nearly it attains perfection, becomes the more sublime and spiritual and the more completely freed from the bonds of nature. Cf. Elucidatio, Pt. II, Chap. iii, p. 180.

301. [embelesamiento, a word denoting a pleasurable condition somewhere between a reverie and a swoon.]

302. [Lit., appear to be necessary in order to journey to spirit.']

CHAPTER XIV

Wherein is proved the fitness of these signs, and the reason is given why that which has been said in speaking of them is necessary to progress.

With respect to the first sign whereof we are speaking -- that is to say, that the spiritual person who would enter upon the spiritual road (which is that of contemplation) must leave the way of imagination and of meditation through sense when he takes no more pleasure therein and is unable to reason -- there are two reasons why this should be done, which may almost be comprised in one. The first is, that in one way the soul has received all the spiritual good which it would be able to derive from the things of God by the path of meditation and reasoning, the sign whereof is that it can no longer meditate or reason as before, and finds no new sweetness or pleasure therein as it found before, because up to that time it had not progressed as far as the spirituality which was in store for it; for, as a rule, whensoever the soul receives some spiritual blessing, it receives it with pleasure, at least in spirit, in that means whereby it receives it and profits by it; otherwise it is astonishing if it profits by it, or finds in the cause of it that help and that sweetness which it finds when it receives it. For this is in agreement with a saying of the philosophers, Quod sapit, nutrit. This is: That which is palatable nourishes and fattens. Wherefore holy Job said: Numquid poterit comedi insulsum, quod non est sale conditum? [303] Can that which is unsavory perchance be eaten when it is not seasoned with salt? It is this cause that the soul is unable to meditate or reason as before: the little pleasure which the spirit finds therein and the little profit which it gains.

2. The second reason is that the soul at this season has now both the substance and the habit of the spirit of meditation. For it must be known that the end of reasoning and meditation on the things of God is the gaining of some knowledge and love of God, and each time that the soul gains this through meditation, it is an act; and just as many acts, of whatever kind, end by forming a habit in the soul, just so, many of these acts of loving knowledge which the soul has been making one after another from time to time come through repetition to be so continuous in it that they become habitual. This end God is wont also to effect in many souls without the intervention of these acts (or at least without many such acts having preceded it), by setting them at once in contemplation. And thus that which aforetime the soul was gaining gradually through its labour of meditation upon particular facts has now through practice, as we have been saying, become converted and changed into a habit and substance of loving knowledge, of a general kind, and not distinct or particular as before. Wherefore, when it gives itself to prayer, the soul is now like one to whom water has been brought, so that he drinks peacefully, without labour, and is no longer forced to draw the water through the aqueducts of past meditations and forms and figures [304] So that, as soon as the soul comes before God, it makes an act of knowledge, confused, loving, passive and tranquil, wherein it drinks of wisdom and love and delight.

3. And it is for this cause that the soul feels great weariness and distaste, when, although it is in this condition of tranquillity, men try to make it meditate and labour in particular acts of knowledge. For it is like a child, which, while receiving the milk that has been collected and brought together for it in the breast, is taken from the breast and then forced to try to gain and collect food by its own diligent squeezing and handling. Or it is like one who has removed the rind from a fruit, and is tasting the substance of the fruit, when he is forced to cease doing this and to try to begin removing the said rind, which has been removed already. He finds no rind to remove, and yet he is unable to enjoy the substance of the fruit which he already had in his hand; herein he is like to one who leaves a prize [305] which he holds for another which he holds not.

4. And many act thus when they begin to enter this state; they think that the whole business consists in a continual reasoning and learning to understand particular things by means of images and forms, which are to the spirit as rind. When they find not these in that substantial and loving quiet wherein their soul desires to remain, and wherein it understands nothing clearly, they think that they are going astray and wasting time, and they begin once more to seek the rind of their imaginings and reasonings, but find it not, because it has already been removed. And thus they neither enjoy the substance nor make progress in meditation, and they become troubled by the thought that they are turning backward and are losing themselves. They are indeed losing themselves, though not in the way they think, for they are becoming lost to their own senses and to their first manner of perception; and this means gain in that spirituality which is being given them. The less they understand, however, the farther they penetrate into the night of the spirit, whereof we are treating in this book, through the which

Ascent of Mount Carmel

night they must pass in order to be united with God, in a union that transcends all knowledge.

5. With respect to the second sign, there is little to say, for it is clear that at this season the soul cannot possibly take pleasure in other and different objects of the imagination, which are of the world, since, as we have said, and for the reasons already mentioned, it has no pleasure in those which are in closest conformity with it -- namely, those of God. Only as has been noted above, the imaginative faculty in this state of recollection is in the habit of coming and going and varying of its own accord; but neither according to the pleasure nor at the will of the soul, which is troubled thereby, because its peace and joy are disturbed.

6. Nor do I think it necessary to say anything here concerning the fitness and necessity of the third sign whereby the soul may know if it is to leave the meditation aforementioned, which is a knowledge of God or a general and loving attentiveness to Him. For something has been said of this in treating of the first sign, and we shall treat of it again hereafter, when we speak in its proper place of this confused and general knowledge, which will come after our description of all the particular apprehensions of the understanding. But we will speak of one reason alone by which it may clearly be seen how, when the contemplative has to turn aside from the way of meditation and reasoning, he needs this general and loving attentiveness or knowledge of God. The reason is that, if the soul at that time had not this knowledge of God or this realization of His presence, the result would be that it would do nothing and have nothing; for, having turned aside from meditation (by means whereof the soul has been reasoning with its faculties of sense), and being still without contemplation, which is the general knowledge whereof we are speaking, wherein the soul makes use of its spiritual faculties [306] -- namely, memory, understanding and will -- these being united in this knowledge which is then wrought and received in them, the soul would of necessity be without any exercise in the things of God, since the soul can neither work, nor can it receive that which has been worked in it, save only by way of these two kinds of faculty, that of sense and that of spirit. For, as we have said, by means of the faculties of sense it can reason and search out and gain knowledge of things and by means of the spiritual faculties it can have fruition of the knowledge which it has already received in these faculties aforementioned, though the faculties themselves take no part herein.

7. And thus the difference between the operation of these two kinds of faculty in the soul is like the difference between working and enjoying the fruit of work which has been done; or like that between the labour of journeying and the rest and quiet which comes from arrival at the goal; or, again, like that between preparing a meal and partaking and tasting of it, when it has been both prepared and masticated, without having any of the labour of cooking it, or it is like the difference between receiving something and profiting by that which has been received. Now if the soul be occupied neither with respect to the operation of the faculties of sense, which is meditation and reasoning, nor with respect to that which has already been received and effected in the spiritual faculties, which is the contemplation and knowledge whereof we have spoken, it will have no occupation, but will be wholly idle, and there would be no way in which it could be said to be employed. This knowledge, then, is needful for the abandonment of the way of meditation and reasoning.

8. But here it must be made clear that this general knowledge whereof we are speaking is at times so subtle and delicate, particularly when it is most pure and simple and perfect, most spiritual and most interior, that, although the soul be occupied therein, it can neither realize it nor perceive it. This is most frequently the case when we can say that it is in itself most clear, perfect and simple; and this comes to pass when it penetrates a soul that is unusually pure and far withdrawn from other particular kinds of knowledge and intelligence, which the understanding or the senses might fasten upon. Such a soul, since it no longer has those things wherein the understanding and the senses have the habit and custom of occupying themselves, is not conscious of them, inasmuch as it has not its accustomed powers of sense. And it is for this reason that, when this knowledge is purest and simplest and most perfect, the understanding is least conscious of it and thinks of it as most obscure. And similarly, in contrary wise, when it is in itself least pure and simple in the understanding, it seems to the understanding to be clearest and of the greatest importance, since it is clothed in, mingled with or involved in certain intelligible forms which understanding or sense may seize upon. [307]

9. This will be clearly understood by the following comparison. If we consider a ray of sunlight entering through a window, we see that, the more the said ray is charged with atoms and particles of matter, the more palpable, visible and bright it appears to the eye of sense; [308] yet it is clear that the ray is in itself least pure, clear, simple and perfect at that time, since it is full of so many particles and atoms. And we see likewise that, when it is purest and freest from those particles and atoms, the least palpable and the darkest does it appear to the material eye; and the purer it is, the darker and less apprehensible it appears to it. And if the ray were completely pure and free from all these atoms and particles, even from the minutest specks of dust, it would appear completely dark and invisible to the eye, since everything that could be seen would be absent from it -- namely, the objects of sight. For the eye would find no objects whereon to rest, since light is no proper object of vision, but the means whereby that which is visible is seen; so that, if there be no visible objects wherein the sun's ray or any

light can be reflected, nothing will be seen. Wherefore, if the ray of light entered by one window and went out by another, without meeting anything that has material form, it would not be seen at all; yet, notwithstanding, that ray of light would be purer and clearer in itself than when it was more clearly seen and perceived through being full of visible objects.

10. The same thing happens in the realm of spiritual light with respect to the sight of the soul, which is the understanding, and which this general and supernatural knowledge and light whereof we are speaking strikes so purely and simply. So completely is it detached and removed from all intelligible forms, which are objects of the understanding, that it is neither perceived nor observed. Rather, at times (that is, when it is purest), it becomes darkness, because it withdraws the understanding from its accustomed lights, from forms and from fancies, and then the darkness is more clearly felt and realized. But, when this Divine light strikes the soul with less force, it neither perceives darkness nor observes light, nor apprehends aught that it knows, from whatever source; hence at times the soul remains as it were in a great forgetfulness, so that it knows not where it has been or what it has done, nor is it aware of the passage of time. Wherefore it may happen, and does happen, that many hours are spent in this forgetfulness, and, when the soul returns to itself, it believes that less than a moment has passed, or no time at all.

11. The cause of this forgetfulness is the purity and simplicity of this knowledge which occupies the soul and simplifies, purifies and cleanses it from all apprehensions and forms of the senses and of the memory, through which it acted when it was conscious of time, [309] and thus leaves it in forgetfulness and without consciousness of time. [310] This prayer, therefore, seems to the soul extremely brief, although, as we say, it may last for a long period; for the soul has been united in pure intelligence, which belongs not to time; and this is the brief prayer which is said to pierce the heavens, because it is brief and because it belongs not to time. [311] And it pierces the heavens, because the soul is united in heavenly intelligence; and when the soul awakens, this knowledge leaves in it the effects which it created in it without its being conscious of them, which effects are the lifting up of the spirit to the heavenly intelligence, and its withdrawal and abstraction from all things and forms and figures and memories thereof. It is this that David describes as having happened to him when he returned to himself out of this same forgetfulness, saying: Vigilavi, et factus sum sicut passer solitarius in tecto. [312] Which signifies: I have watched and I have become like the lonely bird [313] on the house-top. He uses the word lonely' to indicate that he was withdrawn and abstracted from all things. And by the house-top he means the elevation of the spirit on high; so that the soul remains as though ignorant of all things, for it knows God only, without knowing how. Wherefore the Bride declares in the Songs that among the effects which that sleep and forgetfulness of hers produced was this unknowing. She says that she came down to the garden, saying: Nescivi. [314] That is: I knew not whence. Although, as we have said, the soul in this state of knowledge believes itself to be doing nothing, and to be entirely unoccupied, because it is working neither with the senses nor with the faculties, it should realize that it is not wasting time. For, although the harmony of the faculties of the soul may cease, its intelligence is as we have said. For this cause the Bride, who was wise, answered this question herself in the Songs, saying: Ego dormio et cor meum vigilat. [315] As though she were to say: Although I sleep with respect to my natural self, ceasing to labour, my heart waketh, being supernaturally lifted up in supernatural knowledge. [316]

12. But, it must be realized, we are not to suppose that this knowledge necessarily causes this forgetfulness when the soul is in the state that we are here describing: this occurs only when God suspends in the soul the exercise of all its faculties, both natural and spiritual, which happens very seldom, for this knowledge does not always fill the soul entirely. It is sufficient for the purpose, in the case which we are treating, that the understanding should be withdrawn from all particular knowledge, whether temporal or spiritual, and that the will should not desire to think with respect to either, as we have said, for this is a sign that the soul is occupied. And it must be taken as an indication that this is so when this knowledge is applied and communicated to the understanding only, which sometimes happens when the soul is unable to observe it. For, when it is communicated to the will also, which happens almost invariably, the soul does not cease to understand in the very least degree, if it will reflect hereon, that it is employed and occupied in this knowledge, inasmuch as it is conscious of a sweetness of love therein, without particular knowledge or understanding of that which it loves. It is for this reason that this knowledge is described as general and loving; for, just as it is so in the understanding, being communicated to it obscurely, even so is it in the will, sweetness and love being communicated to it confusedly, so that it cannot have a distinct knowledge of the object of its love.

13. Let this suffice now to explain how meet it is that the soul should be occupied in this knowledge, so that it may turn aside from the way of spiritual meditation, and be sure that, although it seem to be doing nothing, it is well occupied, if it discern within itself these signs. It will also be realized, from the comparison which we have made, that if this light presents itself to the understanding in a more comprehensible and palpable manner, as the sun's ray presents itself to the eye when it is full of particles, the soul must not for that reason consider it purer, brighter and more sublime. It is clear that, as Aristotle and the theologians say, the higher and more sublime is the Divine light, the darker is it

Ascent of Mount Carmel
to our understanding.

14. Of this Divine knowledge there is much to say, concerning both itself and the effects which it produces upon contemplatives. All this we reserve for its proper place, [317] for, although we have spoken of it here, there would be no reason for having done so at such length, save our desire not to leave this doctrine rather more confused than it is already, for I confess it is certainly very much so. Not only is it a matter which is seldom treated in this way, either verbally or in writing, being in itself so extraordinary and obscure, but my rude style and lack of knowledge make it more so. Further, since I have misgivings as to my ability to explain it, I believe I often write at too great length and go beyond the limits which are necessary for that part of the doctrine which I am treating. Herein I confess that I sometimes err purposely; for that which is not explicable by one kind of reasoning will perhaps be better understood by another, or by others yet; and I believe, too, that in this way I am shedding more light upon that which is to be said hereafter.

15. Wherefore it seems well to me also, before completing this part of my treatise, to set down a reply to one question which may arise with respect to the continuance of this knowledge, and this shall be briefly treated in the chapter following.

Footnotes:

303. Job vi, 6.
304. [Cf. the simile of the Waters in St. Teresa, Life, Chap. xi, and Interior Castle, IV, ii, iii.]
305. [Lit., booty,' prey.']
306. [Lit., the soul keeps in act its spiritual facilities.']
307. [The verb is tropezar en, which may mean either 'stumble upon' -- i.e., come across (and make use of),' or 'stumble over' -- i.e., the forms may be a stumbling-block, or a snare. I think there is at least a suggestion of the latter meaning.]
308. [Lit., to the sight of sense.']
309. [Or: when it was dependent on time,' Lit., acted in time.']
310. [Or: and independent of time.' Lit., without time.']
311. E.p. modifies these lines thus: . . . it has been in pure intelligence, which is the brief prayer that is said to pierce the heavens. Because it is brief and because the soul is not conscious or observant of time.' P. José de Jesús María comments thus upon this passage: In contemplation the soul withdraws itself from the seashore, and entirely loses sight of land, in order to whelm itself in that vast sea and impenetrable abyss of the Divine Essence; hiding itself in the region of time, it enters within the most extensive limits of eternity. For the pure and simple intelligence whereinto the soul is brought in this contemplation, as was pointed out by the ancient Dionysius (Myst. Theol., Chap. ii), and by our own Father, is not subject to time. For, as St. Thomas says (Pt. I, q. 118, a. 3, et alibi), the soul is a spiritual substance, which is above time and superior to the movements of the heavens, to which it is subject only because of the body. And therefore it seems that, when the soul withdraws from the body, and from all created things, and by means of pure intelligence whelms itself in eternal things, it recovers its natural dominion and rises above time, if not according to substance, at least according to its most perfect being; for the noblest and most perfect being of the soul resides rather in its acts than in its faculties. Wherefore St. Gregory said (Morals, Bk. VIII): "The Saints enter eternity even in this life, beholding the eternity of God."'
312. Psalm ci, 8 [A.V., cii, 7].
313. [The Spanish pájaro, bird,' is derived from passer, 'sparrow.']
314. Canticles vi, 11.
315. Canticles v, 2.
316. The words which conclude this paragraph in the edition of 1630 (The sign by which we may know if the soul is occupied in this secret intelligence is if it is seen to have no pleasure in thinking of aught, whether high or low') are not found either in the Codices or in e.p. When St. John of the Cross uses the words cessation,' idleness' [ocio, Lat. otium], quiet,' annihilation,' 'sleep' (of the faculties), etc., he does not mean, as the Illuminists did, that the understanding and will in the act of contemplation are so passive as to have lost all their force and vitality, and that the contemplative is therefore impeccable, although he commit the grossest sins. The soul's vital powers, according to St. John of the Cross, are involved even in the highest contemplation; the understanding is attentive to God and the will is loving Him. They are not working, it is true, in the way which is usual and natural with them -- that is, by reason and imagination -- but supernaturally, through the unction of the Holy Spirit, which they receive passively, without any effort of their own. It is in this sense that such words as those quoted above (cessation,' idleness,' etc.) are both expressively and appropriately used by the Saint, for what is done without labour and effort may better be described by images of passivity than by those of activity. Further, the soul is unaware that its faculties are working in this sublime contemplation, though they undoubtedly do work. St. John of the Cross, philosopher as well as mystic, would not deny the vital and

intrinsic activity of the understanding and the will in contemplation. His reasoning is supported by P. José de Jesús María (Apologia Mística de la Contemplación Divina, Chap. ix) [quoted at length by P. Silverio, Obras, etc., Vol. II, p. 130, note].

317. In spite of this promise, the Saint does not return to this subject at such length as his language here would suggest.

CHAPTER XV

Wherein is explained how it is sometimes well for progressives who are beginning to enter upon this general knowledge of contemplation to make use of natural reasoning and the work of the natural faculties.

With regard to that which has been said, there might be raised one question -- if progressives (that is, those whom God is beginning to bring into this supernatural knowledge of contemplation whereof we have spoken) must never again, because of this that they are beginning to experience, return to the way of meditation and reasoning and natural forms. To this the answer is that it is not to be understood that such as are beginning to experience this loving knowledge must, as a general rule, never again try to return to meditation; for, when they are first making progress in proficiency, the habit of contemplation is not yet so perfect that they can give themselves to the act thereof whensoever they wish, nor, in the same way, have they reached a point so far beyond meditation that they cannot occasionally meditate and reason in a natural way, as they were wont, using the figures and the steps that they were wont to use, and finding something new in them. Rather, in these early stages, when, by means of the indications already given, they are able to see that the soul is not occupied in that repose and knowledge, they will need to make use of meditation until by means of it they come to acquire in some degree of perfection the habit which we have described. This will happen when, as soon as they seek to meditate, they experience this knowledge and peace, and find themselves unable to meditate and no longer desirous of doing so, as we have said. For until they reach this stage, which is that of the proficient in this exercise, they use sometimes the one and sometimes the other, at different times.

2. The soul, then, will frequently find itself in this loving or peaceful state of waiting upon God [318] without in any way exercising its faculties -- that is, with respect to particular acts -- and without working actively at all, but only receiving. In order to reach this state, it will frequently need to make use of meditation, quietly and in moderation; but, when once the soul is brought into this other state, it acts not at all with its faculties, as we have already said. It would be truer to say that understanding and sweetness work in it and are wrought within it, than that the soul itself works at all, save only by waiting upon God and by loving Him without desiring to feel or to see anything. Then God communicates Himself to it passively, even as to one who has his eyes open, so that light is communicated to him passively, without his doing more than keep them open. And this reception of light which is infused supernaturally is passive understanding. We say that the soul works not at all, not because it understands not, but because it understands things without taxing its own industry and receives only that which is given to it, as comes to pass in the illuminations and enlightenments or inspirations of God.

3. Although in this condition the will freely receives this general and confused knowledge of God, it is needful, in order that it may receive this Divine light more simply and abundantly, only that it should not try to interpose other lights which are more palpable, whether forms or ideas or figures having to do with any kind of meditation; for none of these things is similar to that pure and serene light. So that if at this time the will desires to understand and consider particular things, however spiritual they be, this would obstruct the pure and simple general light of the spirit, by setting those clouds in the way; even as a man might set something before his eyes which impeded his vision and kept from him both the light and the sight of things in front of him.

4. Hence it clearly follows that, when the soul has completely purified and voided itself of all forms and images that can be apprehended, it will remain in this pure and simple light, being transformed therein into a state of perfection. For, though this light never fails in the soul, it is not infused into it because of the creature forms and veils wherewith the soul is veiled and embarrassed; but, if these impediments and these veils were wholly removed (as will be said hereafter), the soul would then find itself in a condition of pure detachment and poverty of spirit, and, being simple and pure, would be transformed into simple and pure Wisdom, which is the Son of God. For the enamoured soul finds that that which is natural has failed it, and it is then imbued with that which is Divine, both naturally and supernaturally, so that there may be no vacuum in its nature.

5. When the spiritual person cannot meditate, let him learn to be still in God, fixing his loving attention upon Him, in the calm of his understanding, although he may think himself to be doing nothing. For thus, little by little and very quickly, Divine calm and peace will be infused into his soul, together with a wondrous and sublime knowledge of God, enfolded in Divine love. And let him not meddle with forms, meditations and imaginings, or with any kind of reasoning, lest his soul be

disturbed, and brought out of its contentment and peace, which can only result in its experiencing distaste and repugnance. And if, as we have said, such a person has scruples that he is doing nothing, let him note that he is doing no small thing by pacifying the soul and bringing it into calm and peace, unaccompanied by any act or desire, for it is this that Our Lord asks of us, through David, saying: Vacate, et videte quoniam ego sum Deus.[319] As though he had said: Learn to be empty of all things (that is to say, inwardly and outwardly) and you will see that I am God.

Footnotes:

318. [Lit., in this loving or peaceful presence,' the original of presence' having also the sense of attendance.']

319. Psalm xlv, 11 [A.V., xlvi, 10].

CHAPTER XVI

Which treats of the imaginary apprehensions that are supernaturally represented in the fancy. Describing how they cannot serve the soul as a proximate means to union with God.

Now that we have treated of the apprehensions which the soul can receive within itself by natural means, and whereon the fancy and the imagination can work by means of reflection, it will be suitable to treat here of the supernatural apprehensions, which are called imaginary visions, which likewise belong to these senses, since they come within the category of images, forms and figures, exactly as do the natural apprehensions.

2. It must be understood that beneath this term imaginary vision' we purpose to include all things which can be represented to the imagination supernaturally by means of any image, form, figure and species. For all the apprehensions and species which, through all the five bodily senses, are represented to the soul, and dwell within it, after a natural manner, may likewise occur in the soul after a supernatural manner, and be represented to it without any assistance of the outward senses. For this sense of fancy, together with memory, is, as it were, an archive and storehouse of the understanding, wherein are received all forms and images that can be understood; and thus the soul has them within itself as it were in a mirror, having received them by means of the five senses, or, as we say, supernaturally; and thus it presents them to the understanding, whereupon the understanding considers them and judges them. And not only so, but the soul can also prepare and imagine others like to those with which it is acquainted.

3. It must be understood, then, that, even as the five outward senses represent the images and species of their objects to these inward senses, even so, supernaturally, as we say, without using the outward senses, both God and the devil can represent the same images and species, and much more beautiful and perfect ones. Wherefore, beneath these images, God often represents many things to the soul, and teaches it much wisdom; this is continually seen in the Scriptures, as when Isaias saw God in His glory beneath the smoke which covered the Temple, and beneath the seraphim who covered their faces and their feet with wings; [320] and as Jeremias saw the rod watching, [321] and Daniel a multitude of visions, [322] etc. And the devil, too, strives to deceive the soul with his visions, which in appearance are good, as may be seen in the Book of the Kings, when he deceived all the prophets of Achab, presenting to their imaginations the horns wherewith he said the King was to destroy the Assyrians, which was a lie. [323] Even such were the visions of Pilate's wife, warning him not to condemn Christ; [324] and there are many other places where it is seen how, in this mirror of the fancy and the imagination, these imaginary visions come more frequently to proficients than do outward and bodily visions. These, as we say, differ not in their nature (that is, as being images and species) from those which enter by the outward senses; but, with respect to the effect which they produce, and in the degree of their perfection, there is a great difference; for imaginary visions are subtler and produce a deeper impression upon the soul, inasmuch as they are supernatural, and are also more interior than the exterior supernatural visions. Nevertheless, it is true that some of these exterior bodily visions may produce a deeper impression; the communication, after all, is as God wills. We are speaking, however, merely as concerns their nature, and in this respect they are more spiritual.

4. It is to these senses of imagination and fancy that the devil habitually betakes himself with his wiles -- now natural, now supernatural; [325] for they are the door and entrance to the soul, and here, as we have said, the understanding comes to take up or set down its goods, as it were in a harbour or in a store-house where it keeps its provisions. And for this reason it is hither that both God and the devil always come with their jewels of supernatural forms and images, to offer them to the understanding; although God does not make use of this means alone to instruct the soul, but dwells within it in substance, and is able to do this by Himself and by other methods.

5. There is no need for me to stop here in order to give instruction concerning the signs by which it may be known which visions are of God and which not, and which are of one kind and which of another; for this is not my intention, which is only to instruct the understanding herein, that it may not be hindered or impeded as to union with Divine Wisdom by the good visions, neither may be deceived by those which are false.

6. I say, then, that with regard to all these imaginary visions and apprehensions and to all other forms and species whatsoever, which present themselves beneath some particular kind of knowledge or image or form, whether they be false and come from the devil or are recognized as true and coming

from God, the understanding must not be embarrassed by them or feed upon them, neither must the soul desire to receive them or to have them, lest it should no longer be detached, free, pure and simple, without any mode or manner, as is required for union.

7. The reason of this is that all these forms which we have already mentioned are always represented, in the apprehension of the soul, as we have said, beneath certain modes and manners which have limitations; and that the Wisdom of God, wherewith the understanding is to be united, has no mode or manner, neither is it contained within any particular or distinct kind of intelligence or limit, because it is wholly pure and simple. And as, in order that these two extremes may be united -- namely, the soul and Divine Wisdom -- it will be necessary for them to attain to agreement, by means of a certain mutual resemblance, hence it follows that the soul must be pure and simple, neither bounded by, nor attached to, any particular kind of intelligence, nor modified by any limitation of form, species and image. As God comes not within any image or form, neither is contained within any particular kind of intelligence, so the soul, in order to reach God, [326] must likewise come within no distinct form or kind of intelligence.

8. And that there is no form or likeness in God is clearly declared by the Holy Spirit in Deuteronomy, where He says: Vocem verborum ejus audistis, et formam penitus non vidistis. [327] Which signifies: Ye heard the voice of His words, and ye saw in God no form whatsoever. But He says that there was darkness there, and clouds and thick darkness, which are the confused and dark knowledge whereof we have spoken, wherein the soul is united with God. And afterwards He says further: Non vidistis aliquam similitudinem in die, qua locutus est vobis Dominus in Horeb de medio ignis. That is: Ye saw no likeness in God upon the day when He spoke to you on Mount Horeb, out of the midst of the fire. [328]

9. And that the soul cannot reach the height of God, even as far as is possible in this life, by means of any form and figure, is declared likewise by the same Holy Spirit in the Book of Numbers, where God reproves Aaron and Miriam, the brother and sister of Moses, because they murmured against him, and, desiring to convey to them the loftiness of the state of union and friendship with Him wherein He had placed him, said: Si quis inter vos fuerit Propheta Domini, in visione apparebo ei, vel per somnium loquar ad illum. At non talis servus meus Moyses, qui in omni domo mea fidelissimus est: ore enim ad os loquor ei, et palem, et non per aenigmata, et figuras Dominum videt. [329] Which signifies: If there be any prophet of the Lord among you, I will appear to him in some vision or form, or I will speak with him in his dreams; but there is none like My servant Moses, who is the most faithful in all My house, and I speak with him mouth to mouth, and he sees not God by comparisons, similitudes and figures. Herein He says clearly that, in this lofty state of union whereof we are speaking, God is not communicated to the soul by means of any disguise of imaginary vision or similitude or form, neither can He be so communicated; but mouth to mouth -- that is, in the naked and pure essence of God, which is the mouth of God in love, with the naked and pure essence of the soul, which is the mouth of the soul in love of God.

10. Wherefore, in order to come to this essential union of love in God, the soul must have a care not to lean upon [330] imaginary visions, nor upon forms or figures or particular objects of the understanding; for these cannot serve it as a proportionate and proximate means to such an end; rather they would disturb it, and for this reason the soul must renounce them and strive not to have them. For if in any circumstances they were to be received and prized, it would be for the sake of profit which true visions bring to the soul and the good effect which they produce upon it. But, for this to happen, it is not necessary to receive them; indeed, for the soul's profit, it is well always to reject them. For these imaginary visions, like the outward bodily visions whereof we have spoken, do the soul good by communicating to it intelligence or love or sweetness; but for this effect to be produced by them in the soul it is not necessary that it should desire to receive them; for, as has also been said above, at this very time when they are present to the imagination, they produce in the soul and infuse into it intelligence and love, or sweetness, or whatever effect God wills them to produce. And not only do they produce this joint effect, but principally, although not simultaneously, they produce their effect in the soul passively, without its being able to hinder this effect, even if it so desired, just as it was also powerless to acquire it, although it had been able previously to prepare itself. For, even as the window is powerless to impede the ray of sunlight which strikes it, but, when it is prepared by being cleansed, receives its light passively without any diligence or labour on its own part, even so the soul, although against its will, cannot fail to receive in itself the influences and communications of those figures, however much it might desire to resist them. For the will that is negatively inclined cannot, if coupled with loving and humble resignation, resist supernatural infusions; only the impurity and imperfections of the soul can resist them even as the stains upon a window impede the brightness of the sunlight. [331]

11. From this it is evident that, when the soul completely detaches itself, in its will and affection, from the apprehensions of the strains of those forms, images and figures wherein are clothed the spiritual communications which we have described, not only is it not deprived of these communications and the blessings which they cause within it, but it is much better prepared to receive them with greater

abundance, clearness, liberty of spirit and simplicity, when all these apprehensions are set on one side, for they are, as it were, curtains and veils covering the spiritual thing that is behind them. And thus, if the soul desire to feed upon them, they occupy spirit and sense in such a way that the spirit cannot communicate itself simply and freely; for, while they are still occupied with the outer rind, it is clear that the understanding is not free to receive the substance. Wherefore, if the soul at that time desires to receive these forms and to set store by them, it would be embarrassing itself, and contenting itself with the least important part of them -- namely, all that it can apprehend and know of them, which is the form and image and particular object of the understanding in question. The most important part of them, which is the spiritual part that is infused into the soul, it can neither apprehend nor understand, nor can it even know what it is, or be able to express it, since it is purely spiritual. All that it can know of them, as we say, according to its manner of understanding, is but the least part of what is in them -- namely, the forms perceptible by sense. For this reason I say that what it cannot understand or imagine is communicated to it by these visions, passively, without any effort of its own to understand and without its even knowing how to make such an effort.

12. Wherefore the eyes of the soul must ever be withdrawn from all these apprehensions which it can see and understand distinctly, which are communicated through sense, and do not make for a foundation of faith, or for reliance on faith, and must be set upon that which it sees not, and which belongs not to sense, but to spirit, which can be expressed by no figure of sense; and it is this which leads the soul to union in faith, which is the true medium, as has been said. And thus these visions will profit the soul substantially, in respect of faith, when it is able to renounce the sensible and intelligible part of them, and to make good use of the purpose for which God gives them to the soul, by casting them aside; for, as we said of corporeal visions, God gives them not so that the soul may desire to have them and to set its affection upon them.

13. But there arises here this question: If it be true that God gives the soul supernatural visions, but not so that it may desire to have them or be attached to them or set store by them, why does He give them at all, since by their means the soul may fall into many errors and perils, or at the least may find in them such hindrances to further progress as are here described, especially since God can come to the soul, and communicate to it, spiritually and substantially, that which He communicates to it through sense, by means of the sensible forms and visions aforementioned?

14. We shall answer this question in the following chapter: it involves important teaching, most necessary, as I see it, both to spiritual persons and to those who instruct them. For herein is taught the way and purpose of God with respect to these visions, which many know not, so that they cannot rule themselves or guide themselves to union, neither can they guide others to union, through these visions. For they think that, just because they know them to be true and to come from God, it is well to receive them and to trust them, not realizing that the soul will become attached to them, cling to them and be hindered by them, as it will by things of the world, if it know not how to renounce these as well as those. And thus they think it well to receive one kind of vision and to reject another, causing themselves, and the souls under their care, great labour and peril in discerning between the truth and the falsehood of these visions. But God does not command them to undertake this labour, nor does He desire that sincere and simple souls should be led into this conflict and danger; for they have safe and sound teaching, which is that of the faith, wherein they can go forward.

15. This, however, cannot be unless they close their eyes to all that is of particular and clear intelligence and sense. For, although Saint Peter was quite certain of that vision of glory which he saw in Christ at the Transfiguration, yet, after having described it in his second canonical Epistle, he desired not that it should be taken for an important and sure testimony, but rather directed his hearers to faith, saying: Et habemus firmiorem propheticum sermonem: cui benefacitis attendentes, quasi lucernae lucenti in caliginoso loco, donec dies elucescat. [332] Which signifies: And we have a surer testimony than this vision of Tabor -- namely, the sayings and words of the prophets who bear testimony to Christ, whereunto ye must indeed cling, as to a candle which gives light in a dark place. If we will think upon this comparison, we shall find therein the teaching which we are now expounding. For, in telling us to look to the faith whereof the prophets spake, as to a candle that shines in a dark place, he is bidding us remain in the darkness, with our eyes closed to all these other lights; and telling us that in this darkness, faith alone, which likewise is dark, will be the light to which we shall cling; for if we desire to cling to these other bright lights -- namely, to distinct objects of the understanding -- we cease to cling to that dark light, which is faith, and we no longer have that light in the dark place whereof Saint Peter speaks. This place, which here signifies the understanding, which is the candlestick wherein this candle of faith is set, must be dark until the day when the clear vision of God dawns upon it in the life to come, or, in this life, until the day of transformation and union with God to which the soul is journeying.

Footnotes:
- 320. Isaias vi, 4.
- 321. Jeremias i, 11.
- 322. Daniel viii, 10.
- 323. Kings xxii, 11 [A.V., 1 Kings xxii, 11].
- 324. [St. Matthew xxvii, 19.]
- 325. E.p. omits: now natural, now supernatural.' The Saint employs this last word, in this passage, with the sense of preternatural.' Only God can transcend the bounds of nature, but the devil can act in such a way that he appears to be doing so, counterfeiting miracles, and so forth.
- 326. [Lit., to come within God.'] E.p.: to be united with God.'
- 327. Deuteronomy iv, 12.
- 328. Deuteronomy iv, 15.
- 329. Numbers xii, 6-8, [D.V. has Mary' for Miriam'.]
- 330. [The progressive form is used in the Spanish: not to go (or be') leaning upon.']
- 331. [Lit., impede the brightness.']
- 332. St. Peter i, 19.

CHAPTER XVII

Wherein is described the purpose and manner of God in His communication of spiritual blessings to the soul by means of the senses. Herein is answered the question which has been referred to.

There is much to be said concerning the purpose of God, and concerning the manner wherein He gives these visions in order to raise up the soul from its lowly estate to His Divine union. All spiritual books deal with this and in this treatise of ours the method which we pursue is to explain it; therefore I shall only say in this chapter as much as is necessary to answer our question, which was as follows: Since in these supernatural visions there is so much hindrance and peril to progress, as we have said, why does God, Who is most wise and desires to remove stumbling-blocks and snares from the soul, offer and communicate them to it?

2. In order to answer this, it is well first of all to set down three fundamental points. The first is from Saint Paul ad Romanos, where he says: Quae autem sunt, a Deo ordinatoe sunt. [333] Which signifies: The works that are done are ordained of God. The second is from the Holy Spirit in the Book of Wisdom, where He says: Disponit omnia suaviter. [334] And this is as though He had said: The wisdom of God, although it extends from one end to another -- that is to say, from one extreme to another -- orders all things with sweetness. The third is from the theologians, who say that Omnia movet secundum modum eorum. That is, God moves all things according to their nature.

3. It is clear, then, from these fundamental points, that if God is to move the soul and to raise it up from the extreme depth of its lowliness to the extreme height of His loftiness, in Divine union with Him, He must do it with order and sweetness and according to the nature of the soul itself. Then, since the order whereby the soul acquires knowledge is through forms and images of created things, and the natural way wherein it acquires this knowledge and wisdom is through the senses, it follows that, if God is to raise up the soul to supreme knowledge, and to do so with sweetness, He must begin to work from the lowest and extreme end of the senses of the soul, in order that He may gradually lead it, according to its own nature, to the other extreme of His spiritual wisdom, which belongs not to sense. Wherefore He first leads it onward by instructing it through forms, images and ways of sense, according to its own method of understanding, now naturally, now supernaturally, and by means of reasoning, to this supreme Spirit of God.

4. It is for this reason that God gives the soul visions and forms, images and other kinds of sensible and intelligible knowledge of a spiritual nature; not that God would not give it spiritual wisdom immediately, and all at once, if the two extremes -- which are human and Divine, sense and spirit -- could in the ordinary way concur and unite in one single act, without the previous intervention of many other preparatory acts which concur among themselves in order and sweetness, and are a basis and a preparation one for another, like natural agents; so that the first acts serve the second, the second the third, and so onward, in exactly the same way. And thus God brings man to perfection according to the way of man's own nature, working from what is lowest and most exterior up to what is most interior and highest. First, then, He perfects his bodily senses, impelling him to make use of good things which are natural, perfect and exterior, such as hearing sermons and masses, looking on holy things, mortifying the palate at meals and chastening the sense of touch by penance and holy rigour. And, when these senses are in some degree prepared, He is wont to perfect them still further, by bestowing on them certain supernatural favours and gifts, in order to confirm them the more completely in that which is good, offering them certain supernatural communications, such as visions of saints or holy things, in corporeal shape, the sweetest perfumes, locutions, and exceeding great delights of touch, wherewith sense is greatly continued in virtue and is withdrawn from a desire for evil things. And besides this He continues at the same time to perfect the interior bodily senses, whereof we are here treating, such as imagination and fancy, and to habituate them to that which is good, by means of considerations, meditations, and reflections of a sacred kind, in all of which He is instructing the spirit. And, when these are prepared by this natural exercise, God is wont to enlighten and spiritualize them still more by means of certain supernatural visions, which are those that we are here calling imaginary; wherein, as we have said, the spirit, at the same time, profits greatly, for both kinds of vision help to take away its grossness and gradually to reform it. And after this manner God continues to lead the soul step by step till it reaches that which is the most interior of all; not that it is always necessary for Him to observe this order, and to cause the soul to advance exactly in this way, from the first step to the last; sometimes He allows the soul to attain one stage and not another, or leads it from the more interior to the less, or

effects two stages of progress together. This happens when God sees it to be meet for the soul, or when He desires to grant it His favours in this way; nevertheless His ordinary method is as has been said.

5. It is in this way, then, that God instructs [335] the soul and makes it more spiritual, communicating spirituality to it first of all by means of outward and palpable things, adapted to sense, on account of the soul's feebleness and incapacity, so that, by means of the outer husk of those things which in themselves are good, the spirit may make [336] particular acts and receive so many spiritual communications [337] that it may form a habit as to things spiritual, and may acquire actual and substantial spirituality, which is completely removed from every sense. To this, as we have said, the soul cannot attain except very gradually, and in its own way -- that is, by means of sense -- to which it has ever been attached. And thus, in proportion as the spirit attains more nearly to converse with God, it becomes ever more detached and emptied of the ways of sense, which are those of imaginary meditation and reflection. Wherefore, when the soul attains perfectly to spiritual converse with God, it must of necessity have been voided of all that relates to God and yet might come under the head of sense. Even so, the more closely a thing grows attracted to one extreme, the farther removed and withdrawn [338] it becomes from the other; and, when it comes to rest perfectly in the one, it will also have withdrawn itself perfectly from the other. Wherefore there is a commonly quoted spiritual adage which says: Gustato spiritu, desipit omni caro. Which signifies: After the taste and sweetness of the spirit have been experienced, everything carnal is insipid. That is: No profit or enjoyment is afforded by all the ways of the flesh, wherein is included all communication of sense with the spiritual. And this is clear: for, if it is spirit, it has no more to do with sense; and, if sense can comprehend it, it is no longer pure spirit. For, the more can be known of it by natural apprehension and sense, the less it has of spirit and of the supernatural, as has been explained above.

6. The spirit that has become perfect, therefore, pays no heed to sense, nor does it receive anything through sense, nor make any great use of it, neither does it need to do so, in its relations with God, as it did aforetime when it had not grown spiritually. It is this that is signified by that passage from Saint Paul's Epistle to the Corinthians which says: Cum essem parvulus, loquebar ut parvulus, sapiebam ut parvulus, cogitabam ut parvulus. Quando autem factus sum vir, evacuavi quae erant parvuli. [339] This signifies: When I was a child, I spake as a child, I knew as a child, I thought as a child; but, when I became a man, I put away [340] childish things. We have already explained how the things of sense, and the knowledge that spirit can derive from them, are the business of a child. Thus, if the soul should desire to cling to them for ever, and not to throw them aside, it would never be aught but a little child; it would speak ever of God as a child, and would know God as a child, and would think of God as a child; for, clinging to the outer husk of sense, which pertains to the child, it would never attain to the substance of the spirit, which pertains to the perfect man. And thus the soul must not desire to receive the said revelations in order to continue in growth, even though God offer them to it, just as the child must leave the breast in order to accustom its palate to strong meat, which is more substantial.

7. You will ask, then, if, when the soul is immature, it must take these things, and, when it is grown, must abandon them; even as an infant must take the breast, in order to nourish itself, until it be older and can leave it. I answer that, with respect to meditation and natural reflection by means of which the soul begins to seek God, it is true that it must not leave the breast of sense in order to continue taking in nourishment until the time and season to leave it have arrived, and this comes when God brings the soul into a more spiritual communion, which is contemplation, concerning which we gave instruction in the eleventh chapter of this book. [341] But, when it is a question of imaginary visions, or other supernatural apprehensions, which can enter the senses without the co-operation of man's free will, I say that at no time and season must it receive them, whether the soul be in the state of perfection, or whether in a state less perfect -- not even though they come from God. And this for two reasons. The first is that, as we have said, He produces His effect in the soul, without its being able to hinder it, although, as often happens, it can and may hinder visions; and consequently that effect which was to be produced in the soul is communicated to it much more substantially, although not after that manner. For, as we said likewise, the soul cannot hinder the blessings that God desires to communicate to it, since it is not in the soul's power to do so, save when it has some imperfection and attachment; and there is neither imperfection nor attachment in renouncing these things with humility and misgiving. The second reason is that the soul may free itself from the peril and effort inherent in discerning between evil visions and good, and in deciding whether an angel be of light or of darkness. This effort brings the soul no advantage; it merely wastes its time, and hinders it, and becomes to it an occasion of many imperfections and of failure to make progress. The soul concerns not itself, in such a case, with what is important, nor frees itself of trifles in the shape of apprehensions and perceptions of some particular kind. This has already been said in the discussion of corporeal visions; and more will be said on the subject hereafter.

8. Let it be believed, too, that, if Our Lord were not about to lead the soul in a way befitting its own nature, as we say here, He would never communicate to it the abundance of His Spirit through these aqueducts, which are so narrow -- these forms and figures and particular perceptions -- by means

whereof He gives the soul enlightenment by crumbs. For this cause David says: Mittit crystallum suam sicut buccellas. [342] Which is as much as to say: He sent His wisdom to the souls as in morsels. It is greatly to be lamented that, though the soul has infinite capacity, it should be given its food by morsels conveyed through the senses, by reason of the small degree of its spirituality and its incapacitation by sense. Saint Paul was also grieved by this lack of preparation and this incapability of men for receiving the Spirit, when he wrote to the Corinthians, saying: I, brethren, when I came to you, could not speak to you as to spiritual persons, but as to carnal; for ye could not receive it, neither can ye now.' Tamquam parvulis in Christo lac potum vobis dedi, non escam. [343] That is: I have given you milk to drink, as to infants in Christ, and not solid food to eat.

9. It now remains, then, to be pointed out that the soul must not allow its eyes to rest upon that outer husk -- namely, figures and objects set before it supernaturally. These may be presented to the exterior senses, as are locutions and words audible to the ear; or, to the eyes, visions of saints, and of beauteous radiance; or perfumes to the sense of smell; or tastes and sweetnesses to the palate; or other delights to the touch, which are wont to proceed from the spirit, a thing that very commonly happens to spiritual persons. Or the soul may have to avert its eyes from visions of interior sense, such as imaginary visions, all of which it must renounce entirely. It must set its eyes only upon the spiritual good which they produce, striving to preserve it in its works and to practise that which is for the due service of God, paying no heed to those representations nor desiring any pleasure of sense. And in this way the soul takes from these things only that which God intends and wills -- namely, the spirit of devotion -- for there is no other important purpose for which He gives them; and it casts aside that which He would not give if these gifts could be received in the spirit without it, as we have said -- namely, the exercise and apprehension of the senses.

Footnotes:
- 333. Romans xiii, 1.
- 334. Wisdom viii, 1.
- 335. [The verb is progressive (goes (on) instructing').]
- 336. [This verb also is progressive: may go (on) making.']
- 337. [Lit., mouthfuls of spiritual communication.']
- 338. [All the verbs in the last two clauses are in the progressive form.]
- 339. 1 Corinthians xiii, 11.
- 340. [Lit., I emptied.']
- 341. In reality, this instruction is given in Chap. xiii.
- 342. Psalm cxlvii, 17.
- 343. 1 Corinthians iii, 1-2.

CHAPTER XVIII

Which treats of the harm that certain spiritual masters may do to souls when they direct them not by a good method with respect to the visions aforementioned. Describes also how these visions may cause deception even though they be of God.

In this matter of visions we cannot be as brief as we should desire, since there is so much to say about them. Although in substance we have said what is relevant in order to explain to the spiritual person how he is to behave with regard to the visions aforementioned, and to the master who directs him, the way in which he is to deal with his disciple, yet it will not be superfluous to go into somewhat greater detail about this doctrine, and to give more enlightenment as to the harm which can ensue, either to spiritual souls or to the masters who direct them, if they are over-credulous about them, although they be of God.

2. The reason which has now moved me to write at length about this is the lack of discretion, as I understand it, which I have observed in certain spiritual masters. Trusting to these supernatural apprehensions, and believing that they are good and come from God, both masters and disciples have fallen into great error and found themselves in dire straits, wherein is fulfilled the saying of Our Saviour: Si caecus caeco ducatum praestet, ambo in foveam cadunt. [344] Which signifies: If a blind man lead another blind man, both fall into the pit. And He says not 'shall fall,' but fall.' For they may fall without falling into error, since the very venturing of the one to guide the other is going astray, and thus they fall in this respect alone, at the very least. And, first of all, there are some whose way and method with souls that experience these visions cause them to stray, or embarrass them with respect to their visions, or guide them not along the road in some way (for which reason they remain without the true spirit of faith) and edify them not in faith, but lead them to speak highly of those things. By doing this they make them realize that they themselves set some value upon them, or make great account of them, and, consequently, their disciples do the same. Thus their souls have been set upon these apprehensions, instead of being edified in faith, so that they may be empty and detached, and freed from those things and can soar to the heights of dark faith. All this arises from the terms and language which the soul observes its master to employ with respect to these apprehensions; somehow it very easily develops a satisfaction and an esteem for them, which is not in its own control, and which averts its eyes from the abyss of faith.

3. And the reason why this is so easy must be that the soul is so greatly occupied with these things of sense that, as it is inclined to them by nature, and is likewise disposed to enjoy the apprehension of distinct and sensible things, it has only to observe in its confessor, or in some other person, a certain esteem and appreciation for them, and not merely will it at once conceive the same itself, but also, without its realizing the fact, its desire will become lured away by them, so that it will feed upon them and will be ever more inclined toward them and will set a certain value upon them. And hence arise many imperfections, at the very least; for the soul is no longer as humble as before, but thinks that all this is of some importance and productive of good, and that it is itself esteemed by God, and that He is pleased and somewhat satisfied with it, which is contrary to humility. And thereupon the devil secretly sets about increasing this, without the soul's realizing it, and begins to suggest ideas to it about others, as to whether they have these things or have them not, or are this or are that; which is contrary to holy simplicity and spiritual solitude.

4. There is much more to be said about these evils, and of how such souls, unless they withdraw themselves, grow not in faith, and also of how there are other evils of the same kind which, although they be not so palpable and recognizable as these, are subtler and more hateful in the Divine eyes, and which result from not living in complete detachment. Let us, however, leave this subject now, until we come to treat of the vice of spiritual gluttony and of the other six vices, whereof, with the help of God, many things will be said, concerning these subtle and delicate stains which adhere to the spirit when its director cannot guide it in detachment.

5. Let us now say something of this manner wherein certain confessors deal with souls, and instruct them ill. And of a truth I could wish that I knew how to describe it, for I realize that it is a difficult thing to explain how the spirit of the disciple grows in conformity with that of his spiritual father, in a hidden and secret way; and this matter is so tedious that it wearies me, for it seems impossible to speak of the one thing without describing the other also, as they are spiritual things, and the one corresponds with the other.

6. But it is sufficient to say here that I believe, if the spiritual father has an inclination toward revelations of such a kind that they mean something to him, or satisfy or delight his soul, it is impossible but that he will impress that delight and that aim upon the spirit of his disciple, even without realizing it, unless the disciple be more advanced than he; and, even in this latter case, he may well do him grievous harm if he continue with him. For, from that inclination of the spiritual father toward such visions, and the pleasure which he takes in them, there arises a certain kind of esteem for them, of which, unless he watch it carefully, he cannot fail to communicate some indication or impression to other persons; and if any other such person is like-minded and has a similar inclination, it is impossible, as I understand, but that there will be communicated from the one to the other a readiness to apprehend these things and a great esteem for them.

7. But we need not now go into detail about this. Let us speak of the confessor who, whether or no he be inclined toward these things, has not the prudence that he ought to have in disencumbering the soul of his disciple and detaching his desire from them, but begins to speak to him about these visions and devotes the greater part of his spiritual conversation to them, as we have said, giving him signs by which he may distinguish good visions from evil. Now, although it is well to know this, there is no reason for him to involve the soul in such labour, anxiety and peril. By paying no heed to visions, and refusing to receive them, all this is prevented, and the soul acts as it should. Nor is this all, for such confessors, when they see that their penitents are receiving visions from God, beg them to entreat God to reveal them to themselves also, or to say such and such things to them, with respect to themselves or to others, and the foolish souls do so, thinking that it is lawful to desire knowledge by this means. For they suppose that, because God is pleased to reveal or say something by supernatural means, in His own way or for His own purpose, it is lawful for them to desire Him to reveal it to them, and even to entreat Him to do so.

8. And, if it come to pass that God answers their petition and reveals it, they become more confident, thinking that, because God answers them, it is His will and pleasure to do so; whereas, in reality, it is neither God's will nor His pleasure. And they frequently act or believe according to that which He has revealed to them, or according to the way wherein He has answered them; for, as they are attached to that manner of communion with God, the revelation makes a great impression upon them and their will acquiesces in it. They take a natural pleasure in their own way of thinking and therefore naturally acquiesce in it; and frequently they go astray. Then they see that something happens in a way they had not expected; and they marvel, and then begin to doubt if the thing were of God,[345] since it happens not, and they see it not, according to their expectations. At the beginning they thought two things: first, that the vision was of God, since at the beginning it agreed so well with their disposition, and their natural inclination to that kind of thing may well have been the cause of this agreement, as we have said; and secondly that, being of God, it would turn out as they thought or expected.

9. And herein lies a great delusion, for revelations or locutions which are of God do not always turn out as men expect or as they imagine inwardly. And thus they must never be believed or trusted blindly, even though they are known to be revelations or answers or sayings of God. For, although they may in themselves be certain and true, they are not always so in their causes, and according to our manner of understanding, as we shall prove in the chapter following. And afterwards we shall further say and prove that, although God sometimes gives a supernatural answer to that which is asked of Him, it is not His pleasure to do so, and sometimes, although He answers, He is angered.

Footnotes:

344. St. Matthew xv, 14.
345. [Lit., if it were of God.']

CHAPTER XIX

Wherein is expounded and proved how, although visions and locutions which come from God are true, we may be deceived about them. This is proved by quotations from Divine Scripture.

For two reasons we have said that, although visions and locutions which come from God are true, and in themselves are always certain, they are not always so with respect to ourselves. One reason is the defective way in which we understand them; and the other, the variety of their causes. In the first place, it is clear that they are not always as they seem, nor do they turn out as they appear to our manner of thinking. The reason for this is that, since God is vast and boundless, He is wont, in His prophecies, locutions and revelations, to employ ways, concepts and methods of seeing things which differ greatly from such purpose and method as can normally be understood by ourselves; and these are the truer and the more certain the less they seem so to us. This we constantly see in the Scriptures. To many of the ancients many prophecies and locutions of God came not to pass as they expected, because they understood them after their own manner, in the wrong way, and quite literally. This will be clearly seen in these passages.

2. In Genesis, God said to Abraham, when He had brought him to the land of the Chanaanites: Tibi dabo terram hanc. [346] Which signifies, I will give thee this land. And when He had said it to him many times, and Abraham was by now very Domine, unde scire possum, quod possessurus sim eam? That old, and He had never given it to him, though He had said this to him, Abraham answered God once again and said: Lord, whereby or by what sign am I to know that I am to possess it? Then God revealed to him that he was not to possess it in person, but that his sons would do so after four hundred years; and Abraham then understood the promise, which in itself was most true; for, in giving it to his sons for love of him, God was giving it to himself. And thus Abraham was deceived by the way in which he himself had understood the prophecy. If he had then acted according to his own understanding of it, those that saw him die without its having been given to him might have erred greatly; for they were not to see the time of its fulfilment. And, as they had heard him say that God would give it to him, they would have been confounded and would have believed it to have been false.

3. Likewise to his grandson Jacob, when Joseph his son brought him to Egypt because of the famine in Chanaan, and when he was on the road, God appeared and said: Jacob, Jacob, noli timere, descende in Aegiptum, quia in gentem magnam faciam te ibi. Ego descendam tecum illuc. . . . Et inde adducam te revertentem. [347] Which signifies: Jacob, fear not; go down into Egypt, and I will go down there with thee; and, when thou goest forth thence again, I will bring thee out and guide thee. This promise, as it would seem according to our own manner of understanding, was not fulfilled, for, as we know, the good old man Jacob died in Egypt and never left it alive. The word of God was to be fulfilled in his children, whom He brought out thence after many years, being Himself their guide upon the way. It is clear that anyone who had known of this promise made by God to Jacob would have considered it certain that Jacob, even as he had gone to Egypt alive, in his own person, by the command and favour of God, would of a certainty leave it, alive and in his own person, in the same form and manner as he went there, since God had promised him a favourable return; and such a one would have been deceived, and would have marvelled greatly, when he saw him die in Egypt, and the promise, in the sense in which he understood it, remain unfulfilled. And thus, while the words of God are in themselves most true, it is possible to be greatly mistaken with regard to them.

4. In the Judges, again, we read that, when all the tribes of Israel had come together to make war against the tribe of Benjamin, in order to punish a certain evil to which that tribe had been consenting, they were so certain of victory because God had appointed them a captain for the war, that, when twenty-two thousand of their men were conquered and slain, they marvelled very greatly; and, going into the presence of God, they wept all that day, knowing not the cause of the fall, since they had understood that the victory was to be theirs. And, when they enquired of God if they should give battle again or no, He answered that they should go and fight against them. This time they considered victory to be theirs already, and went out with great boldness, and were conquered again the second time, with the loss of eighteen thousand of their men. Thereat they were greatly confused, and knew not what to do, seeing that God had commanded them to fight and yet each time they were vanquished, though they were superior to their enemies in number and strength, for the men of Benjamin were no more than twenty-five thousand and seven hundred and they were four hundred thousand. And in this way they were mistaken in their manner of understanding the words of God. His words were not deceptive, for He

Ascent of Mount Carmel

had not told them that they would conquer, but that they should fight; for by these defeats God wished to chastise a certain neglect and presumption of theirs, and thus to humble them. But, when in the end He answered that they would conquer, it was so, although they conquered only after the greatest stratagem and toil. [348]

5. In this way, and in many other ways, souls are oftentimes deceived with respect to locutions and revelations that come from God, because they interpret them according to their apparent sense [349] and literally; whereas, as has already been explained, the principal intention of God in giving these things is to express and convey the spirit that is contained in them, which is difficult to understand. And the spirit is much more pregnant in meaning than the letter, and is very extraordinary, and goes far beyond its limits. And thus, he that clings to the letter, or to a locution or to the form or figure of a vision, which can be apprehended, will not fail to go far astray, and will forthwith fall into great confusion and error, because he has guided himself by sense according to these visions, and not allowed the spirit to work in detachment from sense. Littera enim occidit, spiritus autem vivificat, [350] as Saint Paul says. That is: The letter killeth and the spirit giveth life. Wherefore in this matter of sense the letter must be set aside, and the soul must remain in darkness, in faith, which is the spirit, and this cannot be comprehended by sense.

6. For which cause, many of the children of Israel, because they took the sayings and prophecies of the prophets according to the strict letter, and these were not fulfilled as they expected, came to make little account of them and believed them not; so much so, that there grew up a common saying among them -- almost a proverb, indeed -- which turned prophets into ridicule. Of this Isaias complains, speaking and exclaiming in the manner following: Quem docebit Dominus scientiam? et quem intelligere faciet auditum? ablactatos a lacte, avulsos ab uberibus. Quia manda remanda, manda remanda, expecta reexpecta, expecta reexpecta, modicum ibi, modicum ibi. In loquela enim labii, et lingua altera loquetur ad populum istum. [351] This signifies: To whom shall God teach knowledge? And whom shall He make to understand His word and prophecy? Only them that are already weaned from the milk and drawn away from the breasts. For all say (that is, concerning the prophecies): Promise and promise again; wait and wait again; wait and wait again; [352] a little there, a little there; for in the words of His lips and in another tongue will He speak to this people. Here Isaias shows quite clearly that these people were turning prophecies into ridicule, and that it was in mockery that they repeated this proverb: Wait and then wait again.' They meant that the prophecies were never fulfilled for them, for they were wedded to the letter, which is the milk of infants, and to their own sense, which is the breasts, both of which contradict the greatness of spiritual knowledge. Wherefore he says: To whom shall He teach the wisdom of His prophecies? And whom shall He make to understand His doctrine, save them that are already weaned from the milk of the letter and from the breasts of their own senses? For this reason these people understand it not, save according to this milk of the husk and letter, and these breasts of their own sense, since they say: Promise and promise again; wait and wait again, etc. For it is in the doctrine of the mouth of God, and not in their own doctrine, and it is in another tongue than their own, that God shall speak to them.

7. And thus, in interpreting prophecy, we have not to consider our own sense and language, knowing that the language of God is very different from ours, and that it is spiritual language, very far removed from our understanding and exceedingly difficult. So much so is it that even Jeremias, though a prophet of God, when he sees that the significance of the words of God is so different from the sense commonly attributed to them by men, is himself deceived by them and defends the people, saying: Heu, heu, heu, Domine Deus, ergone decipisti populum istum et Jerusalem, dicens: Pax erit vobis; et ecce pervenit gladius usque ad animam? [353] Which signifies: Ah, ah, ah, Lord God, hast Thou perchance deceived this people and Jerusalem, saying, Peace will come upon you,' and seest Thou here that the sword reacheth unto their soul? For the peace that God promised them was that which was to be made between God and man by means of the Messiah Whom He was to send them, whereas they understood it of temporal peace; and therefore, when they suffered wars and trials, they thought that God was deceiving them, because there befell them the contrary of that which they expected. And thus they said, as Jeremias says likewise: Exspectavimus pacem, et non erat bonum. [354] That is: We have looked for peace and there is no boon of peace. And thus it was impossible for them not to be deceived, since they took the prophecy merely in its literal sense. For who would fail to fall into confusion and to go astray if he confined himself to a literal interpretation of that prophecy which David spake concerning Christ, in the seventy-first Psalm, and of all that he says therein, where he says: Et dominabitur a mari usque ad mare; et a flumine usque ad terminos orbis terrarum. [355] That is: He shall have dominion from one sea even to the other sea, and from the river even unto the ends of the earth. And likewise in that which he says in the same place: Liberabit pauperem a potente, et pauperem, cui non erat adjutor. [356] Which signifies: He shall deliver the poor man from the power of the mighty, and the poor man that had no helper. But later it became known that Christ was born [357] in a low state and lived in poverty and died in misery; not only had He no dominion over the earth, in a temporal sense, while He lived, but He was subject to lowly people, until He died under the power of Pontius Pilate. And not only did He not

deliver poor men -- namely, His disciples -- from the hands of the mighty, in a temporal sense, but He allowed them to be slain and persecuted for His name's sake.

8. The fact is that these prophecies concerning Christ had to be understood spiritually, in which sense they were entirely true. For Christ was not only Lord of earth alone, but likewise of Heaven, since He was God; and the poor who were to follow Him He was not only to redeem and free from the power of the devil, that mighty one against whom they had no helper, but also to make heirs of the Kingdom of Heaven. And thus God was speaking, in the most important sense, of Christ, and of the reward of His followers, [358] which was an eternal kingdom and eternal liberty; and they understood this, after their own manner, in a secondary sense, of which God takes small account, namely that of temporal dominion and temporal liberty, which in God's eyes is neither kingdom nor liberty at all. Wherefore, being blinded by the insufficiency of the letter, and not understanding its spirit and truth, they took the life of their God and Lord, even as Saint Paul said in these words: Qui enim habitabant Jerusalem, et principes ejus, hunc ignorantes et voces prophetarum, quae per omne Sabbatum leguntur, judicantes impleverunt. [359] Which signifies: They that dwelt in Jerusalem, and her rulers, not knowing Who He was, nor understanding the sayings of the prophets, which are read every Sabbath day, have fulfilled them by judging Him.

9. And to such a point did they carry this inability to understand the sayings of God as it behoved them, that even His own disciples, who had gone about with Him, were deceived, as were those two who, after His death, were going to the village of Emmaus, sad and disconsolate, saying: Nos autem sperabamus quod ipse esset redempturus Israel. [360] We hoped that it was He that should have redeemed Israel. They, too, understood that this dominion and redemption were to be temporal; but Christ our Redeemer, appearing to them, reproved them as foolish and heavy and gross of heart as to their belief in the things that the prophets had spoken. [361] And, even when He was going to Heaven, some of them were still in that state of grossness of heart, and asked Him, saying: Domine, si in tempore hoc restitues Regnum Israel. [362] That is: Lord, tell us if Thou wilt restore at this time the kingdom of Israel. The Holy Spirit causes many things to be said which bear another sense than that which men understand; as can be seen in that which he caused to be said by Caiphas concerning Christ: that is was meet that one man should die lest all the people should perish. [363] This he said not of his own accord; and he said it and understood it in one sense, and the Holy Spirit in another.

10. From this it is clear that, although sayings and revelations may be of God, we cannot always be sure of their meaning; for we can very easily be greatly deceived by them because of our manner of understanding them. For they are all an abyss and a depth of the spirit, and to try to limit them to what we can understand concerning them, and to what our sense can apprehend, is nothing but to attempt to grasp the air, and to grasp some particle in it that the hand touches: the air disappears and nothing remains.

11. The spiritual teacher must therefore strive that the spirituality of his disciple be not cramped by attempts to interpret all supernatural apprehensions, which are no more than spiritual particles, lest he come to retain naught but these, and have no spirituality at all. But let the teacher wean his disciple from all visions and locutions, and impress upon him the necessity of dwelling in the liberty and darkness of faith, wherein are received spiritual liberty and abundance, and consequently the wisdom and understanding necessary to interpret sayings of God. For it is impossible for a man, if he be not spiritual, to judge of the things of God or understand them in a reasonable way, and he is not spiritual when he judges them according to sense; and thus, although they come to him beneath the disguise of sense, he understands them not. This Saint Paul well expresses in these words: Animalis autem homo non percipit ea quoe sunt spiritus Dei: stultitia enim est illi, et non potest intelligere: quia de spiritualibus examinatur. Spiritualis autem judicat omnia. [364] Which signifies: The animal man perceives not the things which are of the Spirit of God, for unto him they are foolishness and he cannot understand them because they are spiritual; but he that is spiritual judges all things. By the animal man is here meant one that uses sense alone; by the spiritual man, one that is not bound or guided by sense. Wherefore it is temerity to presume to have intercourse with God by way of a supernatural apprehension effected by sense, or to allow anyone else to do so.

12. And that this may be the better understood let us here set down a few examples. Let us suppose that a holy man is greatly afflicted because his enemies persecute him, and that God answers him, saying: I will deliver thee from all thine enemies. This prophecy may be very true, yet, notwithstanding, his enemies may succeed in prevailing, and he may die at their hands. And so if a man should understand this after a temporal manner he would be deceived; for God might be speaking of the true and principal liberty and victory, which is salvation, whereby the soul is delivered, free and made victorious [365] over all its enemies, and much more truly so and in a higher sense than if it were delivered from them here below. And thus, this prophecy was much more true and comprehensive than the man could understand if he interpreted it only with respect to this life; for, when God speaks, His words are always to be taken in the sense which is most important and profitable, whereas man, according to his own way and purpose, may understand the less important sense, and thus may be deceived. This we see

in that prophecy which David makes concerning Christ in the second Psalm saying: Reges eos in virga ferrea, et tamquam vas figuli confringes eos.[366] That is: Thou shalt rule all the people with a rod of iron and thou shalt dash them in pieces like a vessel of clay. Herein God speaks of the principal and perfect dominion, which is eternal dominion; and it was in this sense that it was fulfilled, and not in the less important sense, which was temporal, and which was not fulfilled in Christ during any part of His temporal life.

13. Let us take another example. A soul has great desires to be a martyr. It may happen that God answers him, saying: Thou shalt be a martyr. This will give him inwardly great comfort and confidence that he is to be martyred; yet it may come to pass that he dies not the death of a martyr, and notwithstanding this the promise may be true. Why, then, is it not fulfilled literally? Because it will be fulfilled, and is capable of being fulfilled, according to the most important and essential sense of that saying -- namely, in that God will have given that soul the love and the reward which belong essentially to a martyr; and thus in truth He gives to the soul that which it formally desired and that which He promised it. For the formal desire of the soul was, not that particular manner of death, but to do God a martyr's service, and to show its love for Him as a martyr does. For that manner of death is of no worth in itself without this love, the which love and the showing forth thereof and the reward belonging to the martyr may be given to it more perfectly by other means. So that, though it may not die like a martyr, the soul is well satisfied that it has been given that which it sired. For, when they are born of living love, such desires, and others like them, although they be not fulfilled in the way wherein they are described and understood, are fulfilled in another and a better way, and in a way which honours God more greatly than that which they might have asked. Wherefore David says: Desiderium pauperum exaudivit Dominus.[367] That is: The Lord has granted the poor their desire. And in the Proverbs Divine Wisdom says: Desiderium suum justis dabitur.[368] The just shall be given their desire.' Hence, then, since we see that many holy men have desired many particular things for God's sake, and that in this life their desires have not been granted them, it is a matter of faith that, as their desires were just and true, they have been fulfilled for them perfectly in the next life. Since this is truth, it would also be truth for God to promise it to them in this life, saying to them: Your desire shall be fulfilled; and for it not to be fulfilled in the way which they expected.

14. In this and other ways, the words and visions of God may be true and sure and yet we may be deceived by them, through being unable to interpret them in a high and important sense, which is the sense and purpose wherein God intends them. And thus the best and surest course is to train souls in prudence so that they flee from these supernatural things, by accustoming them, as we have said, to purity of spirit in dark faith, which is the means of union.

Footnotes:

346. Genesis xv, 7.
347. Genesis xlvi, 3-4.
348. Judges xx, 12 ff.
349. [Lit., according to the rind.' Cf. bk. II ch. viii, above.]
350. 2 Corinthians iii, 6.
351. Isaias xxviii, 9-11.
352. [For wait,' we may also read hope,' the Spanish word (esperar) here used expressing both these ideas.]
353. Jeremias iv, 10.
354. Jeremias viii, 15.
355. Psalm lxxi, 8 [A.V., lxxii, 8].
356. Psalm lxxi, 12 [A.V., lxxii, 12.]
357. [Lit., 'seeing Him later to be born.']
358. [Lit., of Christ and of His followers.' The addition is necessary to the sense.]
359. Acts xiii, 27.
360. St. Luke xxiv, 21.
361. St. Luke xxiv, 25.
362. Acts i, 6.
363. St. John xi, 50.
364. 1 Corinthians ii, 14.
365. [Lit., free and victorious.']
366. Psalm ii, 9.
367. Psalm ix, 17 [A.V., x, 18].
368. Proverbs x, 24.

CHAPTER XX

Wherein is proved by passages from Scripture how the sayings and words of God, though always true, do not always rest upon stable causes.

We have now to prove the second reason why visions and words which come from God, although in themselves they are always true, are not always stable in their relation to ourselves. This is because of their causes, whereon they are founded; for God often makes statements founded upon creatures and their effects, which are changeable and liable to fail, for which reason the statements which are founded upon them are liable also to be changeable and to fail; for, when one thing depends on another, if one fails, the other fails likewise. It is as though God should say: In a year's time I shall send upon this kingdom such or such a plague; and the cause and foundation for this warning is a certain offence which has been committed against God in that kingdom. If the offence should cease or change, the punishment might cease; yet the threat was true because it was founded upon the fault committed at the time, and, if this had continued, it would have been carried out.

2. This, we see, happened in the city of Ninive, where God said: Adhuc quadraginta dies, et Ninive subvertetur. [369] Which signifies: Yet forty days and Ninive shall be destroyed. This was not fulfilled, because the cause of the threat ceased -- namely, the sins of the city, for which it did penace -- but, if this had not been so, the prophecy would have been carried into effect. We read likewise in the Third Book of the Kings that, when King Achab had committed a very great sin, God sent to prophesy [370] a great punishment -- our father Elias being the messenger -- which should come upon his person, upon his house and upon his kingdom. [371] And, because Achab rent his garments with grief and clothed himself in haircloth and fasted, and slept in sackcloth and went about in a humble and contrite manner, God sent again, by the same prophet, to declare to him these words: Quia igitur humiliatus est mei causa, non inducam malum in diebus ejus, sed in diebus filii sui. [372] Which signifies: Inasmuch as Achab has humbled himself for love of Me, I will not send the evil whereof I spake in his days, but in the days of his son. Here we see that, because Achab changed his spirit and his former affection, God likewise changed His sentence.

3. From this we may deduce, as regards the matter under discussion, that, although God may have revealed or affirmed something to a soul, whether good or evil, and whether relating to that soul itself or to others, this may, to a greater or a lesser extent, be changed or altered or entirely withdrawn, according to the change or variation in the affection of this soul, or the cause whereon God based His judgment, and thus it would not be fulfilled in the way expected, and oftentimes none would have known why, save only God. For God is wont to declare and teach and promise many things, not that they may be understood or possessed at the time, but that they may be understood at a later time, when it is fitting that a soul may have light concerning them, or when their effect is attained. This, as we see, He did with His disciples, to whom He spake many parables, and pronounced many judgments, the wisdom whereof they understood not until the time when they had to preach it, which was when the Holy Spirit came upon them, of Whom Christ had said to them that He would explain to them all the things that He had spoken to them in His life. And, when Saint John speaks of that entry of Christ into Jerusalem, he says: Haec non cognoverunt discipuli ejus primum: sed quando glorificatus est Jesus, tunc recordati sunt quia haec erant scripta de eo. [373] And thus there may pass through the soul many detailed messages from God which neither the soul nor its director will understand until the proper time.

4. Likewise, in the First Book of the Kings, we read that, when God was wroth against Heli, a priest of Israel, for his sins in not chastising his sons, he sent to him by Samuel to say, among other words, these which follow: Loquens locutus sum, ut domus tua, et domus patris tui, ministraret in conspectu meo, usque in sempiternum. Verumtamen absit hoc a me. And this is as though He had said: [374] In very truth I said aforetime that thy house and the house of thy father should serve Me continually in the priesthood in my presence for ever, but this purpose is far from Me; I will not do this thing. For this office of the priesthood was founded for giving honour and glory to God, and to this end God has promised to give it to the father of Heli for ever if he failed not. But, when Heli failed in zeal for the honour of God (for, as God Himself complained when He sent him the message, he honoured his sons more than God, overlooking their sins so as not to offend them), the promise also failed which would have held good for ever if the good service and zeal of Heli had lasted for ever. And thus there is no reason to think that, because sayings and revelations come from God, they must invariably come to pass in their apparent sense, especially when they are bound up with human causes which may vary, change, or alter.

5. And when they are dependent upon these causes God Himself knows, though He does not

Ascent of Mount Carmel

always declare it, but pronounces the saying, or makes the revelation, and sometimes says nothing of the condition, as when He definitely told the Ninivites that they would be destroyed after forty days. [375] At other times, he lays down the condition, as He did to Roboam, saying to him: If thou wilt keep My commandments, as my servant David, I will be with thee even as I was with him, and will set thee up a house as I did to My servant David'. [376] But, whether He declares it or no, the soul must not rely upon its own understanding; for it is impossible to understand the hidden truths of God which are in His sayings, and the multitude of their meanings. He is above the heavens, and speaks according to the way of eternity; [377] we blind souls are upon the earth and understand only the ways of flesh and time. It was for that reason, I believe, that the Wise Man said: God is in Heaven, and thou are upon earth; wherefore be not thou lengthy or hasty in speaking.' [378]

6. You will perhaps ask me: Why, if we are not to understand these things, or to play any part in them, does God communicate them to us? I have already said that everything will be understood in its own time by the command of Him Who spake it, and he whom God wills shall understand it, and it will be seen that it was fitting; for God does naught save with due cause and in truth. Let it be realized, therefore, that there is no complete understanding of the meaning of the sayings and things of God, and that this meaning cannot be decided by what it seems to be, without great error, and, in the end, grievous confusion. This was very well known to the prophets, into whose hands was given the word of God, and who found it a sore trial to prophesy concerning the people; for, as we have said, many of the people saw that things came not to pass literally, as they were told them, for which cause they laughed at the prophets and mocked them greatly; so much that Jeremias went as far as to say: They mock me all the day long, they scorn and despise me every one, for I have long been crying against evil and promising them destruction; and the word of the Lord has been made a reproach and a derision to me continually. And I said, I must not remember Him, neither speak any more in His name.' [379] Herein, although the holy prophet was speaking with resignation and in the form of a weak man who cannot endure the ways and workings of God, he clearly indicates the difference between the way wherein the Divine sayings are fulfilled and the ordinary meaning which they appear to have; for the Divine prophets were treated as mockers, and suffered so much from their prophecy that Jeremias himself said elsewhere: Formido et laqueus facta est nobis vaticinatio et contritio. [380] Which signifies: Prophecy has become to us fear and snares and contradiction of spirit.

7. And the reason why Jonas fled when God sent him to preach the destruction of Ninive was this, namely, that he knew the different meanings of the sayings of God with respect to the understanding of men and with respect to the causes of the sayings. And thus, lest they should mock him when they saw that his prophecy was not fulfilled, he went away and lied in order not to prophesy; and thus he remained waiting all the forty days outside the city, to see if his prophecy was fulfilled; and, when it was not fulfilled, he was greatly afflicted, so much so that he said to God: Obsecro, Domine, numquid non hoc est verbum meum, cum adhuc essem in terra mea? propter hoc praeoccupavi, ut fugerem in Tharsis. [381] That is: I pray Thee, O Lord, is not this what I said when I was yet in my own country? Therefore was I vexed, and fled away to Tharsis. And the saint was wroth and besought God to take away his life.

8. Why, then, must we marvel that God should speak and reveal certain things to souls which come not to pass in the sense wherein they understand them? For, if God should affirm or represent such or such a thing to the soul, whether good or evil, with respect to itself or to another, and if that thing be founded upon a certain affection or service or offence of that soul, or of another, at that time, with respect to God, so that, if the soul persevere therein, it will be fulfilled; yet even then its fulfillment is not certain, since it is not certain that the soul will persevere. Wherefore we must rely, not upon understanding, but upon faith.

Footnotes:

369. Jonas iii, 4.
370. [Lit., to promise.']
371. 3 Kings [A.V., 1 Kings] xxi, 21.
372. 3 Kings [A.V., 1 Kings] xxi, 27-9.
373. St. John xii, 16.
374. 1 Kings [A.V., 1 Samuel] ii, 30.
375. Jonas iii, 4.
376. 3 Kings [A.V., 1 Kings] xi, 38. [Actually it was to Jeroboam that this was said.]
377. [Lit., on the road of eternity.']
378. Ecclestiastes v, 1 [A.V., v, 2].
379. Jeremias xx, 7-9.
380. Lamentations iii, 47.
381. Jonas iv, 2.

CHAPTER XXI

Wherein is explained how at times, although God answers the prayers that are addressed to Him, He is not pleased that we should use such methods. It is also shown how, although He condescend to us and answer us, He is oftentimes wroth.

Certain spiritual men, as we have said, assure themselves that it is a good thing to display curiosity, as they sometimes do, in striving to know certain things by supernatural methods, thinking that, because God occasionally answers their importunity, this is a good method and pleasing to Him. Yet the truth is that, although He may answer them, the method is not good, neither is it pleasing to God, but rather it is displeasing to Him; and not only so, but oftentimes He is greatly offended and wroth. The reason for this is that it is lawful for no creature to pass beyond the limits that God has ordained for its governance after the order of nature. He has laid down rational and natural limits for man's governance; wherefore to desire to pass beyond them is not lawful, and to desire to seek out and attain to anything by supernatural means is to go beyond these natural limits. It is therefore an unlawful thing, and it is therefore not pleasing to God, for He is offended by all that is unlawful. King Achaz was well aware of this, since, although Isaias told him from God to ask for a sign, he would not do so, saying: Non petam, et non tentabo Dominum. [382] That is: I will not ask such a thing, neither will I tempt God. For it is tempting God to seek to commune with Him by extraordinary ways, such as those that are supernatural.

2. But why, you will say, if it be a fact that God is displeased, does He sometimes answer? I reply that it is sometimes the devil who answers. And, if it is God Who answers, I reply that He does so because of the weakness of the soul that desires to travel along that road, lest it should be disconsolate and go backward, or lest it should think that God is wroth with it and should be overmuch afflicted; or for other reasons known to God, founded upon the weakness of that soul, whereby God sees that it is well that He should answer it and deigns to do so in that way. In a like manner, too, does He treat many weak and tender souls, granting them favours and sweetness in sensible converse with Himself, as has been said above; this is not because He desires or is pleased that they should commune with Him after that manner or by these methods; it is that He gives to each one, as we have said, after the manner best suited to him. For God is like a spring, whence everyone draws water according to the vessel which he carries. Sometimes a soul is allowed to draw it by these extraordinary channels; but it follows not from this that it is lawful to draw water by them, but only that God Himself can permit this, when, how and to whom He wills, and for what reason He wills, without the party concerned having any right in the matter. And thus, as we say, He sometimes deigns to satisfy the desire and the prayer of certain souls, whom, since they are good and sincere, He wills not to fail to succour, lest He should make them sad, but it is not because He is pleased with their methods that He wills it. This will be the better understood by the following comparison.

3. The father of a family has on his table many and different kinds of food, some of which are better than others. A child is asking him for a certain dish, not the best, but the first that meets its eye, and it asks for this dish because it would rather eat of it than any other; and as the father sees that, even if he gives it the better kind of food, it will not take it, but will have that which it asks for, since that alone pleases it, he gives it that, regretfully, lest it should take no food at all and be miserable. In just this way, we observe, did God treat the children of Israel when they asked Him for a king: He gave them one, but unwillingly, because it was not good for them. And thus He said to Samuel: Audi vocem populi in omnibus quae loquuntur tibi: non enim te objecerunt, sed me. [383] Which signifies: Hearken unto the voice of this people and grant them the king whom they ask of thee, for they have not rejected thee but Me, that I should not reign over them. In this same way God condescends to certain souls, and grants them that which is not best for them, because they will not or cannot walk by any other road. And thus certain souls attain to tenderness and sweetness of spirit or sense; and God grants them this because they are unable to partake of the stronger and more solid food of the trials of the Cross of His Son, which He would prefer them to take, rather than aught else.

4. I consider, however, that the desire to know things by supernatural means is much worse than the desire for other spiritual favours pertaining to the senses; for I cannot see how the soul that desires them can fail to commit, at the least, venial sin, however good may be its aims, and however far advanced it may be on the road to perfection; and if anyone should bid the soul desire them, and consent to it, he sins likewise. For there is no necessity for any of these things, since the soul has its natural

Ascent of Mount Carmel

reason and the doctrine and law of the Gospel, which are quite sufficient for its guidance, and there is no difficulty or necessity that cannot be solved and remedied by these means, which are very pleasing to God and of great profit to souls; and such great use must we make of our reason and of Gospel doctrine that, if certain things be told us supernaturally, whether at our desire or no, we must receive only that which is in clear conformity with reason and Gospel law. And then we must receive it, not because it is revelation, but because it is reason, and not allow ourselves to be influenced by the fact that it has been revealed. Indeed, it is well in such a case to look at that reason and examine it very much more closely than if there had been no revelation concerning it; inasmuch as the devil utters many things that are true, and that will come to pass, and that are in conformity with reason, in order that he may deceive.

5. Wherefore, in all our needs, trials and difficulties, there remains to us no better and surer means than prayer and hope that God will provide for us, by such means as He wills. This is the advice given to us in the Scriptures, where we read that, when King Josaphat was greatly afflicted and surrounded by enemies, the saintly King gave himself to prayer, saying to God: Cum ignoremus quid facere debeamus, hoc solum habemus residue, ut oculos nostros dirigamus ad re.[384] Which is as though he had said: When means fail and reason is unable to succour us in our necessities, it remains for us only to lift up our eyes to Thee, that Thou mayest succour us as is most pleasing to Thee.

6. And further, although this has also been made clear, it will be well to prove, from certain passages of Scripture, that, though God may answer such requests, He is none the less sometimes wroth. In the First Book of the Kings it is said that, when King Saul begged that the prophet Samuel, who was now dead, might speak to him, the said prophet appeared to him, and that God was wroth with all this, since Samuel at once reproved Saul for having done such a thing, saying: Quare inquietasti me, ut suscitarer?[385] That is: Why hast thou disquieted me, in causing me to arise? We also know that, in spite of having answered the children of Israel and given them the meat that they besought of Him, God was nevertheless greatly incensed against them; for He sent fire from Heaven upon them as a punishment, as we read in the Pentateuch, and as David relates in these words: Adhuc escape eorum erant in ore ipsorum, et ira Dei descendit super eos.[386] Which signifies: Even as they had the morsels in their mouths, the wrath of God came down upon them. And likewise we read in Numbers that God was greatly wroth with Balaam the prophet, because he went to the Madianites when Balac their king sent for him, although God had bidden him go, because he desired to go and had begged it of God; and while he was yet in the way there appeared to him an angel with a sword, who desired to slay him, and said to him: Perversa est via tua, mihique contraria.[387] Thy way is perverse and contrary to Me.' For which cause he desired to slay him.

7. After this manner and many others God deigns to satisfy the desires of souls though He be wroth with them. Concerning this we have many testimonies in Scripture, and, in addition, many illustrations, though in a matter that is so clear these are unnecessary. I will merely say that to desire to commune with God by such means is a most perilous thing, more so than I can express, and that one who is affectioned to such methods will not fail to err greatly and will often find himself in confusion. Anyone who in the past has prized them will understand me from his own experience. For over and above the difficulty that there is in being sure that one is not going astray in respect of locutions and visions which are of God, there are ordinarily many of these locutions and visions which are of the devil; for in his converse with the soul the devil habitually wears the same guise as God assumes in His dealings with it, setting before it things that are very like to those which God communicates to it, insinuating himself, like the wolf in sheep's clothing, among the flock, with a success so nearly complete that he can hardly be recognized. For, since he says many things that are true, and in conformity with reason, and things that come to pass as he describes them,[388] it is very easy for the soul to be deceived, and to think that, since these things come to pass as he says, and the future is correctly foretold, this can be the work of none save God; for such souls know not that it is a very easy thing for one that has clear natural light to be acquainted, as to their causes, with things, or with many of them, which have been or shall be. And since the devil has a very clear light of this kind, he can very easily deduce effect from cause, although it may not always turn out as he says, because all causes depend upon the will of God. Let us take an example.

8. The devil knows that the constitution of the earth and the atmosphere, and the laws ruling the sun, are disposed in such manner and in such degree that, when a certain moment has arrived, it will necessarily follow, according to the laws of nature laid down for these elements, that they will infect people with pestilence, and he knows in what places this will be more severe and in what places less so. Here you have a knowledge of pestilence in respect of its causes. What a wonderful thing it seems when the devil reveals this to a soul, saying: In a year or in six months from now there will be pestilence,' and it happens as he says! And yet this is a prophecy of the devil. In the same way he may have a knowledge of earthquakes, and, seeing that the bowels of the earth are filling with air, will say: At such a time there will be an earthquake.' Yet this is only natural knowledge, for the possession of which it suffices for the spirit to be free from the passions of the soul, even as Boetius says in these words: Si vis claro lumine cernere verum, gaudia pelle, timorem, spemque fugato, nec dolor adsit.[389] That is: If thou desire to

know truths with the clearness of nature, cast from thee rejoicing and fear and hope and sorrow.

9. And likewise supernatural events and happenings may be known, in their causes, in matters concerning Divine Providence, which deals most justly and surely as is required by their good or evil causes as regards the sons of men. For one may know by natural means that such or such a person, or such or such a city, or some other place, is in such or such necessity, or has reached such or such a point, so that God, according to His providence and justice, must deal with such a person or thing in the way required by its cause, and in the way that is fitting for it, whether by means of punishment or of reward, as the cause merits. And then one can say: At such a time God will give you this, or will do this, or that will come to pass, of a surety.' It was this that holy Judith said to Holofernes, [390] when, in order to persuade him that the children of Israel would without fail be destroyed, she first related to him many of their sins and the evil deeds that they did. And then she said: Et, quoniam haec faciunt, certum est quod in perditionem dabuntur. Which signifies: Since they do these things, it is certain that they will be destroyed. This is to know the punishment in the cause, and it is as though she had said: It is certain that such sins must be the cause of such punishments, at the hand of God Who is most just. And as the Divine Wisdom says: Per quae quis peccat, per haec et torquetur. [391] With respect to that and for that wherein a man sins, therein is he punished.

10. The devil may have knowledge of this, not only naturally, but also by the experience which he has of having seen God do similar things, and he can foretell it and do so correctly. Again, holy Tobias was aware of the punishment of the city of Ninive because of its cause, and he thus admonished his son, saying: Behold, son, in the hour when I and thy mother die, go thou forth from this land, for it will not remain.' Video enim quia iniquitas ejus finem dabit ei. [392] I see clearly that its own iniquity will be the cause of its punishment, which will be that it shall be ended and destroyed altogether. This might have been known by the devil as well as by Tobias, not only because of the iniquity of the city, but by experience, since they had seen that for the sins of the world God destroyed it in the Flood, and that the Sodomites, too, perished for their sins by fire; but Tobias knew it also through the Divine Spirit.

11. And the devil may know that one Peter [393] cannot, in the course of nature, live more than so many years, and he may foretell this; and so with regard to many other things and in many ways that it is impossible to recount fully -- nor can one even begin to recount many of them, since they are most intricate and subtle -- he insinuates falsehoods; from which a soul cannot free itself save by fleeing from all revelations and visions and locutions that are supernatural. Wherefore God is justly angered with those that receive them, for He sees that it is temerity on their part to expose themselves to such great peril and presumption and curiosity, and things that spring from pride, and are the root and foundation of vainglory, and of disdain for the things of God, and the beginning of many evils to which many have come. Such persons have succeeded in angering God so greatly that He has of set purpose allowed them to go astray and be deceived and to blind their own spirits and to leave the ordered paths of life and give rein to their vanities and fancies, according to the word of Isaias, where he says: Dominus miscuit in medio ejus spiritum vertiginis. [394] Which is as much to say: The Lord hath mingled in the midst thereof the spirit of dissension and confusion. Which in our ordinary vernacular signifies the spirit of misunderstanding. What Isaias is here very plainly saying is to our purpose, for he is speaking of those who were endeavouring by supernatural means to know things that were to come to pass. And therefore he says that God mingled in their midst the spirit of misunderstanding; not that God willed them, in fact, to have the spirit of error, or gave it to them, but that they desired to meddle with that to which by nature they could not attain. Angered by this, God allowed them to act foolishly, giving them no light as to that wherewith He desired not that they should concern themselves. And thus the Prophet says that God mingled that spirit in them, privatively. And in this sense God is the cause of such an evil -- that is to say, He is the privative cause, which consists in His withdrawal of His light and favour, to such a point that they must needs fall into error.

12. And in this way God gives leave to the devil to blind and deceive many, when their sins and audacities merit it; and this the devil can do and does successfully, and they give him credence and believe him to be a good spirit; to such a point that, although they may be quite persuaded that he is not so, they cannot undeceive themselves, since, by the permission of God, there has already been insinuated into them the spirit of misunderstanding, even as we read was the case with the prophets of King Achab, whom God permitted to be deceived by a lying spirit, giving the devil leave to deceive them, and saying: Decipies, et praevalebis; egredere, et fac ita. [395] Which signifies: Thou shalt prevail with thy falsehood, and shalt deceive them; go forth and do so. And so well was he able to work upon the prophets and the King, in order to deceive them, that they would not believe the prophet Micheas, who prophesied the truth to them, saying the exact contrary of that which the others had prophesied, and this came to pass because God permitted them to be blinded, since their affections were attached to that which they desired to happen to them, and God answered them according to their desires and wishes; and this was a most certain preparation and means for their being blinded and deceived, which God allowed of set purpose.

13. Thus, too, did Ezechiel prophesy in the name of God. Speaking against those who began to

Ascent of Mount Carmel

desire to have knowledge direct from God, from motives of curiosity, according to the vanity of their spirit, he says: When such a man comes to the prophet to enquire of Me through him, I, the Lord, will answer him by Myself, and I will set my face in anger against that man; and, as to the prophet, when he has gone astray in that which was asked of him, Ego Dominus decepi prophetam illum.[396] That is: I, the Lord, have deceived that prophet. This is to be taken to mean, by not succouring him with His favour so that he might not be deceived; and this is His meaning when He says: I the Lord will answer him by Myself in anger[397] -- that is, God will withdraw His grace and favour from that man. Hence necessarily follows deception by reason of his abandonment by God. And then comes the devil and makes answer according to the pleasure and desire of that man, who, being pleased thereat, since the answers and communications are according to his will, allows himself to be deceived greatly.

14. It may appear that we have to some extent strayed from the purpose that we set down in the title of this chapter, which was to prove that, although God answers, He sometimes complains. But, if it be carefully considered, all that has been said goes to prove or intention; for it all shows that God desires not that we should wish for such visions, since He makes it possible for us to be deceived by them in so many ways.

Footnotes:

382. Isaias vii, 12. [The Spanish has Achab' for Achaz.']
383. 1 Kings [A.V., 1 Samuel] viii, 7.
384. 2 Paralipomenon [A.V., 2 Chronicles] xx, 12.
385. 1 Kings [A.V., 1 Samuel] xxviii, 15.
386. Psalm lxxvii, 30-1 [A.V., lxxviii, 30-1].
387. Numbers xxii, 32.
388. [Lit., that come out true.']
389. The exact reading in Boetius is: Tu quoque si vis lumine claro cernere vernum -- Tramite recto carpere callem -- Gaudia pelle -- Pelle timorem -- Spemque fugato -- Nec dolor adsit' (Migne, Vol. LXXV, p. 122).
390. Judith xi, 12.
391. Wisdom xi, 17 [A.V., xi, 16].
392. Tobias xiv, 13.
393. [i.e., any individual.]
394. Isaias xix, 14.
395. 3 Kings [A.V., 1 Kings] xxii, 22.
396. Ezechiel xiv, 7-9.
397. [Ezechiel xiv, 7.]

CHAPTER XXII

Wherein is solved a difficulty -- namely, why it is not lawful, under the law of grace, to ask anything of God by supernatural means, as it was under the old law. This solution is proved by a passage from Saint Paul.

Difficulties keep coming to our mind, and thus we cannot progress with the speed that we should desire. For as they occur to us, we are obliged of necessity to clear them up, so that the truth of this teaching may ever be plain and carry its full force. But there is always this advantage in these difficulties, that, although they somewhat impede our progress, they serve nevertheless to make our intention the clearer and more explicit, [398] as will be the case with the present one.

2. In the previous chapter, we said that it is not the will of God that souls should desire to receive anything distinctly, by supernatural means, through visions, locutions, etc. Further, we saw in the same chapter, and deduced from the testimonies which were there brought forward from Scripture, that such communion with God was employed in the Old Law and was lawful; and that not only was it lawful, but God commanded it. And when they used not this opportunity, God reproved them, as is to be seen in Isaias, where God reproves the children of Israel because they desired to go down to Egypt without first enquiring of Him, saying: Et os meum non interrogastis. [399] That is: Ye asked not first at My own mouth what was fitting. And likewise we read in Josue that, when the children of Israel themselves are deceived by the Gabaonites, the Holy Spirit reproves them for this fault, saying: Susceperunt ergo de cibariis eorum, et os Domini non interrogaverunt. [400] Which signifies: They took of their victuals and they enquired not at the mouth of God. Furthermore, we see in the Divine Scripture that Moses always enquired of God, as did King David and all the kings of Israel with regard to their wars and necessities, and the priests and prophets of old, and God answered and spake with them and was not wroth, and it was well done; and if they did it not it would be ill done; and this is the truth. Why, then, in the new law -- the law of grace -- may it not now be as it was aforetime?

3. To this it must be replied that the principal reason why in the law of Scripture the enquiries that were made of God were lawful, and why it was fitting that prophets and priests should seek visions and revelations of God, was because at that time faith had no firm foundation, neither was the law of the Gospel established; and thus it was needful that men should enquire of God and that He should speak, whether by words or by visions and revelations or whether by figures and similitudes or by many other ways of expressing His meaning. For all that He answered and spake and revealed belonged to the mysteries of our faith and things touching it or leading to it. And, since the things of faith are not of man, but come from the mouth of God Himself, God Himself reproved them because they enquired not at His mouth in their affairs, so that He might answer, and might direct their affairs and happenings toward the faith, of which at that time they had no knowledge, because it was not yet founded. But now that the faith is founded in Christ, and in this era of grace, the law of the Gospel has been made manifest, there is no reason to enquire of Him in that manner, nor for Him to speak or to answer as He did then. For, in giving us, as He did, His Son, which is His Word -- and He has no other -- He spake to us all together, once and for all, in this single Word, and He has no occasion to speak further.

4. And this is the sense of that passage with which Saint Paul begins, when he tries to persuade the Hebrews that they should abandon those first manners and ways of converse with God which are in the law of Moses, and should set their eyes on Christ alone, saying: Multifariam multisque modis olim Deus loquens patribus in Prophetis: novissime autem diebus istis locutus est nobis in Filio. [401] And this is as though he had said: That which God spake of old in the prophets to our fathers, in sundry ways and divers manners, He has now, at last, in these days, spoken to us once and for all in the Son. Herein the Apostle declares that God has become, as it were, dumb, and has no more to say, since that which He spake aforetime, in part to the prophets, He has now spoken altogether in Him, giving us the All, which is His Son.

5. Wherefore he that would now enquire of God, or seek any vision or revelation, would not only be acting foolishly, but would be committing an offence against God, by not setting his eyes altogether upon Christ, and seeking no new thing or aught beside. And God might answer him after this manner, saying: If I have spoken all things to thee in My Word, Which is My Son, and I have no other word, what answer can I now make to thee, or what can I reveal to thee which is greater than this? Set thine eyes on Him alone, for in Him I have spoken and revealed to thee all things, and in Him thou shalt find yet more than that which thou askest and desirest. For thou askest locutions and revelations, which are

Ascent of Mount Carmel

the part; but if thou set thine eyes upon Him, thou shalt find the whole; for He is My complete locution and answer, and He is all My vision and all My revelation; so that I have spoken to thee, answered thee, declared to thee and revealed to thee, in giving Him to thee as thy brother, companion and master, as ransom and prize. For since that day when I descended upon Him with My Spirit on Mount Tabor, saying: Hic est filius meus dilectus, in quo mihi bene complacui, ipsum audite [402] (which is to say: This is My beloved Son, in Whom I am well pleased; hear ye Him), I have left off all these manners of teaching and answering, and I have entrusted this to Him. Hear Him; for I have no more faith to reveal, neither have I any more things to declare. For, if I spake aforetime, it was to promise Christ; and, if they enquired of Me, their enquiries were directed to petitions for Christ and expectancy concerning Him, in Whom they should find every good thing (as is now set forth in all the teaching of the Evangelists and the Apostles); but now, any who would enquire of Me after that manner, and desire Me to speak to him or reveal aught to him, would in a sense be asking Me for Christ again, and asking Me for more faith, and be lacking in faith, which has already been given in Christ; and therefore he would be committing a great offence against My beloved Son, for not only would he be lacking in faith, but he would be obliging Him again first of all to become incarnate and pass through life and death. Thou shalt find naught to ask Me, or to desire of Me, whether revelations or visions; consider this well, for thou shalt find that all has been done for thee and all has been given to thee -- yea, and much more also -- in Him.

6. If thou desirest Me to answer thee with any word of consolation, consider My Son, Who is subject to Me, and bound by love of Me, and afflicted, and thou shalt see how fully He answers thee. If thou desirest Me to expound to thee secret things, or happenings, set thine eyes on Him alone, and thou shalt find the most secret mysteries, and the wisdom and wondrous things of God, which are hidden in Him, even as My Apostle says: In quo sunt omnes thesauri sapientiae et scientiae Dei absconditi. [403] That is: In this Son of God are hidden all the treasures of wisdom and knowledge of God. These treasures of wisdom shall be very much more sublime and delectable and profitable for thee than the things that thou desiredst to know. Herein the same Apostle gloried, saying: That he had not declared to them that he knew anything, save Jesus Christ and Him crucified. [404] And if thou shouldst still desire other Divine or bodily revelations and visions, look also at Him made man, and thou shalt find therein more than thou thinkest, for the Apostle says likewise: In ipso habitat omnis plenitudo Divinitatis corporaliter. [405] Which signifies: In Christ dwelleth all the fullness of the Godhead bodily.

7. It is not fitting, then, to enquire of God by supernatural means, nor is it necessary that He should answer; since all the faith has been given us in Christ, and there is therefore no more of it to be revealed, nor will there ever be. And he that now desires to receive anything in a supernatural manner, as we have said, is, as it were, finding fault with God for not having given us a complete sufficiency in His Son. For, although such a person may be assuming the faith, and believing it, nevertheless he is showing a curiosity which belongs to faithlessness. We must not expect, then, to receive instruction, or aught else, in a supernatural manner. For, at the moment when Christ gave up the ghost upon the Cross, saying, Consummatum est, [406] which signifies, It is finished,' an end was made, not only of all these forms, but also of all those other ceremonies and rites of the Old Law. And so we must now be guided in all things by the law of Christ made man, and by that of His Church, and of His ministers, in a human and a visible manner, and by these means we must remedy our spiritual weaknesses and ignorances, since in these means we shall find abundant medicine for them all. If we leave this path, we are guilty not only of curiosity, but of great audacity: nothing is to be believed in a supernatural way, save only that which is the teaching of Christ made man, as I say, and of His ministers, who are men. So much so that Saint Paul says these words: Quod si Angelus de coelo evengelizaverit, praterquam quod evangelizavimus vobis, anathema sit. [407] That is to say: If any angel from Heaven preach any other gospel unto you than that which we men preach unto you, let him be accursed and excommunicate.

8. Wherefore, since it is true that we must ever be guided by that which Christ taught us, and that all things else are as nothing, and are not to be believed unless they are in conformity with it, he who still desires to commune with God after the manner of the Old Law acts vainly. Furthermore, it was not lawful at that time for everyone to enquire of God, neither did God answer all men, but only the priests and prophets, from whose mouths it was that the people had to learn law and doctrine; and thus, if a man desire to know anything of God, he enquired of Him through the prophet or the priest and not of God Himself. And, if David enquired of God at certain times upon his own account, he did this because he was a prophet, and yet, even so, he did it not without the priestly vestment as it is clear was the case in the First Book of the Kings, where he said to Abimelech the priest: Applica ad me Ephod [408] -- which ephod was one of the priestly vestments, having which he then spake with God. But at other times he spake with God through the prophet Nathan and other prophets. And by the mouths of these prophets and of the priests men were to believe that that which was said to them came from God; they were not to believe it because of their own opinions.

9. And thus, men were not authorized or empowered at that time to give entire credence to what was said by God, unless it were approved by the mouths of priests and prophets. For God is so desirous that the government and direction of every man should be undertaken by another man like himself, and

that every man should be ruled and governed by natural reason, that He earnestly desires us not to give entire credence to the things that He communicates to us supernaturally, nor to consider them as being securely and completely confirmed until they pass through this human aqueduct of the mouth of man. And thus, whenever He says or reveals something to a soul, He gives this same soul to whom He says it a kind of inclination to tell it to the person to whom it is fitting that it should be told. Until this has been done, it is not wont to give entire satisfaction, because the man has not taken it from another man like himself. We see in the Book of the Judges that the same thing happened to the captain Gedeon, to whom God had said many times that he should conquer the Madianites, yet he was fearful and full of doubts (for God had allowed him to retain that weakness) until he heard from the mouth of men what God had said to him. And it came to pass that, when God saw he was weak, He said to him: Rise up and go down to the camp.' Et cum audieris quid loquantur, tunc confortabuntur manus tuae, et securior ad hostium castra descendes. [409] That is: When thou shalt hear what men are saying there, then shalt thou receive strength in that which I have said to thee, and thou shalt go down with greater security to the hosts of the enemy. And so it came to pass that, having heard a dream related by one of the Madianites to another, wherein the Madianite had dreamed that Gedeon should conquer them, he was greatly strengthened, and began to prepare for the battle with great joy. From this it can be seen that God desired not that he should feel secure, since He gave him not the assurance by supernatural means alone, but caused him first to be strengthened by natural means.

10. And even more surprising is the thing that happened in this connection to Moses, when God had commanded him, and given him many instructions, which He continued with the signs of the wand changed into a serpent and of the leprous hand, enjoining him to go and set free the children of Israel. So weak was he and so uncertain [410] about this going forward that, although God was angered, he had not the courage to summon up the complete faith necessary for going, until God encouraged him through his brother Aaron, saying: Aaron frater tuus Levites, scio quod eloquent sit: ecce ipse egredietur in occursum tuum, vidensque te, laetabitur corde. Loquere ad eum, en pone verba mea in ore ejus: et ego ero in ore tuo, et in ore illius, etc. [411] Which is as though He had said: I know that thy brother Aaron is an eloquent man: behold, he will come forth to meet thee, and, when he seeth thee, he will be glad at heart; speak to him and tell him all My words, and I will be in thy mouth and in his mouth, so that each of you shall believe that which is in the mouth of the other.

11. Having heard these words, Moses at once took courage, in the hope of finding consolation in the counsel which his brother was to give him; for this is a characteristic of the humble soul, which dares not converse alone with God, neither can be completely satisfied without human counsel and guidance. And that this should be given to it is the will of God, for He draws near to those who come together to converse of truth, in order to expound and confirm it in them, upon a foundation of natural reason, even as He said that He would do when Moses and Aaron should come together -- namely, that He would be in the mouth of the one and in the mouth of the other. Wherefore He said likewise in the Gospel that Ubi fuerint duo vel tres congregati in nomine meo, ibi sum ego in medio eorum. [412] That is: Where two or three have come together, in order to consider that which is for the greater honour and glory of My name, there am I in the midst of them. That is to say, I will make clear and confirm in their hearts the truths of God. And it is to be observed that He said not: Where there is one alone, there will I be; but: Where there are at least two. In this way He showed that God desires not that any man by himself alone should believe his experiences to be of God, [413] or should act in conformity with them, or rely upon them, but rather should believe the Church and [414] her ministers, for God will not make clear and confirm the truth in the heart of one who is alone, and thus such a one will be weak and cold.

12. Hence comes that whereon the Preacher insists, where he says: Vae soli, quia cum ceciderit, non habet sublevantem se. Si dormierint duo, fovebuntur mutuo; unus quomodo calefiet? et si quispiam praevaluerit contra unum, duo resistent ei. [415] Which signifies: Woe to the man that is alone, for when he falleth he hath none to raise him up. If two sleep together, the one shall give warmth to the other (that is to say: with the warmth of God Who is between them); but one alone, how shall he be warm? That is to say: How shall he be other than cold as to the things of God? And if any man can fight and prevail against one enemy (that is, the devil, who can fight and prevail against those that are alone and desire to be alone as regards the things of God), two men together will resist him -- that is, the disciple and the master [416] who come together to know and dost the truth. And until this happens such a man is habitually weak and feeble in the truth, however often he may have heard it from God; so much so that, despite the many occasions on which Saint Paul preached the Gospel, which he said that he had heard, not of men, but of God, he could not be satisfied until he had gone to consult with Saint Peter and the Apostles, saying: Ne forte in vacuum currerem, aut cucurrissem. [417] Which signifies: Perchance he should run, or had run, in vain, having no assurance of himself, until man had given him assurance. This seems a noteworthy thing, O Paul, that He Who revealed to thee this Gospel could not likewise reveal to thee the assurance of the fault which thou mightest have committed in preaching the truth concerning Him.

13. Herein it is clearly shown that a man must not rely upon the things that God reveals, save in

the way that we are describing; for, even in cases where a person is in possession of certainty, as Saint Paul was certain of his Gospel (since he had already begun to preach it), yet, although the revelation be of God, man may still err with respect to it, or in things relating to it. For, although God reveals one thing, He reveals not always the other; and oftentimes He reveals something without revealing the way in which it is to be done. For ordinarily He neither performs nor reveals anything that can be accomplished by human counsel and effort, although He may commune with the soul for a long time, very lovingly. Of this Saint Paul was very well aware, since, as we say, although he knew that the Gospel was revealed to him by God, he went to take counsel with Saint Peter. And we see this clearly in the Book of Exodus, where God had communed most familiarly with Moses, yet had never given him that salutary counsel which was given him by his father-in-law Jethro -- that is to say, that he should choose other judges to assist him, so that the people should not be waiting from morning till night. [418] This counsel God approved, though it was not He Who had given it to him, for it was a thing that fell within the limits of human judgment and reason. With respect to Divine visions and revelations and locutions, God is not wont to reveal them, for He is ever desirous that men should make such use of their own reason as is possible, and all such things have to be governed by reason, save those that are of faith, which transcend all judgment and reason, although these are not contrary to faith.

14. Wherefore let none think that, because it may be true that God and the saints commune with him familiarly about many things, they will of necessity explain to him the faults that he commits with regard to anything, if it be possible for him to recognize these faults by other means. He can have no assurance about this; for, as we read came to pass in the Acts of the Apostles, Saint Peter, though a prince of the Church, who was taught directly by God, went astray nevertheless with respect to a certain ceremony that was in use among the Gentiles, and God was silent. So far did he stray that Saint Paul reproved him, as he affirms, saying: Cum vidissem, quod non recte ad veritatem Evangelii ambularent, dixi coram omnibus: Si tu judaeus cum sis, gentiliter vivis, quomodo Gentes cogis judaizare? [419] Which signifies: When I saw (says Saint Paul) that the disciples walked not uprightly according to the truth of the Gospel, I said to Peter before them all: If thou, being a Jew, as thou art, livest after the manner of the Gentiles, how feignest thou to force the Gentiles to live as do the Jews? And God reproved not Saint Peter Himself for this fault, for that stimulation was a thing that had to do with reason, and it was possible for him to know it by rational means.

15. Wherefore on the day of judgment God will punish for their many faults and sins many souls with whom He may quite habitually have held converse here below, and to whom He may have given much light and virtue; for, as to those things that they have known that they ought to do, they have been neglectful, and have relied upon that converse that they have had with God and upon the virtue that He has given them. And thus, as Christ says in the Gospel, they will marvel at that time, saying: Domine, Domine, nonne in nomine tuo prophetavimus, et in nomine tuo daemonia ejecimus, et in nomine tuo virtutes multas fecimus? [420] That is: Lord, Lord, were the prophecies that Thou spakest to us perchance not prophesied in Thy name? And in Thy name cast we not out devils? And in Thy name performed we not many miracles and mighty works? And the Lord says that He will answer them in these words: Et tunc confitebor illis, quia numquam novi vos: discedite a me omnes qui operamini iniquitatem. [421] That is to say: Depart from Me, ye workers of iniquity, for I never knew you. Of the number of these was the prophet Balaam and others like to him, who, though God spake with them and gave them thanks, were sinners. But the Lord will likewise give their proportion of reproof to His friends and chosen ones, with whom He communed familiarly here below, as to the faults and sins of neglect that they may have committed; whereof there was no need that God should Himself warn them, since He had already warned them through the natural reason and law that He had given to them.

16. In concluding this part of my subject, therefore, I say, and I infer from what has already been said, that anything, of whatsoever kind, received by the soul through supernatural means, must clearly and plainly, fully and simply, be at once communicated to the spiritual director. For although there may seem no reason to speak of it, or to spend time upon doing so, since the soul is acting safely, as we have said, if it rejects it and neither pays heed to it nor desires it -- especially if it be a question of visions or revelations or other supernatural communications, which are either quite clear or very nearly so -- nevertheless, it is very necessary to give an account of all these, although it may seem to the soul that there is no reason for so doing. And this for three causes. First, because, as we have said, God communicates many things, the effect, power, light and certainty whereof He confirms not wholly in the soul, until, as we have said, the soul consults him whom God has given to it as a spiritual judge, which is he that has the power to bind or to loose, and to approve or to blame, as we have shown by means of the passages quoted above; and we can show it clearly by experience, for we see humble souls to whom these things come to pass, and who, after discussing them with the proper persons, experience a new satisfaction, power, light and certainty; so much so that to some it seems that they have no effect upon them, nor do they even belong to them, until they have communicated them to the director, whereupon they are given to them anew.

17. The second cause is that the soul habitually needs instruction upon the things that come to pass

within it, so that it may be led by that means to spiritual poverty and detachment, which is the dark night. For if it begins to relinquish this instruction -- even when it desires not the things referred to -- it will gradually, without realizing it, become callous as it treads the spiritual road, and draw near again to the road of sense; and it is partly with respect to this that these distinct things happen.

18. The third cause is that, for the sake of the humility and submission and mortification of the soul, it is well to relate everything to the director, even though he make [422] no account of it all and consider it of no importance. There are some souls who greatly dislike speaking of such things, because they think them to be unimportant, and know not how the person to whom they should relate them will receive them; but this is lack of humility, and for that very reason it is needful for them to submit themselves and relate these things. And there are others who are very timid in relating them, because they see no reason why they should have these experiences, which seem to belong to saints, as well as other things which they are sorry to have to describe; for which cause they think there is no reason to speak of them because they make no account of them; but for this very reason it is well for them to mortify themselves and relate them, until in time they come to speak of them humbly, unaffectedly, submissively and readily, and after this they will always find it easy to do so.

19. But, with respect to what has been said, it must be pointed out that, although we have insisted so much that such things should be set aside, and that confessors should not encourage their penitents to discuss them, it is not well that spiritual fathers should show displeasure in regard to them, or should seek to avoid speaking of them or despise them, or make their penitents reserved and afraid to mention them, for it would be the means of causing them many inconveniences if the door were closed upon their relating them. For, since they are a means and manner whereby God guides such souls, there is no reason for thinking ill of them or for being alarmed or scandalized by them; but rather there is a reason for proceeding very quietly and kindly, for encouraging these souls and giving them an opportunity to speak of these things; if necessary, they must be exhorted to speak; and, in view of the difficulty that some souls experience in describing such matters, this is sometimes quite essential. Let confessors direct their penitents into faith, [423] advising them frankly to turn away their eyes from all such things, teaching them how to void the desire and the spirit of them, so that they may make progress, and giving them to understand how much more precious in God's sight is one work or act of the will performed in charity than are all the visions and communications that they may receive from Heaven, since these imply neither merit nor demerit. Let them point out, too, that many souls who have known nothing of such things have made incomparably greater progress than others who have received many of them.

Footnotes:

398. [Lit., they serve nevertheless for the greater doctrine and clearness of our intention.']
399. Isaias xxx, 2.
400. Josue ix, 14.
401. Hebrews i, 1.
402. St. Matthew xvii, 5.
403. Colossians ii, 3.
404. 1 Corinthians ii, 2.
405. Colossians ii, 9.
406. St. John xix, 30.
407. Galatians i, 8.
408. [It was to Abiathar that this was said.] 1 Kings [A.V., 1 Samuel] xxiii, 9.
409. Judges vii, 11.
410. [Lit., and so dark.']
411. Exodus iv, 14-15.
412. St. Matthew xviii, 20.
413. [Lit., the things which he has to be of God.']
414. [Lit., . . . with them, without the Church or . . .']
415. Ecclesiastes iv, 10-12.
416. [i.e., the penitent and the confessor or director.]
417. Galatians ii, 2.
418. Exodus xviii, 21-2.
419. Galatians ii, 14.
420. St. Matthew vii, 22.
421. St. Matthew vii, 23.
422. [The Spanish phrase equally admits the reading: even though the soul make.']
423. [i.e., into the night of faith: cf. Chap. xxiii, 4, below.]

CHAPTER XXIII

Which begins to treat of the apprehensions of the understanding that come in a purely spiritual way, and describes their nature.

Although the instruction that we have given with respect to the apprehensions of the understanding which come by means of sense is somewhat brief, in comparison with what might be said about them, I have not desired to write of them at greater length; I believe, indeed, that I have already been too lengthy for the fulfillment of my present intention, which is to disencumber the understanding of them and direct the soul into the night of faith. Wherefore we shall now begin to treat of those other four apprehensions of the understanding, which, as we said in the tenth chapter, [424] are purely spiritual -- namely, visions, revelations, locutions and spiritual feelings. These we call purely spiritual, for they do not (as do those that are corporeal and imaginary) communicate themselves to the understanding by way of the corporeal senses; but, without the intervention of any inward or outward corporeal sense, they present themselves to the understanding, clearly and distinctly, by supernatural means, passively -- that is to say, without the performance of any act or operation on the part of the soul itself, at the least actively.

2. It must be known, then, that, speaking broadly and in general terms, all these four apprehensions may be called visions of the soul; for we term the understanding of the soul also its sight. And since all these apprehensions are intelligible to the understanding, they are described, in a spiritual sense, as visible.' And thus the kinds of intelligence that are formed in the understanding may be called intellectual visions. Now, since all the objects of the other senses, which are all that can be seen, and all that can be heard, and all that can be smelt and tasted and touched, are objects of the understanding in so far as they fall within the limits of truth or falsehood, it follows that, just as to the eyes of the body all that is visible in a bodily way causes bodily vision, even so, to the spiritual eyes of the soul -- namely, the understanding -- all that is intelligible causes spiritual vision; for, as we have said, for the soul to understand is for it to see. And thus, speaking generally, we may call these four apprehensions visions. This cannot be said, however, of the other senses, for no one of them is capable, as such, of receiving the object of another one.

3. But, since these apprehensions present themselves to the soul in the same way as they do to the various senses, it follows that, speaking properly and specifically, we shall describe that which the understanding receives by means of sight (because it can see things spiritually, even as the eyes can see bodily) as a vision; and that which it receives by apprehending and understanding new things (as it were through the hearing, when it hears things that are not heard) we describe as revelation; and that which it receives by means of hearing we call locution; and that which it receives through the other senses, such as the perception of sweet spiritual fragrance, and spiritual taste and of spiritual delight which the soul may joy supernaturally, we call spiritual feelings. From all these the soul derives spiritual vision or intelligence, without any kind of apprehension concerning form, image or figure of natural fancy or imagination; these things are communicated to the soul directly by supernatural means and a supernatural process.

4. Of these, likewise (even as we said of the other imaginary corporeal apprehensions), it is well that we should here disencumber the understanding, leading and directing it by means of them into the spiritual night of faith, to the Divine and substantial union of God; lest, by letting such things encumber and stultify it, it should be hindered upon the road to solitude and detachment from all things, which is necessary to that end. For, although these apprehensions are nobler and more profitable and much more certain than those which are corporeal and imaginary, inasmuch as they are interior and purely spiritual, and are those which the devil is least able to counterfeit, since they are communicated to the soul more purely and subtly without any effort of its own or of the imagination, at least actively, yet not only may the understanding be encumbered by them upon this road, but it is possible for it, through its own imprudence, to be sorely deceived.

5. And although, in one sense, we might conclude with these four kinds of apprehension, by treating them all together and giving advice which applies to them all, as we have given concerning all the others -- namely, that they should neither be desired nor aspired to -- yet, since we shall presently throw more light upon the way in which this is to be done, and certain things will be said in connection with them, it will be well to treat of each one of them in particular, and thus we shall now speak of the first apprehensions, which are intellectual or spiritual visions.

Footnotes:

424. It is in Chapter x (and not in viii, as is said in A, B and e.p.) that the author treats of these spiritual apprehensions.

CHAPTER XXIV

Which treats of two kinds of spiritual vision that come supernaturally.

Speaking now strictly of those visions which are spiritual, and are received without the intervention of any bodily sense, I say that there are two kinds of vision than can be received by the understanding: the one kind is of corporeal substances; the other, of incorporeal or separated substances. The corporeal visions have respect to all material things that are in Heaven and on earth, which the soul is able to see, even while it is still in the body, by the aid of a certain supernatural illumination, derived from God, wherein it is able to see all things that are not present, both in Heaven and on earth, even as Saint John saw, as we read in the twenty-first chapter of the Apocalypse, where he describes and relates the excellence of the celestial Jerusalem, which he saw in Heaven. Even so, again, we read of Saint Benedict that in a spiritual vision he saw the whole world. [425] This vision, says Saint Thomas in the first of his Quodlibets, was in the light that is derived from above, as we have said.

2. The other visions, which are of incorporeal substances, cannot be seen by the aid of this derived illumination, whereof we are here speaking, but only by another and a higher illumination which is called the illumination of glory. And thus these visions of incorporeal substances, such as angels and soul, are not of this life, neither can they be seen in the mortal body; for, if God were pleased to communicate them to the soul, in essence as they are, the soul would at once go forth from the flesh and would be loosed from this mortal life. For this reason God said to Moses, when he entreated Him to show him His Essence: Non videbit me homo, et vivet. [426] That is: Man shall not see Me and be able to remain alive. Wherefore, when the children of Israel thought that they were to see God, or had seen Him, or some angel, they feared death, as we read in the Book of Exodus, where, fearing these things, they said: Non loquatur nobis Dominus, ne forte moriamur. [427] As if they had said: Let not God communicate Himself to us openly, lest we die. And likewise in the Book of Judges, Manue, father of Samson, thought that he and his wife had seen in essence the angel who spake with them (and who had appeared to them in the form of a most beautiful man) and he said to his wife: Morte moriemur, quida vidimus Dominum. [428] Which signifies: We shall die, because we have seen the Lord. [429]

3. And thus these visions occur not in this life, save occasionally and fleetingly, when, making an exception to the conditions which govern our natural life, God so allows it. At such times He totally withdraws the spirit from this life, and the natural functions of the body are supplied by His favour. This is why, at the time when it is thought that Saint Paul saw these (namely, the incorporeal substances in the third heaven), that Saint says: Sive in corpore, nescio, sive extra corpus, nescio, Deus scit. [430] That is, he was raptured, and of that which he saw he says that he knows not if it was in the body or out of the body, but that God knows. Herein it is clearly seen that the limits of natural means of communication were passed, and that this was the work of God. Likewise, it is believed that God showed His Essence to Moses, for we read that God said to him that He would set him in the cleft of the rock, and would protect him, by covering him with His right hand, and protecting him so that he should not die when His glory passed; the which glory passed indeed, and was shown to him fleetingly, and the natural life of Moses was protected by the right hand of God. [431] But these visions that were so substantial -- like that of Saint Paul and Moses, and that of our father Elias, when he covered his face at the gentle whisper of God -- although they are fleeting, occur only very rarely -- indeed, hardly ever and to very few; for God performs such a thing in those that are very strong in the spirit of the Church and the law of God, as were the three men named above.

4. But, although these visions of spiritual substances cannot be unveiled and be clearly seen in this life by the understanding, they can nevertheless be felt in the substance of the soul, with the sweetest touches and unions, all of which belongs to spiritual feelings, whereof, with the Divine favour, we shall treat presently; for our pen is being directed and guided to these -- that is to say, to the Divine bond and union of the soul with Divine Substance. We shall speak of this when we treat of the dark and confused mystical understanding which remains to be described, wherein we shall show how, by means of this dark and loving knowledge, God is united with the soul in a lofty and Divine degree; [432] for, after some manner, this dark and loving knowledge, which is faith, serves as a means to Divine union in this life, even as, in the next life, the light of glory serves as an intermediary to the clear vision of God.

5. Let us, then, now treat of the visions of corporeal substances, received spiritually in the soul, which come after the manner of bodily visions. For, just as the eyes see bodily visions by means of natural light, even so does the soul, through the understanding, by means of supernaturally derived light,

as we have said, see those same natural things inwardly, together with others, as God wills; the difference between the two kinds of vision is only in the mode and manner of them. For spiritual and intellectual visions are much clearer and subtler than those which pertain to the body. For, when God is pleased to grant this favour to the soul, He communicates to it that supernatural light whereof we speak, wherein the soul sees the things that God wills it to see, easily and most clearly, whether they be of Heaven or of earth, and the absence or presence of them is no hindrance to the vision. And it is at times as though a door were opened before it into a great brightness, through which the soul sees a light, after the manner of a lightning flash, which, on a dark night, reveals things suddenly, and causes them to be clearly and distinctly seen, and then leaves them in darkness, although the forms and figures of them remain in the fancy. This comes to pass much more perfectly in the soul, because those things that the spirit has seen in that light remain impressed upon it in such a way that whensoever it observes them it sees them in itself as it saw them before; even as in a mirror the forms that are in it are seen whensoever a man looks in it, and in such a way that those forms of the things that he has seen are never wholly removed from his soul, although in course of time they become somewhat remote.

6. The effect which these visions produce in the soul is that of quiet, illumination, joy like that of glory, sweetness, purity and love, humility and inclination or elevation of the spirit in God; sometimes more so, at other times less; with sometimes more of one thing, at other times more of another, according to the spirit wherein they are received and according as God wills.

7. The devil likewise can produce these visions, by means of a certain natural light, whereby he brings things clearly before the mind, through spiritual suggestion, whether they be present or absent. There is that passage in Saint Matthew, which says of the devil and Christ: Ostendit omnia regna mundi, et gloriam eorum. [433] That is so say: He showed Him all the kingdoms of the world and the glory of them. Concerning this certain doctors say that he did it by spiritual suggestion, [434] for it was not possible to make Him see so much with the bodily eyes as all the kingdoms of the world and the glory of them. But there is much difference between these visions that are caused by the devil and those that are of God. For the effects produced in the soul by the devil's visions are not like those produced by good visions; the former produce aridity of spirit as to communion with God and an inclination to esteem oneself highly, and to receive and set store by the visions aforesaid, and in no wise do they produce the gentleness of humility and love of God. Neither do the forms of such visions remain impressed upon the soul with the sweetness and brightness of the others; nor do they last, but are quickly effaced from the soul, save when the soul greatly esteems them, in which case this high esteem itself causes it to recall them naturally, but with great aridity of spirit, and without producing that effect of love and humility which is produced by good visions when the soul recalls them.

8. These visions, inasmuch as they are of creatures, wherewith God has no essential conformity or proportion, cannot serve the understanding as a proximate means to union with God. And thus the soul must conduct itself in a purely negative way concerning them, as in the other things that we have described, in order that it may progress by the proximate means -- namely, by faith. Wherefore the soul must make no store of treasure of the forms of such visions as remain impressed upon it, neither must it lean upon them; for to do this would be to be encumbered with those forms, images and persons which remain inwardly within it, and thus the soul would not progress toward God by denying itself all things. For, even if these forms should be permanently set before the soul, they will not greatly hinder this progress, if the soul has no desire to set store by them. For, although it is true that the remembrance of them impels the soul to a certain love of God and contemplation, yet it is impelled and exalted much more by pure faith and detachment in darkness from them all, without its knowing how or whence it comes to it. And thus it will come to pass that the soul will go forward, enkindled with yearnings of purest love for God, without knowing whence they come to it, or on what they are founded. The fact is that, while faith has become ever more deeply rooted and infused in the soul by means of that emptiness and darkness and detachment from all things, or spiritual poverty, all of which may be spoken of as one and the same thing, at the same time the charity of God has become rooted and infused in the soul ever more deeply also. Wherefore, the more the soul desires obscurity and annihilation with respect to all the outward or inward things that it is capable of receiving, the more is it infused by faith, and, consequently, by love and hope, since all these three theological virtues go together.

9. But at certain times the soul neither understands this love nor feels it; for this love resides, not in sense, with its tender feelings, but in the soul, with fortitude and with a courage and daring that are greater than they were before, though sometimes it overflows into sense and produces gentle and tender feelings. Wherefore, in order to attain to that love, joy and delight which such visions produce and cause in the soul, it is well that soul should have fortitude and mortification and love, so that it may desire to remain in emptiness and darkness as to all things, and to build its love and joy upon that which it neither sees nor feels, neither can see nor feel in this life, which is God, Who is incomprehensible and transcends all things. It is well, then, for us to journey to Him by denying ourselves everything. For otherwise, even if the soul be so wise, humble and strong that the devil cannot deceive it by visions or cause it to fall into some sin of presumption, as he is wont to do, he will not allow it to make progress;

Ascent of Mount Carmel

for he set obstacles in the way of spiritual detachment and poverty of spirit and emptiness in faith, which is the essential condition for union of the soul with God.

10. And, as the same teaching that we gave in the nineteenth and twentieth chapters, concerning supernatural apprehensions and visions of sense, holds good for these visions, we shall not spend more time here in describing them.

Footnotes:

425. St. Gregory: Dial., Bk. 11, Chap. xxxv. Omnis etiam mundus velut sub uno solis radio collectus, ante oculos eius adductus est.'

426. Exodus xxxiii, 20.

427. Exodus xx, 19.

428. Judges xiii, 22.

429. E.p. abbreviates this paragraph thus: The other visions, which are of incorporeal substances, demand another and a higher illumination; and thus these visions of incorporeal substances, such as angels and souls, do not occur habitually, nor are they proper to this life; still less is that of the Divine Essence, which is proper to the Blessed in Heaven, save that it may be communicated to a soul fleetingly and as in passing.' The next two paragraphs are omitted from e.p. P. Jerónimo de San José, in the edition of 1630, copies from e.p. the lines given in this note above, and then continues: [save when] God so allows, in spite of the condition of our natural life, withdrawing the spirit from it occasionally, as happened to the apostle Saint Paul, when he says that he saw unspeakable secrets in the third heaven.' The adjustments made by P. Salablanca and amplified by P. Jerónimoin the rest of the paragraph [cf. notes below] follow the most usual scholastic doctrine. Among the Discalced Carmelite writers who deal most fully and competently with this doctrine of spiritual visions are the authors of the Cursas Theologiae Mysticae, Vol. IV, Disp. xx, xxi; Felipe de la Santísima Trinidad: Summa Theologiae Mysticae, Pt. II, Tract. III, Disc. iv; Médula Mística, Trat. VI. St. Thomas (I p., q. 88, a. 1) says that we cannot quidditative know separated substances.

430. 2 Corinthians xii, 2.

431. Exodus xxxiii, 22.

432. This description the Saint probably accomplished, or intended to accomplish, in his commentaries on the last five stanzas of the Dark Night, which have not come down to us.

433. St. Matthew iv, 8.

434. E.p.: . . . by intelligible suggestion.' On this passage, cf. Cornelius a Lapide (Commentaria in Matthaeum, Cap. IV) and St. Thomas (III p., q. 41, ad. 3).

CHAPTER XXV

Which treats of revelations, describing their nature and making a distinction between them.

According to the order which we are here following, we have next to treat of the second kind of spiritual apprehension, which we have described above as revelations, and which properly belongs to the spirit of prophecy. With respect to this, it must first be known that revelation is naught else than the discovery of some hidden truth or the manifestation of some secret or mystery. Thus God may cause the soul to understand something by making clear to the understanding the truth concerning it, or He may reveal to the soul certain things which He is doing or proposes to do.

2. Accordingly, we may say that there are two kinds of revelation. The first is the disclosure to the understanding of truths which are properly called intellectual knowledge or intelligence; the second is the manifestation of secrets, which are called revelations with more propriety than the others. For the first kind cannot strictly be called revelations, since they consist in this, that God causes the soul to understand naked truths, not only with respect to temporal things, but likewise with respect to spiritual things, revealing them to the soul clearly and openly. These I have desired to treat under the heading of revelations: first, because they have close kinship and similarity with them: secondly, in order not to multiply distinctions.

3. According to this method, then, we shall now be well able to divide revelations into two kinds of apprehension. The one kind we shall call intellectual knowledge, and the other, the manifestation of secrets and hidden mysteries of God. With these we shall conclude in two chapters as briefly as we may, and in this chapter following we shall treat of the first.

CHAPTER XXVI

Which treats of the intuition of naked truths in the understanding, explaining how they are of two kinds and how the soul is to conduct itself with respect to them.

In order to speak properly of this intuition of naked truths which is conveyed to the understanding, the writer would need God to take his hand and to guide his pen; for know, dear reader, that what they are to the soul cannot be expressed in words. But, since I speak not of them here of set purpose, but only that through them I may instruct the soul and lead it to Divine union, I shall suffer myself to speak of them here in a brief and modified form, as is sufficient for the fulfillment of that intention.

2. This kind of vision (or, to speak more properly, of knowledge of naked truths) is very different from that of which we have just spoken in the twenty-fourth chapter. For it is not like seeing bodily things with the understanding; it consists rather in comprehending and seeing with the understanding the truths of God, whether of things that are, that have been or that will be, which is in close conformity with the spirit of prophecy, as perchance we shall explain hereafter.

3. Here it is to be observed that this kind of knowledge is distinguishable according to two divisions: the one kind comes to the soul with respect to the Creator; the other with respect to creatures, as we have said. And, although both kinds are very delectable to the soul, yet the delight caused in it by the kind that relates to God is comparable to nothing whatsoever, and there are no words or terms wherein it can be described. This kind of knowledge is of God Himself, and the delight is in God Himself, whereof David says: There is naught soever like to Him.' [435] For this kind of knowledge comes to the soul in direct relation to God, when the soul, after a most lofty manner, has a perception of some attribute of God -- of His omnipotence, of His might, of His goodness and sweetness, etc.; and, whensoever it has such a perception, that which is perceived cleaves to the soul. Inasmuch as this is pure contemplation, the soul clearly sees that there is no way wherein it can say aught concerning it, save to speak in certain general terms, of the abundance of delight and blessing which it has felt, and this is expressed by souls that experience it; but not to the end that what the soul has experienced and perceived may be wholly apprehended.

4. And thus David, speaking for himself when something of this kind had happened to him, used only common and general terms, saying: Judicia Domini vera, justificata in semetipsa. Desiderabilia super aurum et lapidem pretiosum multum; et dulciora super mel et favum. [436] Which signifies: The judgments of God -- that is, the virtues and attributes which we perceive in God -- are in themselves true, justified, more to be desired than gold and very much more than precious stones, and sweeter than the honeycomb and honey. And concerning Moses we read that, when God gave him a most lofty manifestation of knowledge from Himself on an occasion when He passed before him, he said only that which can be expressed in the common terms above mentioned. And it was so that, when the Lord passed before him in that manifestation of knowledge, Moses quickly prostrated himself upon the ground, saying: Dominator Domine Deus, misericors et clemens, patiens, et multae miserationis, ac verax. Qui custodis misericordiam in millia. [437] Which signifies: Ruler, [438] Lord, God, merciful and clement, patient, and of great compassion, and true, that keepest mercy promised unto thousands. Here it is seen that Moses could not express that which he had learned from God in one single manifestation of knowledge, and therefore he expressed and gave utterance to it in all these words. And although at times, when such knowledge is given to a soul, words are used, the soul is well aware that it has expressed no part of what it has felt; for it knows that there is no fit name by which it can name it. And thus Saint Paul, when he was granted that lofty knowledge of God, made no attempt to describe it, saying only that it was not lawful for man to speak of it.

5. These Divine manifestations of knowledge which have respect to God never relate to particular matters, inasmuch as they concern the Chief Beginning, and therefore can have no particular reference, unless it be a question of some truth concerning a thing less than God, which is involved in the perception of the whole; but these Divine manifestations themselves -- no, in no way whatsoever. And these lofty manifestations of knowledge can come only to the soul that attains to union with God, for they are themselves that union; and to receive them is equivalent to a certain contact with the Divinity which the soul experiences, and thus it is God Himself Who is perceived and tasted therein. And, although He cannot be experienced manifestly and clearly, as in glory, this touch of knowledge and delight is nevertheless so sublime and profound that it penetrates the substance of the soul, and the devil cannot meddle with it or produce any manifestation like to it, for there is no such thing, neither is there aught that compares with it, neither can he infuse pleasure or delight that is like to it; for such kinds of

knowledge savour of the Divine Essence and of eternal life, and the devil cannot counterfeit a thing so lofty.

6. Nevertheless he might make some pretence of imitating it, by representing to the soul certain great matters and things which enchant the senses and can readily be perceived by them, and endeavoring to persuade the soul that these are God; but he cannot do this in such wise that they enter into the substance of the soul and of a sudden renew it and enkindle it with love, as do the manifestations of God. For there are certain kinds of knowledge, and certain of these touches effected by God in the substance of the soul, which enrich it after such wise that not only does one of them suffice to take from the soul once and for all the whole of the imperfections that it had itself been unable to throw off during its whole life, but it leaves the soul full of virtues and blessings from God.

7. And these touches are so delectable to the soul, and the delight they produce is so intimate, that if it received only one of them it would consider itself well rewarded for all the trials that it had suffered in this life, even had they been innumerable; and it is so greatly encouraged and given such energy to suffer many things for God's sake that it suffers especially in seeing that it is not suffering more.

8. The soul cannot attain to these lofty degrees of knowledge by means of any comparison or imagination of its own, because they are loftier than all these; and so God works them in the soul without making use of its own capacities. Wherefore, at certain times, when the soul is least thinking of it and least desiring it, God is wont to give it these Divine touches, by causing it certain remembrances of Himself. And these are sometimes suddenly caused in the soul by its mere recollection of certain things -- sometimes of very small things. And they are so readily perceived that at times they cause not only the soul, but also the body, to tremble. But at other times they come to pass in the spirit when it is very tranquil, without any kind of trembling, but with a sudden sense of delight and spiritual refreshment.

9. At other times, again, they come when the soul repeats or hears some word, perhaps from Scripture or possibly from some other source; but they are not always equally efficacious and sensible, for oftentimes they are extremely faint; yet, however faint they may be, one of these recollections and touches of God is more profitable to the soul than many other kinds of knowledge or many meditations upon the creatures and the works of God. And, since these manifestations of knowledge come to the soul suddenly, and independently of its own free will, it must neither desire to have them, nor desire not to have them; but must merely be humble and resigned concerning them, and God will perform His work how and when He wills.

10. And I say not that the soul should behave in the same negative manner with regard to these apprehensions as with regard to the rest, for, as we have said, they are a part of the union towards which we are leading the soul, to which end we are teaching it to detach and strip itself of all other apprehensions. And the means by which God will do this must be humility and suffering for love of God with resignation as regards all reward; for these favours are not granted to the soul which still cherishes attachments, inasmuch as they are granted through a very special love of God toward the soul which loves Him likewise with great detachment. It is to this that the Son of God referred, in Saint John, when He said: Qui autem diligit rag, diligetur a Patre meo, et ego diligam eum, et manifestabo ei me ipsum. [439] Which signifies: He that loves Me shall be loved by My Father, and I will love him and will manifest Myself to him. Herein are included the kinds of knowledge and touches to which we are referring, which God manifests to the soul that truly loves Him.

11. The second kind of knowledge or vision of interior truths is very different from this that we have described, since it is of things lower than God. And herein is included the perception of the truth of things in themselves, and that of the events and happenings which come to pass among men. And this knowledge is of such a kind that, when the soul learns these truths, they sink into it, independently of any suggestion from without, to such an extent that, although it may be given a different interpretation of them, it cannot make inward assent to this, even though it endeavor to do so by putting forth a great effort; for within the spirit it is learning otherwise through the spirit that is teaching it that thing, which is equivalent to seeing it clearly. This pertains to the spirit of prophecy and to the grace which Saint Paul calls the gift of the discernment of spirits. [440] Yet, although the soul holds something which it understands to be quite certain and true, as we have said, and although it may be unable to cease giving it that passive interior consent, it must not therefore cease to believe and to give the consent of reason to that which its spiritual director tells it and commands it, even though this may be quite contrary to its own feelings, so that it may be directed in faith to Divine union, to which a soul must journey by believing rather than by understanding.

12. Concerning both these things we have clear testimonies in Scripture. For, with respect to the spiritual knowledge of things that may be acquired, the Wise Man says these words: Ipse dedit mihi horum, quae sunt, scientiam veram, ut sciam dispositionem orbis terrarum, et virtutes elementorum, initium et consummationem temporum, viccissitudinum permutationes, et consummationes temporum, et morum mutationes, divisiones temporum, et anni cursus, et stellarum dispositiones, naturas animalium et iras bestiarum, vim ventorum, et cogitationes hominum, differentias virgultorum, et

virtutes radicum, et quaecumque sunt abscondita, et improvisa didici: omnium enim artifex docuit me sapientia. [441] Which signifies: God hath given me true knowledge of things that are: to know the disposition of the round world [442] and the virtues of the elements; the beginning, and ending, and midst of the times, the alterations in the changes and the consummations of the seasons, and the changes of customs, the divisions of the seasons, the courses of the year and the dispositions of the stars; the natures of animals, and the furies of the beasts, the strength and virtue of the winds, and the thoughts of men; the diversities in plants and trees and the virtues of roots and all things that are hidden, and those that are not foreseen: all these I learned, for Wisdom, which is the worker of all things, taught me. And although this knowledge which the Wise Man here says that God gave him concerning all things was infused and general, the passage quoted furnishes sufficient evidence for all particular kinds of knowledge which God infuses into souls, by supernatural means, when He wills. And this not that He may give them a general habit of knowledge as He gave to Solomon in the matters aforementioned; but that He may reveal to them at times certain truths with respect to any of all these things that the Wise Man here enumerates. Although it is true that into many souls Our Lord infuses habits which relate to many things, yet these are never of so general a kind as they were in the case of Solomon. The differences between them are like to those between the gifts distributed by God which are enumerated by Saint Paul; among these he sets wisdom, knowledge, faith, prophecy, discernment or knowledge of spirits, understanding of tongues, interpretation of spoken words, etc. [443] All these kinds of knowledge are infused habits, which God gives freely to whom He will, whether naturally or supernaturally; naturally, as to Balaam, to other idolatrous prophets and to many sybils, to whom He gave the spirit of prophecy; and supernaturally, as to the holy prophets and apostles and other saints.

13. But over and above these habits or graces freely bestowed, [444] what we say is that persons who are perfect or are making progress in perfection are wont very commonly to receive enlightenment and knowledge of things present or absent; these they know through their spirit, which is already enlightened and purged. We can interpret that passage from the Proverbs in this sense, namely: Quomodo in aquis resplendent vultus prospicientium sic corda hominum manifesta sunt proudentibus. [445] Even as there appear in the waters the faces of those that look therein, so the hearts of men are manifest to the prudent. This is understood of those that have the wisdom of saints, which the sacred Scripture calls prudence. And in this way these spirits sometimes learn of other things also, although not whensoever they will; for this belongs only to those that have the habit, and even to these it belongs not always and with respect to all things, for it depends upon God's will to help them.

14. But it must be known that those whose spirits are purged can learn by natural means with great readiness, and some more readily than others, that which is in the inward spirit or heart, and the inclinations and talents of men, and this by outward indications, albeit very slight ones, as words, movements and other signs. For, even as the devil can do this, since he is spirit, even so likewise can the spiritual man, according to the words of the Apostle, who says: Spiritualis autem judicat omnia. [446] He that is spiritual judgeth all things.' And again he says: Spiritus enim omnia scrutatur, etiam profunda Dei. [447] The spirit searcheth all things, yea, the deep things of God.' Wherefore, although spiritual persons cannot by nature know thoughts, or things that are in the minds of others, [448] they may well interpret them through supernatural enlightenment or by signs. And, although they may often be deceived in their interpretation of signs, they are more generally correct. Yet we must trust neither to the one means nor to the other, for the devil meddles herein greatly, and with much subtlety, as we shall afterwards say, and thus we must ever renounce such kinds of knowledge.

15. And that spiritual persons may have knowledge of the deeds and happenings of men, even though they be elsewhere, we have witness and example in the Fourth Book of the Kings, where Giezi, the servant of our father Eliseus, desired to hide from him the money which he had received from Naaman the Syrian, and Eliseus said: Nonne cor meum in praesenti erat, quando reversus est homo de curru suo in occursum tui? [449] Was not my heart perchance present, when Naaman turned back from his chariot and went to meet thee? This happens spiritually; the spirit sees it as though it were happening in its presence. And the same thing is proved in the same book, where we read likewise of the same Eliseus, that, knowing all that the King of Syria did with his princes in his privy chamber, he told it to the King of Israel, and thus the counsels of the King of Syria were of no effect; so much so that, when the King of Syria saw that all was known, he said to his people: Why do ye not tell me which of you is betraying me to the King of Israel? And then one of his servants said: Nequaquam, Domine mi Rex, sed Eliseus Propheta, qui est in Israel, indicat Regi Israel omnia verba, quaecumque locutus fueris in conclavi tuo. [450] It is not so, my lord, O King, but Eliseus, the prophet that is in Israel, telleth the king of Israel all the words that thou speakest in thy privy chamber.'

16. Both kinds of this knowledge of things, as well as other kinds of knowledge, come to pass in the soul passively, so that for its own part it does naught. For it will come to pass that, when a person is inattentive to a matter and it is far from his mind, there will come to him a vivid understanding of what he is hearing or reading, and that much more clearly than could be conveyed by the sound of the words; and at times, though he understand not the words, as when they are in Latin and he knows not that

tongue, the knowledge of their meaning comes to him, despite his not understanding them.

17. With regard to the deceptions which the devil can bring about, and does bring about, concerning this kind of knowledge and understanding, there is much that might be said, for the deceptions which he effects in this way are very great and very difficult to unmask. Inasmuch as, through suggestion, he can represent to the soul many kinds of intellectual knowledge and implant them so firmly that it appears impossible that they should not be true, he will certainly cause the soul to believe innumerable falsehoods if it be not humble and cautious. For suggestion has sometimes great power over the soul, above all when it is to some extent aided by the weakness of sense, causing the knowledge which it conveys to sink into the soul with such great power, persuasiveness and determination that the soul needs to give itself earnestly to prayer and to exert great strength if it is to cast it off. For at times the devil is accustomed to represent to the soul the sins of others, and evil consciences and evil souls, falsely but very vividly, and all this he does to harm the soul, trusting that it may spread abroad his revelations, and that thus more sins may be committed, for which reason he fills the soul with zeal by making it believe that these revelations are granted it so that it may commend the persons concerned to God. Now, though it is true that God sometimes sets before holy souls the necessities of their neighbours, so that they may commend them to God or relieve them, even as we read that He revealed to Jeremias the weakness of the prophet Baruch, that he might give him counsel concerning it,[451] yet it is more often the devil who does this, and speaks falsely about it, in order to cause infamy, sin and discouragement, whereof we have very great experience. And at other times he implants other kinds of knowledge with great assurance, and persuades the soul to believe them.

18. Such knowledge as this, whether it be of God or no, can be of very little assistance to the progress of the soul on its journey to God if the soul desire it and be attached to it; on the contrary, if it were not scrupulous in rejecting it, not only would it be hindered on its road, but it would even be greatly harmed and led far astray. For all the perils and inconveniences which, as we have said, may be involved in the supernatural apprehensions whereof we have treated up to this point, may occur here, and more also. I will not, therefore, treat more fully of this matter here, since sufficient instruction about it has already been given in past chapters; I will only say that the soul must always be very scrupulous in rejecting these things, and seek to journey to God by the way of unknowing; and must ever relate its experiences to its spiritual confessor, and be ever attentive to his counsel. Let the confessor guide the soul past this, laying no stress upon it, for it is of no kind of importance for the road to union; for when these things are granted to the soul passively they always leave in it such effect as God wills shall remain, without necessity for the soul to exert any diligence in the matter. And thus it seems to me that there is no reason to describe here either the effect which is produced by true knowledge, or that which comes from false knowledge, for this would be wearisome and never-ending. For the effects of this knowledge cannot all be described in a brief instruction, the knowledge being great and greatly varied, and its effects being so likewise, since good knowledge produces good effects, and evil knowledge, evil effects, etc. In saying that all should be rejected, we have said sufficient for the soul not to go astray.

Footnotes:

435. [Psalm xxxix, 6: cf. A.V., xl, 5.]
436. Psalm xviii, 10-11 [A.V., xix, 9-10].
437. Exodus xxxiv, 6-7.
438. [Lit., Emperor.']
439. St. John xiv, 21.
440. 1 Corinthians xii, 10.
441. Wisdom vii, 17-21.
442. [Lit., of the roundness of the lands.']
443. [Lit., exposition of words'; the reference is clearly to 1 Corinthians xii, 8-10.]
444. [The original has gratis datas.]
445. Proverbs xxvii, 19.
446. 1 Corinthians ii, 15.
447. 1 Corinthians ii, 10.
448. [Lit., in the interior.']
449. 4 Kings [A.V., 2 Kings] v, 26.
450. 4 Kings [A.V., 2 Kings] vi, 12.
451. Jeremias xlv, 3.

CHAPTER XXVII

Which treats of the second kind of revelation, namely, the disclosure of hidden secrets. Describes the way in which these may assist the soul toward union with God, and the way in which they may be a hindrance; and how the devil may deceive the soul greatly in this matter.

We were saying that the second kind of revelation was the manifestation of hidden mysteries and secrets. This may come to pass in two ways. The first with respect to that which God is in Himself, wherein is included the revelation of the mystery of the Most Holy Trinity and Unity of God. The second is with respect to that which God is in His works, and herein are included the other articles of our Catholic faith, and the propositions deducible from them which may be laid down explicitly as truths. In these are included and comprised a great number of the revelations of the prophets, of promises and threatenings of God, and of other things which have happened and shall happen concerning this matter of faith. Under this second head we may also include many other particular things which God habitually reveals, both concerning the universe in general as also in particular concerning kingdoms, provinces and states and families and particular persons. Of these we have examples in abundance in the Divine writings, both of the one kind and of the other, especially in all the Prophets, wherein are found revelations of all these kinds. As this is a clear and plain matter, I will not here spend time in quoting these examples, but will only say that these revelations do not come to pass by word alone, but that God gives them in many ways and manners, sometimes by word alone, sometimes by signs and figures alone, and by images and similitudes alone, sometimes in more than one way at once, as is likewise to be seen in the Prophets, particularly throughout the Apocalypse, where we find not only all the kinds of revelation which we have described, but likewise the ways and manners to which we are here referring.

2. As to these revelations which are included under our second head, God grants them still in our time to whom He will. He is wont, for example, to reveal to some persons how many days they still have to live, or what trials they are to suffer, or what is to befall such and such a person, or such and such a kingdom, etc. And even as regards the mysteries of our faith, He will reveal and expound to the spirit the truths concerning them, although, since this has already been revealed once, it is not properly to be termed revelation, but is more correctly a manifestation or explanation of what has been revealed already.

3. In this kind of revelation the devil may meddle freely. For, as revelations of this nature come ordinarily through words, figures and similitudes, etc., the devil may very readily counterfeit others like them, much more so than when the revelations are in spirit alone. Wherefore, if with regard to the first and the second kind of revelation which we are here describing, as touching our faith, there be revealed to us anything new, or different, we must in no wise give our consent to it, even though we had evidence that it was spoken by an angel from Heaven. For even so says Saint Paul, in these words: Licet nos, gut Angelus de coelo evangelizet vobis praeterquam quod evangelizavimus vobis, anathema sit. [452] Which signifies: Even though an angel from Heaven declare or preach unto you aught else than that which we have preached unto you, let him be anathema.

4. Since, then, there are no more articles to be revealed concerning the substance of our faith than those which have already been revealed to the Church, not only must anything new which may be revealed to the soul concerning this be rejected, but it behoves the soul to be cautious and pay no heed to any novelties implied therein, and for the sake of the purity of the soul it behoves it to rely on faith alone. Even though the truths already revealed to it be revealed again, it will believe them, not because they are now revealed anew, but because they have already been sufficiently revealed to the Church: indeed, it must close its understanding to them, holding simply to the doctrine of the Church and to its faith, which, as Saint Paul says, enters through hearing. [453] And let not its credence and intellectual assent be given to these matters of the faith which have been revealed anew, however fitting and true they may seem to it, if it desire not to be deceived. For, in order to deceive the soul and to instil falsehoods into it, the devil first feeds it with truths and things that are probable in order to give it assurance and afterwards to deceive it. He resembles one that sews leather with a bristle, first piercing the leather with the sharp bristle, after which enters the soft thread; the thread could not enter unless the bristle guided it.

5. And let this be considered carefully; for, even were it true that there was no peril in such deception, yet it greatly behoves the soul not to desire to understand clearly things that have respect to

the faith, so that it may preserve the merit of faith, in its purity and entirety, and likewise that it may come, in this night of the understanding, to the Divine light of Divine union. And it is equally necessary to consider any new revelation with ones eyes closed, and holding fast the prophecies of old, for the Apostle Saint Peter, though he had seen the glory of the Son of God after some manner on Mount Tabor, wrote, in his canonical epistle, these words: Et habemus firmiorem propheticum sermonem; cui bene factitis attendentes, etc. [454] Which is as though he had said: Although the vision that we have seen of Christ on the Mount is true, the word of the prophecy that is revealed to us is firmer and surer, and, if ye rest your soul upon it, ye do well.

6. And if it is true that, for the reasons already described, it behoves the soul to close its eyes to the aforementioned revelations which come to it, and which concern the propositions of the faith, how much more necessary will it be neither to receive nor to give credit to other revelations relating to different things, wherein the devil habitually meddles so freely that I believe it impossible for a man not to be deceived in many of them unless he strive to reject them, such an appearance of truth and security does the devil give them? For he brings together so many appearances and probabilities, in order that they may be believed, and plants them so firmly in the sense and the imagination, that it seems to the person affected that what he says will certainly happen; and in such a way does he cause the soul to grasp and hold them, that, if it have not humility, it will hardly be persuaded to reject them and made to believe the contrary. Wherefore, the soul that is pure, cautious, simple and humble must resist revelations and other visions with as much effort and care as though they were very perilous temptations. For there is no need to desire them; on the contrary, there is need not too desire them, if we are to reach the union of love. It is this that Solomon meant when he said: What need has a man to desire and seek things that are above his natural capacity?' [455] As though we were to say: He has no necessity, in order to be perfect, to desire supernatural things by supernatural means, which are above his capacity.

7. And as the objections that can be made to this have already been answered, in the nineteenth and twentieth chapter of this book, I refer the reader to these, saying only that the soul must keep itself from all revelations in order to journey, in purity and without error, in the night of faith, to union.

Footnotes:

452. Galatians i, 8.
453. Romans x, 17.
454. 2 St. Peter i, 19.
455. Ecclesiastes vii, 1.

CHAPTER XXVIII

Which treats of interior locutions that may come to the spirit supernaturally. Says of what kinds they are.

The discreet reader has ever need to bear in mind the intent and end which I have in this book, which is the direction of the soul, through all its apprehensions, natural and supernatural, without deception or hindrance, in purity of faith, to Divine union with God. If he does this, he will understand that, although with respect to apprehensions of the soul and the doctrine that I am expounding I give not such copious instruction neither do I particularize so much or make so many divisions as the understanding perchance requires, I am not being over-brief in this matter. For with respect to all this I believe that sufficient cautions, explanations and instructions are given for the soul to be enabled to behave prudently in every contingency, outward or inward, so as to make progress. And this is the reason why I have so briefly dismissed the subject of prophetic apprehensions and the other subjects allied to it; for there is so much more to be said of each of them, according to the differences and the ways and manners that are wont to be observed in each, that I believe one could never know it all perfectly. I am content that, as I believe, the substance and the doctrine thereof have been given, and the soul has been warned of the caution which it behoves it to exercise in this respect, and also concerning all other things of the same kind that may come to pass within it.

2. I will now follow the same course with regard to the third kind of apprehension, which, we said, was that of supernatural locutions, which are apt to come to the spirits of spiritual persons without the intervention of any bodily sense. These, although they are of many kinds, may, I believe, all be reduced to three, namely: successive, formal and substantial. I describe as successive certain words and arguments which the spirit is wont to form and fashion when it is inwardly recollected. Formal words are certain clear and distinct words [456] which the spirit receives, not from itself, but from a third person, sometimes when it is recollected and sometimes when it is not. Substantial words are others which also come to the spirit formally, sometimes when it is recollected and sometimes when it is not; these cause in the substance of the soul that substance and virtue which they signify. All these we shall here proceed to treat in their order.

Footnotes:

456. [Lit., certain distinct and formal words.']

CHAPTER XXIX

Which treats of the first kind of words that the recollected spirit sometimes forms within itself. Describes the cause of these and the profit and the harm which there may be in them.

These successive words always come when the spirit is recollected and absorbed very attentively in some meditation; and, in its reflections upon that same matter whereon it is thinking, it proceeds from one stage to another, forming words and arguments which are very much to the point, with great facility and distinctiveness, and by means of its reasoning discovers things which it knew not with respect to the subject of its reflections, so that it seems not to be doing this itself, but rather it seems that another person is supplying the reasoning within its mind or answering its questions or teaching it. And in truth it has good cause for thinking this, for the soul itself is reasoning with itself and answering itself as though it were two persons convening together; and in some ways this is really so; for, although it is the spirit itself that works as an instrument, the Holy Spirit oftentimes aids it to produce and form those true reasonings, words and conceptions. And thus it utters them to itself as though to a third person. For, as at that time the understanding is recollected and united with the truth of that whereon it is thinking, and the Divine Spirit is likewise united with it in that truth, as it is always united in all truth, it follows that, when the understanding communicates in this way with the Divine Spirit by means of this truth, it begins to form within itself, successively, those other truths which are connected with that whereon it is thinking, the door being opened to it and illumination being given to it continually by the Holy Spirit Who teaches it. For this is one of the ways wherein the Holy Spirit teaches.

2. And when the understanding is illumined and taught in this way by this master, and comprehends these truths, it begins of its own accord to form the words which relate to the truths that are communicated to it from elsewhere. So that we may say that the voice is the voice of Jacob and the hands are the hand of Esau. [457] And one that is in this condition will be unable to believe that this is so, but will think that the sayings and the words come from a third person. For such a one knows not the facility with which the understanding can form words inwardly, as though they came from a third person, and having reference to conceptions and truths which have in fact been communicated to it by a third person.

3. And although it is true that, in this communication and enlightenment of the understanding, no deception is produced in the soul itself, nevertheless, deception may, and does, frequently occur in the formal words and reasonings which the understanding bases upon it. For, inasmuch as this illumination which it receives is at times very subtle and spiritual, so that the understanding cannot attain to a clear apprehension of it, and it is the understanding that, as we say, forms the reasonings of its own accord, it follows that those which it forms are frequently false, and on other occasions are only apparently true, or are imperfect. For since at the outset the soul began to seize the truth, and then brought into play the skilfulness or the clumsiness of its own weak understanding, its perception of the truth may easily be modified by the instability of its own faculties of comprehension, and act all the time exactly as though a third person were speaking.

4. I knew a person who had these successive locutions: among them were some very true and substantial ones concerning the most holy Sacrament of the Eucharist, but others were sheer heresy. And I am appalled at what happens in these days -- namely, when some soul with the very smallest experience [458] of meditation, if it be conscious of certain locutions of this kind in some state of recollection, at once christens them all as coming from God, and assumes that this is the case, saying: 'God said to me . . ,'; 'God answered me . . ,'; whereas it is not so at all, but, as we have said, it is for the most part they who are saying these things to themselves.

5. And, over and above this, the desire which people have for locutions, and the pleasure which comes to their spirits from them, lead them to make answer to themselves and then to think that it is God Who is answering them and speaking to them. They therefore commit great blunders unless they impose a strict restraint upon themselves, and unless their director obliges them to abstain from these kinds of reflection. For they are apt to gain from them mere nonsensical talk and impurity of soul rather than humility and mortification of spirit, if they think, 'This was indeed a great thing' and 'God was speaking'; whereas it will have been little more than nothing, or nothing at all, or less than nothing. For, if humility and charity be not engendered by such experiences, and mortification and holy simplicity and silence, etc., what can be the value of them? I say, then, that these things may hinder the soul greatly in its progress to Divine union because, if it pay heed to them, it is led far astray from the abyss

of faith, where the understanding must remain in darkness, and must journey in darkness, by love and in faith, and not by much reasoning.

6. And if you ask me why the understanding must be deprived of these truths, since through them it is illumined by the Spirit of God, and thus they [459] cannot be evil, I reply that the Holy Spirit illumines the understanding which is recollected, and illumines it according to the manner of its recollection, [460] and that the understanding cannot find any other and greater recollection than in faith; and thus the Holy Spirit will illumine it in naught more than in faith. For the purer and the more refined in faith is the soul, the more it has of the infused charity of God; and the more charity it has, the more is it illumined and the more gifts of the Holy Spirit are communicated to it, for charity is the cause and the means whereby they are communicated to it. And although it is true that, in this illumination of truths, the Holy Spirit communicates a certain light to the soul, this is nevertheless as different in quality from that which is in faith, wherein is no clear understanding, as is the most precious gold from the basest metal; and, with regard to its quantity, the one is as much greater than the other as the sea is greater than a drop of water. For in the one manner there is communicated to the soul wisdom concerning one or two or three truths, etc., but in the other there is communicated to it all the wisdom of God in general, which is the Son of God, Who communicates Himself to the soul in faith.

7. And if you tell me that this is all good, and that the one impedes not the other, I reply that it impedes it greatly if the soul sets store by it; for to do this is to occupy itself with things which are clear and of little importance, yet which are sufficient to hinder the communication of the abyss of faith, wherein God supernaturally and secretly instructs the soul, and exalts it in virtues and gifts in a way that it knows not. And the profit which these successive communications will bring us cannot come by our deliberately applying the understanding to them, for if we do this they will rather lead us astray, even as Wisdom says to the soul in the Songs: Turn away thine eyes from me, for they make me to fly away.' [461] That is so say: They make me to fly far away from thee and to set myself higher. We must therefore not apply the understanding to that which is being supernaturally communicated to it, but simply and sincerely apply the will to God with love, for it is through love that these good things are communicated and through love they will be communicated in greater abundance than before. For if the ability of the natural understanding or of other faculties be brought actively to bear upon these things which are communicated supernaturally and passively, its imperfect nature will not reach them, and thus they will perforce be modified according to the capacity of the understanding, and consequently will perforce be changed; and thus the understanding will necessarily go astray and begin to form reasonings within itself, and there will no longer be anything supernatural or any semblance thereof, but all will be merely natural and most erroneous and unworthy.

8. But there are certain types of understanding so quick and subtle that, when they become recollected during some meditation, they invent conceptions, and begin naturally, and with great facility, to form these conceptions into the most lifelike words and arguments, which they think, without any doubt, come from God. Yet all the time they come only from the understanding, which, with its natural illumination, being to some extent freed from the operation of the senses, is able to effect all this, and more, without any supernatural aid. This happens very commonly, and many persons are greatly deceived by it, thinking that they have attained to a high degree of prayer and are receiving communications from God, wherefore they either write this down or cause it to be written. And it turns out to be nothing, and to have the substance of no virtue, and it serves only to encourage them in vanity.

9. Let these persons learn to be intent upon naught, save only upon grounding the will in humble love, working diligently, suffering and thus imitating the Son of God in His life and mortifications, for it is by this road that a man will come to all spiritual good, rather than by much inward reasoning.

10. In this type of locution -- namely, in successive interior words -- the devil frequently intervenes, especially in the case of such as have some inclination or affection for them. At times when such persons begin to be recollected, the devil is accustomed to offer them ample material for distractions, forming conceptions or words by suggestion in their understanding, and then corrupting [462] and deceiving it most subtly with things that have every appearance of being true. And this is one of the manners wherein he communicates with those who have made some implicit or expressed compact with him; as with certain heretics, especially with certain heresiarchs, whose understanding he fills with most subtle, false and erroneous conceptions and arguments.

11. From what has been said, it is evident that these successive locutions may proceed in the understanding from three causes, namely: from the Divine Spirit, Who moves and illumines the understanding; from the natural illumination of the same understanding; and from the devil, who may speak to the soul by suggestion. To describe now the signs and indications by which a man may know when they proceed from one cause and when from another would be somewhat difficult, as also to give examples and indications. It is quite possible, however, to give some general signs, which are these. When in its words and conceptions the soul finds itself loving God, and at the same time is conscious not only of love but also of humility and reverence, it is a sign that the Holy Spirit is working within it, for, whensoever He grants favours, He grants them with this accompaniment. [463] When the locutions

proceed solely from the vivacity and brilliance of the understanding, it is the understanding that accomplishes everything, without the operation of the virtues (although the will, in the knowledge and illumination of those truths, may love naturally); and, when the meditation is over, the will remains dry, albeit inclined neither to vanity nor to evil, unless the devil should tempt it afresh about this matter. This, however, is not the case when the locutions have been prompted by a good spirit; for then, as a rule, the will is afterwards affectioned to God and inclined to well-doing. At certain times, nevertheless, it will happen that, although the communication has been the work of a good spirit, the will remains in aridity, since God ordains it so for certain causes which are of assistance to the soul. At other times the soul will not be very conscious of the operations or motions of those virtues, yet that which it has experienced will be good. Wherefore I say that the difference between these locutions is sometimes difficult to recognize, by reason of the varied effects which they produce; but these which have now been described are the most common, although sometimes they occur in greater abundance and sometimes in less. But those that come from the devil are sometimes difficult to understand and recognize, for, although it is true that as a rule they leave the will in aridity with respect to love of God, and the mind inclined to vanity, self-esteem or complacency, nevertheless they sometimes inspire the soul with a false humility and a fervent affection of the will rooted in self-love, so that at times a person must be extremely spiritually-minded to recognize it. And this the devil does in order the better to protect himself; for he knows very well how sometimes to produce tears by the feelings which he inspires in a soul, in order that he may continue to implant in it the affections that he desires. But he always strives to move its will so that it may esteem those interior communications, attach great importance to them, and, as a result, give itself up to them and be occupied in that which is not virtue, but is rather the occasion of losing virtue as the soul may have.

12. Let us remember, then, this necessary caution, both as to the one type of locution and as to the other, so that we may not be deceived or hindered by them. Let us treasure none of them, but think only of learning to direct our will determinedly to God, fulfilling His law and His holy counsels perfectly, which is the wisdom of the Saints, and contenting ourselves with knowing the mysteries and truths

with the simplicity and truth wherewith the Church sets them before us. For this is sufficient to enkindle the will greatly, so that we need not pry into other deep and curious things wherein it is a wonder if there is no peril. For with respect to this Saint Paul says: It is not fitting to know more than it behoves us [464] to know. [465] And let this suffice with respect to this matter of successive words.

Footnotes:

457. Genesis xxvii, 22.

458. [Lit., with four maravedís' worth of experience.' The maravedí was a small coin, worth 1/375 of a gold ducat, the unit of coinage at this time in Castile.]

459. [Lit., and thus it.']

460. This profound and important principle, which has often been developed in mystical theology, is well expounded by P. José de Jesús María in a treatise called Reply to a question [Respuesta a una duda]. Here, among other things, he says: As St. Thomas proves (De Veritate, q. 12, a. 6), Divine illumination, like every other spiritual form, is communicated to the soul after the manner of the receiver of it, whether according to sense or according to spirit, to the particular or to the universal. And thus, he that receives it must prepare himself for it to be communicated to him further, whether in small measure (as we say) or according to sense, or in large measure or intellectually.'

461. [Canticles vi, 4.]

462. [Lit., and then throwing it down.']

463. [Lit., He grants them wrapped up in this.']

464. [The verbs used in the Spanish for is fitting' and behoves' are the same.]

465. Romans xii, 3.

CHAPTER XXX

Which treats of the interior words that come to the spirit formally by supernatural means. Warns the reader of the harm which they may do and of the caution that is necessary in order that the soul may not be deceived by them.

The interior words belonging to the second type are formal words, which at certain times come to the spirit by supernatural means, without the intervention of any of the senses, sometimes when the spirit is recollected and at other times when it is not. I call them formal because they are communicated to the spirit formally by a third person, the spirit itself playing no part in this. And they are therefore very different from those which we have just described; because not only is there this difference, that they come without any such intervention of the spirit itself as takes place in the other case; but also, as I say, they sometimes come when the spirit is not recollected and even when it is far from thinking of the subject of what is being said to it. This is not so in the first type of locution -- namely, that of successive words -- which always has some relation to the subject which the soul is considering.

2. These words are sometimes very clearly formed and sometimes less so; for they are frequently like conceptions in which something is said to the spirit, whether in the form of a reply to it or in that of another manner of address. Sometimes there is only one word; sometimes there are two or more; sometimes the words succeed one another like those already described, for they are apt to be continuous, either instructing the soul or discussing something with it; and all this comes to pass without any part being played therein by the spirit, for it is just as though one person were speaking with another. In this way, we read, it came to pass with Daniel, who says that the angel spoke within him. [466] This was a formal and successive discourse within his spirit, which instructed him, even as the angel declared at the time, saying that he had come to instruct him.

3. When these words are no more than formal, the effect which they produce upon the soul is not great. For ordinarily they serve only to instruct or illumine with respect to one thing; and, in order to produce this effect, it is not necessary that they should produce any other effect more efficacious than the purpose to which they are leading. And when they are of God they invariably work this in the soul; for they make it ready and quick to do that which it is commanded or instructed to do; yet at times they take not from it the repugnance or the difficulty which it feels, but are rather wont to increase these, according as God ordains for the better instruction, increased humility and greater good of the soul. And this repugnance most commonly occurs when the soul is commanded to do things of a high order, or things of a kind that may exalt it; when things are commanded it that conduce to its greater lowliness and humility, it responds with more readiness and ease. And thus we read in Exodus that, when God commanded Moses to go to Pharao and driver the people, he showed such great repugnance that He had to command him three times to do it and to perform signs for him; and all this was of no avail until God gave him Aaron for a companion to take part of the honour. [467]

4. When, on the other hand, the words and communications are of the devil, it comes to pass that the soul responds with more ease and readiness to things that are of greater weight, [468] and for lowlier things it conceives repugnance. The fact is that God so greatly abhors seeing souls attracted by high position that, even when He commands and obliges them to accept such positions, He desires them not to be ready and anxious to command. It is this readiness which God commonly inspires in the soul, through these formal words, that constitutes one great difference between them and those other successive words: the latter move not the spirit so much, neither do they inspire it with such readiness, since they are less formal, and since the understanding has more to do with them. Nevertheless successive words may sometimes produce a greater effect by reason of the close communication that there is at times between the Divine Spirit and the human. It is in the manner of their coming that there is a great difference between the two kinds of locution. With respect to formal words the soul can have no doubt as to whether or no it is pronouncing them itself, for it sees quite ready that it is not, especially when it has not been thinking of the subject of that which has been said to it; and even when it has been so thinking it feels very clearly and distinctly that the words come from elsewhere.

5. The soul must no more attach importance to all these formal words than to the other, or successive, words; for, apart from the fact that to do so would occupy the spirit with that which is not a legitimate and proximate means to union with God -- namely, faith -- it might also very easily cause it to be deceived by the devil. For sometimes it is hardly possible to know what words are spoken by a good spirit, and what by an evil spirit. By their effects they can hardly be distinguished at all, since

neither kind produces effects of much importance: sometimes, indeed, with imperfect souls, words which come from the devil have more efficacy than have these others, which come from a good spirit, with souls that are spiritual. The soul, then, must take no account of what these words may express, nor attach any importance to them, whether the spirit from which they come be good or evil. But the words must be repeated to an experienced confessor, or to a discreet and learned person, that he may give instruction and see what it is well to do, and impart his advice; and the soul must behave, with regard to them, in a resigned and negative way. And, if such an expert person cannot be found, it is better to attach no importance to these words and to repeat them to nobody; for it is easy to find persons who will ruin the soul rather than edify it. Souls must not be given into the charge of any kind of director, since in so grave a matter it is of the greatest importance whether one goes astray or acts rightly.

6. And let it be carefully noted that a soul should never act according to its own opinion or accept anything of what these locutions express, without much reflection and without taking advice of another. For strange and subtle deceptions may arise in this matter; so much so that I myself believe that the soul that does not set itself against accepting such things cannot fail to be deceived by many of them.

7. And since we have treated of these deceptions and perils, and of the caution to be observed with regard to them, in Chapters seventeen, eighteen, nineteen and twenty of this book, I refer the reader to these and say no more on this matter here; I only repeat that my chief instruction is that the soul should attach no importance to these things in any way.

Footnotes:

466. Daniel ix, 22.
467. Exodus iii, iv.
468. [Lit., greater worth.']

CHAPTER XXXI

Which treats of the substantial words that come interiorly to the spirit. Describes the difference between them and formal words, and the profit which they bring and the resignation and respect which the soul must observe with regard to them. [469]

The third kind of interior words, we said, is called substantial. These substantial words, although they are likewise formal, since they are impressed upon the soul in a definitely formal way, differ, nevertheless, in that substantial words produce vivid and substantial effects upon the soul, whereas words which are merely formal do not. So that, although it is true that every substantial word is formal, every formal word is not therefore substantial, but only, as we said above, such a word as impresses substantially on the soul that which it signifies. It is as if Our Lord were to say formally to the soul: Be thou good'; it would then be substantially good. Or as if He were to say to it: Love thou Me'; it would then have and feel within itself the substance of love for God. Or as if it feared greatly and He said to it: Fear thou not'; it would at once feel within itself great fortitude and tranquility. For the saying of God, and His word, as the Wise Man says, is full of power; [470] and thus that which He says to the soul He produces substantially within it. For it is this that David meant when he said: See, He will give to His voice a voice of virtue.' [471] And even so with Abraham, when He said to him: Walk in My presence and be perfect': [472] he was then perfect and walked ever in the fear of God. And this is the power of His word in the Gospel, wherewith He healed the sick, raised the dead, etc., by no more than a word. And after this manner He gives certain souls locutions which are substantial; and they are of such moment and price that they are life and virtue and incomparable good to the soul; for one of these words works greater good within the soul than all that the soul itself has done throughout its life.

2. With respect to these words, the soul should do nothing. It should neither desire them nor refrain from desiring them; it should neither reject them nor fear them. It should do nothing in the way of executing what these words express, for these substantial words are never pronounced by God in order that the soul may translate them into action, but that He may so translate them within the soul; herein they differ from formal and successive words. And I say that the soul must neither desire nor refrain from desiring, since its desire is not necessary for God to translate these words into effect, nor is it sufficient for the soul to refrain from desiring in order for the said effect not to be produced. Let the soul rather be resigned and humble with respect to them. It must not reject them, since the effect of these words remains substantially within it and is full of the good which comes from God. As the soul receives this good passively, its action is at no time of any importance. Nor should it fear any deception; for neither the understanding nor the devil can intervene herein, nor can they succeed in passively producing this substantial effect in the soul, in such a way that the effect and habit of the locution may be impressed upon it, unless the soul should have given itself to the devil by a voluntary compact, and he should have dwelt in it as its master, and impressed upon it these effects, not of good, but of evil. Inasmuch as that soul would be already voluntarily united to him in perversity, the devil might easily impress upon it the effects of his sayings and words with evil intent. For we see by experience that in many things and even upon good souls he works great violence, by means of suggestion, making his suggestions very efficacious; and if they were evil he might work in them the consummation of these suggestions. But he cannot leave upon a soul effects similar to those of locutions which are good; for there is no comparison between the locutions of the devil and those of God. The former are all as though they were not, in comparison with the latter, neither do they produce any effect at all compared with the effect of these. For this cause God says through Jeremias: What has the chaff to do with the wheat? Are not My words perchance as fire, and as a hammer that breaketh the rock in pieces?' [473] And thus these substantial words are greatly conducive to the union of the soul with God; and the more interior they are, the more substantial are they, and the greater is the profit that they bring. Happy is the soul to whom God addresses these words. Speak, Lord, for Thy servant heareth. [474]

[469] This chapter is notable for the hardly surpassable clarity and precisions with which the Saint defines substantial locutions. Some critics, however, have found fault with him for saying that the soul should not fear these locutions, but accept them humbly and passively, since they depend wholly on God. The reply is that, when God favours the soul with these locutions, its own restless effort can only impede His work in it, as has already been said. The soul is truly co-operating with God by preparing itself with resignation and humble affection to receive His favours: it should not, as some critics have

asserted, remain completely inactive. As to the fear of being deceived by these locutions, both St. Thomas and all the principal commentators are in conformity with the Saint's teaching. St. Teresa, too, took the same attitude as St. John of the Cross. Cf. her Life, Chap. xxv, and Interior Castle, VI, iii.

Footnotes:

470. Ecclesiastes viii, 4.
471. Psalm lxvii, 34 [A.V., lxviii, 33].
472. Genesis xvii, 1.
473. Jeremias xxiii, 28-9.
474. 1 Kings [A.V., 1 Samuel] iii, 10.

CHAPTER XXXII

Which treats of the apprehensions received by the understanding from interior feelings which come supernaturally to the soul. Describes their cause, and the manner wherein the soul must conduct itself so that they may not obstruct its road to union with God.

It is now time to treat of the fourth and last kind of intellectual apprehension which we said might come to the understanding through the spiritual feelings which are frequently produced supernaturally in the souls of spiritual persons and which we count amongst the distinct apprehensions of the understanding.

2. These distinct spiritual feelings may be of two kinds. The first kind is in the affection of the will. The second, in the substance of the soul. Each of these may be of many kinds. Those of the will, when they are of God, are most sublime; but those that are of the substance of the soul are very high and of great good and profit. As to these, neither the soul nor he that treats with it can know or understand the cause whence they proceed, or what are the acts whereby God may grant it these favours; for they depend not upon any works performed by the soul, nor upon its meditations, although both these things are a good preparation for them: God grants these favours to whom He wills and for what reason He wills. [475] For it may come to pass that a person will have performed many good works, yet that He will not give him these touches of His favour; and another will have done far fewer good works, yet He will give him them to a most sublime degree and in great abundance. And thus it is not needful that the soul should be actually employed and occupied in spiritual things (although it is much better that it should be so employed if it is to have these favours) for God to give it these touches in which the soul experiences the said feelings; for in the majority of cases the soul is completely heedless of them. Of these touches, some are distinct and pass quickly away; others are less distinct and last longer.

3. These feelings, inasmuch as they are feelings only, belong not to the understanding but to the will; and thus I refrain, of set purpose, from treating of them here, nor shall I do so until we treat of the night and purgation of the will in its affections: this will be in the third book, which follows this. [476] But since frequently, and even in the majority of cases, apprehensions and knowledge and intelligence overflow from them into the understanding, it would be well to make mention of them here, for that reason only. It must be known, then, that from these feelings, both from those of the will and from those which are in the substance of the soul, whether they are caused suddenly by the touches of God, or are durable and successive, an apprehension of knowledge or intelligence frequently overflows, as I say, into the understanding; and this is normally a most sublime perception of God, most delectable to the understanding, to which no name can be given, any more than to the feeling whence it overflows. And these manifestations of knowledge are sometimes of one kind and sometimes of another; sometimes they are clearer and more sublime, according to the nature of the touches which come from God and which produce the feelings whence they proceed, and according also to their individual characteristics.

4. It is unnecessary here to spend a great store of words in cautioning and directing the understanding, through these manifestations of knowledge, in faith, to union with God. For albeit the feelings which we have described are produced passively in the soul, without any effective assistance to that end on its own part, even so likewise is the knowledge of them received passively in the understanding, in a way called by the philosophers passible,' wherein the understanding plays no part. Wherefore, in order not to go astray on their account nor to impede the profit which comes from them, the understanding must do nothing in connection with these feelings, but must conduct itself passively, and not interfere by applying to them its natural capacity. For, as we have said is the case with successive locutions, the understanding, with its activity, would very easily disturb and ruin the effect of these delicate manifestations of knowledge, which are a delectable supernatural intelligence that human nature cannot attain or apprehend by its own efforts, but only by remaining in a state of receptivity. [477] And thus the soul must not strive to attain them or desire to receive them, lest the understanding should form other manifestations of its own, or the devil should make his entry with still more that are different from them and false. This he may very well do by means of the feelings aforementioned, or of those which he can himself infuse into the soul that devotes itself to these kinds of knowledge. Let the soul be resigned, humble and passive herein, for, since it receives this knowledge passively from God, He will communicate it whensoever He is pleased, if He sees the soul to be humble and detached. And in this way the soul will do nothing to counteract the help which these kinds of knowledge give it in its progress toward Divine union, which help is great; for these touches are all touches of union, which is

wrought passively in the soul.⁴⁷⁸

5. What has been said concerning this suffices, for no matter what may happen to the soul with respect to the understanding, cautions and instructions have been given it in the sections already mentioned. And although a case may appear to be different and to be in no way included herein, there is none that cannot be referred to one of these, and thus may be deduced the instruction necessary for it.⁴⁷⁹

Footnotes:

475. A, B: and how He wills.' Note that the Saint does not deprecate good works, as did the Illuminists [alumbrados], who bade the perfect soul set them aside for contemplation, even though they were works of obligation. On the contrary, he asserts that good works have a definite, though a preparatory, part to play in the life of a contemplative.

476. Alc. alone has: which follows this.' The Saint does not, in fact, return to this matter, either in the third book or elsewhere.

477. [Lit., or apprehend by doing, but by receiving.']

478. Some editions here add a long paragraph, which, however, is the work of P. Jerónimo de San José, who was responsible for the edition of 1630. It appears neither in the MSS. nor in e.p. It runs as follows: All the instruction which has been given in this book on total abstraction and passive contemplation, wherein, oblivious to all created things and detached from images and figures, we allow ourselves to be guided by God, dwelling with simple regard upon supreme truth, is applicable not only to that act of most perfect contemplation, the lofty and wholly supernatural repose of which is still prevented by the daughters of Jerusalem (namely, good reflections and meditations), if at that time the soul desires them, but also to the whole of the time during which Our Lord communicates the simple, general and loving attentiveness aforementioned, or during which the soul, aided by grace, places itself in that state. For at that time the soul must always strive to keep its understanding in repose, without the interference of other forms, figures or particular kinds of knowledge, save very fleetingly and quite superficially; and it must have a loving sweetness which will enkindle it ever more. But, except at this time, in all its exercises, acts and works, the soul must make use of good meditations and remembrances, so as to experience the greater devotion and profit, most of all with respect to the life, passion and death of Our Lord Jesus Christ, so that its actions, practices and life may be made like to His.

479. Thus Alc. A, B, e.p. read: This suffices to conclude (our treatment of) the supernatural apprehensions of the understanding, so far as concerns the guidance of the understanding, by their means, in faith, to Divine union. And I think that what has been said with regard to this suffices, for, no matter what happens to the soul with respect to the understanding, instructions and cautions concerning it will be found in the sections already mentioned. And, if something should happen, apparently so different that none of them deals with it (although I think there will be nothing relating to the understanding which cannot be referred to one of the four kinds of distinct knowledge), instructions and cautions concerning it can be deduced from what has been said of others similar to it. And with this we will pass to the third book, where, with the Divine favour, we shall treat of the interior spiritual purgation of the will with regard to its interior affections which we here call active night.' C, D have: From what has been said may be deduced instructions and cautions for guidance in whatever may happen to the soul with regard to the understanding, even if it seem so different that it includes none of the four distinct kinds, although I think there will be nothing relating to the understanding which cannot be referred to one of them. And so we will pass to the third book.' The edition of 1630 follows A, B and e.p., and adds further: I therefore beg the discreet reader to read these things in a benevolent and simple spirit; for, when this spirit is not present, however sublime and perfect be the instruction, it will not yield the profit that it contains, nor will it earn the esteem that it merits. How much truer is this in the present case, since my style is in so many ways deficient!'

BOOK THE THIRD

Which treats of the purgation of the active night of the memory and will. Gives instruction how the soul is to behave with respect to the apprehensions of these two faculties, that it may come to union with God, according to the two faculties aforementioned, in perfect hope and charity.

CHAPTER I

The first faculty of the soul, which is the understanding, has now been instructed, through all its apprehensions, in the first theological virtue, which is faith, to the end that, according to this faculty, the soul may be united with God by means of the purity of faith. It now remains to do likewise with respect to the other two faculties of the soul, which are memory and will, and to purify them likewise with respect to their apprehensions, to the end that, according to these two faculties also, the soul may come to union with God in perfect hope and charity. This will briefly be effected in this third book. We have now concluded our treatment of the understanding, which is the receptacle of all other objects according to its mode of operation; and in treating of this we have gone a great part of the whole way. It is therefore unnecessary for us to write at equal length with respect to these faculties; for it is not possible that, if the spiritual man instructs his understanding in faith according to the doctrine which has been given him, he should not, in so doing, instruct the other two faculties in the other two virtues likewise; for the operations of each faculty depend upon the others.

2. But since, in order to follow our manner of procedure, and in order, too, that we may be the better understood, we must necessarily speak of the proper and determinate matter, we shall here be obliged to set down the apprehensions proper to each faculty, and first, those of the memory, making here such distinction between them as suffices for our purpose. This we shall be able to deduce from the distinction between their objects, which are three: natural, imaginary and spiritual; according to which there are likewise three kinds of knowledge which come from the memory, namely: natural and supernatural, [480] imaginary and spiritual.

3. All these, by the Divine favour, we shall treat here in due course, beginning with natural knowledge, which pertains to the most exterior objects. And we shall then treat of the affections of the will, wherewith we shall conclude this third book of the active spiritual night.

Footnotes:

480. It will be seen from what follows that in practice the Saint preserves the strictly tripartite division given in the text above, supernatural knowledge being found in each of the sections.

CHAPTER II

Which treats of the natural apprehensions of the memory and describes how the soul must be voided of them in order to be able to attain to union with God according to this faculty.

It is necessary that, in each of these books, the reader should bear in mind the purpose of which we are speaking. For otherwise there may arise within him many such questions with respect to what he is reading as might by this time be occurring to him with respect to what we have said of the understanding, and shall say now of the memory, and afterwards shall say of the will. For, seeing how we annihilate the faculties with respect to their operations, it may perhaps seem to him that we are destroying the road of spiritual practice rather than constructing it.

2. This would be true if we were seeking here only to instruct beginners, who are best prepared through these apprehensible and discursive apprehensions. But, since we are here giving instruction to those who would progress farther in contemplation, even to union with God, to which end all of these means and exercises of sense concerning the faculties must recede into the background, and be put to silence, to the end that God may of His own accord work Divine union in the soul, it is necessary to proceed by this method of disencumbering and emptying the soul, and causing it to reject the natural jurisdiction and operations of the faculties, so that they may become capable of infusion and illumination from supernatural sources; for their capacity cannot attain to so lofty an experience, but will rather hinder it, if it be not disregarded.

3. And thus, if it be true, as it is, that the soul must proceed in its growing knowledge of God by learning that which He is not rather than that which He is, in order to come to Him, it must proceed by renouncing and rejecting, to the very uttermost, everything in its apprehensions that it is possible to renounce, whether this be natural or supernatural. We shall proceed with this end in view with regard to the memory, drawing it out from its natural state and limitations, and causing it to rise above itself -- that is, above all distinct knowledge and apprehensible possession -- to the supreme hope of God, Who is incomprehensible.

4. Beginning, then, with natural knowledge, I say that natural knowledge in the memory consists of all the kinds of knowledge that the memory can form concerning the objects of the five bodily senses -- namely: hearing, sight, smell, taste and touch -- and all kinds of knowledge of this type which it is possible to form and fashion. Of all these forms and kinds of knowledge the soul must strip and void itself, and it must strive to lose the imaginary apprehension of them, so that there may be left in it no kind of impression of knowledge, nor trace of aught soever, but rather the soul must remain barren and bare, as if these forms had never passed through it, and in total oblivion and suspension. And this cannot happen unless the memory be annihilated as to all its forms, if it is to be united with God. For it cannot happen save by total separation from all forms which are not God; for God comes beneath no definite form or kind of knowledge whatsoever, as we have said in treating of the night of the understanding. And since, as Christ says, no man can serve two masters, [481] the memory cannot be united both with God and with forms and distinct kinds of knowledge and, as God has no form or image that can be comprehended by the memory, it follows that, when the memory is united with God (as is seen, too, every day by experience), it remains without form and without figure, its imagination being lost and itself being absorbed in a supreme good, and in a great oblivion, remembering nothing. For that Divine union voids its fancy and sweeps it clean of all forms and kinds of knowledge and raises it to the supernatural.

5. Now there sometimes comes to pass here a notable thing; for occasionally, when God brings about these touches of union in the memory, the brain (where memory has its seat) is so perceptibly upset that it seems as if it becomes quite inert, and its judgment and sense are lost. This is sometimes more perceptible and sometimes less so, according to the strength of this touch, and then, by reason of this union, the memory is voided and purged, as I say, of all kinds of knowledge. It remains in oblivion -- at times in complete oblivion -- so that it has to put forth a great effort and to labour greatly in order to remember anything.

6. And sometimes this oblivion of the memory and suspension of the imagination reach such a point, because of the union of the memory with God, that a long time passes without the soul's perceiving it, or knowing what has taken place during that period. And, as the imaginative faculty is then in suspension, it feels naught that is done to it, not even things that cause pain; for without imagination there is no feeling, not even coming through thought, since this exists not. And, to the end

that God may bring about these touches of union, the soul must needs withdraw its memory from all apprehensible kinds of knowledge. And it is to be noted that these suspensions come not to pass in those that are already perfect, since they have attained to perfect union, and these suspensions belong to the beginnings of union.

7. Someone will remark that all this seems very well, but that it leads to the destruction of the natural use and course of the faculties, and reduces man to the state of a beast -- a state of oblivion and even worse -- since he becomes incapable of reasoning or of remembering his natural functions and necessities. It will be argued that God destroys not nature, but rather perfects it; and that from this teaching there necessarily follows its destruction, when that which pertains to morality and reason is not practised and is forgotten, neither is that which is natural practised; for (it will be said) none of these things can be remembered, as the soul is deprived of forms and kinds of knowledge which are the means of remembrance.

8. To this I reply that, the more nearly the memory attains to union with God, the more do distinct kinds of knowledge become perfected within it, until it loses them entirely -- namely, when it attains to the state of union in perfection. And thus, at the beginning, when this is first taking place, the soul cannot but fall into great oblivion with respect to all things, since forms and kinds of knowledge are being erased from it; and therefore it is very negligent concerning its outward behaviour and usage -- forgetting to eat or drink, and being uncertain if it has done this or no, if it has seen this or no, if it has said this or no -- because of the absorption of the memory in God. But when once it attains to the habit of union, which is a supreme blessing, it no longer has these periods of oblivion, after this manner, in that which pertains to natural and moral reason; actions which are seemly and necessary, indeed, it performs with a much greater degree of perfection, although it performs them no longer by means of forms and manners of knowledge pertaining to the memory. For, when it has the habit of union, which is a supernatural state, memory and the other faculties fail it completely in their natural functions, and pass beyond their natural limitations, even to God, Who is supernatural. And thus, when the memory is transformed in God, it cannot receive impressions of forms or kinds of knowledge. Wherefore the functions of the memory and of the other faculties in this state are all Divine; for, when at last God possesses the faculties and has become the entire master of them, through their transformation into Himself, it is He Himself Who moves and commands them divinely, according to His Divine Spirit and will; and the result of this is that the operations of the soul are not distinct, but all that it does is of God, and its operations are Divine, so that, even as Saint Paul says, he that is joined unto God becomes one spirit with Him. [482]

9. Hence it comes to pass that the operations of the soul in union are of the Divine Spirit and are Divine. And hence it comes that the actions of such souls are only those that are seemly and reasonable, and not those that are ill-beseeming. For the Spirit of God teaches them that which they ought to know, and causes them to be ignorant of that which it behoves them not to know, and to remember that which they have to remember, with or without forms, and to forget that which they should forget; and it makes them love that which they have to love, and not to love that which is not in God. And thus, all the first motions of the faculties of such souls are Divine and it is not to be wondered at that the motions and operations of these faculties should be Divine, since they are transformed in the Divine Being. [483]

10. Of these operations I will give a few examples. Let this be one. A person asks another who is in this state to commend him to God. This person will not remember to do so by means of any form or kind of knowledge that remains in his memory concerning that other person; if it be right that he should recommend him to God (which will be if God desires to receive a prayer for that person), He will move his will and give him a desire to pray for him; and if God desires not such prayer, that other person will not be able nor will desire to pray,' though he make great efforts to do so; and at times God will cause him to pray for others of whom he has no knowledge nor has ever heard. And this is because, as I have said, God alone moves the faculties of these souls to do those works which are meet, according to the will and ordinance of God, and they cannot be moved to do others; and thus the works and prayers of these souls are always effectual. Such were those of the most glorious Virgin Our Lady, who, being raised to this high estate from the beginning, had never the form of any creature imprinted in her soul, neither was moved by such, but was invariably guided by the Holy Spirit.

11. Another example. At a certain time a person in this state has to attend to some necessary business. He will remember it by no kind of form, but, without his knowing how, it will come to his soul, at the time and in the manner that it ought to come, and that without fail.

12. And not only in these things does the Holy Spirit give such persons light, but also in many others, relating both to the present and to the future, and even, in many cases, as regards those absent from them; and although at times this comes to pass through intellectual forms, it frequently happens without the intervention of any forms that can be apprehended, so that these persons know not how they know. But this comes to them from the Divine Wisdom; for, since these souls exercise themselves in knowing and apprehending nothing with the faculties, they come in general, as we have said in the Mount, [484] to know everything, according to that which the Wise Man says: The worker of all things,

who is Wisdom, taught me all things.[1] [485]

13. You will say, perhaps, that the soul will be unable to void and deprive its memory of all forms and fancies to such an extent as to be able to attain to so lofty a state; for there are two things so difficult that their accomplishment surpasses human ability and strength, namely, to throw off with one's natural powers that which is natural, which is hard enough, [486] and to attain and be united to the supernatural, which is much more difficult -- indeed, to speak the truth, is impossible with natural ability alone. The truth, I repeat, is that God must place the soul in this supernatural state; but the soul, as far as in it lies, must be continually preparing itself; and this it can do by natural means, especially with the help that God is continually giving it. And thus, as the soul, for its own part, enters into this renunciation and self-emptying of forms, so God begins to give it the possession of union; and this God works passively in the soul, as we shall say, Deo dante, when we treat of the passive night of the soul. And thus, when it shall please God, and according to the manner of the soul's preparation, He will grant it the habit of perfect and Divine union.

14. And the Divine effects which God produces in the soul when He has granted it this habit, both as to the understanding and as to the memory and will, we shall not describe in this account of the soul's active purgation and night, for this alone will not bring the soul to Divine union. We shall speak of these effects, however, in treating of the passive night, by means of which is brought about the union of the soul with God. [487] And so I shall speak here only of the necessary means whereby the memory may place itself actively in this night and purgation, as far as lies in its power. And these means are that the spiritual man must habitually exercise caution, after this manner. All the things that he hears, sees, smells, tastes, or touches, he must be careful not to store up or collect in his memory, but he must allow himself to forget them immediately; and this he must accomplish, if need be, with the same efficacy as that with which others contrive to remember them, so that there remains in his memory no knowledge or image of them whatsoever. It must be with him as if they existed not in the world, and his memory must be left free and disencumbered of them, and be tied to no consideration, whether from above or from below; as if he had no faculty of memory; he must freely allow everything to fall into oblivion as though all things were a hindrance to him; and in fact everything that is natural, if one attempt to make use of it in supernatural matters, is a hindrance rather than a help.

15. And if those questions and objections which arose above with respect to the understanding should also arise here (the objections, that is to say, that the soul is doing nothing, is wasting its time and is depriving itself of spiritual blessings which it might well receive through the memory), the answer to this has already been given, and will be given again farther on, in our treatment of the passive night; wherefore there is no need for us to dwell upon it here. It is needful only to observe that, although at certain times the benefit of this suspension of forms and of all knowledge may not be realized, the spiritual man must not for that reason grow weary, for in His own time God will not fail to succour him. To attain so great a blessing it behoves the soul to endure much and to suffer with patience and hope.

16. And, although it is true that hardly any soul will be found that is moved by God in all things and at all times, and has such continual union with God that, without the mediation of any form, its faculties are ever moved divinely, there are nevertheless souls who in their operations are very habitually moved by God, and these are not they that are moved of themselves, for, as Saint Paul says, the sons of God who are transformed and united in God, are moved by the Spirit of God, [488] that is, are moved to perform Divine work in their faculties. And it is no marvel that their operations should be Divine, since the union of the soul is Divine.

Footnotes:

481. [St. Matthew vi, 24.]

482. 1 Corinthians vi, 17.

483. P. José de Jesús María, in his Vida y excelencias de la Santísima Virgen María (I, xl), quotes this and part of the last paragraph from what he claims to be an original MS. of St. John of the Cross, but his text varies considerably from that of any MS. now known. [P. Silverio considers that this and other similar citations are quite untrustworthy.]

484. The reference is to the drawing of the Mount of Perfection. Cf. The General Introduction, I, above.

485. Wisdom vii, 21.

486. [Lit., which cannot be' (que no puede ser), but this is a well-known Spanish hyperbole describing what is extremely difficult.]

487. E.p. omits all the rest of this paragraph, substituting the following passage, which it introduces in order [says P. Silverio] to describe the scope of the Saint's teaching, and which is copied in the edition of 1630: In [treating of] this purgation of the memory, I speak here only of the necessary means whereby the memory may place itself actively in this night and purgation, as far as lies in its power. And these means are that the spiritual man must habitually exercise caution, after this manner.

Ascent of Mount Carmel
Of all the things that he sees, hears, smells, tastes or touches he must make no particular store in the memory, or pay heed to them, or dwell upon them, but must allow them to pass and must remain in holy oblivion without reflecting upon them, save when necessary for some good reflection or meditation. And this care to forget and forsake knowledge and images is never applicable to Christ and His Humanity. For, although occasionally, at the height of contemplation and simple regard of the Divinity, the soul may not remember this most sacred Humanity, because God, with His own hand, has raised the soul to this, as it were, confused and most supernatural knowledge, yet it is in no wise seemly to study to forget it, since looking and meditating lovingly upon it will aid the soul to [attain] all that is good, and it is by its means that the soul will most readily rise to the most lofty state of union. And it is clear that, although other bodily and visible things are a hindrance and ought to be forgotten, we must not include among these Him Who became man for our salvation, and Who is the truth, the door, the way and the guide to all good things. This being assumed, let the soul strive after complete abstraction and oblivion, so that, in so far as is possible, there may remain in its memory no more knowledge or image of created things than though they existed not in the world; and let it leave the memory free and disencumbered for God, and, as it were, lost in holy oblivion.

    488. Romans viii, 14.

CHAPTER III

Wherein are described three kinds of evil which come to the soul when it enters not into darkness with respect to knowledge and reflections in the memory. Herein is described the first.

To three kinds of evil and inconvenience the spiritual man is subject when he persists in desiring to make use of all natural knowledge and reflections of the memory in order to journey toward God, or for any other purpose: two of these are positive and one is privative. The first comes from things of the world; the second, from the devil; the third, which is privative, is the impediment and hindrance to Divine union caused and effected in the soul.

2. The first evil, which comes from the world, consists in the subjection of the soul, through knowledge and reflection, to many kinds of harm, such as falsehoods, imperfections, desires, opinions, loss of time, and many other things which breed many kinds of impurity in the soul. And it is clear that the soul must of necessity fall into many perils of falsehood, when it admits knowledge and reasoning; for oftentimes that which is true must appear false, and that which is certain, doubtful; and contrariwise; for there is scarcely a single truth of which we can have complete knowledge. From all these things the soul is free if the memory enters into darkness with respect to every kind of reflection and knowledge.

3. Imperfections meet the soul at every step if it sets its memory upon that which it has heard, seen, touched, smelt and tasted; for there must then perforce cling to it some affection, whether this be of pain, of fear, of hatred, of vain hope, vain enjoyment, vainglory, etc.; for all these are, at the least, imperfections, and at times are downright [489] venial sins; and they leave much impurity most subtly in the soul, even though the reflections and the knowledge have relation to God. And it is also clear that they engender desires within the soul, for these arise naturally from the knowledge and reflections aforementioned, and if one wishes only to have this knowledge and these reflections, even that is a desire. And it is clearly seen that many occasions of judging others will come likewise; for, in using its memory, the soul cannot fail to come upon that which is good and bad in others, and, in such a case, that which is evil oftentimes seems good, and that which is good, evil. I believe there is none who can completely free himself from all these kinds of evil, save by blinding his memory and leading it into darkness with regard to all these things.

4. And if you tell me that a man is well able to conquer all these things when they come to him, I reply that, if he sets store by knowledge, this is simply and utterly impossible; for countless imperfections and follies insinuate themselves into such knowledge, some of which are so subtle and minute that, without the soul's realization thereof, they cling to it of their own accord, even as pitch clings to the man that touches it; so that it is better to conquer once for all by denying the memory completely. You will say likewise that by so doing the soul deprives itself of many good thoughts and meditations upon God, which are of great profit to it and whereby God grants it favours. I reply that to this end purity of soul is of the greatest profit, which means that there clings to the soul no creature affection, or temporal affection, or effective advertence; which I believe cannot but cling to the soul because of the imperfection which the faculties have in their own operations. Wherefore it is best to learn to silence the faculties and to cause them to be still, so that God may speak. For, as we have said, in order to attain to this state the natural operations must be completely disregarded, and this happens, as the Prophet says, when the soul comes into solitude, according to these its faculties, and God speaks to its heart. [490]

5. And if you again reply, saying that the soul will have no blessing unless it meditates upon God and allows its memory to reflect upon Him, and that many distractions and negligences will continually enter it, I say that it is impossible, if the memory be recollected with regard both to things of the next life and to things here below, that evils or distractions should enter it, nor any other follies or vices (the which things always enter when the memory wanders), since there is no exit or entrance for them. This would come to pass if, when we had shut the door upon considerations and reflections concerning things above, we opened it to things below; but in this state we shut the door to all things whence distraction may come, [491] causing the memory to be still and dumb, and the ear of the spirit to be attentive, in silence, to God alone, saying with the Prophet: Speak, Lord, for Thy servant heareth.' [492] It was thus that the Spouse in the Songs said that his Bride should be, in these words: My sister is a garden enclosed and a fountain sealed up' [493] -- that is to say, enclosed and sealed up against all things that may enter.

6. Let the soul, then, remain enclosed,' without anxieties and troubles, and He that entered in

Ascent of Mount Carmel

bodily form to His disciples when the doors were shut, and gave them peace, [494] though they neither knew nor thought that this was possible nor knew how it was possible, will enter spiritually into the soul, without its knowing how He does so, when the doors of its faculties -- memory, understanding and will -- are enclosed against all apprehensions. And He will fill them with peace, coming down upon the soul, as the prophet says, like a river of peace, [495] and taking it from all the misgivings and suspicions, disturbances and darknesses which caused it to fear that it was lost or was on the way to being so. Let it not grow careless about prayer, and let it wait in detachment and emptiness, for its blessings will not tarry.

Footnotes:

[489] [Lit., good.']
[490] Osee ii, 14.
[491] [Lit., whence that may come.']
[492] 1 Kings [A.V., 1 Samuel] iii, 10.
[493] Canticles iv, 12.
[494] [St. John xx, 19].
[495] Isaiah xlviii, 18.

CHAPTER IV

Which treats of the second kind of evil that may come to the soul from the devil by way of the natural apprehensions of the memory.

The second positive evil that may come to the soul by means of the knowledge of the memory proceeds from the devil, who by this means obtains great influence over it. For he can continually bring it new forms, kinds of knowledge and reflections, by means whereof he can taint the soul with pride, avarice, wrath, envy, etc., and cause it unjust hatred, or vain love, and deceive it in many ways. And besides this, he is wont to leave impressions, [496] and to implant them in the fancy, in such wise that those that are false appear true, and those that are true, false, And finally all the worst deceptions which are caused by the devil, and the evils that he brings to the soul, enter by way of knowledge and reflections of the memory, Thus if the memory enter into darkness with respect to them all, and be annihilated in its oblivion to them, it shuts the door altogether upon this evil which proceeds from the devil, and frees itself from all these things, which is a great blessing. For the devil has no power over the soul unless it be through the operations of its faculties, principally by means of knowledge, whereupon depend almost all the other operations of the other faculties. Wherefore, if the memory be annihilated with respect to them, the devil can do naught; for he finds no foothold, and without a foothold he is powerless. [497]

2. I would that spiritual persons might clearly see how many kinds of harm are wrought by evil spirits in their souls by means of the memory, when they devote themselves frequently to making use of it, and how many kinds of sadness and affliction and vain and evil joys they have, both with respect to their thoughts about God, and also with respect to the things of the world; and how many impurities are left rooted in their spirits; and likewise how greatly they are distracted from the highest recollection, which consists in the fixing of the whole soul, according to its faculties, upon the one incomprehensible Good, and in withdrawing it from all things that can be apprehended, since these are not incomprehensible Good. This is a great good (although less good results from this emptiness than from the soul's fixing itself upon God), simply because it is the cause whereby the soul frees itself from any griefs and afflictions and sorrows, over and above the imperfections and sins from which it is freed.

Footnotes:

496. [Lit., to leave things.']
497. [Lit., he finds nothing to seize upon, and with nothing he can do nothing.']

CHAPTER V

Of the third evil which comes to the soul by way of the distinct natural knowledge or the memory.

The third evil which comes to the soul through the natural apprehensions of the memory is privative; for these apprehensions can hinder moral good and deprive us of spiritual good. And, in order that we may first of all explain how these apprehensions hinder moral good in the soul, it must be known that moral good consists in the restraining of the passions and the curbing of disorderly desires, from which restraint there come to the soul tranquillity, peace and rest, and moral virtues, all of which things are moral good. This restraining and curbing of the passions cannot be truly accomplished by the soul that forgets not and withdraws not itself from things pertaining to itself, whence arise the affections; and no disturbances ever arise in the soul save through the apprehensions of the memory. For, when all things are forgotten, there is naught that can disturb peace or that moves the desires; since, as they say, that which the eye sees not the heart desires not.

2. This we are constantly learning by experience; for we observe that, whenever the soul begins to think of any matter, it is moved and disturbed, either much or little, with respect to that thing, according to the nature of its apprehension. If it be a troublesome and grievous matter, the soul finds sadness in it; if pleasant, desire and joy, and so forth. Wherefore the result of the changing of that apprehension is necessarily disturbance; and thus the soul is now joyful, now sad; now it hates, now loves; and it cannot continue in one and the same attitude (which is an effect of moral tranquillity save when it strives to forget all things. It is clear, then, that knowledge greatly hinders the good of the moral virtues in the soul.

3. Again, what has been said clearly proves that an encumbered memory also hinders spiritual good; for the soul that is disturbed, and has no foundation of moral good, is to that extent incapable of spiritual good, which impresses itself only upon souls that are restrained and at peace. And besides this, if the soul pays attention and heed to the apprehensions of the memory -- seeing that it can attend to but one thing at a time -- and busies itself with things that can be apprehended, such as the knowledge of the memory, it is not possible for it to be free to attend to the incomprehensible, which is God. For, in order to approach God, the soul must proceed by not comprehending rather than by comprehending; it must exchange the mutable and comprehensible for the immutable and incomprehensible.

CHAPTER VI

Of the benefits which come to the soul from forgetfulness and emptiness of all thoughts and knowledge which it may have in a natural way with respect to the memory.

From the evils which, as we have said, come to the soul through the apprehensions of the memory, we can likewise infer the benefits which are contrary to them and come to the soul as a result of its forgetting them and emptying itself of them. For, as natural philosophy puts it, the same doctrine which serves for one thing serves likewise for the contrary. In the first place, the soul enjoys tranquillity and peace of mind, since it is freed from the disturbance and the changeableness which arise from thoughts and ideas of the memory, and consequently, which is more important, it enjoys purity of conscience and soul. And herein the soul has ample preparation for the acquiring of Divine and human wisdom, and of the virtues.

2. In the second place, it is freed from many suggestions, temptations and motions of the devil, which he infuses into the soul by means of thoughts and ideas, causing it to fall into many impurities and sins, as David says in these words: They have thought and spoken wickedness.'[498] And thus, when these thoughts have been completely removed, the devil has naught wherewith to assault the soul by natural means.

3. In the third place, the soul has within itself, through this recollection of itself and this forgetfulness as to all things, a preparedness to be moved by the Holy Spirit and taught by Him, for, as the Wise Man says, He removes Himself from thoughts that are without understanding.[499] Even if a man received no other benefit from this forgetfulness and emptiness of the memory than being freed thereby from troubles and disturbances, it would be a great gain and good for him. For the troubles and storms which adverse things and happenings arouse in the soul are of no use or help for bringing peace and calm;[500] indeed, as a rule, they make things worse and also harm the soul itself. Wherefore David said: Of a truth every man is disquieted in vain.'[501] For it is clear that to disquiet oneself is always vain since it brings profit to none. And thus, even if everything came to an end and were destroyed, and if all things went wrong and turned to adversity, it would be vain to disturb oneself; for such disturbance hurts a man rather than relieves him. Whereas to bear everything with equable and peaceful tranquillity not only brings the soul the profit of many blessings, but likewise causes it, even in the midst of its adversities, to form a truer judgment about them and to find a fitting remedy.

4. For this reason Solomon, being well acquainted both with the evil and with the benefit of which we are speaking, said: I knew that there was naught better for man than to rejoice and to do good in his life.'[502] By this he meant that, in everything that happens to us, howsoever adverse it be, we should rejoice rather than be disturbed, so that we may not lose a blessing which is greater than any kind of prosperity -- namely, tranquillity and peace of mind in all things, which, whether they bring adversity or prosperity, we must bear in the same manner. This a man would never lose if he were not only to forget all kinds of knowledge and put aside all thoughts, but would even withdraw himself from hearing, sight and commerce with others, in so far as was possible for him. Our nature is so frail and unstable that, however well it be disciplined, it will hardly fail to stumble upon the remembrance of things which will disturb and change a mind that was in peace and tranquillity when it remembered them not. For this cause said Jeremias: With memory I will remember, and my soul will fail me for pain.'[503]

Footnotes:

498. Psalm lxxii, 8 [A.V., lxxiii, 8].
499. Wisdom i, 5.
500. [Lit., for the peace and calm of the same things and happenings.']
501. Psalm xxxviii, 7 [A.V., xxxix, 6].
502. Ecclesiastes iii, 12.
503. Lamentations iii, 20.

CHAPTER VII

Which treats or the second kind or apprehension of the memory -- namely, imaginary apprehensions -- and of supernatural knowledge.

Although in writing of natural apprehensions of the first kind we also gave instruction concerning the imaginary, which are likewise natural, it was well to make this division because of the love which the memory always has for other forms and kinds of knowledge, which are of supernatural things, such as visions, revelations, locutions and feelings which come in a supernatural way. When these things have passed through the soul, there is wont to remain impressed upon it some image, form, figure or idea, whether in the soul or in the memory or fancy, at times very vividly and effectively. Concerning these images it is also needful to give advice, lest the memory be encumbered with them and they be a hindrance to its union with God in perfect and pure hope.

2. I say that the soul, in order to attain that blessing, must never reflect upon the clear and distinct objects which may have passed through its mind by supernatural means, in such a way as to preserve within itself the forms and figures and knowledge of those things. For we must ever bear in mind this principle: the greater heed the soul gives to any clear and distinct apprehensions, whether natural or supernatural, the less capacity and preparation it has for entering into the abyss of faith, wherein are absorbed all things else. For, as has been said, no supernatural forms or kinds of knowledge which can be apprehended by the memory are God, and, in order to reach God, the soul must void itself of all that is not God. The memory must also strip itself of all these forms and kinds of knowledge, that it may unite itself with God in hope. For all possession is contrary to hope, which, as Saint Paul says, belongs to that which is not possessed. [504] Wherefore, the more the memory dispossesses itself, the greater is its hope; and the more it has of hope, the more it has of union with God; for, with respect to God, the more the soul hopes, the more it attains. And it hopes most when it is most completely dispossessed; and, when it shall be perfectly dispossessed, it will remain with the perfect possession of God, in Divine union. But there are many who will not deprive themselves of the sweetness and delight which memory finds in those forms and notions, wherefore they attain not to supreme possession and perfect sweetness. For he that renounces not all that he possesses cannot be the disciple of Christ. [505]

Footnotes:

504. Hebrews xi, 1.
505. St. Luke xiv, 33.

CHAPTER VIII

Of the evils which may be caused in the soul by the knowledge of supernatural things, if it reflect upon them. Says how many these evils are.

The spiritual man incurs the risk of five kinds of evil if he pays heed to, and reflects upon, these forms and ideas which are impressed upon him by the things which pass through his mind in a supernatural way.

2. The first is that he is frequently deceived, and mistakes one thing for another. The second is that he is like to fall, and is exposed to the danger of falling, into some form of presumption or vanity. The third is that the devil has many occasions of deceiving him by means of the apprehensions aforementioned. The fourth is that he is hindered as to union in hope with God. The fifth is that, for the most part, he has a low judgment of God.

3. As to the first evil, it is clear that, if the spiritual man pays heed to these forms and notions, and reflects upon them, he must frequently be deceived in his judgment of them; for, as no man can have a complete understanding of the things that pass through his imagination naturally, nor a perfect and certain judgment about them, he will be much less able still to have this with respect to supernatural things, which are above our capacity to understand, and occur but rarely. Wherefore he will often think that what comes but from his fancy pertains to God; and often, too, that what is of God is of the devil, and what is of the devil is of God. And very often there will remain with him deap-seated impressions of forms and ideas concerning the good and evil of others, or of himself, together with other figures which have been presented to him: these he will consider to be most certain and true, when in fact they will not be so, but very great falsehoods. And others will be true, and he will judge them to be false, although this error I consider safer, as it is apt to arise from humility.

4. And, even if he be not deceived as to their truth, he may well be deceived as to their quantity or quality, thinking that little things are great, and great things, little. And with respect to their quality, he may consider what is in his imagination to be this or that, when it is something quite different; he may put, as Isaias says, darkness for light, and light for darkness, or bitter for sweet, and sweet for bitter. [506] And finally, even though he be correct as to one thing, it will be a marvel if he goes not astray with respect to the next; for, although he may not desire to apply his judgment to the judging of them, yet, if he apply it in paying heed to them, this will be sufficient to make some evil to cling to him as a result of it, at least passively; if not evil of this kind, then of one of the four other kinds of which we shall shortly speak.

5. It behoves the spiritual man, therefore, lest he fall into this evil of being deceived in his judgment, not to desire to apply his judgment in order to know the nature of his own condition or feelings, or the nature of such and such a vision, idea or feeling; neither should he desire to know it or to pay heed to it. This he should only desire in order to speak of it to his spiritual father, and to be taught by him how to void his memory of these apprehensions. For, whatever may be their intrinsic nature, they cannot help him to love God as much as the smallest act of living faith and hope performed in the emptiness and renunciation of all things.

Footnotes:

506. Isaias v, 20.

CHAPTER IX

Of the second kind of evil, which is the peril of falling into self-esteem and vain presumption.

The supernatural apprehensions of the memory already described are also a frequent occasion to spiritual persons of falling into some kind of presumption or vanity, if they give heed to them and set store by them. For, even as he who knows nothing of them is quite free from falling into this vice, since he sees in himself no occasion of presumption, even so, in contrary wise, he that has experience of them has close at hand an occasion for thinking himself to be something, since he possesses these supernatural communications. For, although it is true that he may attribute them to God, hold himself to be unworthy of them, and give God the thanks, yet nevertheless there is wont to remain in his spirit a certain secret satisfaction, and a self-esteem and a sense of their value, from which, without his knowledge, there will come to him great spiritual pride.

2. This may be observed very clearly by such as will consider the dislike and aversion caused them by any who do not praise their spirituality, or esteem the experiences which they enjoy, and the mortification which they suffer when they think or are told that others have just those same experiences, or even superior ones. All this arises from secret self-esteem and pride, and they can never quite realize that they are steeped in pride up to their very eyes. For they think that a certain degree of recognition of their own wretchedness suffices, and, although they have this, they are full of secret self-esteem and self-satisfaction, taking more delight in their own spirituality and spiritual gifts than in those of others. They are like the Pharisee who gave thanks to God that he was not as other men, and that he practised such and such virtues, whereat he was satisfied with himself and presumed thereon. [507] Such men, although they may not use the Pharisee's actual words, habitually resemble him in spirit. And some of them even become so proud that they are worse than the devil. For, observing in themselves, as they imagine, certain apprehensions and feelings concerning God which are devout and sweet, they become self-satisfied to such an extent that they believe themselves to be very near God; and those that are not like themselves they consider very low and despise them after the manner of the Pharisee.

3. In order to flee from this pestilent evil, abhorrent in the eyes of God, they must consider two things. First, that virtue consists not in apprehensions and feelings concerning God, howsoever sublime they be, nor in anything of this kind that a man can feel within himself; but, on the contrary, in that which has nothing to do with feeling -- namely, a great humility and contempt of oneself and of all that pertains to oneself, firmly rooted in the soul and keenly felt by it; and likewise in being glad that others feel in this very way concerning oneself and in not wishing to be of any account in the esteem [508] of others.

4. Secondly, it must be noted that all visions, revelations and feelings coming from Heaven, and any thoughts that may proceed from these, are of less worth than the least act of humility. And humility is one of the effects of charity, which esteems not its own things nor strives to attain them; nor thinks evil, save of itself; nor thinks any good thing of itself, but only of others. It is well, therefore, that these supernatural apprehensions should not attract men's eyes, but that they should strive to forget them in order that they may be free.

Footnotes:

507. St. Luke xviii, 11-12.
508. [Lit., in the heart.']

CHAPTER X

Of the third evil that may come to the soul from the devil, through the imaginary apprehensions of the memory.

From all that has been said above it may be clearly understood and inferred how great is the evil that may come to the soul from the devil by way of these supernatural apprehensions. For not only can he represent to the memory and the fancy many false forms and ideas, which seem true and good, impressing them on spirit and sense with great effectiveness and certifying them to be true by means of suggestion (so that it appears to the soul that it cannot be otherwise, but that everything is even as he represents it; for, as he transfigures himself into an angel of light, he appears as light to the soul); but he may also tempt the soul in many ways with respect to true knowledge, which is of God, moving its desires and affections, whether spiritual or sensual, in unruly fashion with respect to these; for, if the soul takes pleasure in such apprehensions, it is very easy for the devil to cause its desires and affections to grow within it, and to make it fall into spiritual gluttony and other evils.

2. And, in order the better to do this, he is wont to suggest and give pleasure, sweetness and delight to the senses with respect to these same things of God, so that the soul is corrupted and bewildered [509] by that sweetness, and is thus blinded with that pleasure and sets its eyes on pleasure rather than on love (or, at least, very much more than upon love), and gives more heed to the apprehensions than to the detachment and emptiness which are found in faith and hope and love of God. And from this he may go on gradually to deceive the soul and cause it to believe his falsehoods with great facility. For to the soul that is blind falsehood no longer appears to be falsehood, nor does evil appear to be evil, etc.; for darkness appears to be light, and light, darkness; and hence that soul comes to commit a thousand foolish errors, whether with respect to natural things, or to moral things, or to spiritual things; so that that which was wine to it becomes vinegar. All this happens to the soul because it began not, first of all, by denying itself the pleasure of those supernatural things. At first this is a small matter, and not very harmful, and the soul has therefore no misgivings, and allows it to continue, and it grows, like the grain of mustard seed, into a tall tree. For a small error at the beginning, as they say, becomes a great error in the end.

3. Wherefore, in order to flee from this great evil, which comes from the devil, the soul must not desire to have any pleasure in such things, because such pleasure will most surely lead it to become blind and to fall. For of their own nature, and without the help of the devil, pleasure and delight and sweetness blinds the soul. And this was the meaning of David when he said: Perhaps darkness shall blind me in my delights and I shall have the night for my light.' [510]

Footnotes:

509. [The two verbs, in the original, have very definite and concrete meanings, 'sweetened with honey' and dazzled by a lamp' respectively.]

510. Psalm cxxxviii, 11 [A.V., cxxxix, 11].

CHAPTER XI

Of the fourth evil that comes to the soul from the distinct supernatural apprehensions of the memory, which is the hindrance that it interposes to union.

Concerning this fourth evil there is not much to be said, since it has already been treated again and again in this third book, wherein we have proved how, in order that the soul may come to union with God in hope, it must renounce every possession of the memory; for, in order that its hope in God may be perfect, it must have naught in the memory that is not God. And, as we have likewise said, no form or figure or image or other kind of knowledge that may come to the memory can be God, neither can be like Him, whether it be of heaven or of earth, natural or supernatural, even as David teaches, when he says: Lord, among the gods there is none like unto Thee.[511]

2. Wherefore, if the memory desires to pay heed to any of these things, it hinders the soul from reaching God; first, because it encumbers it, and next because, the more the soul has of possession, the less it has of hope. Wherefore it is needful for the soul to be stripped of the distinct forms and the knowledge of supernatural things, and to become oblivious to them, so that the memory may cause no hindrance to its union with God in perfect hope.

Footnotes:

511. Psalm lxxxv, 8 [A.V., lxxxvi, 8].

CHAPTER XII

Of the fifth evil that may come to the soul in supernatural imaginary forms and apprehensions, which is a low and unseemly judgment or God.

No less serious is the fifth evil that comes to the soul from its desire to retain in the memory and imagination the said forms and images of things that are supernaturally communicated to it, above all if it desires to use them as a means to Divine union. For it is a very easy thing to judge of the Being and greatness of God less worthily and nobly than befits His incomprehensible nature; for, although our reason and judgment may form no express conception that God is like any one of these things, yet the very esteeming of these apprehensions, if in fact the soul esteems them, makes and causes it not to esteem God, or not to feel concerning Him, as highly as faith teaches, since faith tells us that He is incomparable, incomprehensible, and so forth. For, quite apart from the fact that the soul takes from God all that it gives to the creature, it is natural that its esteem of these apprehensible things should lead it to make a certain inward comparison between such things and God, which would prevent it from judging and esteeming God as highly as it ought. For the creatures, whether terrestrial or celestial, and all distinct images and kinds of knowledge, both natural and supernatural, that can be encompassed by the faculties of the soul, however lofty they be in this life, have no comparison or proportion with the Being of God, since God falls within no genus and no species, whereas the creatures do, or so the theologians tell us. And the soul in this life is not capable of receiving in a clear and distinct manner aught save that which falls within genus and species. For this cause Saint John says that no man hath seen God at any time. [512] And Isaias says it has not entered into the heart of man what God is like. [513] And God said to Moses that he could not see Him while he was in this mortal state. [514] Wherefore he that encumbers his memory and the other faculties of the soul with that which they can comprehend cannot esteem God, neither feel concerning Him, as he ought.

2. Let us make a comparison on a lower level. It is clear that the more a man fixes his eyes upon the servants of a king, and the more notice he takes of them, the less notice does he take of the king himself, and the less does he esteem him; for, although this comparison may not be formally and distinctly present in the understanding, it is inherent in the act, since, the more attention the man gives to the servants, the more he takes from their lord; and he cannot have a very high opinion of the king if the servants appear to him to be of any importance while they are in the presence of the king, their lord. Even so does the soul treat its God when it pays heed to the creatures aforementioned. This comparison, however, is on a very low level, for, as we have said, God is of another being than His creatures in that He is infinitely far from them all. For this reason they must all be banished from sight, and the soul must withdraw its gaze from them in all their forms, that it may yet gaze on God through faith and hope.

3. Wherefore those who not only pay heed to the imaginary apprehensions aforementioned, but suppose God to be like some of them, and think that by means of them they will be able to attain to union with God, have already gone far astray and will ever continue to lose the light of faith in the understanding, through which this faculty is united with God; neither will they grow in the loftiness of hope, by means whereof the memory is united with God in hope, which must be brought about through disunion from all that is of the imagination.

Footnotes:

512. St. John i, 18.
513. Isaias lxiv, 4.
514. Exodus xxxiii, 20.

CHAPTER XIII

Of the benefits which the soul receives through banishing from itself the apprehensions of the imagination. This chapter answers a certain objection and explains a difference which exists between apprehensions that are imaginary, natural and supernatural.

The benefits that come from voiding the imagination of imaginary forms can be clearly observed in the five evils aforementioned which they inflict upon the soul, if it desires to retain them, even as we also said of the natural forms. But, apart from these, there are other benefits for the spirit -- namely, those of great rest and quiet. For, setting aside that natural rest which the soul obtains when it is free from images and forms, it likewise becomes free from anxiety as to whether they are good or evil, and as to how it must behave with respect to the one and to the other. Nor has it to waste the labour and time of its spiritual masters by requiring them to decide if these things are good or evil, and if they are of this kind or of another; for the soul has no need to desire to know all this if it pays no heed to them. The time and energies which it would have wasted in dealing with these images and forms can be better employed in another and a more profitable exercise, which is that of the will with respect to God, and in having a care to seek detachment and poverty of spirit and sense, which consists in desiring earnestly to be without any consoling support that can be apprehended, whether interior or exterior. This we practise well when we desire and strive to strip ourselves of these forms, since from this there will proceed no less a benefit than that of approach to God (Who has no image, neither form nor figure), and this will be the greater according as the soul withdraws itself the more completely from all forms, images and figures of the imagination.

2. But perchance you will say: Why do many spiritual persons counsel the soul to strive to profit by the communications and feelings which come from God, and to desire to receive them from Him, that it may have something to give Him; since, if He gives us nothing, we shall give Him nothing likewise? And wherefore does Saint Paul say: Quench not the spirit?" [515] And the Spouse to the Bride: "Set Me as a seal upon thy heart and as a seal upon thine arm?" [516] This certainly denotes some kind of apprehension. And, according to the instruction given above, not only must all this not be striven after, but, even though God sends it, it must be rejected and cast aside. But surely it is clear that, since God gives it, He gives it to a good purpose, and it will have a good effect. We must not throw away pearls. And it is even a kind of pride to be unwilling to receive the things of God, as if we could do without them and were self-sufficient.'

3. In order to meet this objection it is necessary to recall what we said in the fifteenth and sixteenth chapters [517] of the second book, where to a great extent the difficulty is solved. For we said there that the good that overflows in the soul from supernatural apprehensions, when they come from a good source, is produced passively in the soul at that very instant when they are represented to the senses, without the working of any operation of the faculties. Wherefore it is unnecessary for the will to perform the act of receiving them; for, as we have also said, if at that time the soul should try to labour with its faculties, the effect of its own base and natural operation would be to hinder the supernatural graces [518] which God is even then working in it rather than that, through these apprehensions, God should cause it to derive any benefit from its active labour. Nay, rather, as the spirituality coming from those imaginary apprehensions is given passively to the soul, even so must the soul conduct itself passively with respect to them, setting no store by its inward or outward actions. To do this is to preserve the feelings that have their source in God, for in this way they are not lost through the soul's base manner of working. And this is not quenching the spirit; for the spirit would be quenched by the soul if it desired to behave in any other manner than that whereby God is leading it. And this it would be doing if, when God had given it spiritual graces [519] passively, as He does in these apprehensions, it should then desire to exert itself actively with respect to them, by labouring with its understanding or by seeking to find something in them. And this is clear because, if the soul desires to labour at that time with its own exertions, its work cannot be more than natural, for of itself it is capable of no more; for supernaturally it neither moves itself nor can move itself -- it is God that moves it and brings it to this state. And thus, if the soul at that time desires to labour with its own exertions (as far as lies in its power), its active working will hinder the passive work that God is communicating to it, which is spirit.[520] It will be setting itself to its own work, which is of another and an inferior kind than that which God communicates to it; for the work of God is passive and supernatural, and that of the soul is active and natural; and in this way the soul would therefore be quenching the spirit.

4. That this activity of the soul is an inferior one is also clear from the fact that the faculties of the soul cannot, of their own power, reflect and act, save upon some form, figure and image, and this is the rind and accident of the substance and spirit which lie beneath this rind and accident. This substance and spirit unite not with the faculties of the soul in true understanding and love, save when at last the operation of the faculties ceases. For the aim and end of this operation is only that the substance which can be understood and loved and which lies beneath these forms may come to be received in the soul. The difference, therefore, between active and passive operation, and the superiority of the latter, corresponds to the difference between that which is being done and that which is done already, or between that which a man tries to attain and effect and that which is already effected. Hence it may likewise be inferred that, if the soul should desire to employ its faculties actively on these supernatural apprehensions, wherein God, as we have said, bestows the spirit of them passively, it would be doing nothing less than abandoning what it had already done, in order to do it again, neither would it enjoy what it had done, nor could it produce any other result by these actions of its own, save that of impeding what had been done already. For, as we say, the faculties cannot of their own power attain to the spirituality which God bestows upon the soul without any operation of their own. And thus the soul would be directly quenching the spirituality [521] which God infuses through these imaginary apprehensions aforementioned if it were to set any store by them; wherefore it must set them aside, and take up a passive and negative attitude with regard to them. For at that time God is moving the soul to things which are above its own power and knowledge. For this cause the Prophet said: I will stand upon my watch and set my step upon my tower, and I will watch to see that which will be said to me.'[522] This is as though he were to say: I will stand on guard over my faculties and I will take no step forward as to my actions, and thus I shall be able to contemplate that which will be said to me -- that is, I shall understand and enjoy that which will be communicated to me supernaturally.

5. And the passage which has been quoted concerning the Spouse is to be understood as referring to the love that He entreats of the Bride, the office of which love between two lovers is to make one like to the other in the most vital part of them. Wherefore He tells her to set Him as a seal upon her heart,[523] where all the arrows strike that leave the quiver of love, which arrows are the actions and motives of love. So they will all strike Him Who is there as a mark for them; and thus all will be for Him, so that the soul will become like Him through the actions and motions of love, until it be transformed in Him. Likewise he bids her set Him as a seal upon her arm, because the arm performs[524] the exercise of love, for by the arm the Beloved is sustained and comforted.

6. Therefore all that the soul has to endeavour to do with respect to all the apprehensions which come to it from above, whether imaginary or of any other kind -- it matters not if they be visions, locutions, feelings or revelations -- is to make no account of the letter or the rind (that is, of what is signified or represented or given to be understood), but to pay heed only to the possession of the love of God which they cause interiorly within the soul. And in this case the soul will make account, not of feelings of sweetness or delight, nor of figures, but of the feelings of love which they cause it. And with this sole end in view it may at times recall that image and apprehension caused it by love, in order to set the spirit on its course of love. For, though the effect of that apprehension be not so great afterwards, when it is recalled, as it was on the first occasion when it was communicated, yet, when it is recalled, love is renewed, and the mind is lifted up to God, especially when the recollection is of certain figures, images or feelings which are supernatural, and are wont to be sealed and imprinted upon the soul in such a way that they continue for a long time -- some of them, indeed, never leave the soul. And those that are thus sealed upon the soul produce in it Divine effects of love, sweetness, light and so forth, on almost every occasion when the soul returns to them, sometimes more so and sometimes less; for it was to this end that they were impressed upon it. And thus this is a great favour for the soul on which God bestows it, for it is as though it had within itself a mine of blessings.

7. The figures which produce effects such as these are deeply implanted in the soul, and are not like other images and forms that are retained in the fancy. And thus the soul has no need to have recourse to this faculty when it desires to recall them, for it sees that it has them within itself, and that they are as an image seen in the mirror. When it comes to pass that any soul has such figures formally within itself, it will then do well to recall them to the effect of love to which I have referred, for they will be no hindrance to the union of love in faith, since the soul will not desire to be absorbed in the figure, but only to profit by the love; it will immediately set aside the figure, which thus will rather be a help to it.

8. Only with great difficulty can it be known when these images are imprinted upon the soul, and when upon the fancy. For those which touch the fancy are as apt to occur very frequently as are the others; for certain persons are accustomed habitually to have imaginary visions in their imagination and fancy, which are presented to them in one form with great frequency; sometimes because the apprehensive power of the organ concerned is very great, and, however little they reflect upon it, that habitual figure is at once presented to, and outlined upon, their fancy; sometimes because it is the work of the devil; sometimes, again, because it is the work of God; but the visions are not formally imprinted

upon the soul. They may be known, however, by their effects. For those that are natural, or that come from the devil, produce no good effect upon the soul, however frequently they be recalled, nor work its spiritual renewal, but the contemplation of them simply produces aridity. Those that are good, however, produce some good effect when they are recalled, like that which was produced in the soul upon the first occasion. But the formal images which are imprinted upon the soul almost invariably produce some effect in it, whensoever they are remembered.

9. He that has experienced these will readily distinguish the one kind from the other, for the great difference between them is very clear to anyone that has experience of them. I will merely say that those which are formally and durably imprinted upon the soul are of very rare occurrence. But, whether they be of this kind or of that, it is good for the soul to desire to understand nothing, save God alone, through faith, in hope. And if anyone makes the objection that to reject these things, if they are good, appears to be pride, I reply that it is not so, but that it is prudent humility to profit by them in the best way, as has been said, and to be guided by that which is safest.

Footnotes:

515. 1 Thessalonians v, 19.
516. Canticles viii, 6.
517. More correctly, in Chaps. xvi and xvii.
518. [Lit., the supernatural.']
519. [Lit., had given it spirit' (or 'spirituality').]
520. [Or 'spirituality.']
521. [Or the spirit.']
522. Habacuc ii, 1. [The original has munition' for tower' and contemplate' for watch and see.']
523. Canticles viii, 6.
524. [Lit., because in the arm is.']

CHAPTER XIV

Which treats of spiritual knowledge in so far as it may concern the memory.

We classed spiritual forms of knowledge as the third division of the apprehensions of the memory, not because they belong to the bodily sense of the fancy, as do the others, for they have no bodily form and image, but because they are likewise apprehensible by spiritual memory and reminiscence. Now, after the soul has had experience of one of these apprehensions, it can recall it whensoever it will; and this is not by the effigy and image that the apprehension has left in the bodily sense, for, since this is of bodily form, as we say, it has no capacity for spiritual forms; but because it recalls it, intellectually and spiritually, by means of that form which it has left impressed upon the soul, which is likewise a formal or spiritual form or notion or image, whereby it is recalled, or by means of the effect that it has wrought. It is for this reason that I place these apprehensions among those of the memory, although they belong not to the apprehensions of the fancy.

2. What these kinds of knowledge are, and how the soul is to conduct itself with respect to them in order to attain to union with God, are sufficiently described in the twenty-fourth chapter [525] of the second book, where we treated this knowledge as apprehensions of the understanding. Let this be referred to, for we there described how it was of two kinds: either uncreated or of the creatures. I speak now only of things relating to my present purpose -- namely, how the memory must behave with respect to them in order to attain to union. And I say, as I have just said of formal knowledge in the preceding chapter (for this, being of created things, is of the same kind), that these apprehensions my be recalled when they produce good effects, not that they may be dwelt upon, but that they may quicken the soul's love and knowledge of God. But, unless the recollection of them produces good effects, let the memory never give them even passing attention. With regard to uncreated knowledge, I say that the soul should try to recall it as often as possible, for it will produce most beneficial effects. As we said above, it produces touches and impressions of union with God, which is the aim towards which we are directing the soul. And by no form, image or figure which can be impressed upon the soul does the memory recall these (for these touches and impressions of union with the Creator have no form), but only by the effects which they have produced upon it of light, love, joy and spiritual renewal, and so forth, some of which are wrought anew in the soul whensoever they are remembered.

Footnotes:

525. Really the chapter is the twenty-sixth.

CHAPTER XV

Which sets down the general method whereby the spiritual person must govern himself with respect to this sense.

In order to conclude this discussion on the memory, it will be well at this point to give the spiritual reader an account of the method which he must observe, and which is of universal application, in order that he may be united with God according to this sense. For, although what has been said makes the subject quite clear, it will nevertheless be more easily apprehended if we summarize it here. To this end it must be remembered that, since our aim is the union of the soul with God in hope, according to the memory, and since that which is hoped for is that which is not possessed, and since, the less we possess of other things, the greater scope and the greater capacity have we for hoping, and consequently the greater hope, therefore, the more things we possess, the less scope and capacity is there for hoping, and consequently the less hope have we. Hence, the more the soul dispossesses the memory of forms and things which may be recalled by it, which are not God, the more will it set its memory upon God, and the emptier will its memory become, so that it may hope for Him Who shall fill it. What must be done, then, that the soul may live in the perfect and pure hope of God is that, whensoever these distinct images, forms and ideas come to it, it must not rest in them, but must turn immediately to God, voiding the memory of them entirely, with loving affection. It must neither think of these things nor consider them beyond the degree which is necessary for the understanding and performing of its obligations, if they have any concern with these. And this it must do without setting any affection or inclination upon them, so that they may produce no effects in the soul. And thus a man must not fail to think and recall that which he ought to know and do, for, provided he preserves no affection or attachments, this will do him no harm. For this matter the lines of the Mount, which are in the thirteenth chapter of the first book, will be of profit.

2. But here it must be borne in mind that this doctrine ours does not agree, nor do we desire that it should agree, with the doctrine of those pestilent men, who, inspired by Satanic pride and envy, have desired to remove from the eyes of the faithful the holy and necessary use, and the worthy [526] adoration, of images of God and of the saints. This teaching of ours is very different from that; for we say not here, as they do, that images should not exist, and should not be adored; we simply explain the difference between images and God. We exhort men to pass beyond that which is superficial [527] that they may not be hindered from attaining to the living truth beneath it, and to make no more account of the former than suffices for attainment to the spiritual. For means are good and necessary to an end; and images are means which serve to remind us of God and of the saints. But when we consider and attend to the means more than is necessary for treating them as such, they disturb and hinder us as much, in their own way, as any different thing; the more so, when we treat of supernatural visions and images, to which I am specially referring, and with respect to which arise many deceptions and perils. For, with respect to the remembrance and adoration and esteem of images, which the Catholic Church sets before us, there can be no deception or peril, because naught is esteemed therein other than that which is represented; nor does the remembrance of them fail to profit the soul, since they are not preserved in the memory save with love for that which they represent; and, provided the soul pays no more heed to them than is necessary for this purpose, they will ever assist it to union with God, allowing the soul to soar upwards (when God grants it that favour) from the superficial image [528] to the living God, forgetting every creature and everything that belongs to creatures.

Footnotes:

526. [The Spanish word, ínclita, is stronger than this, meaning distinguished,' illustrious.']
527. [Lit., which is painted.']
528. [Lit., the painted image.']

CHAPTER XVI

Which begins to treat of the dark night of the will. Makes a division between the affections of the will.

We should have accomplished nothing by the purgation of the understanding in order to ground it in the virtue of faith, and by the purgation of the memory in order to ground it in hope, if we purged not the will also according to the third virtue, which is charity, whereby the works that are done in faith live and have great merit, and without it are of no worth. For, as Saint James says: Without works of charity, faith is dead.' [529] And, now that we have to treat of the active detachment and night of this faculty, in order to form it and make it perfect in this virtue of the charity of God, I find no more fitting authority than that which is written in the sixth chapter of Deuteronomy, where Moses says: Thou shalt love the Lord thy God with thy whole heart and with thy whole soul and with thy whole strength.' [530] Herein is contained all that the spiritual man ought to do, and all that I have here to teach him, so that he may truly attain to God, through union of the will, by means of charity. For herein man is commanded to employ all the faculties and desires and operations and affections of his soul in God, so that all the ability and strength of his soul may serve for no more than this, according to that which David says, in these words: Fortitudinem meam ad te custodiam. [531]

2. The strength of the soul consists in its faculties, passions and desires, all of which are governed by the will. Now when these faculties, passions and desires are directed by the will toward God, and turned away from all that is not God, then the strength of the soul is kept for God, and thus the soul is able to love God with all its strength. And, to the end that the soul may do this, we shall here treat of the purgation from the will of all its unruly affections, whence arise unruly operations, affections and desires, and whence also arises its failure to keep all its strength for God. These affections and passions are four, namely: Joy, hope, grief and fear. These passions, when they are controlled by reason according to the way of God, so that the soul rejoices only in that which is purely the honour and glory of God, and hopes for naught else, neither grieves save for things that concern this, neither fears aught save God alone, it is clear that the strength and ability of the soul are being directed toward God and kept for Him. For, the more the soul rejoices in any other thing than God, the less completely will it centre its rejoicing in God; [532] and the more it hopes in aught else, the less will it hope in God; and so with the other passions.

3. And in order to give fuller instructions concerning this, we shall treat, in turn and in detail, as is our custom, of each of these four passions and of the desires of the will. For the whole business of attaining to union with God consists in purging the will from its affections and desires; so that thus it may no longer be a base, human will, but may become a Divine will, being made one [533] with the will of God.

4. These four passions have the greater dominion in the soul, and assail it the more vehemently, when the will is less strongly attached to God and more dependent on the creatures. For then it rejoices very readily at things that merit not rejoicing, hopes in that which brings no profit, grieves over that in which perchance it ought to rejoice, and fears where there is no reason for fearing.

5. From these affections, when they are unbridled, arise in the soul all the vices and imperfections which it possesses, and likewise, when they are ordered and composed, all its virtues. And it must be known that, if one of them should become ordered and controlled by reason, the rest will become so likewise; for these four passions of the soul are so closely and intimately united to one another that the actual direction of one is the virtual direction of the others; and if one be actually recollected the other three will virtually and proportionately be recollected likewise. For, if the will rejoice in anything it will as a result hope for the same thing to the extent of its rejoicing, and herein are virtually included grief and fear with regard to the same thing; and, in proportion as desire for these is taken away, fear and grief concerning them are likewise gradually lost, and hope for them is removed. For the will, with these four passions, is denoted by that figure which was seen by Ezechiel, of four beasts with one body, which had four faces; and the wings of the one were joined to those of the other, and each one went straight before his face, and when they went forward they turned not back. [534] And thus in the same manner the wings of each one of these affections are joined to those of each of the others, so that, in whichever direction one of them turns -- that is, in its operation -- the others of necessity go with it virtually also; and, when one of them descends, as is there said, they must all descend, and, when one is lifted up, they will all be lifted up. Where thy hope is, thither will go thy joy and fear and grief; and, if

Ascent of Mount Carmel

thy hope returns, the others will return, and so of the rest.

6. Wherefore thou must take note that, wheresoever one of these passions is, thither will go likewise the whole soul and the will and the other faculties, and they will all live as captives to this passion, and the other three passions will be living in it also, to afflict the soul with their captivity, and not to allow it to fly upward to the liberty and rest of sweet contemplation and union. For this cause Boetius told thee that, if thou shouldst desire to understand truth with clear light, thou must cast from thee joys, hope, fear and grief. [535] For, as long as these passions reign, they allow not the soul to remain in the tranquillity and peace which are necessary for the wisdom which, by natural or supernatural means, it is capable of receiving.

Footnotes:

529. St. James ii, 20.
530. Deuteronomy vi, 5.
531. Psalm lviii, 10 [A.V., lix, 9].
532. [Lit., the less strongly will its rejoicing be employed in God.']
533. [The original is stronger: one same thing.']
534. Ezechiel i, 5-9.
535. Cf. Bk. III, ch. XVI, above.

CHAPTER XVII

Which begins to treat of the first affections of the will. Describes the nature of joy and makes a distinction between the things in which the will can rejoice.

The first of the passions of the soul and affections of the will is joy, which, in so far as concerns that which we propose to say about it, is naught else than a satisfaction of the will together with esteem for something which it considers desirable; for the will never rejoices save when an object affords it appreciation and satisfaction. This has reference to active joy, which arises when the soul clearly and distinctly understands the reason for its rejoicing, and when it is in its own power to rejoice or not. There is another and a passive joy, a condition in which the will may find itself rejoicing without understanding clearly and distinctly the reason for its rejoicing, and which also occurs at times when it does understand this; but it is not in the soul's power to rejoice or not. Of this condition we shall speak hereafter. For the present we shall speak of joy when it is active and voluntary and arises from things that are distinct and clear.

2. Joy may arise from six kinds of good things or blessings, [536] namely: temporal, natural, sensual, moral, supernatural and spiritual. Of these we shall speak in their order, controlling the will with regard to them so that it may not be encumbered by them and fail to place the strength of its joy in God. To this end it is well to presuppose one fundamental truth, which will be as a staff whereon we should ever lean as we progress; and it will be well to have understood it, because it is the light whereby we should be guided and whereby we may understand this doctrine, and direct our rejoicing in all these blessings to God. This truth is that the will must never rejoice save only in that which is to the honour and glory of God; and that the greatest honour we can show to Him is that of serving Him according to evangelical perfection; and anything that has naught to do with this is of no value and profit to man.

Footnotes:

536. [Lit., things or blessings.' The word here translated blessings' is bienes, often rendered goods.' I use blessings' or good things' in the following chapters, according as best suits the context.]

CHAPTER XVIII

Which treats of joy with respect to temporal blessings. Describes how joy in them must be directed to God.

The first kind of blessing of which we have spoken is temporal. And by temporal blessings we here understand riches, rank, office and other things that men desire; and children, relatives, marriages, etc.: all of which are things wherein the will may rejoice. But it is clear how vain a thing it is for men to rejoice in riches, titles, rank, office and other such things which they are wont to desire; for, if a man were the better servant of God for being rich, he ought to rejoice in riches; but in fact they are rather a cause for his giving offence to God, even as the Wise Man teaches, saying: Son, if thou be rich, thou shalt not be free from sin.' [537] Although it is true that temporal blessings do not necessarily of themselves cause sin, yet, through the frailty of its affections, the heart of man habitually clings to them and fails God (which is a sin, for to fail God is sin); it is for this cause that the Wise Man says: Thou shalt not be free from sin.' For this reason the Lord described riches, in the Gospel, as thorns, [538] in order to show that he who touches them [539] with the will shall be wounded by some sin. And that exclamation which He makes in the Gospel, saying: How hardly shall they that have riches enter the Kingdom of the heavens' -- that is to say, they that have joy in riches -- clearly shows that man must not rejoice in riches, since he exposes himself thereby to such great peril. [540] And David, in order to withdraw us from this peril, said likewise: If riches abound, set not your heart on them.' [541] And I will not here quote further testimony on so clear a matter.

2. For in that case I should never cease quoting Scripture, nor should I cease describing the evils which Solomon imputes to riches in Ecclesiastes. Solomon was a man who had possessed great riches, and, knowing well what they were, said: All things that are under the sun are vanity of vanities, vexation of spirit and vain solicitude of the mind.' [542] And he that loves riches, he said, shall reap no fruit from them. [543] And he adds that riches are kept to the hurt of their owner, [544] as we see in the Gospel, where it was said from Heaven to the man that rejoiced because he had kept many fruits for many years: Fool, this night shall thy soul be required of thee to give account thereof, and whose shall be that which thou has provided?' [545] And finally, David teaches us the same, saying: Let us have no envy when our neighbour becomes rich, for it will profit him nothing in the life to come;' [546] meaning thereby that we might rather have pity on him.

3. It follows, then, that a man must neither rejoice in riches when he has them, nor when his brother has them, unless they help them to serve God. For if ever it is allowable to rejoice in them, it will be when they are spent and employed in the service of God, for otherwise no profit will be derived from them. And the same is to be understood of other blessings (titles, offices, etc.), in all of which it is vain to rejoice if a man feel not that God is the better served because of them and the way to eternal life is made more secure. And as it cannot be clearly known if this is so (if God is better served, etc.), it would be a vain thing to rejoice in these things deliberately, since such a joy cannot be reasonable. For, as the Lord says: If a man gain all the world, he may yet lose his soul.' [547] There is naught, then, wherein to rejoice save in the fact that God is better served.

4. Neither is there cause for rejoicing in children because they are many, or rich, or endowed with natural graces and talents and the good things of fortune, but only if they serve God. For Absalom, the son of David, found neither his beauty nor his riches nor his lineage of any service to him because he served not God. [548] Hence it was a vain thing to have rejoiced in such a son. For this reason it is also a vain thing for men to desire to have children, as do some who trouble and disturb everyone with their desire for them, since they know not if such children will be good and serve God. Nor do they know if their satisfaction in them will be turned into pain; nor if the comfort and consolation which they should have from them will change to disquiet and trial; and the honour which they should bring them, into dishonour; nor if they will cause them to give greater offence to God, as happens to many. Of these Christ says that they go round about the sea and the land to enrich them and to make them doubly the children of perdition which they are themselves. [549]

5. Wherefore, though all things smile upon a man and all that he does turns out prosperously, he ought to have misgivings rather than to rejoice; for these things increase the occasion and peril of his forgetting God. For this cause Solomon says, in Ecclesiastes, that he was cautious: Laughter I counted error and to rejoicing I said, "Why art thou vainly deceived?"' [550] Which is as though he had said: When things smiled upon me I counted it error and deception to rejoice in them; for without doubt it is a great

error and folly on the part of a man if he rejoice when things are bright and pleasant for him, knowing not of a certainty that there will come to him thence some eternal good. The heart of the fool, says the Wise Man, is where there is mirth, but that of the wise man is where there is sorrow.[551] For mirth blinds the heart and allows it not to consider things and ponder them; but sadness makes a man open his eyes and look at the profit and the harm of them. And hence it is that, as he himself says, anger is better than laughter.[552] Wherefore it is better to go to the house of mourning than to the house of feasting; for in the former is figured the end of all men,[553] as the Wise Man says likewise.

6. It would therefore be vanity for a woman or her husband to rejoice in their marriage when they know not clearly that they are serving God better thereby. They ought rather to feel confounded, since matrimony is a cause, as Saint Paul says, whereby each one sets his heart upon the other and keeps it not wholly with God. Wherefore he says: If thou shouldst find thyself free from a wife, desire not to seek a wife; while he that has one already should walk with such freedom of heart as though he had her not.[554] This, together with what we have said concerning temporal blessings, he teaches us himself, in these words: This is certain; as I say to you, brethren, the time is short; it remaineth that they also who have wives be as if they had none; and they that weep, as them that weep not; and they that rejoice, as them that rejoice not; and they that buy, as them that possess not; and they that use this world, as them that use it not.'[555] All this he says to show us that we must not set our rejoicings upon any other thing than that which tends to the service of God, since the rest is vanity and a thing which profits not; for joy that is not according to God can bring the soul no profit.[556]

Footnotes:

537. Ecclesiasticus xi, 10.
538. St. Matthew xiii, 22; St. Luke viii, 14.
539. [Lit., handles them.']
540. St. Matthew xix, 23; St. Luke xviii, 24.
541. Psalm lxi, 11 [A.V., lxii, 10].
542. Ecclesiastes i, 14.
543. Ecclesiastes v, 9.
544. Ecclesiastes v, 12.
545. St. Luke xii, 20.
546. Psalm xlviii, 17-18 [A.V., xlix, 16-17].
547. St. Matthew xvi, 26.
548. 2 Kings [A.V., 2 Samuel] xiv, 25.
549. St. Matthew xxiii, 15.
550. Ecclesiastes ii, 2.
551. Ecclesiastes vii, 5.
552. Ecclesiastes vii, 4.
553. Ecclesiastes vii, 3.
554. 1 Corinthians vii, 27.
555. 1 Corinthians vii, 29-30.
556. [Lit., bring it no profit.']

CHAPTER XIX

Of the evils that may befall the soul when it sets its rejoicing upon temporal blessings.

If we had to describe the evils which encompass the soul when it sets the affections of its will upon temporal blessings, neither ink nor paper would suffice us and our time would be too short. For from very small beginnings a man may attain to great evils and destroy great blessings; even as from a spark of fire, if it be not quenched, may be enkindled great fires which set the world ablaze. All these evils have their root and origin in one important evil of a privative kind that is contained in this joy -- namely, withdrawal from God. For even as, in the soul that is united with Him by the affection of its will, there are born all blessings, even so, when it withdraws itself from Him because of this creature affection, there beset it all evils and disasters proportionately to the joy and affection wherewith it is united with the creature; for this is inherent in [557] withdrawal from God. Wherefore a soul may expect the evils which assail it to be greater or less according to the greater or lesser degree of its withdrawal from God. These evils may be extensive or intensive; for the most part they are both together.

2. This privative evil, whence, we say, arise other privative and positive evils, has four degrees, each one worse than the other. And, when the soul compasses the fourth degree, it will have compassed all the evils and depravities that arise in this connection. [558] These four degrees are well indicated by Moses in Deuteronomy in these words, where he says: The beloved grew fat and kicked. He grew fat and became swollen and gross. He forsook God his Maker and departed from God his Salvation.' [559]

3. This growing fat of the soul, which was loved before it grew fat, indicates absorption in this joy of creatures. And hence arises the first degree of this evil, namely the going backward; which is a certain blunting of the mind with regard to God, an obscuring of the blessings of God like the obscuring of the air by mist, so that it cannot be clearly illumined by the light of the sun. For, precisely when the spiritual person sets his rejoicing upon anything, and gives rein to his desire for foolish things, he becomes blind as to God, and the simple intelligence of his judgment becomes clouded, even as the Divine Spirit teaches in the Book of Wisdom, saying: the use and association of vanity and scorn obscureth good things, and inconstancy of desire overturneth and perverteth the sense and judgment that are without malice.' [560] Here the Holy Spirit shows that, although there be no malice conceived in the understanding of the soul, concupiscence and rejoicing in creatures suffice of themselves to create in the soul the first degree of this evil, which is the blunting of the mind and the darkening of the judgment, by which the truth is understood and each thing honestly judged as it is.

4. Holiness and good judgment suffice not to save a man from falling into this evil, if he gives way to concupiscence or rejoicing in temporal things. For this reason God warned us by uttering these words through Moses: Thou shalt take no gifts, which blind even the prudent.' [561] And this was addressed particularly to those who were to be judges; for these have need to keep their judgment clear and alert, which they will be unable to do if they covet and rejoice in gifts. And for this cause likewise God commanded Moses to appoint judges from those who abhorred avarice, so that their judgment should not be blunted with the lust of the passions. [562] And thus he says not only that they should not desire it, but that they should abhor it. For, if a man is to be perfectly defended from the affection of love, he must preserve an abhorrence of it, defending himself by means of the one thing against its contrary. The reason why the prophet Samuel, for example, was always so upright and enlightened a judge is that (as he said in the Book of the Kings) he had never received a gift from any man. [563]

5. The second degree of this privative evil arises from the first, which is indicated in the words following the passage already quoted, namely: He grew fat and became swollen and gross.' [564] And thus this second degree is dilation of the will through the acquisition of greater liberty in temporal things; which consists in no longer attaching so much importance to them, nor troubling oneself about them, nor esteeming so highly the joy and pleasure that come from created blessings. And this will have arisen in the soul from its having in the first place given rein to rejoicing; for, through giving way to it, the soul has become swollen with it, as is said in that passage, and that fatness of rejoicing and desire has mused it to dilate and extend its will more freely toward the creatures. And this brings with it great evils. For this second degree causes the soul to withdraw itself from the things of God, and from holy practices, and to take no pleasure in them, because it takes pleasure in other things and devotes itself continually to many imperfections and follies and to joys and vain pleasures.

6. And when this second degree is consummated, it withdraws a man wholly from the practices which he followed continually and makes his whole mind and covetousness to be given to secular

things. And those who are affected by this second degree not only have their judgment and understanding darkened so that they cannot recognize truth and justice, like those who are in the first degree, but they are also very weak and lukewarm and careless in acquiring knowledge of, and in practising, truth and justice, even as Isaias says of them in these words: They all love gifts and allow themselves to be carried away by rewards, and they judge not the orphan, neither doth the cause of the widow come unto them that they may give heed to it.'[565] This comes not to pass in them without sin, especially when to do these things is incumbent upon them because of their office. For those who are affected by this degree are not free from malice as are those of the first degree. And thus they withdraw themselves more and more from justice and virtues, since their will reaches out more and more in affection for creatures. Wherefore, the characteristics of those who are in this second degree are great lukewarmness in spiritual things and failure to do their duty by them; they practise them from formality or from compulsion or from the habit which they have formed of practising them, rather than because they love them.

7. The third degree of this privative evil is a complete falling away from God, neglect to fulfil His law in order not to lose worldly things and blessings, and relapse into mortal sin through covetousness. And this third degree is described in the words following the passage quoted above, which says: He forsook God his Maker.'[566] In this degree are included all who have the faculties of the soul absorbed in things of the world and in riches and commerce, in such a way that they care nothing for fulfilling the obligations of the law of God. And they are very forgetful and dull with respect to that which touches their salvation, and have a correspondingly greater ardour and shrewdness with respect to things of the world. So much so that in the Gospel Christ calls them children of this world, and says of them that they are more prudent and acute in their affairs than are the children of light in their own.[567] And thus they are as nothing in God's business, whereas in the world's business they are everything. And these are the truly avaricious, who have extended and dispersed their desire and joy on things created, and this with such affection that they cannot be satisfied; on the contrary, their desire and their thirst grow all the more because they are farther withdrawn from the only source that could satisfy them, which is God. For it is of these that God Himself speaks through Jeremias, saying: They have forsaken Me, Who am the fountain of living water, and they have digged to themselves broken cisterns that can hold no water.'[568] And this is the reason why the covetous man finds naught among the creatures wherewith he can quench his thirst, but only that which increases it. These persons are they that fall into countless kinds of sin through love of temporal blessings and the evils which afflict them are innumerable. And of these David says: Transierunt in affectum cordis.[569]

8. The fourth degree of this privative evil is indicated in the last words of our passage, which says: And he departed from God his Salvation.'[570] To this degree come those of the third degree whereof we have just spoken. For, through his not giving heed to setting his heart upon the law of God because of temporal blessings, the soul of the covetous man departs far from God according to his memory, understanding and will, forgetting Him as though He were not his God, which comes to pass because he has made for himself a god of money and of temporal blessings, as Saint Paul says when he describes avarice as slavery to idols.[571] For this fourth degree leads a man as far as to forget God, and to set his heart, which he should have set formally upon God, formally upon money, as though he had no god beside.

9. To this fourth degree belong those who hesitate not to subject Divine and supernatural things to temporal things, as to their God, when they ought to do the contrary, and subject temporal things to God, if they considered Him as their God, as would be in accordance with reason. To these belonged the iniquitous Balaam, who sold the grace that God had given to him.[572] And also Simon Magus, who thought to value the grace of God in terms of money, and desired to buy it.[573] In doing this he showed a greater esteem for money; and he thought there were those who similarly esteemed it, and would give grace for money. There are many nowadays who in many other ways belong to this fourth degree; their reason is darkened to spiritual things by covetousness; they serve money and not God, and are influenced by money and not by God, putting first the cost of a thing and not its Divine worth and reward, and in many ways making money their principal god and end, and setting it before the final end, which is God.

10. To this last degree belong also those miserable souls who are so greatly in love with their own goods that they take them for their god, so much so that they scruple not to sacrifice their lives for them, when they see that this god of theirs is suffering some temporal harm. They abandon themselves to despair and take their own lives for their miserable ends, showing by their own acts how wretched is the reward which such a god as theirs bestows. For when they can no longer hope for aught from him he gives them despair and death; and those whom he pursues not to this last evil of death he condemns to a dying life in the griefs of anxiety and in many other miseries, allowing no mirth to enter their heart, and naught that is of earth to bring them satisfaction. They continually pay the tribute of their heart to money by their yearning for it and hoarding of it for the final calamity of their just perdition, as the Wise Man warns them, saying: Riches are kept to the hurt of their owner.'[574]

Ascent of Mount Carmel

11. And to this fourth degree belong those of whom Saint Paul says: Tradidit illos in reprobum sensum.[575] For joy, when it strives after possessions as its final goal, drags man down to these evils. But those on whom it inflicts lesser evils are also to be sorely pitied, since, as we have said, their souls are driven far backward upon the way of God. Wherefore, as David says: Be not thou afraid when a man shall be made rich: that is, envy him not, thinking that he outstrips thee, for, when he dieth, he shall carry nothing away, neither shall his glory nor his joy descend with him.[576]

Footnotes:

557. [Lit., for this is.']
558. [Lit., that can be told in this case.']
559. Deuteronomy xxxii, 15.
560. Wisdom iv, 12.
561. Exodus xxiii, 8.
562. Exodus xxiii, 21-2.
563. 1 Kings [A.V., 1 Samuel] xii, 3.
564. Deuteronomy xxxii, 15.
565. Isaiah i, 23.
566. Deuteronomy xxxii, 15.
567. St. Luke xvi, 8.
568. Jeremias ii, 13.
569. [They have passed into the affection of the heart.'] Psalm lxxii, 7 [A.V., lxxiii, 7].
570. Deuteronomy xxxii, 15.
571. Colossians iii, 5.
572. Numbers xxii, 7.
573. Acts viii, 18-19.
574. Ecclesiastes v, 11-12.
575. [He delivered them up to a reprobate sense.'] Romans i, 28.
576. Psalm xlviii, 17-18 [A.V., xlix, 16-17].

CHAPTER XX

Of the benefits that come to the soul from its withdrawal of joy from temporal things.

The spiritual man, then, must look carefully to it that his heart and his rejoicing begin not to lay hold upon temporal things; he must fear lest from being little it should grow to be great, and should increase from one degree to another. For little things, in time, become great; and from a small beginning there comes in the end a great matter, even as a spark suffices to set a mountain on fire and to burn up the whole world. And let him never be self-confident because his attachment is small, and fail to uproot it instantly because he thinks that he will do so later. For if, when it is so small and in its beginnings, he has not the courage to make an end of it, how does he suppose, and presume, that he will be able to do so when it is great and more deeply rooted. The more so since Our Lord said in the Gospel: He that is unfaithful in little will be unfaithful also in much.' [577] For he that avoids the small sin will not fall into the great sin; but great evil is inherent in the small sin, [578] since it has already penetrated within the fence and wall of the heart; and as the proverb says: Once begun, half done. Wherefore David warns us, saying: Though riches abound, let us not apply our heart to them.' [579]

2. Although a man might not do this for the sake of God and of the obligations of Christian perfection, he should nevertheless do it because of the temporal advantages that result from it, to say nothing of the spiritual advantages, and he should free his heart completely from all rejoicing in the things mentioned above. And thus, not only will he free himself from the pestilent evils which we have described in the last chapter, but, in addition to this, he will withdraw his joy from temporal blessings and acquire the virtue of liberality, which is one of the principal attributes of God, and can in no wise coexist with covetousness. Apart from this, he will acquire liberty of soul, clarity of reason, rest, tranquillity and peaceful confidence in God and a true reverence and worship of God which comes from the will. He will find greater joy and recreation in the creatures through his detachment from them, for he cannot rejoice in them if he look upon them with attachment to them as to his own. Attachment is an anxiety that, like a bond, ties the spirit down to the earth and allows it no enlargement of heart. He will also acquire, in his detachment from things, a clear conception of them, so that he can well understand the truths relating to them, both naturally and supernaturally. He will therefore enjoy them very differently from one who is attached to them, and he will have a great advantage and superiority over such a one. For, while he enjoys them according to their truth, the other enjoys them according to their falseness; the one appreciates the best side of them and the other the worst; the one rejoices in their substance; the other, whose sense is bound to them, in their accident. For sense cannot grasp or attain to more than the accident, but the spirit, purged of the clouds and species of accident, penetrates the truth and worth of things, for this is its object. Wherefore joy, like a cloud, darkens the judgment, since there can be no voluntary joy in creatures without voluntary attachment, even as there can be no joy which is passion when there is no habitual attachment in the heart; and the renunciation and purgation of such joy leave the judgment clear, even as the mists leave the air clear when they are scattered.

3. This man, then, rejoices in all things -- since his joy is dependent upon none of them -- as if he had them all; and this other, through looking upon them with a particular sense of ownership, loses in a general sense all the pleasure of them all. This former man, having none of them in his heart, possesses them all, as Saint Paul says, in great freedom. [580] This latter man, inasmuch as he has something of them through the attachment of his will, neither has nor possesses anything; it is rather they that have possessed his heart, and he is, as it were, a sorrowing captive. Wherefore, if he desire to have a certain degree of joy in creatures, he must of necessity have an equal degree of disquietude and grief in his heart, since it is seized and possessed by them. But he that is detached is untroubled by anxieties, either in prayer or apart from it; and thus, without losing time, he readily gains great spiritual treasure. But the other man loses everything, running to and fro upon the chain by which his heart is attached and bound; and with all his diligence he can still hardly free himself for a short time from this bond of thought and rejoicing by which his heart is bound. The spiritual man, then, must restrain the first motion of his heart towards creatures, remembering the premiss which we have here laid down, that there is naught wherein a man must rejoice, save in his service of God, and in his striving for His glory and honour in all things, directing all things solely to this end and turning aside from vanity in them, looking in them neither for his own joy nor for his consolation.

4. There is another very great and important benefit in this detachment of the rejoicing from creatures -- namely, that it leaves the heart free for God. This is the dispositive foundation of all the

favours which God will grant to the soul, and without this disposition He grants them not. And they are such that, even from the temporal standpoint, for one joy which the soul renounces for love of Him and for the perfection of the Gospel, He will give him a hundred in this life, as His Majesty promises in the same Gospel. [581] But, even were there not so high a rate of interest, the spiritual man should quench these creature joys in his soul because of the displeasure which they give to God. For we see in the Gospel that, simply because that rich man rejoiced at having laid up for many years, God was so greatly angered that He told him that his soul would be brought to account on that same night. [582] Therefore, we must believe that, whensoever we rejoice vainly, God is beholding us and preparing some punishment and bitter draught according to our deserts, so that the pain which results from the joy may sometimes be a hundred times greater than the joy. For, although it is true, as Saint John says on this matter, in the Apocalypse, concerning Babylon, that as much as she had rejoiced and lived in delights, so much torment and sorrow should be given her, [583] yet this is not to say that the pain will not be greater than the joy, which indeed it will be, since for brief pleasures are given eternal torments. The words mean that there shall be nothing without its particular punishment, for He Who will punish the idle word will not pardon vain rejoicing.

Footnotes:
    577. St. Luke xvi, 10.
    578. [The word 'sin' is not in the original of this sentence, which reads the small . . . the great . . .' etc.]
    579. Psalm lxi, 11 [A.V., lxii, 10].
    580. 2 Corinthians vi, 10.
    581. St. Matthew xix, 29.
    582. St. Luke xii, 20.
    583. Apocalypse xviii, 7.

CHAPTER XXI

Which describes how it is vanity to set the rejoicing of the will upon the good things of nature, and how the soul must direct itself, by means of them, to God.

By natural blessings we here understand beauty, grace, comeliness, bodily constitution and all other bodily endowments; and likewise, in the soul, good understanding, discretion and other things that pertain to reason. Many a man sets his rejoicing upon all these gifts, to the end that he himself, or those that belong to him, may possess them, and for no other reason, and gives no thanks to God Who bestows them on him so that He may be better known and loved by him because of them. But to rejoice for this cause alone is vanity and deception, as Solomon says in these words: Deceitful is grace and vain is beauty; the woman who fears God, she shall be praised.'[584] Here he teaches us that a man ought rather to be fearful because of these natural gifts, since he may easily be distracted by them from the love of God, and, if he be attracted by them, he may fall into vanity and be deceived. For this reason bodily grace is said to be deceptive because it deceives a man in the ways and attracts him to that which beseems him not, through vain joy and complacency, either in himself or in others that have such grace. And it is said that beauty is vain because it causes a man to fall in many ways when he esteems it and rejoices in it, for he should rejoice only if he serves God or others through it. But he ought rather to fear and harbour misgivings lest perchance his natural graces and gifts should be a cause of his offending God, either by his vain presumption or by the extreme affection with which he regards them. Wherefore he that has such gifts should be cautious and live carefully, lest, by his vain ostentation, he give cause to any man to withdraw his heart in the smallest degree from God. For these graces and gifts of nature are so full of provocation and occasion of evil, both to him that possesses them and to him that looks upon them, that there is hardly any who entirely escapes from binding and entangling his heart in them. We have heard that many spiritual persons, who had certain of these gifts, had such fear of this that they prayed God to disfigure them, lest they should be a cause and occasion of any vain joy or affection to themselves or to others, and God granted their prayer.

2. The spiritual man, then, must purge his will, and make it to be blind to this vain rejoicing, bearing in mind that beauty and all other natural gifts are but earth, and that they come from the earth and will return thither; and that grace and beauty are the smoke and vapour belonging to this same earth; and that they must be held and esteemed as such by any man who desires not to fall into vanity, but will direct his heart to God in these matters, with rejoicing and gladness, because God is in Himself all these beauties and graces in the most eminent degree, and is infinitely high above all created things. And, as David says, they are all like a garment and shall grow old and pass away, and He alone remains immutable for ever.[585] Wherefore, if in all these matters a man direct not his rejoicing to God, it will ever be false and deceptive. For of such a man is that saying of Solomon to be understood, where he addresses joy in the creatures, saying: To joy I said: "Why art thou vainly deceived?"'[586] That is, when the heart allows itself to be attracted by the creatures.

Footnotes:

584. Proverbs xxxi, 30.
585. Psalm ci, 27 [A.V., cii, 26-7].
586. Ecclesiastes ii, 2.

CHAPTER XXII

Of the evils which come to the soul when it sets the rejoicing of its will upon the good things of nature.

Although many of these evils and benefits that I am describing in treating of these kinds of joy are common to all, yet, because they follow directly from joy and detachment from joy (although comprised under any one of these six divisions which I am treating), therefore I speak under each heading of some evils and benefits which are also found under another, since these, as I say, are connected with that joy which belongs to them all. But my principal intent is to speak of the particular evils and benefits which come to the soul, with respect to each thing, through its rejoicing or not rejoicing in it. These I call particular evils, because they are primarily and immediately caused by one particular kind of rejoicing, and are not, save in a secondary and mediate sense, caused by another. The evil of spiritual lukewarmness, for example, is caused directly by any and every kind of joy, and this evil is therefore common to all these six kinds; but fornication is a particular evil, which is the direct result only of joy in the good things of nature of which we are speaking.

2. The spiritual and bodily evils, then, which directly and effectively come to the soul when it sets its rejoicing on the good things of nature are reduced to six principal evils. The first is vainglory, presumption, pride and disesteem of our neighbour; for a man cannot cast eyes of esteem on one thing without taking them from the rest. From this follows, at the least, a real disesteem for everything else; for naturally, by setting our esteem on one thing, we withdraw our heart from all things else and set it upon the thing esteemed; and from this real contempt it is very easy to fall into an intentional and voluntary contempt for all these other things, in particular or in general, not only in the heart, but also in speech, when we say that such a thing or such a person is not like such another. The second evil is the moving of the senses to complacency and sensual delight and lust. The third evil comes from falling into adulation and vain praise, wherein is deception and vanity, as Isaias says in these words: 'My people, he that praises thee deceives thee.'[587] And the reason is that, although we sometimes speak the truth when we praise grace and beauty, yet it will be a marvel if there is not some evil enwrapped therein or if the person praised is not plunged into vain complacency and rejoicing, or his imperfect intentions and affections are not directed thereto. The fourth evil is of a general kind: it is a serious[588] blunting of the reason and the spiritual sense, such as is effected by rejoicing in temporal good things. In one way, indeed, it is much worse. For as the good things of nature are more closely connected with man than are temporal good things, the joy which they give leaves an impression and effect and trace upon the senses more readily and more effectively, and deadens them more completely. And thus reason and judgment are not free, but are clouded with that affection of joy which is very closely connected with them; and from this arises the fifth evil, which is distraction of the mind by created things. And hence arise and follow lukewarmness and weakness of spirit, which is the sixth evil, and is likewise of a general kind; this is apt to reach such a pitch that a man may find the things of God very tedious and troublesome, and at last even come to abhor them. In this rejoicing purity of spirit is invariably lost -- at least, in its essence. For, if any spirituality is discerned, it will be of such a gross and sensual kind as to be hardly spiritual or interior or recollected at all, since it will consist rather in pleasure of sense than in strength of spirit. Since, then, the spirituality of the soul is of so low and weak a character at that time as not to quench the habit of this rejoicing (for this habit alone suffices to destroy pure spirituality, even when the soul is not consenting to the acts of rejoicing), the soul must be living, so to say, in the weakness of sense rather than in the strength of the spirit. Otherwise, it will be seen in the perfection and fortitude which the soul will have when the occasion demands it. Although I do not deny that many virtues may exist together with serious imperfections, no pure or delectable inward spirituality can exist while these joys are not quenched; for the flesh reigns within, warring against the spirit, and, although the spirit may be unconscious of the evil, yet at the least it causes it secret distraction.

3. Returning now to speak of that second evil, which contains within itself innumerable other evils, it is impossible to describe with the pen or to express in words the lengths to which it can go, but this is not unknown or secret, nor is the extent of the misery that arises from the setting of our rejoicing on natural beauty and graces. For every day we hear of its causing numerous deaths, the loss by many of their honour, the commission of many insults, the dissipation of much wealth, numerous cases of emulation and strife, of adultery, rape and fornication, and of the fall of many holy men, comparable in number to that third part of the stars of Heaven which was swept down by the tail of the serpent on

earth.[589] The fine gold has lost its brilliance and lustre and is become mire; and the notable and noble men of Sion, who were clothed in finest gold, are counted as earthen pitchers that are broken and have become potsherds.[590] How far does the poison of this evil not penetrate?

4. And who drinks not, either little or much, from this golden chalice of the Babylonian woman of the Apocalypse?[591] She seats herself on that great beast, that had seven heads and ten crowns, signifying that there is scarce any man, whether high or low, saint or sinner, who comes not to drink of her wine, to some extent enslaving his heart thereby, for, as is said of her in that place, all the kings of the earth have become drunken with the wine of her prostitution. And she seizes upon all estates of men, even upon the highest and noblest estate -- the service of the sanctuary and the Divine priesthood -- setting her abominable cup, as Daniel says, in the holy place,[592] and leaving scarcely a single strong man without making him to drink, either little or much, from the wine of this chalice, which is vain rejoicing. For this reason it is said that all the kings of the earth have become drunken with this wine, for very few will be found, however holy they may have been, that have not been to some extent stupefied and bewildered by this draught of the joy and pleasure of natural graces and beauty.

5. This phrase have become drunken' should be noted. For, however little a man may drink of the wine of this rejoicing, it at once takes hold upon the heart, and stupefies it and works the evil of darkening the reason, as does wine to those who have been corrupted by it. So that, if some antidote be not at once taken against this poison, whereby it may be quickly expelled, the life of the soul is endangered. Its spiritual weakness will increase, bringing it to such a pass that it will be like Samson, when his eyes were put out and the hair of his first strength was cut off, and like Samson it will see itself grinding in the mills, a captive among its enemies;[593] and afterwards, peradventure, it will die the second death among its enemies, even as did he, since the drinking of this rejoicing will produce in them spiritually all those evils that were produced in him physically, and does in fact produce them in many persons to this day. Let his enemies come and say to him afterwards, to his great confusion: Art thou he that broke the knotted cords, that tore asunder the lions, slew the thousand Philistines, broke down the gates and freed himself from all his enemies?

6. Let us conclude, then, by giving the instruction necessary to counteract this poison. And let it be this: As soon as thy heart feels moved by this vain joy in the good things of nature, let it remember how vain a thing it is to rejoice in aught save the service of God, how perilous and how pernicious. Let it consider how great an evil it was for the angels to rejoice and take pleasure in their natural endowments and beauty, since it was this that plunged them into the depths of shame.[594] Let them think, too, how many evils come to men daily through this same vanity, and let them therefore resolve in good time to employ the remedy which the poet commends to those who begin to grow affectioned to such things. Make haste now,' he says, and use the remedy at the beginning; for when evil things have had time to grow in the heart, remedy and medicine come late.' Look not upon the wine, as the Wise Man says, when its colour is red and when it shines in the glass; it enters pleasantly and bites like a viper and sheds abroad poison like a basilisk.[595]

Footnotes:

587. Isaias iii, 12.
588. [Lit., the great.']
589. Apocalypse xii, 4.
590. Lamentations iv, 1-2.
591. Apocalypse xvii, 3-4.
592. Daniel ix, 27.
593. Judges xvi.
594. [Lit., since it was through this they fell into the vile abysses.']
595. Proverbs xxiii, 31-2.

CHAPTER XXIII

Of the benefits which the soul receives from not setting its rejoicing upon the good things of nature.

Many are the benefits which come to the soul through the withdrawal of its heart from this rejoicing; for, besides preparing itself for the love of God and the other virtues, it makes a direct way for its own humility, and for a general charity toward its neighbours. For, as it is not led by the apparent good things of nature, which are deceitful, into affection for anyone, the soul remains free and able [596] to love them all rationally and spiritually, as God wills them to be loved. Here it must be understood that none deserves to be loved, save for the virtue that is in him. And, when we love in this way, it is very pleasing to the will of God, and also brings great freedom; and if there be attachment in it, there is greater attachment to God. For, in that case, the more this love grows, the more grows our love toward God; and, the more grows our love toward God, the greater becomes our love for our neighbour. For, when love is grounded in God, the reason for all love is one and the same and the cause of all love is one and the same also.

2. Another excellent benefit comes to the soul from its renunciation of this kind of rejoicing, which is that it fulfils and keeps the counsel of Our Saviour which He gives us through Saint Matthew. Let him that will follow Me', He says, deny himself.' [597] This the soul could in no wise do if it were to set its rejoicing upon the good things of nature; for he that makes any account of himself neither denies himself nor follows Christ.

3. There is another great benefit in the renunciation of this kind of rejoicing, which is that it produces great tranquillity in the soul, empties it of distractions and brings recollection to the senses, especially to the eyes. For the soul that desires not to rejoice in these things desires neither to look at them nor to attach the other senses to them, lest it should be attracted or entangled by them. Nor will it spend time or thought upon them, being like the prudent serpent, which stops its ears that it may not hear the charmers lest they make some impression upon it. [598] For, by guarding its doors, which are the senses, the soul guards itself safely and increases its tranquillity and purity.

4. There is another benefit of no less importance to those that have become proficient in the mortification of this kind of rejoicing, which is that evil things and the knowledge of them neither make an impression upon them nor stain them as they do those to whom they still give any delight. Wherefore the renunciation and mortification of this rejoicing result in spiritual cleanness of soul and body; that is, of spirit and sense; and the soul comes to have an angelical conformity with God, and becomes, both in spirit and in body, a worthy temple of the Holy Spirit. This cannot come to pass if the heart rejoices in natural graces and good things. For this reason it is not necessary to have given consent to any evil thing, or to have remembrance of such; for that rejoicing suffices to stain the soul and the senses with impurity by means of the knowledge of evil; for, as the Wise Man says, the Holy Spirit will remove Himself from thoughts that are without understanding -- that is, without the higher reason that has respect to God. [599]

5. Another benefit of a general kind follows, which is that, besides freeing ourselves from the evils and dangers aforementioned, we are delivered also from countless vanities, and from many other evils, both spiritual and temporal; and especially from falling into the small esteem in which are held all those that are seen to glory or rejoice in the said natural gifts, whether in their own or in those of others. And thus these souls are held and esteemed as wise and prudent, as indeed are all those who take no account of these things, but only of that which pleases God.

6. From these said benefits follows the last, which is a generosity of the soul, as necessary to the service of God as is liberty of spirit, whereby temptations are easily vanquished and trials faithfully endured, and whereby, too, the virtues grow and become prosperous.

Footnotes:

596. [Lit., free and clear.']
597. St. Matthew xvi, 24.
598. Psalm lvii, 5 [A.V., lviii, 4-5].
599. Wisdom i, 5.

CHAPTER XXIV

Which treats of the third kind of good thing whereon the will may set the affection of rejoicing, which kind pertains to sense. Indicates what these good things are and of how many kinds, and how the will has to be directed to God and purged of this rejoicing.

We have next to treat of rejoicing with respect to the good things of sense, which is the third kind of good thing wherein we said that the will may rejoice. And it is to be noted that by the good things of sense we here understand everything in this life that can be apprehended by the senses of sight, hearing, smell, taste or touch, and by the interior fashioning of imaginary reflections, all of which things belong to the bodily senses, interior and exterior.

2. And, in order to darken the will and purge it of rejoicing with respect to these sensible objects, and direct it to God by means of them, it is necessary to assume one truth, which is that, as we have frequently said, the sense of the lower part of man which is that whereof we are treating, is not, neither can be, capable of knowing or understanding God as God is. So that the eye cannot see Him, or aught that is like Him; neither can the ear hear His voice, or any sound that resembles it; neither can the sense of smell perceive a perfume so sweet as He; neither can the taste detect a savour so sublime and delectable; neither can the touch feel a movement so delicate and full of delight, nor aught like to it; neither can His form or any figure that represents Him enter into the thought or imagination. Even as says Isaias: Eye hath not seen Him, nor hath ear heard Him, neither hath it entered into the heart of man.'[600]

3. And here it must be noted that the senses may receive pleasure and delight, either from the spirit, by means of some communication that it receives from God interiorly, or from outward things communicated to them. And, as has been said, neither by way of the spirit nor by that of sense can the sensual part of the soul know God. For, since it has no capacity for attaining to such a point, it receives in the senses both that which is of the spirit and that which is of sense, and receives them in no other way. Wherefore it would be at the least but vanity to set the rejoicing of the will upon pleasure caused by any of these apprehensions, and it would be hindering the power of the will from occupying itself with God and from setting its rejoicing upon Him alone. This the soul cannot perfectly accomplish, save by purging itself and remaining in darkness as to rejoicing of this kind, as also with respect to other things.

4. I said advisedly that if the rejoicing of the will were to rest in any of these things it would be vanity. But, when it does not rest upon them, but, as soon as the will finds pleasure in that which it hears, sees and does, soars upward to rejoice in God -- so that its pleasure acts as a motive and strengthens it to that end -- this is very good. In such a case not only need the said motions not be shunned when they cause this devotion and prayer, but the soul may profit by them, and indeed should so profit, to the end that it may accomplish this holy exercise. For there are souls who are greatly moved by objects of sense to seek God. But much circumspection must be observed herein and the resulting effects must be considered; for oftentimes many spiritual persons indulge in the recreations of sense aforementioned under the pretext of offering prayer and devotion to God; and they do this in a way which must be described as recreation rather than prayer, and which gives more pleasure to themselves than to God. And, although the intention that they have is toward God, the effect which they produce is that of recreation of sense, wherein they find weakness and imperfection, rather than revival of the will and surrender thereof to God.

5. I wish, therefore, to propose a test whereby it may be seen when these delights of the senses aforementioned are profitable and when they are not. And it is that, whensoever a person hears music and other things, and sees pleasant things, and is conscious of sweet perfumes, or tastes things that are delicious, or feels soft touches, if his thought and the affection of his will are at once centred upon God and if that thought of God gives him more pleasure than the movement of sense which causes it, and save for that he finds no pleasure in the said movement, this is a sign that he is receiving benefit therefrom, and that this thing of sense is a help to his spirit. In this way such things may be used, for then such things of sense subserve the end for which God created and gave them, which is that He should be the better loved and known because of them. And it must be known, furthermore, that one upon whom these things of sense cause the pure spiritual effect which I describe has no desire for them, and makes hardly any account of them, though they cause him great pleasure when they are offered to him, because of the pleasure which, as I have said, they cause him in God. He is not, however,

Ascent of Mount Carmel

solicitous for them, and when they are offered to him, as I say, his will passes from them at once and he abandons it to God and sets it upon Him.

6. The reason why he cares little for these motives, although they help him on his journey to God, is that the spirit which is ready to go by every means and in every way to God is so completely nourished and prepared and satisfied by the spirit of God that it lacks nothing and desires nothing; or, if it desires anything to that end, the desire at once passes and is forgotten, and the soul makes no account of it. But one that feels not this liberty of spirit in these things and pleasures of sense, but whose will rests in these pleasures and feeds upon them, is greatly harmed by them and should withdraw himself from the use of them. For, although his reason may desire to employ them to journey to God, yet, inasmuch as his desire finds pleasure in them which is according to sense, and their effect is ever dependent upon the pleasure which they give, he is certain to find hindrance in them rather than help, and harm rather than profit. And, when he sees that the desire for such recreation reigns in him, he must mortify it; for, the stronger it becomes, the more imperfection he will have and the greater will be his weakness.

7. So whatever pleasure coming from sense presents itself to the spiritual person, and whether it come to him by chance or by design, he must make use of it only for God, lifting up to Him the rejoicing of his soul so that his rejoicing may be useful and profitable and perfect; realizing that all rejoicing which implies not renunciation [601] and annihilation of every other kind of rejoicing, although it be with respect to something apparently very lofty, is vain and profits not, but is a hindrance towards the union of the will in God.

Footnotes:

600. Isaias lxiv, 4; 1 Corinthians ii, 9.
601. [Lit., that is not in renunciation . . .']

CHAPTER XXV

Which treats of the evils that afflict the soul when it desires to set the rejoicing of its will upon the good things of sense.

In the first place, if the soul does not darken and quench the joy which may arise within it from the things of sense, and direct its rejoicing to God, all the general kinds of evil which we have described as arising from every other kind of rejoicing follow from this joy in the things of sense: such evils are darkness in the reason, lukewarmness, spiritual weariness, etc. But, to come to details, many are the evils, spiritual, bodily and sensual, into which the soul may fall through this rejoicing.

2. First of all, from joy in visible things, when the soul denies not itself therein in order to reach God, there may come to it, directly, vanity of spirit and distraction of the mind, unruly covetousness, immodesty, outward and inward unseemliness, impurity of thought, and envy.

3. From joy in hearing useless things there may directly arise distraction of the imagination, gossiping, envy, rash judgements and vacillating thoughts; and from these arise many other and pernicious evils.

4. From joy in sweet perfumes, there arise loathing of the poor, which is contrary to the teaching of Christ, dislike of serving others, unruliness of heart in humble things, and spiritual insensibility, at least to a degree proportionate with its desire for this joy.

5. From joy in the savour of meat and drink, there arise directly such gluttony and drunkenness, wrath, discord and want of charity with one's neighbours and with the poor, as had that Epulon, who fared sumptuously every day, with Lazarus. [602] Hence arise bodily disorders, infirmities and evil motions, because the incentives to luxury become greater. Directly, too, there arises great spiritual torpor, and the desire for spiritual things is corrupted, so that the soul can derive no enjoyment or satisfaction from them nor can even speak of them. From this joy is likewise born distraction of the other senses and of the heart, and discontent with respect to many things.

6. From joy in the touch of soft things arise many more evils and more pernicious ones, which more quickly cause sense to overflow into spirit, and quench all spiritual strength and vigour. Hence arises the abominable vice of effeminacy, or the incentives thereto, according to the proportion of joy of this kind which is experienced. Hence luxury increases, the mind becomes effeminate and timid, and the senses grow soft and delicate and are predisposed to sin and evil. Vain gladness and joy are infused into the heart; the tongue takes to itself licence and the eyes roam unrestrainedly; and the remaining senses are blunted and deadened, according to the measure [603] of this desire. The judgment is put to confusion, being nourished by spiritual folly and insipidity; moral cowardice and inconstancy increase; and, by the darkness of the soul and the weakness of the heart, fear is begotten even where no fear is. At times, again, this joy begets a spirit of confusion, and insensibility with respect to conscience and spirit; wherefore the reason is greatly enfeebled, and is affected in such a way that it can neither take nor give good counsel, and remains incapable of moral and spiritual blessings and becomes as useless as a broken vessel.

7. All these evils are caused by this kind of rejoicing -- in some more intensely, according to the intensity of their rejoicing, and also according to the complacency or weakness or variableness of the person who yields to it. For there are natures that will receive more detriment from a slight occasion of sin than will others from a great one.

8. Finally, from joy of this kind in touch, a person may fall into as many evils and perils as those which we have described as concerning the good things of nature; and, since these have already been described, I do not detail them here; neither do I describe many other evils wrought thus, such as a falling-off in spiritual exercises and bodily penance and lukewarmness and lack of devotion in the use of the sacraments of penance and of the Eucharist.

Footnotes:

602. St. Luke xvi, 19.
603. [Lit., to the quantity.']

Ascent of Mount Carmel

CHAPTER XXVI

Of the benefits that come to the soul from self-denial in rejoicing as to things of sense, which benefits are spiritual and temporal.

Marvellous are the benefits that the soul derives from self-denial in this rejoicing: some of these are spiritual and some temporal.

2. The first is that the soul, by restraining its rejoicing as to things of sense, is restored from the distraction into which it has fallen through excessive use of the senses, and is recollected in God. The spirituality and the virtues that it has acquired are preserved; nay, they are increased and increase continually. [604]

3. The second spiritual benefit which comes from self-denial in rejoicing as to things of sense is exceeding great. We may say with truth that that which was sensual becomes spiritual, and that which was animal becomes rational; and even that the soul is journeying from a human life to a portion which is angelical; and that, instead of being temporal and human, it becomes celestial and divine. For, even as a man who seeks the pleasure of things of sense and sets his rejoicing upon them neither merits nor deserves any other name than those which we have given him -- that is, sensual, animal, temporal, etc. -- even so, when he exalts his rejoicing above these things of sense, he merits all those other names -- to wit, spiritual, celestial, etc.

4. And it is clear that this is true; for, although the use of the senses and the power of sensuality are contrary, as the Apostle says, to the power and the exercises of spirituality, [605] it follows that, when the one kind of power is diminished and brought to an end, the other contrary kinds, the growth of which was hindered by the first kinds, are increased. And thus, when the spirit is perfected (which is the higher part of the soul and the part that has relations with God and receives His communications), it merits all these attributes aforementioned, since it is perfected in the heavenly and spiritual gifts and blessings of God. Both these things are proved by Saint Paul, who calls the sensual man (namely, the man that directs the exercise of his will solely to sense) the animal man, who perceives not the things of God. But this other man, who lifts up his will to God, he calls the spiritual man, saying that this man penetrates and judges all things, even the deep things of God. [606] Therefore the soul gains herein the marvellous benefit of a disposition well able to receive the blessings and spiritual gifts of God.

5. The third benefit is that the pleasures and the rejoicing of the will in temporal matters are very greatly increased; for, as the Saviour says, they shall receive an hundredfold in this life. [607] So that, if thou deniest thyself one joy, the Lord will give thee an hundredfold in this life, both spiritually and temporally; and likewise, for one joy that thou hast in these things of sense, thou shalt have an hundredfold of affliction and misery. For, through the eye that is purged from the joys of sight, there comes to the soul a spiritual joy, directed to God in all things that are seen, whether Divine or profane. Through the ear that is purged from the joy of hearing, there comes to the soul joy most spiritual an hundredfold, directed to God in all that it hears, whether Divine or profane. Even so is it with the other senses when they are purged. For, even as in the state of innocence all that our first parents saw and said and ate in Paradise furnished them with greater sweetness of contemplation, so that the sensual part of their nature might be duly subjected to, and ordered by, reason; even so the man whose senses are purged from all things of sense and made subject to the spirit receives, in their very first motion, the delight of delectable knowledge and contemplation of God.

6. Wherefore, to him that is pure, all things, whether high or low, are an occasion of greater good and further purity; even as the man that is impure is apt to derive evil from things both high and low, because of his impurity. But he that conquers not the joy of desire will not enjoy the serenity of habitual rejoicing in God through His creatures and works. In the man that lives no more according to sense, all the operations of the senses and faculties are directed to Divine contemplation. For, as it is true in good philosophy that each thing operates according to its being, and to the life that it lives, so it is clear, beyond contradiction, that, if the soul lives a spiritual life, the animal life being mortified, it must be journeying straight to God, since all its spiritual actions and motions pertain to the life of the spirit. Hence it follows that such a man, being pure in heart, finds in all things a knowledge of God which is joyful and pleasant, chaste, pure, spiritual, glad and loving.

7. From what has been said I deduce the following doctrine -- namely that, until a man has succeeded in so habituating his senses to the purgation of the joys of sense that from their first motion he is gaining the benefit aforementioned of directing all his powers to God, he must needs deny himself

joy and pleasure with respect to these powers, so that he may withdraw his soul from the life of sense. He must fear that since he is not yet spiritual, he may perchance derive from the practice of these things a pleasure and an energy which is of sense rather than of spirit; that the energy which is of sense may predominate in all his actions; and that this may lead to an increase of sensuality and may sustain and nurture it. For, as Our Saviour says, that which is born of the flesh is flesh, and that which is born of the spirit is spirit. [608] Let this be closely considered, for it is the truth. And let not him that has not yet mortified his pleasure in things of sense dare to make great use of the power and operation of sense with respect to them, thinking that they will help him to become more spiritual; for the powers of the soul will increase the more without the intervention of these things of sense -- that is, if it quench the joy and desire for them rather than indulge its pleasure in them.

8. There is no need to speak of the blessings of glory that, in the life to come, result from the renunciation of these joys. For, apart from the fact that the bodily gifts of the life of glory, such as agility and clarity, will be much more excellent than in those souls who have not denied themselves, there will be an increase in the essential glory of the soul corresponding to its love of God, for Whose sake it has renounced the things of sense aforementioned. For every momentary, fleeting joy that has been renounced, as Saint Paul says, there shall be laid up an exceeding weight of glory eternally. [609] And I will not here recount the other benefits, whether moral, temporal or spiritual, which result from this night of rejoicing; for they all are those that have already been described, and to a more eminent degree; since these joys that are renounced are more closely linked to the natural man, and therefore he that renounces them acquires thereby a more intimate purity.

Footnotes:

604. [Lit., and gain continually.']
605. Galatians v, 17.
606. 1 Corinthians ii, 9, 10, 14.
607. St. Matthew xix, 29.
608. St. John iii, 6.
609. 2 Corinthians iv, 17.

CHAPTER XXVII

Which begins to treat of the fourth kind of good -- namely, the moral. Describes wherein this consists, and in what manner joy of the will therein is lawful.

The fourth kind of good wherein the will may rejoice is moral. By this we here understand the virtues, and the habits of the virtues, in so far as these are moral, and the practice of any virtue, and the practice of works of mercy, the keeping of the law of God, and of that of the commonweal, [610] and the putting into practice of all good intentions and inclinations.

2. These kinds of moral good, when they are possessed and practised, deserve perhaps more than any of the other kinds aforementioned that the will should rejoice in them. For a man may rejoice in his own affairs for one of two reasons, or for both reasons together -- namely, for that which they are in themselves, or for the good which they imply and bring with them as a means and instrument. We shall find that the possession of the three kinds of good already mentioned merits no rejoicing of the will. For of themselves, as has been said, they do no good to man, nor in themselves have they any good, since they are so fleeting and frail; rather, as we have likewise said, they cause and bring him trouble and grief and affliction of spirit. Now, although they might merit that man should rejoice in them for the second reason -- which is that he may profit by them for journeying to God -- this is so uncertain that, as we commonly see, they more often harm man than bring him profit. But good things of a moral kind merit a certain degree of rejoicing in him that possesses them, and this for the first reason -- namely, for their intrinsic nature and worth. For they bring with them peace and tranquillity, and a right and ordered use of the reason and actions that are consistent therewith, so that a man cannot, humanly speaking, have anything better in this life.

3. Thus, since these virtues deserve to be loved and esteemed, humanly speaking, for their own sakes, a man may well rejoice in the possession of them, and may practise them for that which they are in themselves, and for the blessing which they bring to man in human and temporal form. In this way and for this reason philosophers and wise men and princes of old esteemed and praised them, and endeavoured to possess and practise them; and, although they were heathen, and regarded them only in a temporal manner, merely considering the blessings which they knew would result from them -- temporal, corporeal and natural -- they not only obtained by means of them the temporal renown and benefits which they sought, but, apart from this, God, Who loves all that is good (even in barbarians and heathen) and, as the Wise Man says, hinders the doing of naught that is good, [611] gave them longer life, greater honour, dominion and peace (as He did for example to the Romans), because they made just laws; for He subjected nearly the whole world to them, and gave rewards of a temporal kind for their good customs to those who because of their unbelief were incapable of eternal reward. For God loves moral good so much that, merely because Solomon asked wisdom of Him that he might teach his people, govern them justly and bring them up in good customs, God Himself was greatly pleased with him, and told him that, because he had asked for wisdom to that end, this should be given him, and there should also be given him that which he had not asked, namely, riches and honour, so that no king, either in the past or in the future, should be like him. [612]

4. But, although the Christian should rejoice in this first way in the moral good that he possesses and in the good works of a temporal kind which he does, since they lead to the temporal blessings which we have described, he must not allow his joy to stop at this first stage (as we have said the heathen did, because their spiritual sight extended not beyond the things of this mortal life); but, since he has the light of faith, wherein he hopes for eternal life, without which nothing that belongs to this life and the next will be of any value to him, he must rejoice principally and solely in the possession and employment of this moral good after the second manner -- namely, in that by doing these works for the love of God he will gain eternal life. And thus he should set his eyes and his rejoicing solely on serving and honouring God with his good customs and virtues. For without this intention the virtues are of no worth in the sight of God, as is seen in the ten virgins of the Gospel, who had all kept their virginity and done good works; and yet, because the joy of five of them was not of the second kind (that is, because they had not directed their joy to God), but was rather after the first and vain kind, for they rejoiced in the possession of their good works, they were cast out from Heaven with no acknowledgement or reward from the Bridegroom. And likewise many persons of old had many virtues and practised good works, and many Christians have them nowadays and accomplish great acts, which will profit them nothing for eternal life, because they have not sought in them the glory and honour which belong to God

alone. The Christian, then, must rejoice, not in the performing of good works and the following of good customs, but in doing them for the love of God alone, without respect too aught else soever. For, inasmuch as good works that are done to serve God alone will have the greater reward in glory, the greater will be the confusion in the presence of God of those who have done them for other reasons.

5. The Christian, then, if he will direct his rejoicing to God with regard to moral good, must realize that the value of his good works, fasts, alms, penances, etc., is based, not upon the number or the quality of them, but upon the love of God which inspires him to do them; and that they are the more excellent when they are performed with a purer and sincerer love of God, and when there is less in them of self-interest, joy, pleasure, consolation and praise, whether with reference to this world or to the next. Wherefore the heart must not be set upon pleasure, consolation and delight, and the other interests which good works and practices commonly bring with them, but it must concentrate its rejoicing upon God. It must desire to serve Him in its good works, and purge itself from this other rejoicing, remaining in darkness with respect to it and desiring that God alone shall have joy in its good works and shall take secret pleasure therein, without any other intention and delight than those relating to the honour and glory of God. And thus, with respect to this moral good, the soul will concentrate all the strength of its will upon God.

Footnotes:

610. [Lit., política, the political' virtue of Aristotle and St. Thomas -- i.e., the 'social,' as opposed to the moral,' intellectual' and theological' virtues. P. Silverio glosses the word as meaning good government in the commonweal, courtesy and other social virtues.']

611. Wisdom vii, 22.

612. 3 Kings [A.V., 1 Kings] iii, 11-13.

CHAPTER XXVIII

Of seven evils into which a man may fall if he set the rejoicing of his will upon moral good.

The principal evils into which a man may fall through vain rejoicing in his good works and habits I find to be seven; and they are very hurtful because they are spiritual.

2. The first evil is vanity, pride, vainglory and presumption; for a man cannot rejoice in his works without esteeming them. And hence arise boasting and like things, as is said of the Pharisee in the Gospel, who prayed and congratulated himself before God, [613] boasting that he fasted and did other good works.

3. The second evil is usually linked with this: it is our judging others, by comparison with ourselves, as wicked and imperfect, when it seems to us that their acts and good works are inferior to our own; we esteem them the less highly in our hearts, and at times also in our speech. This evil was likewise that of the Pharisee, for in his prayer he said: I thank Thee that I am not as other men are: robbers, unjust and adulterers.' [614] So that by one single act he fell into these two evils, esteeming himself and despising others, as do many nowadays, saying: I am not like such a man, nor do I do this and that, as does such or such a man. And many of these are even worse than the Pharisee. He, it is true, not only despised others, but also pointed to an individual, saying: Nor am I like this publican.' But they, not satisfied with either of these things, go so far as to be angry and envious when they see that others are praised, or do more, or are of greater use, than themselves.

4. The third evil is that, as they look for pleasure in their good works, they usually perform them only when they see that some pleasure and praise will result from them. And thus, as Christ says, they do everything ut videantur ab hominibus, [615] and work not for the love of God alone.

5. The fourth evil follows from this. It is that they will have no reward from God, since they have desired in this life to have joy or consolation or honour or some other kind of interest as a result of their good works: of such the Saviour says that herein they have received their reward. [616] And thus they have had naught but the labour of their work and are confounded, and receive no reward. There is so much misery among the sons of men which has to do with this evil that I myself believe that the greater number of good works which they perform in public are either vicious or will be of no value to them, or are imperfect in the sight of God, because they are not detached from these human intentions and interests. For what other judgment can be formed of some of the actions which certain men perform, and of the memorials which they set up, when they will not perform these actions at all unless they are surrounded by human respect and honour, which are the vanity of life, or unless they can perpetuate in these memorials their name, lineage or authority, even setting up their emblems and escutcheons in the very churches, as if they wished to set themselves, in the stead of images, in places where all bend the knee? In these good works which some men perform, may it not be said that they are worshipping [617] themselves more than God? This is certainly true if they perform them for the reason described and otherwise would not perform them at all. But leaving aside these, which are the worst cases, how many are there who fall into these evils in their good works in many ways? Some wish to be praised, others to be thanked, others enumerate their good works and desire that this person and that shall know of them, and indeed the whole world; and sometimes they wish an intermediary to present their alms, or to perform other of their charitable deeds, [618] so that more may be known of them; and some desire all these things. This is the sounding of the trumpet, which, says the Saviour in the Gospel, vain men do, for which reason they shall have no reward for their works from God. [619]

6. In order to flee from this evil, such persons must hide their good works so that God alone may see them, and must not desire anyone to take notice of them. And they must hide them, not only from others, but even from themselves. That is to say, they must find no satisfaction in them, nor esteem them as if they were of some worth, nor derive pleasure from them at all. It is this that is spiritually indicated in those words of Our Lord: Let not thy left hand know what they right hand doeth. [620] Which is as much to say: Esteem not with thy carnal and temporal eye the work that thou doest spiritually. And in this way the strength of the will is concentrated upon God, and a good deed bears fruit in His sight; so that not only will it not be lost, but it will be of great merit. And in this sense must be understood that passage from Job: If I have kissed my hand with my mouth, which is a great sin and iniquity, and my heart hath rejoiced in secret.' [621] Here by the hand is understood good works, and by the mouth is understood the will which finds satisfaction in them. And since this is, as we say, finding satisfaction in oneself, he says: If my heart hath rejoiced in secret, which is a great iniquity against God and a denial of

Him. And this is as though he were to say that he had no satisfaction, neither did his heart rejoice in secret.

7. The fifth of these evils is that such persons make no progress on the road of perfection. For, since they are attached to the pleasure and consolation which they find in their good works, it follows that, when they find no such pleasure and consolation in their good works and exercises, which ordinarily happens when God desires to lead them on, by giving them the dry bread of the perfect and taking from them the milk of babes, in order to prove their strength and to purge their delicate appetites so that they may be able to enjoy the food of grown men, they commonly faint and cease to persevere, because their good works give them no pleasure. In this way may be spiritually understood these words of the Wise Man: Dying flies spoil the sweetness of ointment.'[622] For, when any mortification comes to these persons, they die to their good works and cease to practise them; and thus they lose their perseverance, wherein are found sweetness of spirit and interior consolation.

8. The sixth of these evils is that such persons commonly deceive themselves, thinking that the things and good works which give them pleasure must be better than those that give them none. They praise and esteem the one kind and depreciate the other; yet as a rule those works whereby a man is most greatly mortified (especially when he is not proficient in perfection) are more acceptable and precious in the sight of God, by reason of the self-denial which a man must observe in performing them, than are those wherein he finds consolation and which may very easily be an occasion of self-seeking. And in this connection Micheas says of them: Malum manuum suarum dicunt bonum.[623] That is: That which is bad in their works they call good. This comes to them because of the pleasure which they take in their good works, instead of thinking only of giving pleasure to God. The extent to which this evil predominates, whether in spiritual men or in ordinary persons, would take too long to describe, for hardly anyone can be found who is moved to do such works simply for God's sake, without the attraction of some advantage of consolation or pleasure, or some other consideration.

9. The seventh evil is that, in so far as a man stifles not vain rejoicing in moral works, he is to that extent incapable of receiving reasonable counsel and instruction with regard to good works that he should perform. For he is lettered by the habit of weakness that he has acquired through performing good works with attachment to vain rejoicing; so that he cannot consider the counsel of others as best, or, even if he considers it to be so, he cannot follow it, through not having the necessary strength of mind. Such persons as this are greatly weakened in charity toward God and their neighbour; for the self-love with respect to their good works in which they indulge causes their charity to grow cold.

Footnotes:

613. St. Luke xviii, 11-12.
614. St. Luke xviii, 11.
615. St. Matthew xxiii, 5.
616. St. Matthew vi, 2.
617. [Lit., are adoring.']
618. [Lit., to present their alms or that which they do.']
619. St. Matthew vi, 2.
620. St. Matthew vi, 3.
621. Job xxxi, 27-8.
622. Ecclesiastes x, 1.
623. Micheas vii, 3.

CHAPTER XXIX

Of the benefits which come to the soul through the withdrawal of its rejoicing from moral good.

Very great are the benefits which come to the soul when it desires not to set the vain rejoicing of its will on this kind of good. For, in the first place, it is freed from falling into many temptations and deceits of the devil, which are involved in rejoicing in these good works, as we may understand by that which is said in Job, namely: He sleepeth under the shadow, in the covert of the reed and in moist places.' [624] This he applies to the devil, who deceives the soul in the moisture of rejoicing and in the vanity of the reed -- that is, in vain works. And it is no wonder if the soul is secretly deceived by the devil in this rejoicing; for, apart altogether from his suggestions, vain rejoicing is itself deception. This is especially true when there is any boasting of heart concerning these good works, as Jeremias well says in these words: Arrogantia tua decepit te. [625] For what greater deception is there than boasting? And from this the soul that purges itself from this rejoicing is freed.

2. The second benefit is that the soul performs its good works with greater deliberation and perfection than it can if there be in them the passion of joy and pleasure. For, because of this passion of joy, the passions of wrath and concupiscence are so strong that they will not submit to reason, [626] but ordinarily cause a man to be inconsistent in his actions and purposes, so that he abandons some and takes up others, and begins a thing only to abandon it without completing any part of it. For, since he acts under the influence of pleasure, and since pleasure is variable, being much stronger in some natures than in others, it follows that, when this pleasure ceases, both the action and its purpose cease, important though they may be. To such persons the joy which they have in their work is the soul and the strength thereof; and, when the joy is quenched, the work ceases and perishes, and they persevere therein no longer. It is of such persons that Christ says: They receive the word with joy, and then the devil taketh it away from them, lest they should persevere.' [627] And this is because they have no strength and no roots save in the joy aforementioned. To take and to withdraw their will, therefore, from this rejoicing is the cause of their perseverance and success. This benefit, then, is a great one, even as the contrary evil is great likewise. The wise man sets his eyes upon the substance and benefit of his work, not upon the pleasure and delight which it gives him; and so he is not beating the air, but derives from his work a stable joy, without any meed of bitterness.

3. The third benefit is divine. It is that, when vain joy in these good works is quenched, the soul becomes poor in spirit, which is one of the blessings spoken of by the Son of God when He says: Blessed are the poor in spirit, for theirs is the Kingdom of Heaven.' [628]

4. The fourth benefit is that he that denies himself this joy will be meek, humble and prudent in his actions. For he will not act impetuously and rapidly, through being impelled by the wrath and concupiscence which belong to joy; neither presumptuously, through being affected by the esteem of his own work which he cherishes because of the joy that he has in it; neither incautiously, through being blinded by joy.

5. The fifth benefit is that he becomes pleasing to God and man, and is freed from spiritual sloth, gluttony and avarice, and from spiritual envy and from a thousand other vices.

Footnotes:

624. Job xl, 16 [A.V., xl, 21].
625. Jeremias xlix, 16. E.p. adds the translation: Thy arrogance hath deceived thee.'
626. [Lit., will not give place to the weight of reason.']
627. St. Luke viii, 12.
628. St. Matthew v, 3.

CHAPTER XXX

Which begins to treat of the fifth kind of good wherein the will may rejoice, which is the supernatural. Describes the nature of these supernatural good things, and how they are distinguished from the spiritual, and how joy in them is to be directed to God.

It now behoves us to treat of the fifth kind of good thing wherein the soul may rejoice, which is the supernatural. By this term we here understand all the gifts and graces given by God which transcend natural virtue and capacity and are called gratis datae. Such as these are the gifts of wisdom and knowledge which God gave to Solomon, and the graces whereof Saint Paul speaks [629] -- namely, faith, gifts of healing, the working of miracles, prophecy, knowledge and discernment of spirits, interpretation of words and likewise the gift of tongues.

2. These good things, it is true, are also spiritual, like those of the same kind of which we have to speak presently; yet, since the two are so different, I have thought well to make a distinction between them. The practice of these has an intimate relation with the profit of man, and it is with a view to this profit and to this end that God gives them. As Saint Paul says: The spirit is given to none save for the profit of the rest;' [630] this is to be understood of these graces. But the use and practice of spiritual graces has to do with the soul and God alone, and with God and the soul, in the communion of understanding and will, etc., as we shall say hereafter. And thus there is a difference in their object, since spiritual graces have to do only with the Creator and the soul; whereas supernatural graces have to do with the creature, and furthermore differ in substance, and therefore in their operation, and thus of necessity the instruction which we give concerning them differs also.

3. Speaking now of supernatural graces and gifts as we here understand them, I say that, in order to purge ourselves of vain joy in them, it is well here to notice two benefits which are comprised in this kind of gift -- namely, temporal and spiritual. The temporal benefits are the healing of infirmities, the receiving of their sight by the blind, the raising of the dead, the casting out of devils, prophesying concerning the future so that men may take heed to themselves, and other things of the kind. The spiritual and eternal benefit is that God is known and served through these good works by him that performs them, or by those in whom and in whose presence they are performed.

4. With respect to the first kind of benefit -- namely, the temporal -- supernatural works and miracles merit little or no rejoicing on the part of the soul; for, without the second kind of benefit, they are of little or no importance to man, since they are not in themselves a means for uniting the soul with God, as charity is. And these supernatural works and graces may be performed by those who are not in a state of grace and charity, whether they truly give thanks and attribute their gifts to God, [631] as did the wicked prophet Balaam, and Solomon, or whether they perform them falsely, through the agency of the devil, as did Simon Magus, or by means of other secrets of nature. These works and marvels, if any of them were to be of any profit to him that worked them, would be true works given by God. And Saint Paul teaches us what these are worth without the second kind of benefit, saying: Though I speak with the tongues of men and of angels, and have not charity, I am become as a sounding bell or metal. And though I have prophecy and know all mysteries and all knowledge; and though I have all faith, even as much as may remove [632] mountains, and have not charity, I am nothing, etc.' [633] Wherefore Christ will refuse the requests of many who have esteemed their good works in this way, when they beg Him for glory because of them, saying: Lord, have we not prophesied in Thy name and worked many miracles? Then Christ will say to them: Depart from Me, workers of iniquity.' [634]

5. A man, then, should rejoice, not when he has such graces and makes use of them, but when he reaps from them the second spiritual fruit, namely that of serving God in them with true charity, for herein is the fruit of eternal life. For this cause Our Saviour reproved the disciples who were rejoicing because they cast out devils, saying: Desire not to rejoice in this, that devils are subject to you, but rather because your names are written in the book of life.' [635] This, according to good theology, is as much as to say: Rejoice if your names are written in the book of life. By this it is understood that a man should not rejoice save when he is walking in the way of life, which he may do by performing good works in charity; for where is the profit and what is the worth in the sight of God of aught that is not love of God? And this love is not perfect if it be not strong and discreet in purging the will of joy in all things, and if it be not set upon doing the will of God alone. And in this manner the will is united with God through these good things which are supernatural.

Ascent of Mount Carmel
Footnotes:

629. 1 Corinthians xii, 9-10.
630. 1 Corinthians xii, 7.
631. [Lit., give thanks and gifts to God.']
632. [traspasar: lit., go over,' go through.']
633. 1 Corinthians xiii, 1-2.
634. St. Matthew vii, 22-3.
635. St. Luke x, 20.

CHAPTER XXXI

Of the evils which come to the soul when it sets the rejoicing of the will upon this kind of good.

Three principal evils, it seems to me, may come to the soul when it sets its rejoicing upon supernatural good. These are: that it may deceive and be deceived; that it may fall away from the faith; and that it may indulge in vainglory or some other such vanity.

2. As to the first of these, it is a very easy thing to deceive others, and to deceive oneself, by rejoicing in this kind of operation. And the reason is that, in order to know which of these operations are false and which are true, and how and at what time they should be practised, much counsel and much light from God are needful, both of which are greatly impeded by joy in these operations and esteem for them. And this for two reasons: first, because joy blunts and obscures the judgment; second, because, when a man has joy in these things, not only does he the more quickly become eager for them, but he is also the more impelled to practise them out of the proper season. And even supposing the virtues and operations which are practised to be genuine, these two defects suffice for us to be frequently deceived in them, either through not understanding them as they should be understood, or through not profiting by them and not using them at the times and in the ways that are most meet. For, although it is true that, when God gives these gifts and graces, He gives light by which to see them, and the impulse whereby a man may know at what times and in what ways to use them; yet these souls, through the attachment and imperfection which they may have with regard to them, may greatly err, by not using them with the perfection that God desires of them therein, and in the way and at the time that He wills. We read that Balaam desired to do this, when, against the will of God, he determined to go and curse the people of Israel, for which reason God was wroth and purposed to slay him.[636] And Saint James and Saint John desired to call down fire from Heaven upon the Samaritans because they gave not lodging to Our Saviour, and for this He reproved them.[637]

3. Here it is evident that these persons were led to determine to perform these works, when it was not meet for them to do so, by a certain imperfect passion, which was inherent in their joy in them and esteem for them. For, when no such imperfection exists, the soul is moved and determined to perform these virtues only in the manner wherein God so moves it, and at His time, and until then it is not right that they should be performed. It was for this reason that God complained of certain prophets, through Jeremias, saying: I sent not the prophets, and they ran; I spake not to them, and they prophesied.'[638] And later He says: They deceived My people by their lying and their miracles, when I had not commanded them, neither had I sent them.'[639] And in that place He says of them likewise: They see the visions of their heart, and speak of them'[640]; which would not happen if they had not this abominable attachment to these works.

4. From these passages it is to be understood that the evil of this rejoicing not only leads men to make wicked and perverse use of these graces given by God, as did Balaam and those of whom the prophet here says that they worked miracles whereby they deceived the people, but it even leads them to use these graces without having been given them by God, like those who prophesied their own fancies and published the visions which they invented or which the devil represented to them. For, when the devil sees them affectioned to these things, he opens a wide field to them, gives them abundant material and interferes with them in many ways; whereupon they spread their sails and become shamelessly audacious in the freedom wherewith they work these marvels.

5. Nor does the evil stop here. To such a point does their joy in these works and their eagerness for them extend that, if before they had a secret compact with the devil (and many of them do in fact perform these works by such secret compacts), it now makes them bold enough to work with him by an explicit and manifest compact, submitting themselves to him, by agreement, as his disciples and allies. Hence we have wizards, enchanters, magicians, soothsayers and sorcerers. And so far does the joy of these persons in their works carry them that, not only do they seek to purchase gifts and graces with money, as did Simon Magus, in order to serve the devil, but they even strive to obtain sacred things, and (which cannot be said without trembling) Divine things, for even the very Body[641] of our Lord Jesus Christ has been seen to be usurped for the use of their wicked deeds and abominations. May God here extend and show to them His great mercy!

6. Everyone will clearly understand how pernicious are such persons to themselves and how prejudicial to Christianity. It may be noted here that all those magicians and soothsayers who lived among the children of Israel, whom Saul destroyed out of the land, because they desired to imitate the

Ascent of Mount Carmel

true prophets of God, had fallen into such abominations and deceits.

7. He, then, that has supernatural gifts and graces ought to refrain from desiring to practise them, and from rejoicing in so doing, nor ought he to care to exercise them; for God, Who gives Himself to such persons, by supernatural means, for the profit of His Church and of its members, will move them likewise supernaturally in such a manner and at such time as He desires. As He commanded His faithful ones to take no thought as to what they were to say, or as to how they were to say it, since this is the supernatural business of faith, it will likewise be His will (as these operations are no less a supernatural matter) that a man should wait and allow God to work by moving his heart, since it is in the virtue of this working that there will be wrought all virtue. The disciples (so we read in the Acts of the Apostles), although these graces and gifts had been infused within them, prayed to God, beseeching Him to be pleased to stretch forth His hand in making signs and performing works of healing through them, that they might introduce the faith of our Lord Jesus Christ into men's hearts. [642]

8. From this first evil may proceed the second, which is a falling away from the faith; this can come to pass after two manners. The first has respect to others; for, when a man sets out, unseasonably and needlessly, to perform a marvel or a mighty work, apart from the fact that this is tempting God, which is a great sin, it may be that he will not succeed, and will engender in the hearts of men discredit and contempt for the faith. For, although at times such persons may succeed because for other reasons and purposes God so wills it, as in the case of Saul's witch [643] (if it be true that it was indeed Samuel who appeared on that occasion), they will not always so succeed; and, when they do so, they go astray none the less and are blameworthy for having used these graces when it was not fitting. The second manner in which we may fall away is in ourselves and has respect to the merit of faith; for, if a man make much account of these miracles, he ceases to lean upon the substantial practice of faith, which is an obscure habit; and thus, where signs and witnesses abound, there is less merit in believing. In this way Saint Gregory says that faith has no merit when human reason provides experience. [644] And thus these marvels are never worked by God save when they are really necessary for belief. Therefore, to the end that His disciples should not be without merit, though they had experience of His resurrection, He did many things before He showed Himself to them, so that they should believe Him without seeing Him. To Mary Magdalene, first of all, He showed the empty tomb, and afterwards bade the angels speak to her [645] (for, as Saint Paul says, faith comes by hearing); [646] so that, having heard, she should believe before she saw. And, although she saw Him, it was as an ordinary man, [647] that, by the warmth of His presence, He might completely instruct her in the belief which she lacked. And He first sent to tell His disciples, with the women, and afterwards they went to see the tomb. And, as to those who went to Emmaus, He first of all enkindled their hearts in faith so that they might see Him, dissembling with them as He walked. [648] And finally He reproved them all because they had not believed those who had announced to them His resurrection. [649] And He reproved Saint Thomas because he desired to have the witness of His wounds, by telling him that they who saw Him not and yet believed Him were blessed. [650]

9. And thus it is not the will of God that miracles should be wrought: when He works them, He does so, as it were, because He cannot do otherwise. And for this cause He reproved the Pharisees because they believed not save through signs, saying: Unless ye see marvels and signs, ye believe not.' [651] Those, then, who love to rejoice in these supernatural works lose much in the matter of faith.

10. The third evil is that, because of their joy in these works, men commonly fall into vainglory or some other vanity. For even their joy in these wonders, when it is not, as we have said, purely in God and for God, is vanity; which is evident in the reproof given by Our Lord to the disciples because they had rejoiced that devils were subject to them; [652] for which joy, if it had not been vain, He would not have reproved them.

Footnotes:

636. Numbers xxii, 22-3.
637. St. Luke ix, 54-5.
638. Jeremias xxiii, 21.
639. Jeremias xxiii, 32.
640. Jeremias xxiii, 26.
641. [Lit., the awful Body.']
642. Acts iv, 29-30.
643. 1 Kings [A.V., 1 Samuel] xxviii, 7, ff.
644. Nec fides habet meritum cui humana ratio praebet experimentum.' St. Gregory, Hom. 26 in Evang. (Migne, Vol. LXXVI, p. 1,137).
645. [St. Luke xxiv, 6; St. John xx, 2.]
646. [Romans x, 17.]
647. [St. John xx, 15].

648. St. Luke xxiv, 15.
649. [St. Luke xxiv, 25-6.]
650. St. John xx, 29.
651. St. John iv, 48.
652. St. Luke x, 20.

CHAPTER XXXII

Of two benefits which are derived from the renunciation of rejoicing in the matter of the supernatural graces.

Besides the benefits which the soul gains by being delivered from the three evils aforementioned through its renunciation of this joy, it acquires two excellent benefits. The first is that it magnifies and exalts God: the second is that it exalts itself. For God is exalted in the soul after two manners: first, by the withdrawal of the heart and the joy of the will from all that is not God, in order that they may be set upon Him alone. This David signified in the verse which we quoted when we began to speak of the night of this faculty; namely: Man shall attain to a lofty heart, and God shall be exalted.'[653] For, when the heart is raised above all things, the soul is exalted above them all.

2. And, because in this way the soul centres itself in God alone, God is exalted and magnified, when He reveals to the soul His excellence and greatness; for, in this elevation of joy, God bears witness of Who He Himself is. This cannot be done save if the will be voided of joy and consolation with respect to all things, even as David said also, in these words: Be still and see that I am God.'[654] And again he says: In a desert land, dry and pathless, have I appeared before Thee, to see Thy power and Thy glory.'[655] And, since it is true that God is exalted by the fixing of the soul's rejoicing upon detachment from all things, He is much more highly exalted when the soul withdraws itself from the most wondrous of these things in order to fix its rejoicing on Him alone. For these, being supernatural, are of a nobler kind; and thus for the soul to cast them aside, in order to set its rejoicing upon God alone, is for it to attribute greater glory and excellence to God than to them. For, the more and the greater things a man despises for the sake of another, the more does he esteem and exalt that other.

3. Furthermore, God is exalted after the second manner when the will is withdrawn from this kind of operation; for, the more God is believed and served without testimonies and signs, the more He is exalted by the soul, for it believes more concerning God than signs and miracles can demonstrate.

4. The second benefit wherein the soul is exalted consists in this, that, withdrawing the will from all desire for apparent signs and testimonies, it is exalted in purest faith, which God increases and infuses within it much more intensely. And, together with this, He increases in it the other two theological virtues, which are charity and hope, wherein the soul enjoys the highest Divine knowledge by means of the obscure and detached habit of faith; and it enjoys great delight of love by means of charity, whereby the will rejoices in naught else than in the living God; and likewise it enjoys satisfaction in the memory by means of hope. All this is a wondrous benefit, which leads essentially and directly to the perfect union of the soul with God.

Footnotes:

653. Psalm lxiii, 7 [A.V., lxiv, 6-7].
654. Psalm xlv, 11 [A.V., xlvi, 10].
655. Psalm lxii, 3 [A.V., lxii, 1-2].

CHAPTER XXXIII

Which begins to treat of the sixth kind of good wherein the soul may rejoice. Describes its nature and makes the first division under this head.

Since the intention of this work of ours is to lead the spirit through these good things of the spirit even to the Divine union of the soul with God, it will not behove both myself and the reader to give our consideration to this matter with particular care. For, in speaking of this sixth kind of good, we have to treat of the good things of the spirit, which are those that are of the greatest service to this end. For it is quite certain, and quite an ordinary occurrence, [656] that some persons, because of their lack of knowledge, make use of spiritual things with respect only to sense, and leave the spirit empty. There will scarcely be anyone whose spirit is not to a considerable degree corrupted by sweetness of sense; since, if the water be drunk up before it reaches the spirit, the latter becomes dry and barren.

2. Coming to this matter, then, I say that by good things of the spirit I understand all those that influence and aid the soul in Divine things and in its intercourse with God, and the communications of God to the soul.

3. Beginning by making a division between these supreme kinds of good, I say that good things of the spirit are of two kinds: the one kind is delectable and the other painful. And each of these kinds is likewise of two manners; for the delectable kind consists of clear things that are distinctly understood, and also of things that are not understood clearly or distinctly. The painful kind, likewise, may be of clear and distinct things, or of things dark and confused.

4. Between all these we may likewise make distinctions with respect to the faculties of the soul. For some kinds of spiritual good, being of knowledge, pertain to the understanding; others, being of affection, pertain to the will; and others, inasmuch as they are imaginary, pertain to the memory.

5. We shall leave for later consideration those good things that are painful, since they pertain to the passive night, in treating of which we shall have to speak of them; and likewise the delectable blessings which we described as being of things confused and not distinct, of which we shall treat hereafter, since they pertain to that general, confused and loving knowledge wherein is effected the union of the soul with God, and which we passed over in the second book, deferring it so that we might treat of it later [657] when we should make a division between the apprehensions of the understanding. We shall speak here and now of those delectable blessings which are of things clear and distinct.

Footnotes:

656. [Lit., thing.']

657. [In spite of this promise, the Saint does not return to this subject at such length as his language here would suggest.]

CHAPTER XXXIV

Of those good things of the spirit which can be distinctly apprehended by the understanding and the memory. Describes how the will is to behave in the matter of rejoicing in them.

We might spend much time here upon the multitude of the apprehensions of the memory and the understanding, teaching how the will is to conduct itself with regard to the joy that it may have in them, had we not treated of this at length in the second and the third book. But, since we there spoke of the manner wherein it behoves these two faculties to act with respect to them, in order that they may take the road to Divine union, and since it behoves the will to conduct itself likewise as regards rejoicing in them, it is unnecessary to go over this here; for it suffices to say that wheresoever we there said that those faculties should void themselves of this or that apprehension, it is to be understood also that the will should likewise be voided of joy in them. And in the way wherein it is said that memory and understanding are to conduct themselves with regard to all these apprehensions, the will must conduct itself likewise; for, since the understanding and the other faculties cannot admit or reject anything unless the will intervene therein, it is clear that the same teaching that serves for the one will serve also for the other.

2. It may there be seen, then, what is requisite in this case, for the soul will fall into all the evils and perils to which we there referred if it cannot direct the rejoicing of the will to God in all those apprehensions.

CHAPTER XXXV

Of the delectable spiritual good things which can be distinctly apprehended by the will. Describes the kinds of these.

We can reduce all the kinds of good which can distinctly cause joy to the will to four: namely, motive, provocative, directive and perfective. Of these we shall speak in turn, each in its order; and first, of the motive kind -- namely, images and portraits of saints, oratories and ceremonies.

2. As touching images and portraits, there may be much vanity and vain rejoicing in these. For, though they are most important for Divine worship and most necessary to move the will to devotion, as is shown by the approval given to them and the use made of them by our Mother Church (for which reason it is always well that we should employ them, in order to awaken our lukewarmness), there are many persons who rejoice rather in the painting and decoration of them than in what they represent.

3. The use of images has been ordained by the Church for two principal ends -- namely, that we may reverence the saints in them, and that the will may be moved and devotion to the saints awakened by them. When they serve this purpose they are beneficial and the use of them is necessary; and therefore we must choose those that are most true and lifelike, and that most move the will to devotion, and our eyes must ever be fixed upon this motive rather than upon the value and cunning of their workmanship and decoration. For, as I say, there are some who pay more attention to the cunning with which an image is made, and to its value, than to what it represents; and that interior devotion which they ought to direct spiritually to the saint whom they see not, forgetting the image at once, since it serves only as a motive, they squander upon the cunning and the decoration of its outward workmanship. In this way sense is pleased and delighted, and the love and rejoicing of the will remain there. This is a complete hindrance to true spirituality, which demands annihilation of the affections as to all particular things.

4. This will become quite clear from the detestable custom which certain persons observe with regard to images in these our days. Holding not in abhorrence the vain trappings of the world, they adorn images with the garments which from time to time vain persons invent in order to satisfy their own pleasures and vanities. So they clothe images with garments reprehensible even in themselves, a kind of vanity which was, and is still, abhorrent to the saints whom the images represent. Herein, with their help, the devil succeeds in canonizing his vanities, by clothing the saints with them, not without causing them great displeasure. And in this way the honest and grave devotion of the soul, which rejects and spurns all vanity and every trace of it, becomes with them little more than a dressing of dolls; some persons use images merely as idols upon which they have set their rejoicing. And thus you will see certain persons who are never tired of adding one image to another, and wish them to be of this or that kind and workmanship, and to be placed in this or that manner, so as to be pleasing to sense; and they make little account of the devotion of the heart. They are as much attached to them as was Michas to his idols, [658] or as was Laban; [659] for the one ran out of his house crying aloud because they were being taken from him; and the other, having made a long journey and been very wroth because of them, disturbed all the household stuff of Jacob, in searching for them.

5. The person who is truly devout sets his devotion principally upon that which is invisible; he needs few images and uses few, and chooses those that harmonize with the Divine rather than with the human, clothing them, and with them himself, in the garments of the world to come, and following its fashions rather than those of this world. For not only does an image belonging to this world in no way influence his desire; it does not even lead him to think of this world, in spite of his having before his eyes something worldly, akin to the world's interests. Nor is his heart attached to the images that he uses; if they are taken from him, he grieves very little, for he seeks within himself the living image, which is Christ crucified, for Whose sake he even desires that all should be taken from him and he should have nothing. Even when the motives and means which lead him closest to God are taken from him, he remains in tranquility. For the soul is nearer perfection when it is tranquil and joyous, though it be deprived of these motives, than if it has possession of them together with desire and attachment. For, although it is good to be pleased to have such images as assist the soul to greater devotion (for which reason it is those which move it most that must always be chosen), yet it is something far removed from perfection to be so greatly attached to them as to possess them with attachment, so that, if they are taken away from the soul, it becomes sad.

6. Let the soul be sure that, the more closely it is attached to an image or a motive, the less will its

devotion and prayer mount to God. For, although it is true that, since some are more appropriate than others, and excite devotion more than others, it is well, for this reason alone, to be more affectioned to some than to others, as I have just now said, yet there must be none of the attachment and affection which I have described. Otherwise, that which has to sustain the spirit in its flight to God, in total forgetfulness, will be wholly occupied by sense, and the soul will be completely immersed in a delight afforded it by what are but instruments. These instruments I have to use, but solely in order to assist me in devotion; and, on account of my imperfection, they may well serve me as a hindrance, no less so than may affection and attachment to anything else.

7. [660] But, though perhaps in this matter of images you may think that there is something to be said on the other side, if you have not clearly understood how much detachment and poverty of spirit is required by perfection, at least you cannot excuse the imperfection which is commonly indulged with regard to rosaries; for you will hardly find anyone who has not some weakness with regard to these, desiring them to be of this workmanship rather than of that, or of this colour or metal rather than of that, or decorated in some one style or in some other. Yet no one style is better than another for the hearing of a prayer by God, for this depends upon the simple and true heart, which looks at no more than pleasing God, and, apart from the question of indulgences, cares no more for one rosary than for another.

8. Our vain concupiscence is of such a nature and quality that it tries to establish itself in everything; and it is like the worm which destroys healthy wood, and works upon things both good and evil. For what else is your desire to have a rosary of cunning workmanship, and your wish that it shall be of one kind rather than of another, but the fixing of your rejoicing upon the instrument? It is like desiring to choose one image rather than another, and considering, not if it will better awaken Divine love within you, but only if it is more precious and more cunningly made. If you employed your desire and rejoicing solely in the love of God, you would care nothing for any of these considerations. It is most vexatious to see certain spiritual persons so greatly attached to the manner and workmanship of these instruments and motives, and to the curiosity and vain pleasure which they find in them: you will never see them satisfied; they will be continually leaving one thing for another, and forgetting and forsaking spiritual devotion for these visible things, to which they have affection and attachment, sometimes of just the same kind as that which a man has to temporal things; and from this they receive no small harm.

Footnotes:

658. Judges xviii, 22-4.
659. Genesis xxxi, 34-7.
660. [In this and the next paragraph the Saint is more than usually personal in his approach to the reader. The word tú(you) is repeated many times, and placed in emphatic positions, in a way which cannot be exactly reproduced in English.]

CHAPTER XXXVI

Which continues to treat of images, and describes the ignorance which certain persons have with respect to them.

There is much that might be said of the stupidity which many persons display with regard to images; their foolishness reaches such a point that some of them place more confidence in one kind of image than in another, believing that God will hear them more readily because of these than because of those, even when both represent the same thing, as when there are two of Christ or two of Our Lady. And this happens because they have more affection for the one kind of workmanship than for the other; which implies the crudest ideas concerning intercourse with God and the worship and honour that are owed to Him, which has solely to do with the faith and the purity of heart of him that prays. For if God sometimes grants more favours by means of one image rather than by another of the same kind, it is not because there is more virtue to this effect in one than in another (however much difference there may be in their workmanship), but because some persons better awaken their own devotion by one than by another. If they had the same devotion for the one as for the other (or even without the use of either), they would receive the same favours from God.

2. Hence the reason for which God works [661] miracles and grants favours by means of one kind of image rather than by another is not that these should be esteemed more than those, but to the end that, by means of the wonder that they cause, there may be awakened sleeping devotion and the affection of the faithful for prayer. And hence it comes that, as the contemplation of the image at that time enkindles devotion and makes us to continue in prayer (both these being means whereby God hears and grants that which is asked of Him), therefore, at that time and by means of that same image, God continues to work favours and miracles because of the prayer and affection which are then shown; for it is certain that God does it not because of the image, which in itself is no more than a painted thing, but because of the devotion and faith which the person has toward the saint whom it represents. And so, if you had the same devotion and faith in Our Lady before one image representing her as before another, since the person represented is the same (and even, as we have said, if you had no such image at all), you would receive the same favours. For it is clear from experience that, when God grants certain favours and works miracles, He does so as a rule by means of certain images which are not well carved or cunningly formed or painted, so that the faithful may attribute nothing to the figure or the painting.

3. Furthermore, Our Lord is frequently wont to grant these favours by means of those images that are most remote and solitary. One reason for this is that the effort necessary to journey to them causes the affections to be increased and makes the act of prayer more earnest. Another reason is that we may withdraw ourselves from noise and from people when we pray, even as did the Lord. Wherefore he that makes a pilgrimage does well if he makes it at a time when no others are doing so, even though the time be unusual. I should never advise him to make a pilgrimage when a great multitude is doing so; for, as a rule, on these occasions, people return in a state of greater distraction than when they went. And many set out on these pilgrimages and make them for recreation rather than for devotion. Where there is devotion and faith, then, any image will suffice; but, if there is none, none will suffice. Our Saviour was a very living image in the world; and yet those that had no faith, even though they went about with Him and saw His wondrous works, derived no benefit from them. And this was the reason why, as the Evangelist says, He did few mighty works in His own country. [662]

4. I desire also to speak here of certain supernatural effects which are sometimes produced by certain images upon particular persons. To certain images God gives a particular spiritual influence upon such persons, so that the figure of the image and the devotion caused by it remain fixed in the mind, and the person has them ever present before him; and so, when he suddenly thinks of the image, the spiritual influence which works upon him is of the same kind as when he saw it -- sometimes it is less, but sometimes it is even greater -- yet, from another image, although it be of more perfect workmanship, he will not obtain the same spiritual effect.

5. Many persons, too, have devotion to one kind of workmanship rather than to another, and to some they will have no more than a natural inclination and affection, just as we prefer seeing one person's face to another's. And they will naturally become more attracted to a particular image, and will keep it more vividly in their imagination, even though it be not as beautiful as others, just because their nature is attracted to that kind of form and figure which it represents. And some persons will think that the affection which they have for such or such an image is devotion, whereas it will perhaps be no more

than natural inclination and affection. Again, it may happen that, when they look at an image, they will see it move, or make signs and gestures and indications, or speak. This, and the variety of supernatural effects caused by images of which we have here been speaking, are, it is true, quite frequently good and true effects, produced by God either to increase devotion or so that the soul may have some support on which to lean, because it is somewhat weak, and so that it may not be distracted. Yet frequently, again, they are produced by the devil in order to cause deception and harm. We shall therefore give instruction concerning this in the chapter following.

Footnotes:

661. [Lit., awakens.' Cf. the use of the same metaphor below.]
662. St. Luke iv, 24. [Rather St. Matthew xiii, 58 or St. Mark vi, 5.]

CHAPTER XXXVII

Of how the rejoicing of the will must be directed, by way of the images, to God, so that the soul may not go astray because of them or be hindered by them.

Just as images are of great benefit for remembering God and the saints, and for moving the will to devotion when they are used in the ordinary way, as is fitting, so they will lead to great error if, when supernatural happenings come to pass in connection with them, the soul should not be able to conduct itself as is fitting for its journey to God. For one of the means by which the devil lays hold on incautious souls, with great ease, and obstructs the way of spiritual truth for them, is the use of extraordinary and supernatural happenings, of which he gives examples by means of images, both the material and corporeal images used by the Church, and also those which he is wont to fix in the fancy in relation to such or such a saint, or an image of him, transforming himself into an angel of light that he may deceive. For in those very means which we possess for our relief and help the astute devil contrives to hide himself in order to catch us when we are least prepared. Wherefore it is concerning good things that the soul that is good must ever have the greatest misgivings, for evil things bear their own testimony with them.

2. Hence, in order to avoid all the evils which may happen to the soul in this connection, which are its being hindered from soaring upward to God, or its using images in an unworthy and ignorant manner, or its being deceived by them through natural or supernatural means, all of which are things that we have touched upon above; and in order likewise to purify the rejoicing of the will in them and by means of them to lead the soul to God, for which reason the Church recommends their use, I desire here to set down only one warning, which will suffice for everything; and this warning is that, since images serve us as a motive for invisible things, we must strive to set the motive and the affection and the rejoicing of our will only upon that which in fact they represent. Let the faithful soul, then, be careful that, when he sees the image, he desire not that his senses should be absorbed by it, whether the image be corporeal or imaginary, whether beautifully made, whether richly adorned, whether the devotion that it causes be of sense or of spirit, whether it produce supernatural manifestations or no. The soul must on no account set store by these accidents, nor even regard them, but must raise up its mind from the image to that which it represents, centering the sweetness and rejoicing of its will, together with the prayer and devotion of its spirit, upon God or upon the saint who is being invoked; for that which belongs to the living reality and to the spirit should not be usurped by sense and by the painted object. If the soul do this, it will not be deceived, for it will set no store by anything that the image may say to it, nor will it occupy its sense or its spirit in such a way that they cannot travel freely to God, nor will it place more confidence in one image than in another. And an image which would cause the soul devotion by supernatural means will now do so more abundantly, since the soul will now go with its affections directly to God. For, whensoever God grants these and other favours, He does so by inclining the affection of the joy of the will to that which is invisible, and this He wishes us also to do, by annihilating the power and sweetness of the faculties with respect to these visible things of sense.

CHAPTER XXXVIII

Continues to describe motive good. Speaks of oratories and places dedicated to prayer.

I think it has now been explained how the spiritual person may find as great imperfection in the accidents of images, by setting his pleasure and rejoicing upon them, as in other corporeal and temporal things, and perchance imperfection more perilous still. And I say perchance more perilous, because, when a person says that the objects of his rejoicing are holy, he feels more secure, and fears not to cling to them and become attached to them in a natural way. And thus such a person is sometimes greatly deceived, thinking himself to be full of devotion because he perceives that he takes pleasure in these holy things, when, perchance, this is due only to his natural desire and temperament, which lead him to this just as they lead him to other things.

2. Hence it arises (we are now beginning to treat of oratories) that there are some persons who never tire of adding to their oratories images of one kind and then of another, and take pleasure in the order and array in which they set them out, so that these oratories may be well adorned and pleasing to behold. Yet they love God no more when their oratories are ornate than when they are simple -- nay, rather do they love Him less, since, as we have said, the pleasure which they set upon their painted adornments is stolen from the living reality. It is true that all the adornment and embellishment and respect that can be lavished upon images amounts to very little, and that therefore those who have images and treat them with a lack of decency and reverence are worthy of severe reproof, as are those who have images so ill-carved that they take away devotion rather than produce it, for which reason some image-makers who are very defective and unskilled in this art should be forbidden to practise it. But what has that to do with the attachment and affection and desire which you have [663] for these outward adornments and decorations, when your senses are absorbed by them in such a way that your heart is hindered from journeying to God, and from loving Him and forgetting all things for love of Him? If you fail in the latter aim for the sake of the former, not only will God not esteem you for it, but He will even chasten you for not having sought His pleasure in all things rather than your own. This you may clearly gather from the description of that feast which they made for His Majesty when He entered Jerusalem. They received Him with songs and with branches, and the Lord wept; [664] for their hearts were very far removed from Him and they paid Him reverence only with outward adornments and signs. We may say of them that they were making a festival for themselves rather than for God; and this is done nowadays by many, who, when there is some solemn festival in a place, are apt to rejoice because of the pleasure which they themselves will find in it -- whether in seeing or in being seen, or whether in eating or in some other selfish thing -- rather than to rejoice at being acceptable to God. By these inclinations and intentions they are giving no pleasure to God. Especially is this so when those who celebrate festivals invent ridiculous and undevout things to intersperse in them, so that they may incite people to laughter, which causes them greater distraction. And other persons invent things which merely please people rather than move them to devotion.

3. And what shall I say of persons who celebrate festivals for reasons connected with their own interests? They alone, and God Who sees them, know if their regard and desire are set upon such interests rather than upon the service of God. Let them realize, when they act in any of these ways, that they are making festivals in their own honour rather than in that of God. For that which they do for their own pleasure, or for the pleasure of men, God will not account as done for Himself. Yea, many who take part in God's festivals will be enjoying themselves even while God is wroth with them, as He was with the children of Israel when they made a festival, and sang and danced before their idol, thinking that they were keeping a festival in honour of God; of whom He slew many thousands. [665] Or again, as He was with the priests Nabad and Abiu, the sons of Aaron, whom He slew with the censers in their hands, because they offered strange fire. [666] Or as with the man that entered the wedding feast ill-adorned and ill-garbed, whom the king commanded to be thrown into outer darkness, bound hand and foot. [667] By this it may be known how ill God suffers these irreverences in assemblies that are held for His service. For how many festivals, O my God, are made Thee by the sons of men to the devil's advantage rather than to Thine! The devil takes a delight in them, because such gatherings bring him business, as they might to a trader. And how often wilt Thou say concerning them: This people honoureth Me with their lips alone, but their heart is far from Me, for they serve Me from a wrong cause!' [668] For the sole reason for which God must be served is that He is Who He is, and not for any other mediate ends. And thus to serve Him for other reasons than solely that He is Who He is, is to

serve Him without regard for Him as the Ultimate Reason.

4. Returning now to oratories, I say that some persons deck them out for their own pleasure rather than for the pleasure of God; and some persons set so little account by the devotion which they arouse that they think no more of them than of their own secular antechambers; some, indeed, think even less of them, for they take more pleasure in the profane than in the Divine.

5. But let us cease speaking of this and speak only of those who are more particular [669] -- that is to say, of those who consider themselves devout persons. Many of these centre their desire and pleasure upon their oratory and its adornments, to such an extent that they squander on them all the time that they should be employing in prayer to God and interior recollection. They cannot see that, by not arranging their oratory with a view to the interior recollection and peace of the soul, they are as much distracted by it as by anything else, and will find the pleasure which they take in it a continual occasion of unrest, and more so still if anyone endeavors to deprive them of it.

Footnotes:

663. [Again the Saint begins, repeatedly and emphatically, to employ the pronoun tú. Cf. Bk. III, chap. xxxvi, 7, above.]
664. St. Matthew xxi, 9. [Cf. St. Luke xix, 41.]
665. Exodus xxxii, 7-28.
666. Leviticus x, 1-2.
667. St. Matthew xxii, 12-13.
668. St. Matthew xv, 8. [Lit., they serve Me without cause.']
669. [Lit., that spin more finely' -- a common Spanish metaphor.]

CHAPTER XXXIX

Of the way in which oratories and churches should be used, in order to direct the spirit to God.

With regard to the direction of the spirit to God through this kind of good, it is well to point out that it is certainly lawful, and even expedient, for beginners to find some sensible sweetness and pleasure in images, oratories and other visible objects of devotion, since they have not yet weaned or detached their desire [670] from things of the world, so that they can leave the one pleasure for the other. They are like a child holding something in one of its hands; to make it loosen its hold upon it we give it something else to hold in the other hand lest it should cry because both its hands are empty. But the spiritual person that would make progress must strip himself of all those pleasures and desires wherein the will can rejoice, for pure spirituality is bound very little to any of those objects, but only to interior recollection and mental converse with God. So, although he makes use of images and oratories, he does so only fleetingly; his spirit at once comes to rest in God and he forgets all things of sense.

2. Wherefore, although it is best to pray where there is most decency, yet notwithstanding one should choose the place where sense and spirit are least hindered from journeying to God. Here we should consider that answer made by Our Saviour to the Samaritan woman, when she asked Him which was the more fitting place wherein to pray, the temple or the mountain, and He answered her that true prayer was not connected with the mountain or with the temple, but that those who adored the Father and were pleasing to Him were those that adored Him in spirit and in truth. [671] Wherefore, although churches and pleasant places are set apart and furnished for prayer (for a church must not be used for aught else), yet, for a matter as intimate as converse held with God, one should choose that place which gives sense the least occupation and the least encouragement. And thus it must not be a place that is pleasant and delectable to sense (like the places that some habitually contrive to find), for otherwise, instead of the recollection of the spirit in God, naught will be achieved save recreation and pleasure and delight of sense. Wherefore it is good to choose a place that is solitary, and even wild, so that the spirit may resolutely and directly soar upward to God, and not be hindered or detained by visible things; for, although these sometimes help to raise up the spirit, it is better to forget them at once and to rest in God. For this reason Our Saviour was wont to choose solitary places for prayer, and such as occupied the senses but little, in order to give us an example. He chose places that lifted up the soul to God, such as mountains, which are lifted up above the earth, and are ordinarily bare, thus offering no occasion for recreation of the senses.

3. The truly spiritual man, then, is never tied to a place of prayer because of its suitability in this way or in that, nor does he even consider such a thing, for, if he did so, he would still be tied to sense. But, to the end that he may attain interior recollection, and forget everything, he chooses the places most free from sensible objects and attractions, withdrawing his attention from all these, that he may be able to rejoice in his God and be far removed from all things created. But it is a remarkable thing to see some spiritual persons, who waste all their time in setting up oratories and furnishing places which please their temperaments or inclinations, yet make little account of interior recollection, which is the most important thing, but of which they have very little. If they had more of it, they would be incapable of taking pleasure in those methods and manners of devotion, which would simply weary them.

Footnotes:

670. [Lit., their palate.']
671. St. John iv, 23-4.

CHAPTER XL

Which continues to direct the spirit to interior recollection with reference to what has been said.

The reason, then, why some spiritual persons never enter perfectly into the true joys of the spirit is that they never succeed in raising their desire for rejoicing above these things that are outward and visible. Let such take note that, although the visible oratory and temple is a decent place set apart for prayer, and an image is a motive to prayer, the sweetness and delight of the soul must not be set upon the motive or the visible temple, lest the soul should forget to pray in the living temple, which is the interior recollection of the soul. The Apostle, to remind us of this, said: See that your bodies are living temples of the Holy Spirit, Who dwelleth in you.'[672] And this thought is suggested by the words of Christ which we have quoted, namely that they who truly adore God must needs adore Him in spirit and in truth.[673] For God takes little heed of your oratories and your places set apart for prayer if your desire and pleasure are bound to them, and thus you have little interior detachment, which is spiritual poverty and renunciation of all things that you may possess.

2. In order, then, to purge the will from vain desire and rejoicing in this matter, and to lead it to God in your prayer, you must see only to this, that your conscience is pure, and your will perfect with God, and your spirit truly set upon Him. Then, as I have said, you should choose the place that is the farthest withdraw and the most solitary that you can find, and devote all the rejoicing of the will to calling upon God and glorifying Him; and you should take no account of those whims about outward things, but rather strive to renounce them. For, if the soul be attached to the delight of sensible devotion, it will never succeed in passing onward to the power of spiritual delight, which is found in spiritual detachment coming through interior recollection.

Footnotes:

672. 1 Corinthians iii, 16.
673. St. John iv, 24.

CHAPTER XLI

Of certain evils into which those persons fall who give themselves to pleasure in sensible objects and who frequent places of devotion in the way that has been described.

Many evils, both interior and exterior, come to the spiritual person when he desires to follow after sweetness of sense in these matters aforementioned. For, as regards the spirit, he will never attain to interior spiritual recollection, which consists in neglecting all such things, and in causing the soul to forget all this sensible sweetness, and to enter into true recollection, and to acquire the virtues by dint of effort. As regards exterior things, he will become unable to dispose himself for prayer in all places, but will be confined to places that are to his taste; and thus he will often fail in prayer, because, as the saying goes, he can understand no other book than his own village.

2. Furthermore, this desire leads such persons into great inconstancy. Some of them never continue in one place or even always in one state: now they will be seen in one place, now in another; now they will go to one hermitage, now to another; now they will set up this oratory, now that. Some of them, again, wear out their lives in changing from one state or manner of living to another. For, as they possess only the sensible fervour and joy to be found in spiritual things, and have never had the strength to attain spiritual recollection by the renunciation of their own will, and submitting to suffering inconveniences, whenever they see a place which they think well suited for devotion, or any kind of life or state well adapted to their temperament and inclination, they at once go after it and leave the condition or state in which they were before. And, as they have come under the influence of that sensible pleasure, it follows that they soon seek something new, for sensible pleasure is not constant, but very quickly fails.

CHAPTER XLII

Of three different kinds of place for devotion and of how the will should conduct itself with regard to them.

I can think of three kinds of place by means of which God is wont to move the will to devotion. The first consists in certain dispositions of the ground and situation, which, by means of a pleasing effect of variety, whether obtained by the arrangement of the ground or of trees, or by means of quiet solitude, naturally awaken devotion. These places it is beneficial to use, if they at once lead the will to God and cause it to forget the places themselves, even as, in order to reach one's journey's end, it is advisable not to pause and consider the means and motive of the journey more than is necessary. For those who strive to refresh their desires and to gain sensible sweetness will rather find spiritual aridity and distraction; for spiritual sweetness and satisfaction are not found save in interior recollection.

2. When they are in such a place, therefore, they should forget it and strive to be inwardly with God, as though they were not in that place at all. For, if they be attached to the pleasure and delight of the place, as we have said, they are seeking refreshment of sense and instability of spirit rather than spiritual repose. The anchorites and other holy hermits, who in the most vast and pleasing wildernesses selected the smallest places that sufficed for them, built there the smallest cells and caves, in which to imprison themselves. Saint Benedict was in such a place for three years, and another -- namely, Saint Simon [674] -- bound himself with a cord that he might have no more liberty nor go any farther than to places within its reach; and even so did many who are too numerous ever to be counted. Those saints understood very clearly that, if they quenched not the desire and eagerness for spiritual sweetness and pleasure, they could not attain to spirituality.

3. The second kind is of a more special nature, for it relates to certain places (not necessarily deserts, but any places whatsoever) where God is accustomed to grant to a few special persons certain very delectable spiritual favours; ordinarily, such a place attracts the heart of the person who has received a favour there, and sometimes gives him great desires and yearnings to return to it; although, when he goes there, what happened to him before is not repeated, since this is not within his control. For God grants these favours when and how and where He pleases, without being tied to any place or time, nor to the free-will of the person to whom He grants them. Yet it is good to go and pray in such places at times if the desire is free from attachment; and this for three reasons. First, because although, as we said, God is not bound to any place, it would seem that He has willed to be praised by a soul in the place where He has granted it a favour. Secondly, because in that place the soul is more mindful to give thanks to God for that which it has received there. Thirdly, because, by remembering that favour, the soul's devotion is the more keenly awakened.

4. It is for these reasons that a man should go to such places, and not because he thinks that God is bound to grant him favours there, in such a way as to be unable to grant them wheresoever He wills, for the soul is a fitter and more comely place for God than any physical place. Thus we read in Holy Scripture that Abraham built an altar in the very place where God appeared to him, and invoked His holy name there, and that afterwards, coming from Egypt, he returned by the same road where God had appeared to him, and called upon God there once more at the same altar which he had built. [675] Jacob, too, marked the place where God had appeared to him, leaning upon a ladder, by raising there a stone which he anointed with oil. [676] And Agar gave a name to the place where the angel had appeared to her, and prized it highly, saying: Of a truth I have here seen the back of Him that seeth me.' [677]

5. The third kind consists of certain special places which God chooses that He may be called upon and served there, such as Mount Sinai, where He gave the law to Moses. [678] And the place that He showed Abraham, that he might sacrifice his son there. [679] And likewise Mount Horeb, where He appeared to our father Elias. [680]

6. The reason for which God chooses these places rather than others, that He may be praised there, is known to Himself alone. What it behoves us to know is that all is for our advantage, and that He will hear our prayers there, and also in any place where we pray to Him with perfect faith; although there is much greater opportunity for us to be heard in places dedicated to His service, since the Church has appointed and dedicated those places to that end.

Ascent of Mount Carmel
Footnotes:
674. E.p. omits: namely, Saint Simon.' The allusion is, of course, to Saint Simon Stylites.
675. Genesis xii, 8; xiii, 4.
676. Genesis xxviii, 13-19.
677. Genesis xvi, 13.
678. Exodus xxiv, 12.
679. Genesis xxii, 2.
680. 3 Kings [A.V., 1 Kings] xix, 8.

CHAPTER XLIII

Which treats of other motives for prayer that many persons use -- namely, a great variety of ceremonies.

The useless joys and the imperfect attachment which many persons have to the things which we have described are perhaps to some extent excusable, since these persons act more or less innocently with regard to them. But the great reliance which some persons place in many kinds of ceremonies introduced by uninstructed persons who lack the simplicity of faith is intolerable. Let us here disregard those which bear various extraordinary names or use terms that signify nothing, and also other things that are not sacred which persons who are foolish and gross and mistrustful in spirit are wont to interpolate in their prayers. For these are clearly evil, and involve sin, and many of them imply a secret compact with the devil; by such means these persons provoke God to wrath and not to mercy, wherefore I treat them not here.

2. I wish to speak solely of those ceremonies into which enters nothing of a suspicious nature, and of which many people make use nowadays with indiscreet devotion, attributing such efficacy and faith to these ways and manners wherein they desire to perform their devotions and prayers, that they believe that, if they fail to the very slightest extent in them, or go beyond their limits, God will not be served by them nor will He hear them. They place more reliance upon these methods and kinds of ceremony than upon the reality of their prayer, and herein they greatly offend and displease God. I refer, for example, to a Mass at which there must be so many candles, neither more nor fewer; which has to be said by the priest in such or such a way; and must be at such or such an hour, and neither sooner nor later; and must be after a certain day, neither sooner nor later; and the prayers and stations must be made at such and such times, with such or such ceremonies, and neither sooner nor later nor in any other manner; and the person who makes them must have such or such qualities or qualifications. And there are those who think that, if any of these details which they have laid down be wanting, nothing is accomplished.

3. And, what is worse, and indeed intolerable, is that certain persons desire to feel some effect in themselves, or to have their petitions fulfilled, or to know that the purpose of these ceremonious prayers of theirs will be accomplished. This is nothing less than to tempt God and to anger Him greatly, so much so that He sometimes gives leave to the devil to deceive them, making them feel and understand things that are far removed from the benefit of their soul, which they deserve because of the attachment that they show in their prayers, not desiring God's will, rather than their own desires, to be done therein; and thus, because they place not their whole confidence in God, nothing goes well with them. [681]

Footnotes:

681. With the last word of this chapter, which is also the last word of the page in Alc., the copy of P. Juan Evangelista comes to an end. The remainder of Alc. comes from another very early copy which, in the time of P. Andrés, existed at Duruelo (cf. Outline of the Life of St. John of the Cross, above).

CHAPTER XLIV

Of the manner wherein the rejoicing and strength of the will must be directed to God through these devotions.

Let these persons, then, know that, the more reliance they place on these things and ceremonies, the less confidence they have in God, and that they will not obtain of God that which they desire. There are certain persons who pray for their own ends rather than for the honour of God. Although they suppose that a thing will be done if it be for the service of God, and not otherwise, yet, because of their attachment to it and the vain rejoicing which they have in it, they multiply a large number of petitions for a thing, when it would be better for them to substitute others of greater importance to them, such as for the true cleansing of their consciences, and for a real application to things concerning their own salvation, leaving to a much later season all those other petitions of theirs which are not of this kind. And in this way they would attain that which is of the greatest importance to them, and at the same time all the other things that are good for them (although they might not have prayed for them), much better and much earlier than if they had expended all their energy on those things. For this the Lord promised, through the Evangelist, saying: Seek ye first and principally the Kingdom of God and His righteousness, and all these other things shall be added unto you.' [682]

2. This is the seeking and the asking that is most pleasing to God, and, in order to obtain the fulfilment of the petitions which we have in our hearts, there is no better way than to direct the energy of our prayer to the thing that most pleases God. For then not only will He give that which we ask of Him, which is salvation, but also that which He sees to be fitting and good for us, although we pray not for it. This David makes clear in a psalm where he says: The Lord is nigh unto those that call upon Him in truth, [683] that beg Him for the things that are in the highest degree true, such as salvation; for of these he then says: He will fulfill the will of them that fear Him, and will hear their cries, and will save them. For God is the guardian of those that truly love Him.' [684] And thus, this nearness to God of which David here speaks is naught else than His being ready to satisfy them and grant them even that which it has not passed through their minds to ask. Even so we read that, because Solomon did well in asking God for a thing that was pleasing to Him -- namely, wisdom to lead and rule his people righteously -- God answered him, saying: Because more than aught else thou didst desire wisdom, and askedst not victory over thine enemies, with their deaths, nor riches, nor long life, I will not only give thee the wisdom that thou askest to rule My people righteously, but I will likewise give thee that which thou hast not asked -- namely, riches and substance and glory -- so that neither before thee nor after thee shall there be any king like unto thee.' [685] And this He did, giving him peace also from his enemies, so that all around him should pay tribute to him and trouble him not: We read of a similar incident in Genesis, where God promised Abraham to increase the generation of his lawful son, like the stars of Heaven, even as he had asked of Him, and said to him: Likewise I will increase the son of the bondwoman, for he is thy son.' [686]

3. In this way, then, the strength of the will and its rejoicing must be directed to God in our petitions, and we must not be anxious to cling to ceremonial inventions which are not used or approved by the Catholic Church. We must leave the method and manner of saying Mass to the priest, whom the Church sets there in her place, giving him her orders as to how he is to do it. And let not such persons use new methods, as if they knew more than the Holy Spirit and His Church. If, when they pray in their simplicity, God hears them not, let them not think that He will hear them any the more however many may be their inventions. For God is such that, if they behave towards Him as they should, and conformably to His nature, they will do with Him whatsoever they will; but, if they act from selfish ends, they cannot speak with Him.

4. With regard to further ceremonies connected with prayer and other devotions, let not the will be set upon other ceremonies and forms of prayer than those which Christ taught us. [687] For it is clear that, when His disciples besought Him that He would teach them to pray, He would tell them all that is necessary in order that the Eternal Father may hear us, since He knew the Father's nature so well. Yet all that He taught them was the Pater Noster, with its seven petitions, wherein are included all our needs, both spiritual and temporal; and He taught them not many other kinds of prayer, either in words or in ceremonies. On the contrary, He told them that when they prayed they ought not to desire to speak much, since our heavenly Father knows well what is meet for us. He charged them only, but with great insistence, that they should persevere in prayer (that is, in the prayer of the Pater Noster), saying elsewhere: It behoves us always to pray and never to fail.' [688] But He taught not a variety of petitions,

but rather that our petitions should be repeated frequently and with fervour and care. For, as I say, in them is contained all that is the will of God and all that is meet for us. Wherefore, when His Majesty drew near three times to the Eternal Father, He prayed all these three times, using those very words of the Pater Noster, as the Evangelists tell us, saying: Father, if it cannot be but that I must drink this cup, Thy will be done.' [689] And the ceremonies which He taught us to use in our prayers are only two. Either we are to pray in the secret place of our chamber, where without noise and without paying heed to any we can pray with the most perfect and pure heart, as He said in these words: When thou shalt pray, enter into thy chamber and shut the door and pray.' [690] Or else He taught us to go to a solitary and desert place, as He Himself did, and at the best and quietest time of night. And thus there is no reason to fix any limit of time, or any appointed days, or to set apart one time more than another for our devotions, neither is there any reason to use other forms, in our words and prayers, nor phrases with double meanings, but only those which the Church uses and in the manner wherein she uses them; for all are reduced to those which we have described -- namely, the Pater Noster.

5. I do not for this reason condemn -- nay, I rather approve -- the fixing of days on which certain persons sometimes arrange to make their devotions, such as novenas, or other such things. I condemn only their conduct as concerns the fixity of their methods and the ceremonies with which they practise them. Even so did Judith rebuke and reprove the people of Bethulia because they had limited God as to the time wherein they awaited His mercy, saying: Do ye set God a time for his mercies?' To do this, she says, is not to move God to clemency, but to awaken His wrath. [691]

Footnotes:

682. St. Matthew vi, 33.
683. Psalm cxliv, 18 [A.V., cxlv, 18].
684. Psalm cxliv, 19-20 [A.V., cxlv, 19-20].
685. 2 Paralipomenon [A.V., 2 Chronicles] i, 11-12.
686. Genesis xxi, 13.
687. St. Luke xi, 1-4.
688. St. Luke xviii, 1.
689. St. Matthew xxvi, 39.
690. St. Matthew vi, 6.
691. Judith viii, 11-12.

CHAPTER XLV

Which treats of the second kind of distinct good, wherein the will may rejoice vainly.

The second kind of distinct and delectable good wherein the will may rejoice vainly is that which provokes or persuades us to serve God and which we have called provocative. This class comprises preachers, and we might speak of it in two ways, namely, as affecting the preachers themselves and as affecting their hearers. For, as regards both, we must not fail to observe that both must direct the rejoicing of their will to God, with respect to this exercise.

2. In the first place, it must be pointed out to the preacher, if he is to cause his people profit and not to embarrass himself with vain joy and presumption, that preaching is a spiritual exercise rather than a vocal one. For, although it is practised by means of outward words, its power and efficacy reside not in these but in the inward spirit. Wherefore, however lofty be the doctrine that is preached, and however choice the rhetoric and sublime the style wherein it is clothed, it brings as a rule no more benefit than is present in the spirit of the preacher. For, although it is true that the word of God is of itself efficacious, according to those words of David, He will give to His voice a voice of virtue,' [692] yet fire, which has also a virtue -- that of burning -- will not burn when the material is not prepared.

3. To the end that the preacher's instruction may exercise its full force, there must be two kinds of preparation: that of the preacher and that of the hearer; for as a rule the benefit derived from a sermon depends upon the preparation of the teacher. For this reason it is said that, as is the master, so is wont to be the disciple. For, when in the Acts of the Apostles those seven sons of that chief priest of the Jews were wont to cast out devils in the same form as Saint Paul, the devil rose up against them, saying: Jesus I confess and Paul I know, but you, who are ye?' [693] And then, attacking them, he stripped and wounded them. This was only because they had not the fitting preparation, and not because Christ willed not that they should do this in His name. For the Apostles once found a man, who was not a disciple, casting out a devil in the name of Christ, and they forbade him, and the Lord reproved them for it, saying: Forbid him not, for no man that has done any mighty works in My name shall be able to speak evil of Me after a brief space of time.' [694] But He is angry with those who, though teaching the law of God, keep it not, and, which preaching spirituality, possess it not. For this reason God says, through Saint Paul: Thou teachest others and teachest not thyself. Thou who preachest that men should not steal, stealest.' [695] And through David the Holy Spirit says: To the sinner, God said: "Why dost thou declare My justice and take My law in thy mouth, when thou hast hated discipline and cast My words behind thee?"' [696] Here it is made plain that He will give them no spirituality whereby they may bear fruit.

4. It is a common matter of observation that, so far as we can judge here below, the better is the life of the preacher, the greater is the fruit that he bears, however undistinguished his style may be, however small his rhetoric and however ordinary his instruction. For it is the warmth that comes from the living spirit that clings; whereas the other kind of preacher will produce very little profit, however sublime be his style and his instruction. For, although it is true that a good style and gestures and sublime instruction and well-chosen language influence men and produce much effect when accompanied by true spirituality, yet without this, although a sermon gives pleasure and delight to the sense and the understanding, very little or nothing of its sweetness remains in the will. As a rule, in this case, the will remains as weak and remiss with regard to good works as it was before. Although marvelous things may have been marvellously said by the preacher, they serve only to delight the ear, like a concert of music or a peal of bells; the spirit, as I say, goes no farther from its habits than before, since the voice has no virtue to raise one that is dead from his grave.

5. Little does it matter that one kind of music should sound better than another if the better kind move me not more than the other to do good works. For, although marvellous things may have been said, they are at once forgotten if they have not fired the will. For, not only do they of themselves bear little fruit, but the fastening of the sense upon the pleasure that it finds in that sort of instruction hinders the instruction from passing to the spirit, so that only the method and the accidents of what has been said are appreciated, and the preacher is praised for this characteristic or for that, and followed from such motives as these rather than because of the purpose of amendment of life which he has inspired. This doctrine is well explained to the Corinthians by Saint Paul, where he says: I, brethren, when I came to you, came not preaching Christ with loftiness of instruction and of wisdom, and my words and my preaching consisted not in the rhetoric of human wisdom, but in the showing forth of the spirit and of the truth.' [697]

6. Although the intention of the Apostle here, like my own intention, is not to condemn good style and rhetoric and phraseology, for, on the contrary, these are of great importance to the preacher, as in everything else, since good phraseology and style raise up and restore things that are fallen and ruined, even as bad phraseology ruins and destroys good things . . .[698]

Footnotes:
 692. Psalm lxvii, 34 [A.V., lxviii, 33].
 693. Acts xix, 15.
 694. St. Mark ix, 38-9.
 695. Romans ii, 21.
 696. Psalm xlix, 16-17 [A.V., l, 16-17].
 697. 1 Corinthians ii, 1-4.
 698. E.p. adds: End of the Ascent of Mount Carmel.' The treatise thus remains incomplete, the chapter on the preacher being unfinished and no part of any chapter upon the hearer having come down to us. Further, the last two divisions of the four mentioned in Chap. xxxv, 1 are not treated in any of the MSS. or early editions. The fragments which P. Gerardo [Obras, etc., I, 402-10] added to the Ascent, forming two chapters, cannot be considered as a continuation of this book. They are in reality a long and admirable letter [Letter XI in The Complete Works of St. John of the Cross: Vol. III, p. 255], written to a religious, who was one of the Saint's spiritual sons, and copied by P. Jerónimo de San José in his History of St. John of the Cross (Bk. VI, Chap. vii). There is not the slightest doubt that the letter which was written at Segovia, and is fully dated, is a genuine letter, and not an editor's maltreatment of part of a treatise. Only the similarity of its subject with that of these last chapters is responsible for its having been added to the Ascent. It is hard to see how P. Gerardo could have been misled about a matter which is so clear. [This question was re-opened, in 1950, by P. Sobrino (see Vol. III, p. 240), who adds TG and a codex belonging to the Discalced Carmelite Fathers of Madrid to the list of the MSS. which give the fragments as part of the Ascent, making six authorities in all, against which can be set only the proved and admitted reliability of P. Jerónimo de San José. P. Sobrino, who discusses the matter (Estudios, etc., pp. 166-93) in great detail, hazards a plausible and attractive solution, which he reinforces with substantial evidence -- that of a double redaction.' According to this theory, the Saint, in writing to the religious of Letter XI, made use, for the substance of his instruction, of two fragments which were to have gone into the Ascent. Considering how often in his writings he doubled passages, to say nothing of whole works, it is quite understandable that he should have utilized two unincorporated, and indeed unfinished, passages for a private letter.]

www.ingramcontent.com/pod-product-compliance
Lightning Source LLC
Chambersburg PA
CBHW020354170426
43200CB00005B/168